OUTLAWS
of the
OCEAN

OUTLAWS
of the
OCEAN

The Complete Book of Contemporary
Crime on the High Seas

**G.O.W. MUELLER and
FREDA ADLER**

HEARST MARINE BOOKS · NEW YORK

Grateful acknowledgment is made to the following for permission to reprint copyrighted material:

Houghton Mifflin Company, Inc.: One stanza from "The Fisherman" in *Songs of Sixpence* by Abbie Farwell Brown. Copyright 1914 by Abbie Farwell Brown. Copyright renewed 1942 by Barton Corneau.

Library of Congress Cataloging in Publication Data

Mueller, G.O.W.
Outlaws of the ocean.

Bibliography: p.
Includes index.
1. Pirates.   I. Adler, Freda.   II.Title.
G535.M74   1985   364.1'09162   84–19255
ISBN 0–688–04170–1

Printed in the United States of America

2 3 4 5 6 7 8 9 10

BOOK DESIGN BY BERNARD SCHLEIFER

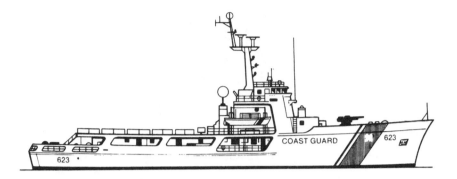

WE DEDICATE THIS BOOK TO the U.S. Coast Guard cutter *Steadfast*, her commanding officer, Commander (U.S.C.G.) Charles ("Chick") W. Murray, her officers, and her crew, and to all marine police officers, in every country of the world, who at the risk of their lives, in the face of the perils of the oceans and their outlaws, are endeavoring to keep the seas from becoming the domain of the earth's lawless elements, in the hope that, someday, the high seas themselves be patrolled by an international force, safeguarding the will of all humankind on the oceans.

Contents

•

Acknowledgments

•

"Wouldst thou,"—So the helmsman answered,
"Learn the secret of the sea?
Only those who brave the dangers
Comprehend its mystery!"

Henry Wadsworth Longfellow,
The Secret of the Sea

We are indeed very grateful for the help that friends and colleagues in some seventy nations have provided us in conceiving, conceptualizing, and completing this long overdue book. They all helped, not as much for personal reasons, but out of a conviction that crime should be "off limits" on the watery two thirds of the globe. To list all helpers would require a second volume. We must resort to a summary "thank you to all," noting only that some of our helpers went out of their way in providing us access to materials and information. This must be specially recorded—with a disclaimer: The responsibility for interpreting such information is ours. Quotes from personal interviews may not always be accurate, since notes were taken hastily and sometimes in thirty-foot seas. We hope, nevertheless, that we have captured the spirit of all information that was so generously imparted to us.

Since our book is being principally dedicated to our own American maritime police force, the U.S. Coast Guard, we shall begin our special thanksgiving list with U.S. Coast Guard personnel:*

*Ranks and post designations are as of the time of encounter.

Admiral James S. Gracey, U.S.C.G., Commandant of the U.S.
Coast Guard, who allowed us access to U.S. Coast Guard
operations and vessels

Rear Admiral D. C. Thompson, U.S.C.G., Commander, Seventh U.S. Coast Guard District, Miami, Florida

Captain Allen Breed, U.S.C.G., Chief of Operations, Seventh
U.S. Coast Guard District, Miami, Florida

Captain W. P. Hewel, U.S.C.G., Liaison Officer, SouthCom,
Panama

Commander Charles ("Chick") W. Murray, U.S.C.G., C.O.,
U.S. Coast Guard cutter *Steadfast,* and all officers and
crew of this steadfast ship

Commander Gary C. Nelson, U.S.C.G., Chief, Intelligence
and Law Enforcement Branch, Seventh U.S. Coast
Guard District, Miami, Florida

Lieutenant Commander David N. Russell, U.S.C.G., Assistant Chief, Intelligence and Law Enforcement Branch,
Seventh U.S. Coast Guard District, Miami, Florida

Lieutenant Commander Terrance P. Hart, U.S.C.G., Chief,
General Law Enforcement Branch, U.S.C.G. H.Q.,
Washington, D.C.

Lieutenant Commander Richard L. Cashdollar, U.S.C.G.,
Current Operations Officer, U.S.C.G. H.Q., Washington, D.C.

Mr. Richard W. ("Pete") Velde, former Administrator of the
Law Enforcement Assistance Administration

Mr. Charles F. Rinkevich, Coordinator, Vice President's
South Florida Task Force, Miami, Florida

Mr. Robert Grimes, Director of Patrol Services, U.S. Customs Service

Mr. Robert N. Battard, Regional Commissioner of Customs,
U.S. Customs Service, Miami, Florida

Mr. David B. Woods, Intelligence Officer, U.S. Customs Service, Region IV, Miami, Florida

Mr. Steve Wust, Librarian, U.S. Merchant Marine Academy,
Kings Point, New York

Mr. George J. Billy, Readers Services Librarian, U.S. Merchant Marine Academy, Kings Point, New York

Mr. Frank O. Braynard, Curator, American Merchant Marine
Museum Foundation, U.S. Merchant Marine Academy,
Kings Point, New York

Professor Jeffery C. Peck, U.S. Merchant Marine Academy, Kings Point, New York

Mr. Andrew Antippes, Chargé d'Affaires, U.S. Embassy, Nassau, Bahamas

Admiral Bror Stefenson, of the Royal Swedish Navy

Ms. Inga-Britt Ericson, Marinstabens, Royal Swedish Navy

Mr. R. V. Burroughs, M.O.M., C.P.M., Commissioner of Police of Trinidad and Tobago

Major Hans Riepel, of the Burgenland (Austria) State Police Force

Mr. Julius Wohlfahrt, of the Neusiedler (Austria) Lake Police Force, and all his colleagues

Mr. Carl Hiaasen, Staff Writer, the *Miami Herald*

Mr. Horace W. Schmahl, Chairman of the Board, Schmahl and Schmahl, Inc., Marine Surveyors, Fort Lauderdale, Florida

Captain Patricia A. Schmahl, Schmahl and Schmahl, Inc., Marine Surveyors, Fort Lauderdale, Florida

Dr. Albert Hess, Professor Emeritus of Sociology, State University of New York

Ms. Lynn Stallings, Reference Librarian, Historical Society of Delaware, Wilmington, Delaware

Ms. Anne R. Bryan, Librarian, Museum and Library of Maryland History, Baltimore, Maryland

Mr. J. T. Knepper, Vice President, Mobil Shipping and Transportation Company, New York

Colonel Issa Shuaib, Director of Police, Kuwait

Mr. Erich Haugk, *New York Times*

Professor Albin Eser, Director of the Max-Planck Institute of Foreign and International Criminal Law, Freiburg, Germany

Mr. Harry LeHuquet, Chief Engineer of the *Contessa Maria II.*

Special thanks are due to Miss Susan Okubo and Messrs. Stephen Perrello and Dennis Kenney, of Rutgers University, for their research assistance.

Only sailors will understand what it means to sail uncharted seas and to anchor in unmarked coves. This book was a cruise on largely uncharted waters. Had it not been for the guideposts provided by news-media coverage, we would never have been able to drop anchor. Without the superb coverage by UPI and AP, or Reuters, through the press of the world, the superb reporting by *The New York Times* (and its competitors around the globe), but particularly by the *New Bedford* (Mass.) *Standard Times*, we could not have completed this book. The coverage of the *Standard Times*, especially regarding the drug war invasion of New England, was so important that we felt compelled to subscribe to the paper, and we have honored it by using the abbreviation *N.B.S.T.* in our References section, the only paper whose title is abbreviated there. Special felicitations are due to its current editor, Mr. James M. Ragsdale, and his predecessor, Mr. Everett S. Allen, the salty author of *The Black Ships*, for publishing a daily that is so helpful to the New England maritime community. Other dailies that have been particularly helpful in our research include the *Miami Herald*, the *Miami News*, the *Express* (Trinidad), and the *Trinidad Guardian*. Among the yachting magazines, *Motor Boating & Sailing, Cruising World, Sail*, and *Yachting* have proven helpful research tools. *Soundings* turned out to be a veritable gold mine of information on law enforcement on the water.

The *Miami Herald* permitted us graciously to reproduce a graph by Rick Brownlee, "Aliens Detained," originally published in the *Herald* on December 8, 1982.

Credit for the photographic portrait of the U.S. Coast Guard cutter *Steadfast* goes to the U.S. Coast Guard, and for the photographs of the seizure of the drug runner *The Four of Us* and her cargo, to Marge Westgate, editor-in-chief of *The Advocate* (Fairhaven, Mass.), in which these pictures first appeared.

Several of the chapter titles were entries in a title contest we held aboard the U.S. Coast Guard cutter *Steadfast*. The winners of the contest (and of a case of Heineken's each, delivered dockside at the end of the patrol) were:

Lieutenant Randy Corrigan, U.S.C.G.
Ensign Bruce Gaudette, U.S.C.G.
S. N. Robert T. Brunke
R. M. Kenneth Faria
S. N. John H. Long

And finally there is the crew at Hearst Marine, captained by Paul Larsen, publisher, who had the vision to see the significance of the topic and who saw it through print to publication!

We are grateful to you all.

Before closing the list, Freda suggests: Why not include Grandpa Mueller, who taught Gerhard, at the ripe old age of ten, to handle a catboat? Why not?

On the East River in Manhattan,
March 15, 1984, the day on which, 2029
years ago, Gaius Julius Caesar, victim
and victor of pirates, was murdered.

Introduction

•

Shrilly squeal the running sheaves,
    the weather gear strains,
Such a clatter of chain-sheets,
    the devil's in the chains;
Over us the bright stars,
    under us the drowned,
"A long pull, a strong pull,
    and we're outward bound."

John Masefield,
A Valediction

Two mighty little tugs are nudging the twenty-thousand-tonner gently off her berth and into the East River. Having unloaded her lumber cargo for New York's busy construction industry, she is riding high in the water, flying the flag of Singapore, the little island republic in Asia that now has the world's tenth largest merchant fleet, bigger than that of the U.S.A., which ranks eleventh.[1] Of course, she may never have been to Singapore, her hailing port. Her captain may be Greek, her mate Spanish, and her crewmen may hail from Pakistan or Nigeria. Her owners may reside in Texas or London, and the cargo she unloaded may have come from Finland. What port is she headed for? *Bon voyage,* stranger, and make it a safe one!

It is an ancient sailors' custom to wish a departing vessel Godspeed. The perils of the sea loomed large: wind and weather, pirates, and the *Flying Dutchman:*

. . . Heaven help the ship near which the demon sailor steers!
The doom of those is sealed, to whom the Phantom Ship appears,
They'll never reach their destin't port;
    they'll never see their homes no more,
They who see the Flying Dutchman,
    never, never reach the shore.[2]

We don't know whether the *Flying Dutchman* is still out there. Those who don't return from the sea can't tell us. But we do know that many of those who don't return found a watery grave because of crime on the ocean. Crime on the ocean? What have the oceans got to do with crime? What have they got to do with anything? People live on land. They are born there and they die there. Nations are created on land, and that is where they cease to exist. Crime occurs on land—just check any book on criminology! Land is where it is all happening. Land! But land is simply composed of the dry spots on a globe of water. Land covers less than a third of the globe. And do you suppose that nothing happens on the other two thirds of the world? Since time immemorial the sea has attracted the more adventurous lot to make their living, to bring in food from the waters, to connect by commerce and transportation land masses and the people confined to them, or to seek their recreation in that alien element. On the waters, too, there always have been those who exploit what others create. These are the criminals of the sea.

For reasons beyond our comprehension, the explanation of crime has remained landlocked, as if there were no crime on the waters. Criminologists have neglected the criminality of that far greater portion of the world called oceans! The chances that our voyager with the flag of Singapore, who now passes beneath our windows, will reach her destination unscathed, are perhaps no greater today than were those of a merchantman two hundred years ago, and it won't be the *Flying Dutchman*'s fault if she were to disappear. More likely, you would have to blame it on crime on the oceans. Piracy, dead for generations, has returned in force within the past decade, in Southeast Asia, where hundreds of thousands of refugees have been robbed, raped, abused, and killed by pirates; in the waters off Singapore, where large vessels are being attacked; in the Caribbean, where hundreds of vessels have disappeared; in West Africa, the Mediterranean—all over the world, where substantial ships vanish at the rate of one a week. What a decade! In the United States, there were some eight hundred stolen boats listed ten years ago; there are over twenty-three thousand on the list today! Terrorism, once confined almost exclusively to land and air, stalks the waterways today. Insurance fraud, a minor risk in the past, appears to have increased tenfold in recent memory. Smuggling, always a problem on the oceans, has now turned deadly and so lucrative that it outstrips the sales volume of the world's largest corporations. Espionage and sabotage on the waters have become daily events. The oceans, it seems, are the New Frontier of the world's mobsters, outlaws, and pariahs.

For all these reasons, we surmise, our book comes none too soon. Ocean crime is challenging the world as never before. It finds that world unprepared for the onslaught and just barely organizing to meet the challenge. On the local level, the Association of the Bar of the City of New York recently held its first meeting on the topic "Crime in the Maritime Industry." On the world level, as we are going to press, the United Nations Conference on Trade and Development (UNCTAD) concludes the first meeting of the conference "Ad Hoc Intergovernmental Group to Consider Means of Combating All Aspects of Maritime Fraud, Including Piracy" (February 6–17, 1984). We studied the documentation and the press releases assiduously, and we are gratified that the world has awakened to the crime threat on our oceans. The realization on the part of the world community that our oceans are in trouble, because we did not mind them, attests to the timeliness of the subject.

It was only a year ago that the nations of the world, assembled at Montego Bay, Jamaica, approved the United Nations Convention on the Law of the Sea, the necessary first step toward ending lawlessness on the oceans. Much remains to be done to implement the good intentions of this convention, in the drafting of which criminologists, unfortunately, had no part. The idealism of the diplomats awaits the touch of realism that comes from an understanding of crime on the oceans and, with it, the analysis of the factors that must be controlled for any program that will ensure *pacem in maribus*—peace on the oceans.

We are datelining this Introduction, and therefore this book, in Manhattan, where these final words are being penned. That is appropriate. In a large measure, this small island controls the world's ocean commerce, suffers the attacks on peaceful trade, and—only a few blocks from here—endeavors to cope with the problems, at the headquarters of the United Nations.

Peace on the oceans! Our friend from Singapore is now rounding the bend in the river, under her own power. With a hoot from their horns the tugs are heading away, a last message, "Safe trip!" But why can't we guarantee it? Why can we only wish it?

We searched every conceivable library for an assessment of the problem of crime on the seas and for proposed solutions. Our search yielded many interesting books and articles concerned with individual cases, incidents, epochs, and episodes. But world literature is devoid of any book that examines criminality on the oceans in its entirety. Short of any such examination, there would of course be no literary effort to come to grips with the problem and to offer solutions. The books we found are full of lore and historical accounts. Yet, as enticing as the history of the outlaws of the oceans appears to be, we were far more concerned about the contemporary world, the crime on the oceans that is happening all around us today.

Dateline Manhattan. But that is not really true. Only the final words were written here. As our readers will soon perceive, the book was really written where crime on the oceans occurs: while on the *Contessa Maria II* in New England waters; on the Panama, Suez, and Kiel canals; in the pirate-infested waters of the Philippines; in Australia; in the "bottlenecks" of the ancient pirate channels of the Caribbean, especially on Tobago; on Isla Bella, off the coast of Brazil; in the Swedish archipelagoes, churned by sub-chasing naval vessels; on peaceful Neusiedler Lake, Austria; and in the Danube river ports of Regensburg and Passau (Germany), Vienna (Austria), Bratislava (Czechoslovakia), and Budapest (Hungary); in a sleazy bar in Tahiti, where yachtsmen tried to enlist the French Foreign Legionnaires (and their machine guns) at our table, because they had to head northwest from safe Tahiti to pirate-infested sea lanes; in the ports of the Ivory Coast of Africa and of the Arabian Sea; in the great harbors of Hamburg and Bremen (Germany), of Copenhagen (Denmark) and Rotterdam (the Netherlands), of Oslo (Norway) and London (England), of Helsinki (Finland), of Monrovia (Liberia), Osaka (Japan), and Mar del Plata (Argentina); and in dozens of little ports all over the world. But foremost, the manuscript was written aboard many marine police patrol vessels, of countries that could be alphabetically arranged from Australia to Zambia. We remember particularly the devout crew of the Kuwaiti patrol vessel who managed to kneel and bow for their prayers aboard, at the prescribed times, without ever losing track of their mission. Faith and dedication are what it takes. The mission is there.

PART · I

Getting into Deep Water

I must down to the seas again
    to the vagrant gypsy life,
To the gull's way and the whale's way
    where the wind's like a whetted knife;
And all I ask is a merry yarn
    from a laughing fellow rover,
And quiet sleep and a sweet dream
    when the long trick's over.

John Masefield,
Sea-Fever

WHILE WE CERTAINLY KNOW why we had to write this book—
indeed, it had to be written—we do not recall exactly when we
made this decision. In fact, we did not realize that we were
writing it until we were in the midst of it. Perhaps the decision
was made in the waning days of World War II, when Mueller
found himself in the British military government, persisting in
his applications until he was transferred to the water police.
Assigned to command a seagoing patrol vessel (a captured German torpedo retriever), duty took him all over the British-
occupied Baltic shores, the Kiel Canal, the Elbe River, and parts
of the North Sea coastline. The service's rewards were primarily
the excitement of cruising through ill-charted minefields. It
wasn't exactly like your average Sunday afternoon sail down
Long Island Sound. The service's charges were grueling: Taking
crew (unharmed, wounded, or dead) off an American Liberty
ship blown up by one of those mines, or fishing hundreds of

corpses out of harbors filled with wrecks and derelicts, the grim harvest of war, or retrieving the bodies of soldiers drowned on transport vessels, sailors who died at their antiaircraft guns during the last days of combat, refugees who drowned on decrepit vessels of escape (anything that would seem to float), Nazi suicides who could not take the defeat, and concentration camp inmates on a last ship's passage on SS-commandeered vessels to nowhere. And then there was the drive to stop war criminals from escaping, to find them so that they would become the first objects of international criminal justice; to keep the stores of leftover German weapons and munitions from finding their way into a vast world black market; to sail picket while British sappers attached the dynamite charges to German naval craft slated for destruction, such as the pocket battleship *Scheer* or the cruiser *Emden*, or wrecks posing a navigational hazard; to block contraband from coming into the occupied zones; to provide safety for the vessels that in increasing numbers brought food, cattle, and machinery to devastated Poland; and, above all, to make the waters safe again for peaceful navigation after six years of an apocalyptic war.

But then, perhaps the decision to write this book was made a few years later when Adler found her stateroom on the liner *Groote Baer* ransacked during a transatlantic passage. Yes, we believe that the thought for the book was also born then, but we realized that we were actually writing it only when our curiosity had driven us south, via Washington to Florida. Clearly, something was happening on the oceans that necessitated criminological inquiry. The media kept referring to a new war at sea—a drug war. In our United Nations offices we had heard of the plight of the Vietnamese boat people, subjected to piracy by the hundreds of thousands. Ocean pollution had been a concern of the United Nations, as well as fisheries rights, and terrorism had concerned us, although mostly on land—but not exclusively so.

Closer to home, one Saturday night, while peacefully asleep on our old *Contessa Maria*, securely tied up at City Island (or so we thought), our docking lines had been cut and we found ourselves adrift on Long Island Sound. There it was, all around us: crime on the water! That discovery was the more startling since, as criminologists, we had dealt with crime as if it existed only on land. All the criminological theories we had rehearsed with our students were rooted in land-based experiences. As hard as we searched in the annals and archives, there was no seafaring criminology, although by now it had become clear that today's waterways were by no means free from crime. As yet we had no idea of its true dimensions.

Washington was to be our first stop.

1

Perspectives from the Crow's Nest

•

Darkness settles on roofs and walls,
    But the sea, the sea in the darkness calls;
The little waves, with their soft, white hands,
    Efface the footprints in the sands,
And the tide rises, the tide falls.

Henry Wadsworth Longfellow,
The Tide Rises, the Tide Falls

MR. ROBERT GRIMES, director of Customs patrols, received us at U.S. Customs headquarters. His service was created only a decade ago, under the onslaught of drug imports. The service started with a staff of 800. By now it was up to over 1,400, operating a fleet of some 600 patrol vessels, 90 percent unmarked. We wondered about the "unmarked." Would not any yachtsman or fisherman experience a rapid flow of adrenaline when a speedboat approached to within a few feet? Wallet-attached badges of the Customs Service are displayed only at the last minute. Yet, no untoward incidents had occurred so far. The U.S. Customs Service works at its best in the coastal zone, where the Coast Guard's heavy cutters cannot operate. It also relies heavily on cooperation with all the other services, the Coast Guard included, and on sophisticated radar scanning devices, located at the Guantánamo naval base and elsewhere, as well as on AWACS planes. The service is proud of its record—and justly so—which shows a steady rise in cocaine seizures during a five-year period, from 1,418.7 pounds seized in 1978 to 11,149.5 pounds in 1982. Customs seized 334 vessels involved in smuggling operations in 1978. That number increased to 1,319 for 1980 and then leveled off to 556 in 1981 and 500 in 1982.[1] "These figures," explained the director of Customs patrol, "reflect the increased cocaine import into the United

25

States. Our effectiveness in interdicting contraband has always been great. Of course, when there was no cocaine smuggled into the United States, none could be seized. But now it is coming in massively and our increasing seizures are both the result of this steady increase and of the service's vigilance, especially through cooperation with other services, under the Vice President's South Florida Task Force. You should go to Miami and observe our operations firsthand."

We had an equally cordial reception and informative visit at U.S. Coast Guard headquarters in Washington, D.C., where, servicewide, all law-enforcement activities were being coordinated by the General Law Enforcement Branch. We had, indeed, come to the right place, said Lt. Cdr. Terrance P. Hart, chief of the branch, as he explained the Coast Guard's nine major law enforcement tasks. These extended to the following crime types: (1) hijacking of yachts and other vessels (internal takeovers); (2) piracy (external takeovers of vessels); (3) marine felonies (crimes committed aboard a vessel subject to the jurisdiction of the United States); (4) drug smuggling; (5) smuggling of aliens into the United States; (6) mutinies (which are sometimes hard to differentiate from labor disputes); (7) marine insurance frauds; (8) theft of vessels; and (9) Neutrality Act violations (illegal export of arms and munitions). Several if not all of these crime types are undoubtedly interconnected. The impact of these crimes was felt especially in South Florida. He went on to say how drug smuggling and piracy had become problems in the midseventies in various parts of the world, but particularly in Bahamian waters, where piracy had been flourishing well into the nineteenth century. Yet it had been dormant for over a hundred years. But why did it recur? "Money is the bottom line," commented Lieutenant Commander Richard L. Cashdollar, the operations officer. Immense fortunes can be made in smuggling marijuana, cocaine, or aliens into the United States, and even greater fortunes are being made by "ripping off" a drug runner. This also subjects innocent boaters to the risk of attack. The area of operations of the drug runners/pirates has become a war zone, which stretches east and south from Florida's shores into Bahamian waters. Indeed, it covers the Caribbean and the Gulf of Mexico, the area of the Seventh and the Tenth U.S. Coast Guard districts. "You should really visit the Miami headquarters of the Seventh U.S. Coast Guard

District and, of course, of the Vice President's South Florida Task Force, of which the Coast Guard is an integral part," added Lieutenant Commander Hart.

Miami, January 1983: As is our custom when we come to a new town, we gather all the local newspapers to canvass the concerns of the community and to gauge the nature of their problems. The contents of Miami's papers are startlingly different from those of New York's. Here were some of the headlines which appeared during our initial three-day stay:

- "Inspectors say 5 night postal workers moved more than mail" (namely, cocaine and Quāaludes)[2]
- "Drug fight trims smuggling here, task force chief says"[3]
- "Drug smugglers convicted in San Juan" (after interception of the vessel *Recife* by the nuclear-powered cruiser U.S.S. *Mississippi*)[4]
- "Metro police seek identity of body" (found floating in a South Dade canal)[5]
- "Motel maid finds body in room" (shot to death)[6]
- "Key residents acquitted in pot case" (the "Islamarada 19" case—with 212 bales of marijuana aboard)[7]
- "South Florida congressman files to rid U.S. of Quāaludes"[8]
- "In blood from wounds, he wrote suspect's name" (a drug-running operation)[9]
- "Plant owner dumped toxic chemical, Dade officials say" (threat of water pollution in canal)[10]
- "Hastings, F.B.I. clash at trial on cash issue" (corruption trial of a federal judge)[11]
- "Poll, drugs are Miamians' top concern"[12]
- "Rush is on for mysterious $800,000 found in car" (drug money)[13]
- "U.S. will streamline drug force"[14]
- "Race-car pot dealer gets 10 years"[15]
- "Judge checks on refugees' release" (Cuban boat people)[16]
- "Haitians need legal aid" (aliens smuggled into the U.S.A.)[17]
- "Saving the whales helps humanity, too" (fight against illegal whale killings)[18]

- "Shipment of turtle soup is seized" (endangered-species-law violation)[19]
- "Ex-Nazi enjoyed torturing Jews, two victims testify" (the capture of Altman-Barbie, whose neo-Nazi thugs had organized drug production in Bolivia and export to the U.S.A.)[20]
- "Gables detective duo earns Officer of the Year honors" (for successful drug seizures)[21]

This brief cross section of a three-day stretch of Miami's dailies includes neither the parallel accounts nor the follow-ups of the news stories; nor does it include the general news about crime in the area which, according to knowledgeable local observers, is mostly drug-related; nor does it include any news about the impact that maritime criminality has on the law-enforcement and criminal-justice situation in South Florida.[22]

We entered the office of Robert Battard, regional commissioner of Customs, U.S.C., with considerable anticipation. The office overlooks the Miami River, a busy waterway plied every day by hundreds of vessels, from day sailors to freighters of a few thousand tons. Commissioner Battard bid us a hearty welcome. We admired his view of the mouth of the Miami River. "Convenient," he said. "I get a good look at every vessel passing through. Having gotten to know vessel design and layout, you get alerted to the unusual. The other day a yacht came in, the crew standing topside, waving at me. They seemed to be standing a little higher than on yachts of that design. So I sent a few of my officers out, and they were there dockside to greet the yacht when she made fast. Sure enough, a false deck had been added, and the between space was filled with marijuana."

The Customs Service, according to Commissioner Battard, is faced with a myriad of tasks. They all boil down to ensuring that Uncle Sam gets his duty on all goods imported into the U.S.A. that are dutiable, and keeping out of the U.S.A. all contraband (goods not legally importable). In this age of narcotics, more service time is spent on the latter duty. While heroin is still coming into New York and other northern ports, as well as into those of the West Coast, the problem of more immediate concern, especially to Customs' Fourth Region (which stretches from the Potomac south to the Virgin Islands), is the importation of cocaine and marijuana, in vast quantities. Points of origin for transshipment to the U.S.A. are almost invariably in Colombia. Points of production of the 95 percent pure cocaine paste, as well as of most of the marijuana, are in Bolivia, Colombia, and, to some extent, Peru, with a smaller load of marijuana still coming in from Jamaica.

How does this contraband come in? Cocaine comes in hidden in air or sea cargo. Sometimes it is concealed in nonoperative diesel cylinders (and then the cocaine has the odor of diesel!), in stanchions or other hollow parts aboard a vessel, or concealed on the body or within the personal luggage of travelers, sometimes diplomats (a Jamaican diplomat was recently seized with thirty pounds of Mexican heroin). Some of the travelers come by plane from South America, some by cruise ship from the Caribbean. Some of the carriers are crew members who take the contraband ashore, out of hiding places aboard the vessel, after Customs has cleared the ship. The carriers are almost always mere "mules," whether Americans, exiled Cubans, or others. The trade itself is firmly controlled by a handful of Colombian crime families, which control the departure and arrival of the mules and the distribution of the contraband.

The bulkier marijuana is brought to our shores primarily by mother ships, small freighters, trawlers, and yachts, frequently converted for the drug-smuggling business in boatyards in southern ports that specialize in the construction of double bulkheads, false bottoms, and concealed compartments. "The same yards that specialized in that kind of ship construction and conversion in the eighteenth century?" we asked. "Who knows?" The last leg, from mother ships to shore, is usually made by ultrafast speedboats of the Scarab or Cigarette type. Customs has risen to the challenge, especially with the increased strength and maneuverability it acquired since being joined with the Vice President's South Florida Task Force, together with all other concerned law-enforcement agencies:

- 160 additional Customs investigators have been sent South from northern duty stations
- "Profiles" have been worked out by which suspect persons, aircraft, and vessels can be identified
- Customs began to focus on Bimini, the Bahamian island closest to our shorelines, and obtained excellent cooperation from Bahamian officials; U.S. Customs preclearance

officers are now also stationed at Freeport Airport, Bahamas[23]

- Customs uses surface radar
- and some 600 undercover vessels
- as well as undercover agents who sometimes sign on as crew on smuggling vessels (one such officer steered a drug-running vessel right into the arms of Customs!)
- An excellent information network for the whole Caribbean has been established, with the cooperation of the maritime community
- Radio frequencies are being monitored
- Customs' air arm flies surveillance, even occasionally over Colombian air space, with the express consent of the Colombian government
- Customs officers, together with the officers of other services, are receiving special training at the training center in Glencoe, outside Brunswick, Georgia
- Above all, Customs works with the other services, as a team, under the umbrella of the Vice President's South Florida Task Force; true, as a task force member, Customs loses a bit of its identity, but since Customs is doing what it always has done successfully but is now doing as a strengthened team member, the overall success is noteworthy[24]

Cocaine seizures by U.S. Customs jumped from an annual 728.9 pounds in 1975 to 1,438.1 pounds in 1979. Only a year later, in 1980, cocaine seizures tripled, to 4,742.9 pounds.[25] With the establishment of the South Florida Task Force, cocaine seizures doubled again, but for the Southern District (which includes Florida) alone, to 9,404 pounds.[26] And the record on marijuana seizures is no less impressive: Customs seized close to 500,000 pounds in 1975, nationwide. That rose to 4.5 million pounds by 1978, slid down to half that amount in 1980, and went back to 500,000 pounds for 1982, the first year of the South Florida Task Force—but for seizures in the Southern District alone![27]

"But, above all, by making it tough to land contraband in Florida, we've added a thousand miles to their problems and taken them to unfamiliar waters," said the Customs commissioner. Through its seizures, Customs has driven up the street price of cocaine and marijuana in the big cities of America. Of course, that could also increase the number of burglaries, robberies, larcenies, and embezzlements by the users to maintain their habit! These seizures have also depressed the price of these drugs f.o.b. Colombia. There remain questions and problems: Exactly how do druggies—and in the trade this means smugglers, not users—deal with the payment problem? Of course, stolen cars, hot off the streets, purloined heavy equipment, arms, and other contraband are leaving in the same freighters that may just have landed a load of drugs. Unhappily, Customs departure clearances had to be somewhat neglected in view of the enormous emphasis on incoming contraband.

Mostly, however, payment for drugs is made in cash. As sure as a river flows downstream, this cash must flow to banks. These may be located in Switzerland or Austria, Luxembourg or Panama, the Cayman Islands, or the Bahamas, countries with secretive banking laws.[28] Take the Bahamas as an example. In 1971, while ostensibly still a reputable banker, Robert L. Vesco created an elaborate banking system in the Bahamas, ingratiated himself with the power structure by making liberal loans, arranged for the vouching of his enterprises (which then permitted him to bilk Investors Overseas Services of $224 million), and finally operated his Bahamian banks as "laundries" for drug money. Vesco was forced out of the Bahamas in 1973. He fled to Costa Rica, returned to the Bahamas later on (albeit briefly), and is on the run again. But his Columbus Trust Company Ltd. (of the Bahamas) had its license revoked only in 1983. A number of American confederates are under federal indictment on various charges.[29]

American banks as well have become deeply involved, especially those in Miami. Federal law requires every transaction of more than $10,000 to be specially reported to the IRS. Yet one organization in Florida made daily deposits of about $2.5 million in the very same bank branch. That requires somebody right inside the bank to conceal these transactions! In one of the major drug money "laundry" trials against major banking officials charged with moving money among banks of Panama, Colombia, Switzerland, the Cayman Islands, Florida, and New York, a New York bank branch manager actually pleaded guilty to two misdemeanor counts and turned state's evidence.[30] If that part of American law were to be faithfully adhered to, it

would become extremely hard to get the laundered money back
into the country. It would be as if the automatic washer-drier
were to miss a cycle!

Commissioner Battard told us: "We have started Operation
Greenback, with Bill Rosenblatt in charge under Andy Hoffman,
head of Customs patrol here. They are tracking down the flow
of cash, from dirty drug money through the laundries, right to
clean and wholesome investments—with no questions asked."

We left the offices of Commissioner Battard filled with respect for the Customs Service's dedication to the common good,
a respect such work did not enjoy before Matthew 9:11, but
whose workers have valiantly tried to gain during the two millennia since then.

Our next stop obviously had to be the command of the Seventh Coast Guard District, charged with policing 2.2 million
square miles of salt water. We were greeted by Captain Allen
Breed, U.S.C.G., chief of operations, an articulate analyst of the
situation and a salty veteran of many commands, including the
U.S. Coast Guard cutter *Albert Gallatin,* named after the venerable Secretary of the Treasury. We also had the good fortune to
meet with Commander Gary C. Nelson, chief, and Lieutenant
Commander David N. Russell, assistant chief of the Intelligence
and Law Enforcement Branch of the Seventh Coast Guard District. In these conversations and in subsequent research and
observation, a fairly complete picture of the drug war at sea
emerged:

The U.S. Coast Guard has gone through many phases in its
two centuries of history, including combat service in many wars,
notably World War II, and subsequent hostilities, especially the
Vietnam War. In its peacetime duties, the service during the
"Rum War" of the Prohibition period stands out. That experience taught the Coast Guard to be ever alert to ships on seas
where they are not expected to sail, vessels engaged in weird
operations, shrimpers with rusty gear, fishermen without nets,
yachts sailing at night with no navigation lights, or profitable
freighters with unprofitable freight.

It started a decade ago, and a pattern swiftly emerged. When
in 1975, due to Mexican cooperation, especially by crop destruction, Mexican marijuana imports turned from a flood into a
trickle,[31] that much-sought-after weed came in from elsewhere,
mostly by sea. And as the drug habit worked its way up from the

deprived to the depraved sectors of more affluent Americans, cocaine, the classless drug, fought its way into the country, by air and by sea. Both cargoes could be traced straight south—to Colombian ports. It naturally fell to the Coast Guard to prevent such contraband from reaching our shores.

Congress expressed its first major concern about the drug onslaught in 1979, when the Subcommittee on Coast Guard and Navigation of the Committee on Merchant Marine and Fisheries held its hearings in Washington, D.C., and Key West, Florida. The federal and local law-enforcement establishments were fully represented. The picture they drew was not a pretty one, yet the conclusions were obvious: Federal legislation and intervention, massive funding, and better cooperation were needed to meet the menace.[32] The Coast Guard has its traditional law-enforcement powers and the right to conduct searches and seizures. Yet were these powers far-reaching enough?

To reach United States shores, smuggling vessels coming from Colombian ports would normally choose one of four passages: (1) Moving in a northwesterly direction, they would traverse the Yucatán Channel, long known as the I-95 of drug traffic, between Cuba and Mexico's Yucatán Peninsula. Once there, druggies could head straight north for Gulf Coast ports, or turn west to the Florida Keys, or, through the Straits of Florida, they could reach the Atlantic Coast ports of Florida and other states. In any event, such vessels would all have to go through one narrow passage, the Yucatán Channel, and possibly a second one, the Straits of Florida. (2) Running straight north, drug runners could keep Jamaica and Cuba on port, and Haiti on starboard, and run through the Windward Passage. Once through that passage, such vessels can easily disappear among the myriad of Bahamian islands until finally reaching the proximity of United States shores. (3) Choosing a northeasterly course, druggies could exit the Caribbean through the Mona Passage, between the island of Hispaniola on port (the eastern part of the island is the Dominican Republic, while the western part is Haiti) and the United States commonwealth of Puerto Rico on starboard. Once through that passage, druggies would face a longer stretch of the open Atlantic before reaching the concealment of the Bahamian islands. (4) There is a fourth possibility, not popular with the druggies in the past: The various Leeward passages through the maze of the many islands and island republics that dot the chart between Puerto Rico, at its northern point, and the coast of Venezuela—the old "Spanish Main"—at its southernmost point, constituting a virtual arc, concave toward the Caribbean, between those two end points. It has not been a popular route because it is far longer; leads into wide stretches of open Atlantic; and requires larger and more seaworthy vessels equipped with better navigation systems, a larger crew, more fuel, and more provisions—it's a headache!

In essence, so our friends of the Coast Guard told us, the Caribbean is a bottle with four necks—not counting the Panama Canal. To bottle up the Caribbean you need four corks. The U.S. Coast Guard provides these corks to prevent the drug-running mother ships from getting through the bottlenecks. How prophetic the reference to corks was to prove we found out a few months later when we bounced on one of these corks in a tropical gale near the Windward Passage. These corks are the Coast Guard's workhorses, ranging from the sleek and large (327 feet) frigate-sized cutters of the Hamilton class to seagoing tugs, with the medium-endurance cutters of the Reliance class (210-footers) constituting the main force.

With the establishment of the Vice President's South Florida Task Force, the Coast Guard is no longer alone in patrolling the sea lanes leading to America's shores. The Drug Enforcement Administration (DEA); the Customs Service; the Immigration and Naturalization Service; the FBI;[33] the Alcohol, Tobacco, and Firearms Division; the IRS; the U.S. Border Patrol, and state and local law-enforcement agencies in southern Florida have all joined in this task force, participating in planning, decision-making, and execution of all plans to stop drugs from getting into the United States of America. It is a distinct advantage that the chain of command emanates straight from the Vice President, putting the whole operation above departmental interests. Admiral Daniel Murphy was designated the Vice President's right hand in running the operation. Early on the State Department had been added to the task force, because, as Vice President Bush said, of "a need for greater cooperation with the Bahamas, Bolivia, Colombia and Peru."[34] The Department of Defense next joined the task force, which also included the Secretaries of State, Defense, Transportation, Treasury, and Health and Human Services, the Attorney General, and presidential counselor Edwin Meese.

Immediate priority was given to bottling up the Caribbean to keep drugs from reaching U.S. shores. The capacity of the Seventh U.S. Coast Guard District, headquartered in Miami, was greatly strengthened, to some extent by transferring cutters and personnel from less affected districts to the Florida peninsula, but also by training of personnel, by improved communications, vastly improved intelligence, and, of course, cooperation with the other agencies. Not since the days of Prohibition has the Coast Guard been showered with as much attention.

We found the reference to the days of Prohibition most appropriate, for whatever was said during our conversations with any Coast Guard officer about today's narcotics interdiction efforts appeared to have had its counterpart during the alcohol interdiction efforts of the fourteen Volstead Act years,[35] such as the following:

- "mother ships"—larger vessels crammed full of marijuana at any of the Colombian ports, hovering off the United States coast and waiting for a
- "contact boat" to pick up any part of the illegal cargo for a fast run ashore. Both types of vessels would, of course, have that
- "profile," which puts any ship or vessel into the suspect category when it fulfills the characteristics of the profile. Of course, that may include any ship or craft of almost any size, ranging from a 20-foot sailboat with a single ton of pot aboard, through the shrimpers (with rusty gear) from 40 to 80 feet, to the island or coastal freighters of 190 feet or more.

Nor have the tricks of the trade changed much in the half century since Prohibition ended. The business of smuggling drugs—like the business of rum running[36]—moved from the Mom and Pop shops into the hands of large syndicates, which today are Colombian. When a smuggling vessel is in danger of being caught, or is seized already, the owner will report her as stolen, to increase his chances of recovering the vessel, which normally would be subject to forfeiture. (This trick usually does not work.) And since, in maritime law, only the master of the vessel can be deemed to know the nature of the cargo, it happens now (as it happened then) that just prior to seizure, the captain simply disappears (by rowboat a hundred miles to shore!), leaving an "innocent-ignorant" crew behind. (That, too, does not work too well, especially when that crew is observed tossing numerous bales of marijuana into the ocean.)

Now as then, the constitutional limitations on search and seizure, restrictively applied by the federal courts, can frustrate dedicated prize interception crews. Now as then, cutters may lose the benefit of their best officers for prolonged periods of time, sitting as witnesses through protracted trials with frequent adjournments. Now as then, the danger of armed encounters looms large, as contraband runners are arming themselves heavily for protection against rip-off pirates. And the yachting community again feels compelled to arm itself against pirates who may want to take its vessels, especially when they believe that contraband is aboard. Now as then, the Coast Guard warns legitimate boaters simply to stay out of the "combat zones" crisscrossed by "contact boats" running at speeds of up to eighty miles per hour. Now as then, a whole industry thrives on converting vessels to smugglers with raised decks, false bulkheads, and concealed compartments. Now as then, the runners resort to ever more sophisticated means of communication and navigation, which the Coast Guard is challenged to match— sometimes with inferior equipment. Occasionally, seizures and forfeitures of the smugglers' superior equipment have augmented the Coast Guard's own procurement program for sophisticated technology.

But two things are vastly different today. First, so far no drug runner has attacked a U.S. Coast Guard cutter, whose size and presence are intimidating, while running battles between rummies and Coast Guard vessels were commonplace during Prohibition. Just remember the case of James "Red" Alderman, a rum runner who killed a skipper of a seventy-five-foot cutter (one of about two hundred "six-bitters"), killed two crew members, temporarily seized control of the cutter, and was about to kill the rest of the crew when he was subdued by two mates. Alderman was convicted of murder and hanged at the U.S. Coast Guard section base in Fort Lauderdale, Florida.[37]

Second, today's Coast Guard operates with a vastly improved intelligence system, which is superior to that of the outlaws. Of course, the druggies have their spotter planes and helicopters, warning drug runners of nearby Coast Guard cutters. (Such pilots earn $1,000 for one surveillance flight, plus expenses, at no risk to them whatsoever!) But the U.S. Coast Guard and the other agencies fighting the drug war are doing far better than the opposition as far as intelligence is concerned. Not only does there exist an extensive network of undercover agents in all areas affected,[38] but also the Coast Guard has the benefit of satellites, with optics so fine that the markings, names, and characteristics of vessels loading marijuana in Barranquilla or Cartagena, Colombia, can be clearly ascertained.[39] The electronic scanning devices at the U.S. naval base at Guantánamo Bay, Cuba, and other U.S. Navy installations are being used; and more recently, Coast Guard HU-25 high-tech computerized jets, AWACS (Advanced Warning and Control Systems) reconnaissance planes, helicopters, flying boats, and radar balloons[40] have taken to the air, and an advanced design blimp is likely to join this sophisticated force in the sky soon.[41]

Having experienced the effectiveness of blimps as aerial observation platforms ourselves, cruising in one of them over South Florida, we can only agree with the U.S. Coast Guard test pilot who reported, after his first flight on the British-built sky-ship 500 blimp: ". . . never have I seen such a platform! Windows [big ones] everywhere. This, combined with a slow search speed, means the visibility is almost unrestricted. . . . Just think [in terms of rough equivalents] of having a search/patrol craft with the speed and maneuverability of an HH-52A, the useful load of a C-130, and the range and endurance of an 82-foot WPB. And that at a fuel consumption of one sixth of any of the Coast Guard's high- or medium-endurance cutters!"[42]

And while the new blimp cruising capacity is being developed, an older ex-Navy blimp is already in the air, tethered at Cudyo Key, where its radar equipment closes the radar gap through which low-flying smugglers' planes had been able to make their way to U.S. soil undetected. Yet the best part of today's intelligence system is EPIC, the El Paso Intelligence Center. It "is a unique, cooperative effort established to collect, process and disseminate information concerning illicit drug trafficking. It is staffed by personnel of six participating agencies: Drug Enforcement Administration, Immigration and Naturalization Service, U.S. Customs Service, U.S. Coast Guard, Bureau of Alcohol, Tobacco and Firearms, and the Federal Aviation Administration."[43] If information pertaining to any suspicious person or vessel exists, EPIC has it and will provide it to an inquiring cutter on the high seas within minutes. Time and again we have seen this process work. Having spotted a suspect vessel matching the profile of a drug runner (such as a shrimper without gear far outside shrimping waters, on a straight course from Colombia running north, etc.), the Coast Guard cutter's skipper would call EPIC, and within minutes he would obtain information such as this: "Ex-shrimper *Marybelle* from Key West, last reported name *Bellweather*, observed four days ago loading marijuana in Cartagena, Colombia, probably skippered by John Doe, U.S. citizen, three previous felony convictions, two additional arrests on narcotics charges, likely armed."

Up to this point drug runners and organized crime have not penetrated the EPIC system. If they were to do so, they could increase their illegitimate success rate considerably. Obviously, then, EPIC is available only to "subscribers"—federal and state law-enforcement agencies operating with closely guarded, coded access information. The only limitation on EPIC is that it is bound by and observes the provisions of the Federal Privacy Act, and that, of course, is the way it should be.

The Coast Guard is justly proud of its successes. But nothing is perfect in this world. The concentration of cutters and personnel in southern waters has left less protection for the northern coastline. The Coast Guard has had to severely restrict its towing services for vessels disabled on the high seas, to the chagrin of fishermen and yachtsmen alike; and fisheries protection, in general, has had to be somewhat reduced. Time and again, Coast Guard officers told us ruefully, and outlaws of the ocean gleefully, that while the Coast Guard has ships, personnel, and the necessary *esprit de corps*, it simply hasn't the bucks to bring the drug war at sea to a victorious conclusion. The Vice President's South Florida Task Force has helped a lot, but mostly by shifting personnel and equipment around, not by increases felt to be badly needed by Coast Guard officers and other law enforcers. We also heard a bit of rumbling by officers of various services to the effect that old interagency rivalries were still smoldering and that the whole task force concept was a gimmick soon to be abandoned.

We had to go to the top to find out.

Charles F. Rinkevich is the coordinator of the Vice President's South Florida Task Force, the superagency designed to

serve as the high command in the drug war. In his speech before
the Miami Citizens Against Crime, on March 16, 1982, Vice
President Bush referred to Charles Rinkevich as "my guy in
Miami . . . [who] will be an enormous help . . . in pulling together
the diverse efforts that will be needed here."[44] An experienced
crime fighter who served in previous administrations, Charles
Rinkevich appeared to have matters well in hand when he
briefed us in his office on the drug war.

The President's resolve to respond with might to the druggies' undeclared war against the United States arose in no small
measure out of the concern of Miami's citizens, who had become
the victims long before anybody had thought about a "drug
war." Not only had Miami become the homicide capital of the
United States, but also other violence and property crime, including illegal financial transactions, had turned the "sunshine
city" into something like the old territory west of Fort Smith.
Anything went, and most of it was drug-related! In 1981, the
Miami Herald documented it all so well in an article by two young
reporters, Jim McGee and Carl Hiaasen: "U.S. Drug Enforcement—The Billion-Dollar Bust: the story of America's hapless
drug war—a failure from the streets to the courtrooms."[45] The
subtitles of the exposé tell the story:

- "U.S. is losing drug war—eight years after the launching
  of the Drug Enforcement Administration, the war on drugs
  is a rout—a lopsided romp for the drug traffickers"
- "Seizures fail to dam the flood of dope"
- "Trouble at top frustrates battle against the dopers"
- "America's eight-year-old, billion-dollar war on drugs has
  become a domestic version of Vietnam. One reason is mis-
  management"
- "An agent's world: unbearable tedium broken by stark
  terror; street unit's job: disruption"
- "An informant's role is vital and perilous"
- "Civil Service rules protect errant agents"
- "Undercover agents are often tempted"
- "DEA's big cases blend triumph and debacle"
- "Controversy has hounded the long war against drugs"
- "A tangled bureaucracy: the drug flow just won't stop"
- "Convicted traffickers soon back on street"
- "Illegal drug trade a major industry inside Colombia"
- "DEA feebly attempts to slay 'drug dragon' in Colombia"

- "How a 'family' stung Bolivians—Dad, Mom, and Junior were all federal drug agents, acting out an elaborate charade"
- "Peru: cocaine flows unchecked through jungle waterways"
- "Big dealers rarely get caught in Peru"
- "New strategy is sought for war on drugs"

A new strategy was indeed needed to come to grips with the crime war in *mare narcoticum,* the narcotics ocean, which seemed beyond control on the part of the victimized United States, with the odds totally in favor of the aggressor. The McGee-Hiaasen exposé sparked the first organized resistance, or counterattack: Miami Citizens Against Crime, a powerful confederation of civic, business, and political leaders intent on winning Miami and the rest of South Florida back to the side of civic order and tranquillity.[46] This group, with a carefully drawn-up strategy, put the pressure on the White House that resulted in the creation of the South Florida Task Force.

By the time of our visit with the Vice President's "guy in Miami," the South Florida Task Force was in full operation. The Vice President, with his chief of staff, Admiral Daniel Murphy, was frequently meeting with all involved Cabinet members, and the Vice President himself visited Miami biweekly. There had even been talk of nationalizing the South Florida Task Force, raising it to Cabinet level, and a year earlier we even had toasted the apparent designee of the new department!

Customs, the Coast Guard, the FBI, the Immigration and Naturalization Service, and other agencies, had been strengthened in South Florida, though the ATF (the Alcohol, Tobacco, and Firearms Agency) fared badly and was facing extinction. But the spirit was distinctly gung-ho if not tally-ho, and the seizure of suspect ships and aircraft was increasing, with record-breaking loads of narcotics contraband.[47]

At the risk of breaking the continuity of our account, we feel compelled now to report on subsequent events. We had seen the silver lining, but a year later it became clear that there is no silver lining without a cloud. Speaking before the Florida congressional delegation on March 28, 1983—the first anniversary of the establishment of the South Florida Task Force—Admiral Murphy gave an admirable account of the work of the task force.

A total of $3 billion worth of drugs, at street value, had been seized. Things were now tough on the smugglers. A pilot who used to demand $100,000 for one drug flight now insisted on $300,000. The admiral had to admit, however, that the amount of cocaine on South Florida's streets had not diminished, and that while marijuana imports to Florida had fallen off, they had increased elsewhere in the United States.

The Florida congressional delegation was less than happy, and it was particularly concerned with the President's plan to withdraw the Vice President as head of the task force and to place the operation under the jurisdiction of the Attorney General. Said Representative Sam Gibbons: "What assurance do we have that the Attorney General is going to have the clout to get the job done?" And Representative Claude Pepper chimed in: "When the Attorney General starts telling the Navy what to do or the Coast Guard, I don't know whether they'd be too receptive or not."[48] The *Miami Herald* portrayed the impending cloudburst of the silver lining diplomatically when it reported on the administration's plans: "U.S. will streamline drug force"; "The South Florida Task Force will be smaller but stronger."[49]

Several months later, long after the completion of our investigation of the war at sea in the drug ocean, the nation's papers reported: "Busted—South Florida Task Force to be disbanded."[50]

Budget cuts and lack of cooperation with the Pentagon were cited as reasons. And the President took a firm stand against the appointment of a federal drug "czar." Twice the President vetoed bills that would have established a Cabinet-level command to fight the drug war.[51] The emphasis was to be on a network of regionally operating task forces coordinated by the Attorney General.[52] Guidelines for the operation of these task forces were issued early in 1983.[53] But nine months later, the House Select Committee on Narcotics Abuse and Control, at hearings in West Palm Beach, expressed its dissatisfaction with the federal effort: "The flow of drugs into the United States has not been significantly reduced. . . ."[54] Matters were to get worse. The 1985 national budget proposed to cut in half Customs' $31 million appropriation for running its surveillance planes. "I can't imagine us operating with the budget they've given us. We're going to have to shut down," said a U.S. Customs official.[55] But when we left the office of the South Florida Task

Force coordinator, long before the fiasco we just related, matters still seemed to hang together: silver lining, no clouds.

It had been a full day in the various federal offices. We were completing our notes at one of the hotels overlooking the Miami River. Freighters from Haiti, shrimpers, and yachts were passing by. It all seemed so tranquil. But it wasn't. Only a few weeks ago the guests of the hotel had complained about having to witness dozens of Haitian refugees jumping from one of those freighters into the river and scrambling up to the premises of the hotel, thereby disturbing their cocktail hour.

There was one person we had yet to see in Miami—Carl Hiaasen, whose exposé with Jim McGee had sparked the creation of the task force and who had followed up with a novel, *Trap Line*, which told the archetypal story of a Key West shrimper gone bad. With prices depressed, mortgages on the ship due, and bad luck (syndicate-created) to boot, just one drug run could get the shrimper off the hook![56]

We met Carl Hiaasen at his news desk at the *Miami Herald*. There is no news source better than an investigative reporter, and Carl Hiaasen is one of the best. By now he had written, with Susan Sacks and Richard Marin, yet another exposé: "Smuggler's Island," the story of Key West.[57] And so we heard from him the accounts of the drug war episodes—of prosecutors who drop charges; of judges who acquit in the face of the evidence; of innocent yachtsmen whose vessels were taken over by druggies; of shrimpers becoming millionaires overnight, of Colombian grandmothers turned chiefs of staff in running drug operations out of Miami; of sheriff's deputies who cordon off a marijuana unloading operation so that nobody can rip off the druggies; of shoot-outs on the high seas between Bimini in the Bahamas and the Florida shore among druggies trying to rip each other off; of the Cigarette speedboat salesman who took two would-be customers for a test drive (they had flashed $80,000 in cash) and who later disappeared but whose blood was found in the speedboat twenty-four hours later, after it was scuttled following a marijuana run from the Bahamas; of innocent boaters forced to leave certain Bahama Keys at gunpoint for no apparent reason; and of boats that simply disappeared in the ocean. "Sea crimes are perfect crimes. The bodies disappear —the evidence is at the bottom of the ocean. The vessel—if she survives—has different colors and a change in name," Carl Hiaasen told us.

"The Coast Guard is doing a creditable job," he continued. "But the odds are against it. There is corruption among all the governments running the Caribbean basin, including Florida. The seas are vast, the Coast Guard is small."

Hiaasen had a recommendation: "Go further South and see for yourself."

2

A Tangled
Caribbean Web

•

From Bermuda's reefs, from edges
   of sunken ledges,
In some far-off, bright Azore;
From Bahama, and the dashing,
   Silver-flashing
Surges of San Salvador;—

   Henry Wadsworth Longfellow,
   Seaweed

The Bahamian Chain

WE ARE IN THE ANTEROOM OF Andrew Antippes, chargé d'affaires
of the United States to the government of the Bahamas. This
embassy is what you would expect the United States embassy in
a small tropical country to look like: kind of a colonial setting,
palm trees around the premises, overhead rotating blades fanning the moist air in the offices, the clickety-clack of typewriters
in the background. We could not help but overhear angry voices
emanating from the office of the chargé d'affaires while we were
reading dog-eared copies of *Customs Today*. At last the visitors
left, Andrew Antippes bade them farewell, and, recognizing us,
bid us hello.

   "I guess you could not help but overhear . . ." Yes, we
answered him, we could not. "Now let me tell you. These folks
really have a justified complaint. They are Americans and a
Canadian, who bought property and vacation houses on Norman's Cay, Bahamas. That's right here," and he pointed to a tiny
speck on the map of the Bahamas. "In 1978, a Colombian national of German background, named Charles Lehder, also
bought property on that island. It appears that Lehder is con-

44

trolled by Vesco—I am sure you have heard his name before."
We had—and we were bound to hear it again and again. "Now,
Lehder brought in heavy equipment, by landing craft, I suppose,
and he bulldozed the landscape until it turned into an airfield
with two runways. Then he constructed hangars. The whole
thing was an efficient paramilitary operation that the Seabees
could not have bested. He also brought in thirty attack-trained
Dobermans and let them loose at night. These dogs terrorized
the other settlers. After all, they had settled there for the superb
marine life the cay offers, not to study the American Kennel
Club's breed specifications of Dobermans. The American and
Canadian settlers were so intimidated that they fled the island.
Then the Lehder people ran the island as if it were their own.
Planes, from Lear Jets to DC-3's, would bring in drug cargoes,
which were then unloaded and brought by fast craft into the
good ol' U.S.A. The druggies made themselves quite at home.
Here, look at these photographs! They left the place in sham-
bles!

"Yes, we intervened with Bahamian authorities. A team of
ten cops was sent in to clean up the place. Next thing that
happened is that the cops were employed unloading the Lear
Jets, for a payment of a case of Heineken's each. The cops were
rotated. Same thing with the next shift. Yes, I got a lot of cooperation from the commissioner of police, who is clean and compe-
tent, as are most of the officials I deal with. But the clincher was
an accident. A private United States plane, overflying the Bahamas, experienced a cockpit fire and had to make an emergency
landing at the nearest airstrip—Norman's Cay. The Colombians
at the island sought to prevent that landing by all means: They
blocked the runway with one of their own planes and with cars,
forcing the American plane to crash-land, severely injuring all
four persons aboard.

"Then I got action! We've cleaned out the place. The druggies are gone, thanks to Bahamian cooperation. And the American and Canadian owners have got their property back—or
what's left of it. Well, you heard the noise!"

The Bahamian islands are indeed a chain—around the neck
of the southeastern United States of America, when it comes to
crime on the crests. And they always have been. When you have
dinner at Nassau, it is bound to be within sight of "Blackbeard's
Tower," the remnants of the fortress of the notorious pirate

Edward Teach, who bled American traders and their ports. The Bahamas simply are there, in front of our southeastern coastline, islands galore, a chain to adore us—or a chain to choke us.

"The Bahamian islands figure prominently," Andrew Antippes continued, "in the drug war against the United States of America—as a transfer point, from air or mother ship to [relatively] small [and usually swift] craft. Assuredly, the success of the Norman's Cay operation has slowed down the drug traffic, but the success is not complete. Bahamian police just seized 418 pounds of cocaine—with help from the United States intelligence sources! And Lehder and his likes will continue their operations as long as they are profitable, if not out of Norman's Cay, then from somewhere else, perhaps Paradise Island—and yes, those fellows have the best lawyers working for them!"

Here is a quick rundown of the Bahamas situation:

By virtue of geography, the Bahamas were destined to become a transfer point for the smuggling of drugs into the United States, just as they had been the staging area for rum running into the United States half a century ago. Once again, the United States Coast Guard, as the front-line force, is pitted against outlaws who attempt that last short run from the Bahamas to the United States shores. The Bahamas are hard to patrol: The sea area they cover is vast, with shoals, cays, bays, and inlets offering ideal hiding places and escape routes. The Bahamian government is friendly and most cooperative; its tiny defense force works closely with the United States Coast Guard.

During the rum war, aliens were smuggled into the United States by the rum runners from time to time. Today, alien smuggling has become a very lucrative supplement to the drug runners' operations—a matter we shall discuss in greater detail in a later chapter. Violence marks today's drug-running operations. Gun battles between or among the vessels, planes, and helicopters of competing organizations have become common. Just a few days ago, we were told, a major gun battle was prevented and seizure of a vessel loaded with drugs was effected off Abaco Island thanks to the cooperation among the United States Customs radar station at Guantánamo Bay, Cuba, the United States Coast Guard, and the Bahamian defense force: One vessel was approaching bales of marijuana that had been dropped by a plane for pickup by a drug runner. While that vessel was engaged in retrieving the bales, a competing drug-running ves-

sel approached to pirate the cargo. It had already attached itself
to the first vessel but was driven off by a Bahamian patrol boat,
which seized the drug-loading vessel. The pirate got away. Actually, the intercepted druggies seemed happy about their fate—
it was preferable to being machine-gunned to death! Hundreds
of vessels, mostly but not necessarily identified as suspect, have
simply disappeared in and around Bahamian waters. Violence is
a necessary concomitant of an illegal business with incredibly
high stakes. The American public had not appeared overly concerned with that shooting war outside its borders—until the
Exuma incident of 1980. That documented the resurgence of
outright piracy, affecting the lives of innocent people, and we
shall tell the story in full when we return to piracy.

Certain areas of the Bahamian chain have become so violent,
corrupt, and drug-saturated that innocent yachtsmen will simply
stay away. The yachts that do go to these areas, including
Bimini, Treasure Cay, Great Inagua, or Andros, will carry plenty
of firepower, and they can be sure that other vessels they encounter are similarly armed—and that includes Vesco's boat,
which they are likely to encounter in those parts from time to
time. Of course, Vesco has now been expelled from the Bahamas and reportedly resides in—of all places—socialist Cuba.

The drug trade is all-pervasive—on land, on water, and in
the air. Of the one hundred aircraft on the grass and tarmac of
Nassau's airport, a third are on the EPIC list of suspect craft, and
none is totally beyond suspicion—not even the fixed-wing patrol
plane with the U.S. Coast Guard markings! As we learned elsewhere, a private party had bought an old and decommissioned
Coast Guard plane out of mothballs. Its markings had never
been removed. The plane was next spotted in the Bahamas,
buzzing a drug-smuggling vessel. In fright, the druggies threw
their cargo overboard, which was promptly picked up by the
plane crew's confederates on water.

Inroads into the drug traffic flowing through the Bahamas
have been made, thanks to the tie-in of the United States embassy in the Bahamas with the Vice President's South Florida
Task Force (of which our chargé d'affaires is a member), on the
one hand, and the close cooperation with Bahamian authorities
on the other. What happened on Bahamian National Day, July
10, 1982, surely was a sign of success and a clear demonstration
of the druggies' concern about having their style cramped: In

the middle of the celebrations, with all the bigwigs of the Bahamian government in the grandstand and the entire diplomatic corps assembled, a small plane appeared overhead, dropping thousands of leaflets over the assembled multitude. The leaflets read: "Nixon—Reagan—DEA go home!" Attached were genuine bills, in denominations of $5, $10, and $20; and a similar drop was made over Bimini, where the leaflets read: "Leave Bahamas to the Bahamians."

As we were leaving Andrew Antippes' office, he pointed to the latest briefings that had just come in:

- Last night two planes were seized by Bahamian police in Bimini with eighteen hundred pounds of marijuana aboard, following a U.S. intelligence tip-off. The crew was United States and Colombian—unhappily, some Bahamian police appear to be implicated
- Four hundred pounds of cocaine seized on Great Anagua
- Gasoline sales dropped 60 percent on Grand Turks and Caicos islands!

That last item surely is a good sign of the success of our overflights, circumnavigations, and undercover work! It means that Grand Turks and Caicos islands are no longer a major staging area in the war on the drug ocean.[1] But nearby island republics stand ready to fill any break that may be created by the success of antinarcotics operations in the Bahamas. The Dominican Republic appears to be the latest "bridge." Dominican Attorney General Antonio Rosario called the situation in his country "extremely dangerous."[2]

Smugglers' Island[3]

Old U.S. 1 runs straight from the border of Maine with New Brunswick, Canada, to America's toes, the Florida Keys. George Washington had recognized the defense implications of this communications artery and entrusted his friend and confidant Polish Cavalry General Pulaski with securing "the road," which promptly became known as the Pulaski Highway. And here and there, between Maine and Florida, a local map or street marker will still refer to it as such. Washington never strayed far from the Pulaski Highway, operating out of New Jersey—the "cockpit of the revolution"[4]—or Pennsylvania, from where he could move his troops on that road, to north or south, depending on the exigencies of the moment.

During World War II the highway, much improved with bridges and by straightening of the route, became known as the National Defense Highway, in anticipation of the attempted implementation of Hitler's wildest plan—the conquest of America. Now U.S. 1 has largely been rendered obsolete by the construction of I-95, which runs parallel to old U.S. 1 and has to some extent incorporated and replaced it. I-95 and U.S. 1 are the drug-run arteries of the narcotics war, only these arteries no longer end at Key West—they continue on the ocean lanes to Colombia, and they are just as busy south of Key West as they are around Boston or Baltimore.

That vacation trailer—a "mobile home"—just passing us, with "Bert and Ethyl from Lima, Ohio" inscribed on its fantail, may be a mere extension of a shrimper called *Ethyl B,* which brought cocaine from Lima, Peru, via Cape LaVela, Colombia, on the watery I-95 to any of the Florida Keys. But then, of course, Bert and Ethyl just might be retired from their grocery store in Lima, Ohio, enjoying the warmth of the sunbelt, totally oblivious to the drug war that has hit our beaches. But then again, how can anyone be totally oblivious to it?

We are traveling U.S. 1 pursuant to Carl Hiaasen's recommendation. The highway across the Keys, a marvel of road construction of which the Roman master road builders would have been envious, is lined with the symbols of affluence: Splashy condominiums, ostentatious homes, elaborate marinas crowded with sail and motor yachts worth millions upon millions of dollars, airports with hundreds of gleaming Lear Jets and lesser flying machines tethered to the tarmac. Surely this cannot be "Bert and Ethyl" country.

We are passing Big Pine Key and the motel at which storyteller Lionel White placed part of the plot to blow up a cabin cruiser, meant to destroy the witnesses and evidence in an imaginary yet not so unrealistic plot of Mafiosi and of government accountants turned bad.[5] In the hot sunlight of South Florida, fact and fiction tend to blur, though fact seems to keep the upper hand. Checking into one of those hotels was an experience. The clerk had been suspicious of the party before us. The lady who wanted the suite was barely literate and obviously needed a shampoo. She had no credit cards but *insisted* on a suite. She managed to convince the clerk of her affluence when she peeled off a few $100 bills from a roll representing a multiple of the cost of a night. The restaurants en route tend to be called "Smuggler's Cove," or "Buccaneer Bar," if not "Pirate's Paradise." At last we made it to Key West, terminal of the dry part of U.S. 1.

Smugglers' Island, U.S.A., is what they call this town. We felt out of place. A kind soul in one of Hemingway's favorite watering holes patiently explained what we had perceived but not digested. "You see, each gold chain around a fella's neck means one successful drug run. Look at that guy—if he falls overboard, he'll sink! On that T-shirt? 'Save the bales!' Get it? Instead of 'Save the whales.' A bale, man, that's a bale of marijuana. They also call them 'square groupers.' Sure, because that's the only catch that half of these fishermen over there bring in. And why shouldn't they? At a hundred thousand bucks for one run, instead of a measely two thousand for a week's hard work on a shrimper. There—half of these shrimpers don't even have their real gear anymore. Don't need no shrimping gear bringing in square groupers. On that T-shirt? 'Coke's the thing!' Get it? That's the new gold coming out of Colombia. And look at that bumper sticker: 'You legalize pot—I go on welfare.' And why do you suppose that fellow has a two-hundred-fifty-thousand-buck helicopter behind his hash joint? 'Ten-buck rides!' He doesn't give rides. But for a good fee he'll help the shrimpers find out where the Coast Guard isn't at. They say it's a thousand bucks a ride." Our friend chuckled. We paid for the rounds. He slouched out, got in his car, and drove off. He, too, had a bumper sticker: "How do you spell relief? 'Colombian'!"

That was our first visit to Key West, where the local real-estate magazine advertised condominiums at a beachfront property as "Smugglers' Special." We visited the premises as "potential buyers." The asking price was in the millions.

Smuggling had always been good business in the Keys. Now it is also a highly profitable sport for young and old. When recently a nervous smuggling vessel had dumped its bales of marijuana prematurely, local teenagers jumped joyfully into the breakers to retrieve the bouncing bundles, and not even four Customs launches and a Coast Guard cutter and helicopter could interrupt the gleeful retrieval.[6] We were told that at Sears that night there was a run on laundry driers. But business in general is good in the Keys, and it gets better every time the harvest is finished in Colombia. And all business is for cash—like fourteen cars the night before Christmas from the local Cadillac dealer, or that other hot item out of the Sears catalogue: compactors! They are a nice trade item with the Colombian pot exporters: The compactors make the square groupers!

For years America's traditional hard-core drug, heroin, has been eclipsed by cocaine and marijuana. Eighty-five percent of all cocaine and marijuana in the United States are imported from Caribbean ports, mostly Colombian, but also, in the case of marijuana, Jamaican. And the natural off-loading point for these drugs is Key West. The names of the Colombian ports from which the cargoes come are legendary in the history of South Florida and of sea crime: Cartagena, Barranquilla, and Santa Marta, where the loot of plundered Spanish colonies once was loaded and where pirates plundered the plunderers. Colombia's legitimate export, coffee, amounts to maximally 20 percent of its total export; the bulk is cocaine and marijuana. Most of the cocaine is grown in Bolivia or Peru, while the marijuana is grown on Colombia's Guajira Peninsula, the northeasternmost part of the country flanking the Gulf of Venezuela. Guajira appears to be a part of Colombia that has been given up by organized government, and Colombia has persistently denied requests for the extradition of Guajira growers and traffickers who have violated U.S. laws. After all, they are Colombian nationals.[7]

Cocaine, while shipped from Colombia, where the refineries are located, derives from coca grown on 86,000 Bolivian and 123,000 Peruvian acres. The crop generates nearly $1 billion in revenue, annually, for Peru (whose entire budget is only $5 billion). No blame appears to attach to the growing of coca bushes. A coca farmer with ten acres may net $65,000 per year in a country with an annual per-capita income of $1,150. From the point of production to the ultimate sale in America, the trade is controlled by ten principal cocaine rings, with an annual earning of $50 million each, and it has been estimated that a hundred thousand Colombians living in the United States "earn major dollar figures in drugs."[8] Our government has found it virtually impossible to persuade the South American governments to eliminate the production and export of narcotics to the United

States. Such efforts are seen as Yankee imperialism. In 1982, Colombia seized a mere 4 percent of the coca leaves grown there,[9] and in Bolivia there was, at best, a token response to each pressure by the United States embassy. In one instance—involving Altman-Barbie and cohorts (about whom more later)—a violent raid by the government's paramilitary thugs was directed against small producers of Santa Cruz, while the biggest producer of them all, Roberto Suarez, stood smilingly by.[10] While the drug economy has brought new wealth to the impoverished producing countries—especially a few families, who donate heavily to charity and Church—drugs have also brought those countries the new factor of drug-related violence. It starts in the Andes, where gangs rip each other off, where growers and exporters constantly endeavor to outsmart and cheat each other. But death is the price of fraud in drug dealings,[11] and retaliatory mass murder is not unheard of. Thus, in April 1983, the skeletal remains of a hundred people were found in a cave near Becerril, in the department of Cesar, Colombia—killed in a clandestine drug operation.[12] This trade can flourish only under the protection of bazookas and machine guns, and not just at the points of production and loading, but also at every point of the way, until final distribution in the United States, as attested to by the ever-increasing number of weapons seizures in connection with vessel seizures by the Coast Guard and other law-enforcement agencies.

At the point of delivery of the drugs, the Colombians assume control once again, all the way to the distribution centers in the U.S.A., where by now there exists a tight organization of illegal Colombian aliens, with their own business and execution machinery. One of the foremost Colombian drug entrepreneurs in Florida happens to be a woman—Martha Libia Cardona. Indicted in Florida, she jumped bail and is now back in Colombia.[13]

As in times past, organized government was initially far too disorganized to meet the novel threat of criminal elements. It took years to organize the South Florida Task Force, yet during our inquisitive visit we saw little if any impact of the task force's efforts in the drug war on the streets and in the harbors of the Florida Keys. Certainly, seizures of contraband and of smuggling vessels have increased. It has become much harder to get the stuff into Florida, but much of it is still making it through the cordon provided by the Coast Guard and its partners in the South Florida Task Force. The highly lucrative contraband is simply coming in elsewhere!

There are those among the old-timers of Key West who will tell you that the Florida Keys are really only a peripheral part of the United States, that the Keys really are and always have been the independent Conch Republic, living by its own laws, customs, and mores, which certainly antedate the laws of the United States and are hard to square with the rules of any other legal system. Even during Spanish sovereignty over these parts, the Conches did as they pleased. Being in the southernmost part of what is now the United States of America, they were the pivot of the illicit trade between the lands and islands claimed by the great powers—the United Kingdom, Spain, France, the Netherlands, and lesser sovereignties, including Sweden, Denmark, and even Brandenburg (later on Prussia and Germany). Conches had always made their comfortable living by accommodating themselves within the loopholes of conflicting interests, conflicting laws, and conflicting powers. Commanding the shortest route between the Gulf of Mexico and the wide-open Atlantic through the Bahama Islands, the Florida Keys were in a unique position to provide and shelter the pirates and to cash in on the flourishing illicit trades. By the time Americans were stirring for independence, this easy mode of living between laws had been well entrenched among the Conches. By then, at least that part of living between laws that is called "smuggle" had become their national sport. The United Kingdom was intent on taking its dues on every piece of colonial trade. Yet the colonials were not willing to provide it, and the Conches cashed in on that form of patriotism. Nor does there appear to be much respect in the Conch Republic for the customs and narcotics laws of today's sovereign, Uncle Sam.[14]

When we inquired of knowledgeable persons how many of the over three hundred Key West fishing vessels were involved in the narcotics trade, the answer was: A lot more than a half, and it may be nine out of ten! Fred W. Long, the supervisory patrol officer of the U.S. Customs Service in Miami, guessed in House testimony that "probably better than 50 percent of South Florida fishing vessels are either continually involved or have been involved at one time or another."[15] That figure boggles the imagination. We found matters in the Conch Republic to be virtually beyond control. The maritime drug trade is open and notorious, and let the South Florida Task Force be damned—such is the attitude we discerned. Hiaasen and the *Miami Herald* team had earlier established the close links among Conch politics, law enforcement, legitimate business, the drug trade, the virtual impunity with which fishermen could operate their drug runs, the virtual guarantee of a dismissal of the charges, or their reduction from a major felony charge of smuggling tons of pot to a misdemeanor slap on the wrist for possession of a minuscule amount of marijuana—subject to probation—if you had the right defense counsel! Time and again we heard the rumor that "the organization" guarantees the busted marijuana smuggling skipper the best defense counsel, coverage of all expenses, and a new vessel if the busted vessel is seized, or maybe return of his old vessel after auction sale by the government.

It is in this environment that the Coast Guard and other marine police establishments, especially Customs, were expected to make a difference, in the war against an unholy alliance between the Conch Republic and Guajira Peninsula, Colombia—though this confederation has not yet been admitted to United Nations membership!

The Eternal Skull and Crossbones

We looked farther south yet, to the Andean origin of what more and more appeared to be the source of America's crime war on the ocean. We had visited these countries earlier. And we had been duly impressed with the gentleness of the people, the evidence of a great past and of present civilizations, and, in the case of Peru, a rather low crime rate. But then, the short-term visitor to Bogotá, La Paz, or Lima, the modern capitals, or to any of the ancient Inca cities, does not and cannot perceive that other part of life in these Andean countries, the part that has created incredible wealth among a few while maintaining misery among the many and bringing a new form of slavery—drug dependency—to North America: the life of drug production, with its elaborate political connections and implications, the manufacture of the illicit cargo that keeps the druggies on their runs and that fuels the drug war in North American waters. But let us start with the skull and crossbones, the archetypal

symbol of death and terror flown on the halyards of the buccaneers who sailed the shores north of the Andean countries in
centuries past. It is not surprising that this very same symbol was
deployed on the banners of Hitler's elite corps, the SS, to strike
terror and the fear of death in all his opponents.

It was the same symbol which graced the lapels of Colonel
Claus Altman-Barbie, the SS commander in occupied Lyons,
France, in 1942. According to the postwar French court that
sentenced him to death *in absentia,* Colonel Altman-Barbie "participated in 4,342 murders in France. He sent 7,591 Jews, including children, to the gas chambers in Auschwitz. He arrested
14,311 Resistance fighters. He tortured many of them."[16] "He
beat me with his fists, he kicked me with riding crops and trun-
cheons. Luckily, I usually fainted," testified a wartime French
Resistance fighter.[17]

And then there is the story of Altman-Barbie's extermination
of the children of Izieu, France: Forty-one children aged three
to thirteen were "terminated" by the colonel.[18] After the war,
Altman-Barbie disappeared. Only in 1983 did the United States
government reveal, with apologies to France, that United States
Army intelligence had hired Altman-Barbie after the war, used
his services as an ardent anti-Communist, and, when these services were no longer needed—or became too embarrassing—
had spirited him out of Europe and installed him in Bolivia.[19]
There he promptly resumed his profession as an organizer of
repression, served as security adviser to various military leaders
and presidents, and became president of that country's maritime
company. It was so simple for Altman-Barbie, who once served
under the skull and crossbones, to enter a trade that traditionally sailed under the same symbol—and to extend his criminal
activities to the organization and protection of the drug trade.
He was indeed needed to build the drug fortunes of Bolivia's
corrupt military leaders and public officials.[20] When France,
having now twice sentenced Altman-Barbie to death *in absentia,*
requested his extradition for trial in France for his wartime
atrocities, the Bolivian regime denied extradition on the
grounds that he had become a Bolivian citizen. It was only when
the military dictatorship was replaced by a democratically
elected government, in October 1982, that France's request for
his extradition was granted, in January 1983.[21] He is now awaiting trial, in the same Lyons prison in which he had tortured

Resistance fighters and imprisoned Lyons' Jews prior to their deportation to death camps.[22] There are still some Bolivian charges pending against the man of the skull and crossbones. He is being accused of violating Bolivia's immigration laws, of illegally "organizing and advising a network of mercenaries and paramilitary," operating under the swastika sign, and securing that country's drug production under the corrupt generals whom he had served.[23] But these charges were filed just the day before his extradition to France. We suppose the government of Bolivia needed a few extra hours of time to perfect the extradition of Altman-Barbie, who was already sitting in a Bolivian jail on a fraud conviction involving his "commercial" activities in Bolivia.

While Altman-Barbie is awaiting trial in France, that country is reaping the harvest from the seedlings whose growth the butcher of Lyons protected with his storm troopers in Bolivia: On January 6, 1984, a Bolivian was arrested at Orly Airport in Paris with 5.5 kilograms of cocaine worth 3.3 million francs—from Bolivia with love.[24]

Even with Altman-Barbie out of the way and a democratic government installed in Bolivia, drug production in Bolivia and its neighboring countries continues to flourish. In October 1983, the Bolivian Minister of the Interior, Federico Alvarez Plata, had to confess that illegal cocaine production in Bolivia is growing "at an alarming rate." The government is virtually powerless to do anything about it. Even the offer of $45 million in United States assistance money to help farmers switch to the planting of legitimate crops is not going to solve the problem. What is $45 million to combat an illegal trade that brings Bolivian growers at least $155 million annually?[25]

On August 5, 1983, the new Bolivian Cabinet resigned because right-wing drug traffickers—Altman-Barbie's former associates—were plotting to overthrow the democratically elected government. This move was intended to give President Hernán Silas Zuazo the opportunity to form a new coalition government involving the labor unions, which are heavily Communist-influenced. This, of course, worried the United States government greatly.[26] Are we, then, to choose between Nazi narcotics and communism? The diplomatic implications are vast!

For those Americans who did not realize what was happening to our country during the current drug war, ABC News provided a shocker with the airing on August 20, 1983, of "The Cocaine

Cartel," a news special that brought to the television screen such unlikely costars as Vice President Bush and Bolivian cocaine producer Fabio Ochoa, drug dealers and law-enforcement officers from Colombia and the United States, U.S. Coast Guard skippers and cocaine addicts, corrupt Colombian politicians, honest political leaders, and financial analysts. America discovered through the tube that our national drug habit costs us $80 billion a year, and the cocaine euphoria alone about $34 billion. Thus the cocaine cartel has a money turnover exceeded only by that of Exxon Corporation. This money flow fuels the inflation in many parts of the United States as well as in Colombia and Bolivia. Wittingly or unwittingly, our largest banks have participated in laundering the drug money from filthy lucre into clean cash, on which no taxes have been paid. It is clear who produces the cocaine, who is being supported by it—in Colombia and Bolivia, especially—and who is supporting it: a new organized crime clan, the cocaine cartel. The vast profits of this organization, the narcobucks, are transferred through any of our large United States banks or money exchange firms to a bank in a country with secretive accounts, and then back to the United States, Colombia, or Bolivia as clean money. Sometimes cash is transferred physically in large bags by plane or vessel out of the United States. Despite the Vice President's South Florida Task Force, cocaine keeps coming into the United States as fast as 23,000 Bolivian farmers, on 35,000 hectares of land, can produce it, and as soon as air- or waterborne mules are ready to bring it to the United States, where it will be sold at an 8,000 percent markup since production, and where, every day, 5,000 Americans try the drug for the first time. While producers in Bolivia and traders, refiners, and politicians in Colombia are growing fat and respectable,[27] millions of Americans—mostly from the middle class—become battle casualties of the drug war. Cocaine is shared by 4 million Americans, half of them between eighteen and twenty-four years old, and probably 20 million Americans have tried it.[28] An estimated 22.5 million Americans, 10 percent of the population, have made cannabis (pot) the drug of their choice.[29] America's illicit drug habit, over which the drug war at sea is now being waged, costs users the equivalent of 6 percent of the national debt of $1.389 trillion.[30] These figures stagger our imagination! Our country is at war, a war financed at a high profit by the cocaine cartel and the marijuana mobsters.

PART·II

The Drug War at Sea

I saw a ship a-sailing, a-sailing, a-sailing,
With emeralds and rubies and saphires in her hold;
And a bosun in a blue coat bawling at the railing,
Piping through a silver call that had a chain of gold;
The summer wind was falling and the tall ship rolled.

> John Masefield,
> *An Old Song Re-sung*

3

El Tiburón Blanco:
On Patrol with the U.S.
Coast Guard's *White Shark*

•

With sloping masts and dipping prow,
As who pursued with yell and blow
Still treads the shadow of his foe,
    and forward bends his head,
The ship drove fast, loud roared the blast,
    and southward aye we fled.

            Samuel Taylor Coleridge,
            The Rime of the Ancient Mariner

ON NAUTICAL CHART 409, which spans the vast sea lanes of the Gulf of Mexico and the Caribbean, the progress of our ship, as measured from navigational fix to fix, appears painfully slow. Yet the ship's wake assures us that we are proceeding at fifteen knots toward the point of interception. We are in the Windward Passage, where three and a half centuries ago Spanish galleons sailed eastward, laden with the gold and silver of the exploited colonies of Mexico and South America, and where Yankee pirates and buccaneers from every seafaring nation pursued the convoys' stragglers for booty, under the skull and crossbones.

Our radar indicates a vessel eighteen thousand yards ahead. There is virtually no visibility on the water, yet the sky is starlit and the moon is bright. The sea is calm, churned only by the wake of our ship, which creates a turbulence of phosphorescence. The U.S. Coast Guard cutter *Steadfast* is closing in on her target. Ten thousand yards. "Professors on the bridge!" the PA system blares. Swiftly we climb the companionway to the bridge. All is dark. Our ship shows the navigation lights of a small coastal freighter, concealing her true identity. Only subdued red lights in the charthouse give a sense of direction topside. The quartermasters are plotting our approach. Eight thousand yards. "Big eyes—any sighting?" The sailor manning the huge binoculars on the flying bridge answers in the negative. Seven thousand yards. "Anything on the nightscope?" That marvel of optics, developed during the Vietnam War, capable of compacting even the dimmest nightlight into daytime visibility, has no contact. Yet our radar clearly shows the suspect vessel, now six thousand yards ahead. She appears to be towing something. A long net? Another vessel? "Nightscope—anything?" "Captain, sir, the nightscope just went out." (The captain's response is not quotable.) We are approaching that blip on the radar screen, holding our breath. "Range?" "A thousand yards, sir." And still no vision! "Port searchlight on the target." A switch is thrown —and a fizzle follows. "What the hell!" "Starboard searchlight on!" Another switch is thrown—a fizzle—the searchlight flares up and burns out. (Unquotable comments from the captain, the officer of the watch, and everybody else!) "Range, five hundred yards on the radar." At this point the lenses pop out of Professor Mueller's eyeglasses. "Light plane overhead," comes the comment from Professor Adler and a lookout. The plane disappears as mysteriously as it had appeared. "Range, four hundred yards on the radar—Captain, sir, it's gone—it's gone." The captain jumps to the radar screen, and where a big blip had been, the sea is empty, the target is gone.

The captain breaks the silence of incredulity with only one comment: "We have just crossed into the Bermuda Triangle."

We shall not comment on the guessing game that occupied the eighty-some officers and crew of the *Steadfast* for the next twenty-four hours, with surmises ranging all the way from Soviet submarines (after all, Cuba is near), to U.S. submarines (the chart marks the area as a submarine operating area), to a school of whales, to a self-destruct smuggler, to mermaids and—to the Bermuda Triangle, with the ghosts of Captain Kidd and Blackbeard. In any event, our target was gone.[1]

Only minutes later, our radar screen picked up another target miles away. We gave chase and, sure enough, found one of the suspect vessels identified to us by the superb but not perfect intelligence network that keeps track of the U.S. bound marijuana and cocaine smugglers. Within a thousand yards we hailed the vessel on channel sixteen. Answer: *"No hablo inglés."* We answered back: *"Hola, barca a mi izquierda. ¿Qué es el nombre de su barca?"* Answer, *"Bismark."* Of all the confounded names! More than four decades after the great Allied hunt for the German battleship *Bismarck,* we encounter this decrepit rusty ex-shrimper that hadn't caught a shrimp in years but that had acquired an enviable reputation as the drug runner *Bismark* out of Cartagena, Colombia, but of no documented nationality. In her converted cargo hold the *Bismark* can easily carry $100 million worth of drugs. Yes, we had been searching for her for days. Orders were piped through the *Steadfast.* The 50mm machine guns were manned, the launch with an armed crew was lowered, and the *Bismark* was boarded. Our boarding party radioed back: "The smell of pot is nauseating—yet there is not a single bale, not a leaf left."

The boarding party returned disappointed. Obviously we had been too late. The *Bismark,* a mother ship of the drug trade, had off-loaded on smaller vessels, in the protection of Bahamian shoals. These smaller vessels were now on their way to points off the shores of Florida or the Carolinas, where Cigarette-type speedboats would run the dope ashore.

The *Bismark* incident, however, was not over. A few days later we encountered her again a bit farther south, toward Colombia. She was drifting with dead engines. She had neither fuel nor food nor water left. And a crew member's leg had been injured. Gangrene had set in. She requested help from the Coast Guard! Due to duty, our ship complied with the request. Our crew barely concealed their anger. "Maybe they'd like to come aboard to watch movies with us," one of the Coast Guardsmen commented, and another suggested we might want to supply them with our code book. Without the intervention of our medical corpsman, the gangrenous sailor would be dead today; in fact, the *Bismark* might have joined her namesake on the bottom of the ocean. As it was, sailor's duty to sailors in distress kept another drug runner on the drug run, for not even on the ocean is anyone guilty until proven so, and sailors in need of help must be helped.

There was another aftermath to the *Bismark* incident. A week or so later, the *Steadfast* intercepted one of the Cigarette boats that had shuttled the *Bismark*'s cargo to Florida, and her crew were charged with narcotics importation offenses.

Following our first encounter with the *Bismark,* our skipper held a "rat-patch" (coded radio conference) with Coast Guard headquarters and with another nearby Coast Guard cutter, the *Hamilton.* We were to pursue two of the off-loaders; the *Hamilton* was to pursue the third. Yes, we caught up with one of the drug runners, and the *Hamilton* with another. But her target vessel, the *Anna I,* refused to stop. Flying the Panamanian flag and running for Bahamian waters, she tried to salvage her fourteen tons of marijuana. Within minutes the Panamanian government, at the Coast Guard's request, had authorized the *Hamilton* to stop and board the vessel, and Coast Guard headquarters authorized the use of disabling artillery fire if necessary. It turned out to be necessary to force the *Anna I,* by artillery fire, to heave to. The vessel was towed to Miami, where all aboard faced trial on charges of conspiracy to import drugs into the United States.

During our patrol on the *Steadfast* we made seven other boardings and had many sightings of suspect vessels, which were promptly communicated to other vessels or authorities ashore. Among the suspect vessels we encountered was a coastal freighter, once German, with a German captain aboard. One of her previous names was still clearly visible under a coat of paint. Under that name, so EPIC informed us within minutes, she had been engaged in the narcotics trade. As she was clearly headed for Port Everglades, we made sure that a Customs welcoming party would greet her at dockside. And there was a million-dollar sailing yacht, likewise a suspect vessel but of the cocaine trade, a cargo that is normally beyond the Coast Guard's search capability, because the white powder is so easy to conceal. It takes Customs' German shepherds to sniff out a cargo like that, and the folks aboard the yacht knew it. In fact, to our radio inquiry they responded cockily: "You chaps wouldn't have a case of cold beer aboard for us?" No, there was no beer on the *Steadfast,* unless one believes the myth that among all the soft-drink cans in the Coke machine there is one can of Budweiser —but only the youngest, greenest sailor fell for this sales trick.

Life aboard one of the Coast Guard's workhorses, the 210-foot medium-endurance cutters, is both exciting and boringly routine. We shared both at the invitation of Admiral James S. Gracey, commandant of the U.S. Coast Guard. We had been waiting anxiously for the phone call that would tell us which vessel to board, when and where. She had to be the right vessel on the right mission. We suppose there was just as much anxiety among the captain, officers, and crew of the designated vessel. Women aboard Coast Guard vessels are still somewhat rare, couples unheard of, and professors of criminology—that had never happened! And then the call came from Commander Charles ("Chick") Murray, commanding officer of the *Steadfast,* WMEC 623. "W" is the Coast Guard's designation for all of the service's vessels, all of which (save small patrol boats) are known as cutters. "MEC" stands for "medium-endurance cutter." A medium-endurance cutter is a vessel designed to patrol any part of the ocean, under all conditions, for several weeks at a time. The range of a WMEC is over 6,000 miles. These vessels are sleek, with the superstructure forward, a 76mm cannon behind the foc's'le and a helicopter flight deck aft. The ship is run by two turbocharged diesels, in sparkling engine rooms, producing 5,000 horsepower. The ship's company of some 80 officers and ratings enjoy the ship's high degree of habitability. Three movies are shown nightly, one in the officers' wardroom, one in the NCOs' wardroom, and one in the crew's mess. (We regret to report that both of us gained weight aboard—the chef had once been a chef at a country club!) Our vessel, of the Reliance class of MECs, displaced 950 tons standard and 1,007 tons fully loaded. In Navy terms that puts her into the corvette category. These vessels are ideal for search and rescue—they could easily tow a 10,000-ton vessel—but also for law-enforcement patrol, and that was to be our mission on the *Steadfast* which, although 15 years old, behaved like a spring chicken of the sea.

We met her dockside at Tampa-St. Petersburg, her superstructure graced with "hash marks" attesting to her success as a drug hunter. She had made it into the "million-pound club" and justly earned the name the Colombian drug runners had bestowed on her: *El Tiburón Blanco* (The White Shark). We could bestow other titles on her: The friendliest ship (except to druggies)—the most efficient ship—the happiest ship.

At first cautiously regarded with detachment, we soon became part of the ship's company, especially when the ship bobbed about like a cork in one of those bottlenecks we had heard about and when only the captain and the professors showed up for dinner in the wardroom! The crew swiftly became acquainted with our mission. We lectured and held discussion sessions. Soon there was a contest for the title of our book and its chapter headings: First prize, a $50 check; the other prizes, a case of Heineken's each—to be delivered dockside at the end of the patrol.

Our ship's assignment was to patrol the Bahamian passages through which drug mother ships would have to exit the Caribbean for their run to the U.S. Atlantic shoreline. We were to hunt on the basis of intelligence information, but also to act on our own in intercepting vessels engaged in conspiracies to violate the laws of the United States, especially the drug laws.

There was not just one life aboard ship; there were two, as there are on any maritime patrol vessel or, for that matter, on any naval vessel, of whatever nation. Life one is the tedium of keeping the ship afloat, her engines running, her paint bright, her brass shiny, her electronics humming, her guns on the ready, and her crew fed and happy. Then there is the other life: It is mission-oriented. Its details are known to the bridge only when the ship is at sea, while the crew is standing watch oiling, scraping, and painting. Details of any given action become known to the crew only when the claxon sounds, the bells shrill, and the captain's voice comes over the PA system: A suspect vessel spotted! A specific task to be accomplished! Sailors drop their brushes, dinner plates are abandoned, or a John Wayne movie—with guns blazing on the Arizona desert—comes to an abrupt halt, and the entire ship's company jumps to their duty stations for the action required for the specific task. Perhaps our skipper was overly cautious when he ordered the guns manned before every encounter. After all, so far, no drug runner or pirate had yet fired a shot at a U.S. Coast Guard cutter (unlike during the "rum war," when armed rum runners were not averse to engage cutters in running gun battles). But some of today's drug runners, seized by the Coast Guard, had virtual arsenals aboard: surface-to-surface missiles, bazookas, machine guns, and bombs. Moreover, more than one cutter has been rammed by a druggie, most recently the *Steadfast*'s sister ship, the *Durable*, which had a sizable hole in her bow after the seventy-five-foot drug runner *Lady Mar* tried to disable the *Durable* and get away with her cargo of twenty-five tons of marijuana.[2]

We spent most of our waking hours on the bridge, but if we were watching a movie, we, too, would leave John Wayne on the Arizona desert and rush to the bridge in balmy Caribbean waters when action was about to occur. The suspect vessel would be ten thousand yards ahead. Is she the one we are searching for? What a disappointment when she turned out to be one of the Bahamian defense force's gunboats, or an old-time schooner that had just crossed the Atlantic with Church missionaries aboard! Frustrations abound! After all, the druggies are out there! Here is an entry from our personal logbook:

> Sailboat dead ahead. Intercept in one-and-one-half minutes. Background noise click-a-dee-clack of the machine gun being oiled like a baby. A gorgeous sailing wind, yet, the sailboat ahead of us, a ketch of about 50 feet, motoring under full engine speed—of about 5 knots—changed course into the Bahamian 3 mile zone and does not respond to our channel 16 radio calls or a signal lamp. If she is a doper, she did the smart thing. Majaguana island, the protection of which the ketch sought, is rocky, no real town, no harbor, no marina, no jetty, just a whole bunch of marked wrecks around it. Yet, says the captain, I cannot permit myself to think that every sailboat, however idiosyncratic its master, is a doper. Odd behavior is not reasonable suspicion! The American constitutional law of search and seizure exercises its powerful influence!

Several times we suffered the frustration of highly suspect vessels escaping into Bahamian shoals, beyond the reach of our cutter with her deep draft. That, too, is an old rum runner's trick. They know when the deep draft of a Coast Guard vessel would prevent the skipper from running the risk of getting sand in his condenser, or grounding his vessel. Smugglers prefer shallow-draft vessels![3] If only we had had our helicopter with us throughout the patrol, we could have intercepted escaping druggies before they reached foreign territorial waters beyond our jurisdiction! Unhappily, our HH-52A chopper was ashore for repairs, and we had the benefit of a chopper only when one of our lieutenants had to be flown ashore to testify in a drug conspiracy case stemming from an earlier seizure.

And then there are the frustrations fostered by the druggies themselves, foremost the diversion trick. We suppose it was invented by the rum runners of Prohibition days, who radioed the *Frying Pan* lightship to be in distress, causing the Coast Guard cutter *Manning* and all other Coast Guard cutters and destroyers in the area to converge on the supposedly hapless lightship, while the rum runners were conveying a huge cargo of liquor through the now unguarded sea lanes.[4] We encountered that trick fifty years later but did not fall for it. A distress signal was received by our ship, and all other Coast Guard vessels on patrol in the Caribbean, from one of the southernmost passages, about a plane having ditched in the pond. A Coast Guard plane was immediately dispatched and found no trace—or even probability —of the emergency, and all patrol vessels guarding the other passages stayed right where they were.

On May 18, 1983, the ploy was repeated. A distress signal was picked up on the Atlantic to the effect that the eighty-two-foot yacht *Sorrento* was sinking two hundred miles southeast of Bermuda, with eighteen people aboard. Even a passing Soviet merchant ship joined in the search by a Coast Guard C-130 and a Navy P-3 Orion. As it turned out, the *Sorrento* was at that time safely in Martinique Harbor, fifteen hundred miles away. But the Coast Guard cutter *Unimac* was alert. She apprehended the sixty-foot fishing trawler *Acoupa* with a cargo of pot, trying to slip through the hole in the net to be created by the false distress signal.[5] But the druggies are not giving up. On November 28, 1983, the Coast Guard received still another major distress signal—the most realistic of them all—of a Panamanian freighter, *The South Wind,* reported ablaze off Orient Point, on Long Island Sound. A $37,000 rescue effort was launched but not a trace of a vessel in distress was found, and the Coast Guard ascertained subsequently that the only two vessels with the same name anywhere in the world were safely afloat elsewhere.[6]

EPIC had alerted us to the yacht *Evening Star,* which had left Fort Lauderdale for a drug pickup from a mother ship in our area. Here is our log entry:

> Last night "Evening Star" [not the true name of the ship] was overheard radioing about leaving Eleuthera [Bahamian] Island for Ft. Lauderdale. We were told she'd be a 55 foot yacht, blue on the hull. We positioned ourselves for intercept at N.W. end of both the N.E. and N.W. Prospect Channel, expecting her about 2h after her departure time from E.I. Sure enough, sails were spotted on the horizon, we got an aspect of the vessel and plotted our intercept. L.E. [law-enforcement] Bill was piped, port boat cleared. She did turn out to be the "Evening Star" (from Maine), 60 ft. long, blue below the waterline, otherwise white, a trim and proper yacht. We were answered on channel 16, then 12, in Maine brogue. All our questions were properly answered. At this moment a twin engine plane flew straight over us. Our lookout saw a little yellow balloon

floating in the water. The "Evening Star" answered our question —yes—they had a semi-automatic and a luger aboard, few people, one of whom a 75-year old doctor. Our L.E. Bill boarded three men. Clean, clear ship, inspected it, found no violation. Of course, no drawers, etc., were opened. This was a pure Coast Guard inspection. They were polite, but not friendly, asked us for weather, which we provided.

Dr. "A" lost her bet—a can of soda on this one. The meticulous care with which this operation was conducted, both in seamanship and L.E.—(law enforcement)—menship is remarkable, intelligence, at this point, had proven less than helpful. While there are 50 registered yachts "Evening Star," it is odd we'd come across the wrong one.

Or did we? The ocean is a haystack. *El Tiburón Blanco* is but a tiny magnet, and some pins are not even magnetic—yet they can prick!

How did the Coast Guard get into this war in the drug ocean? In June 1973 *Mr. Lucky* ran out of luck off the South Florida coastline. This high-powered racing boat's engines stopped dead. A passing pleasure boat took *Mr. Lucky* in tow, but finding the job too difficult, sent out a distress signal, which promptly brought a Coast Guard cutter to the scene. Over the protest of Messrs. Andries and Greenwood, the crew of *Mr. Lucky,* the cutter towed the disabled vessel to Miami. There, during an inspection of the boat's engine, an alert Coast Guardsman found several thousand pounds of marijuana aboard. But luck was with *Mr. Lucky,* after all. Three times a jury was deadlocked in the subsequent trial for conspiracy to import marijuana. The defendants argued, ingeniously, that their mission had been to transport their load from a Colombian vessel, outside the jurisdiction of the United States, to a European vessel likewise outside the jurisdiction of the United States. Thus, although the pot ultimately was seized in Miami, they never intended to bring it there—indeed, the Coast Guard had hauled it there over their protest![7]

The case of *Mr. Lucky* and a few similar incidents in 1973 marked the opening of the drug war in America's southern waters. Until that time, marijuana had come in via Mexico. But the Mexican government, in a spirit of neighborly cooperation, used its armed forces to destroy a good many of the marijuana plantations.[8] The Mexican exports to the United States dwindled. For a while Jamaican growers picked up the slack, sending modest quantities of marijuana to the United States, hidden in tourist luggage. The hollowed-out wood-carved head souvenir was a favorite hiding place.[9] Ultimately the runs were made by small planes, which took off right from the plantation and landed at any of a vast array of private landing strips in Florida. Those drug deals financed the armament with which Jamaica's gangs were fighting their not-so-civil wars during the Manley administration, leading to a complete breakdown of law and order in the country and a collapse of the economy. We were unhappy witnesses of this situation when, in the midseventies, dispatched by U.N. Secretary General Kurt Waldheim and at the request of Prime Minister Manley, we led in Jamaica a U.N. team that, with moderate success, ended the gang fighting and ameliorated the marijuana (ganja in Jamaica)-arms cycle, helped restore order in the country, and brought the tourists back to Jamaica.

Unhappily, Jamaica's new conservative government, with Prime Minister Seaga at the helm, was soon to encounter similar difficulties. " 'Ganja matia' proving too powerful for J'ca gov't?" wrote the Caribbean press.[10] Jamaican ganja seizures in 1983 doubled over the previous year's, to 164,740 pounds, thanks to a strengthening of air patrols and Jamaican Coast Guard vigilance. But armed groups were back in business. There was to be "No respite for Jamaicans,"[11] and Prime Minister Seaga once again had to call on the troops to head off a confrontation.[12]

The demand for pot in the United States continued and increased. Where was the principal supply to come from, with Mexico and Jamaica having drastically reduced their exports? Of course, marijuana merely constituted America's minor drug problem. Heroin was the big one, and, as most American criminologists, we were extremely concerned about the impact that heroin addiction was exercising on the crime rate. In 1970, on the basis of the available evidence, we had estimated that the number of hard-core American heroin addicts on the street was in the neighborhood of a hundred thousand, with a daily habit, or maintenance cost, of $50 on average. Nearly all of the addicts had to sustain these habits by illegitimate means, usually burglary, theft, and robbery, and normally of property other than cash. Stolen items, whether cameras or television sets, could be sold at one fifth of their retail value, at best. Thus, to buy $50 worth of heroin daily, an addict had to steal $250 worth of goods a day, 365 days a year. The daily heroin retail cost thus would add up to 100,000 times $250, or $25 million daily, times 365, for a grand total of $9.125 billion.[13] At the time we thought those figures staggering. Yet they were real, and nothing could convince us more than, as fortunate witnesses to the final arrests, our staring at the millions upon millions in bills, neatly stashed in attaché cases, that the French Connection investigation yielded in New York.

We traveled the route of that French Connection, to Marseille, France, and an island off the coast of Brazil, Isla Bella, which had been turned into the transshipment center of the Marseille organization. There we saw, for the first time, the enormous impact that the criminal cash drug culture can have on a theretofore happy and peaceful community. It was not to be our last time. And then there was, and is, the Golden Triangle, with its enormous capacity to produce and operate heroin (and we shall return to this connection), and there was America's unfortunate involvement in the Vietnam War, which subjected our GI's to heroin addiction and the country to heroin imports in vast quantities, smuggled in returning tanks and bombers, in freighters and military transports of all kinds, and even in body bags.[14]

By now the production of heroin had shifted largely from Turkish areas to the Pakistan-Afghan area. A total of 85 to 90 percent of all heroin sold in the New York City area comes from that region, which is controlled by Pathan tribesmen, on both sides of the Pakistan-Afghan border, with little interference by government agents.[15] But Thailand is still heavily producing as well.[16] In December 1982, Thai police, in an exchange of gunfire, killed or arrested seven traffickers who were about to load 185 pounds of heroin on a vessel at a beach near Bangkok, for shipment abroad.[17]

Yet while we were and still are struggling for solutions to the heroin epidemic,[18] a new danger was building in the Caribbean —that traditional trouble spot of maritime criminality—unexpected, and at first unnoticed by law-enforcement officers and criminologists alike. Perhaps it was the Federal Bureau of Narcotics and Dangerous Drugs that was first alert to the incipient maritime drug trade headed for U.S. shores. Early in 1973 the bureau planted an undercover agent among the crew of one of two American vessels that had been suspected of smuggling drugs into Florida from points south. The investigation resulted in the seizure of both vessels and the arrest of American and Jamaican conspirators, in March 1973. The prosecution was successful.[19]

Thus began the reentry of the Coast Guard into primary maritime law enforcement, a function that, since the end of Prohibition, it had exercised only as a sideline. By the end of 1973 the Coast Guard's cutters had seized 6 drug-smuggling vessels and had cooperated in yet another seizure. By the end of 1974 this number had more than doubled: The Coast Guard seized 11 vessels and assisted in the seizure of 4 others. By the end of 1976 the combined number of seized vessels stood at 33 and by the end of 1977 at 64. A year later the number was 173.[20]

With the concentration of the drug war on America's southernmost shores and the consequent emphasis of the Coast Guard's law-enforcement efforts on the southern waters—the drug ocean—we have to pay particular attention to the success rate of the cutters in that area, comprising the Seventh Coast Guard District, headquartered in Miami. The number of vessels seized there increased from 6 in 1973 to 33 in 1977. The big jump occurred in 1978, with 102 smuggling vessels seized. This number was to reach 145 during 1982, during the height of the South Florida Task Force effort. The number of persons arrested aboard these vessels rose proportionately, from 15 in 1973 to 762 in 1982. Marijuana seizures increased hundredfold, from 20,300 pounds in 1973 to 2,380,061 pounds in 1982.[21] Unhappily, these startling figures document not just the success of El Tiburón Blanco and all her sister ships, but also the enormous increase in marijuana shipped out of Colombia.

Equally revealing are the seizure statistics of the U.S. Customs Service, whose small patrol craft scour the waterways closest to shore. These shallow waters normally are beyond the reach of Coast Guard cutters. Customs encounters smaller vessels, but in greater numbers. In 1975 the Customs Service had seized 129 drug-smuggling vessels. By the end of 1980 it was 1,319 vessels![22]

In terms of contraband cargo, the figures clearly indicate what was happening to the nation. By December 1982, the annual seizures by Coast Guard, Customs, and other agencies had climbed to 3,013,793 pounds of marijuana in the southeastern region of the country alone. Clearly marijuana had become America's first choice of drugs. And South America had become the supplier.

Let us now turn our attention to the routes and sea lanes between Colombia and the United States. We should differentiate between two products traveling those routes. There is the more costly, the more deadly, the more expensive, and the far more compact Bolivian or Peruvian cocaine. This substance is easily concealed, whether in passenger luggage, or strapped to a person, or in air freight, or mixed in with sea shipments of legitimate cargo. The third largest seizure, of 1,065 pounds of cocaine, was made on the Costa Rican ship *Lion Heart,* in Miami on June 1, 1983.[23] The largest single seizure, in March 1982, had occurred at Miami International Airport: 3,676 pounds of pure cocaine, concealed in a shipment of jeans. The second largest seizure, 1,391 pounds, concealed in a shipment of fungicides from Barranquilla, Colombia, had been made aboard the Danish freighter *Sine Boye,* docked at Tampa Bay, in August 1983.[24] Spectacular seizures continue to be made, largely by Customs at points of entry. But the interceptions remain minuscule. It appears to be equally difficult to track cocaine once it has reached the retail level on America's streets. Indeed, the task is formidable.

The story is somewhat different with marijuana, or cannabis, which is an extremely bulky commodity. It is exported by the same countries that are responsible for our cocaine supply. Rarely does cannabis move by air. To make a cannabis shipment economically feasible, it must move across the sea. Shippers and skippers willing to run the risk of a smuggling expedition can easily be found. And what about the dollar figures? The Colombian rings offer a minimum of $100,000 per run. For a working shrimper intent on making the mortgage payments on his vessel, this is an incredible temptation. In lieu of the few thousand dollars or less he can make on a legitimate shrimping trip in the same period of time, he could pay off the mortgage! For the Colombians, this means that it is easier to "buy" a vessel for a week than to overpower and seize one on the high seas. But if a shrimper can yield to a $100,000 temptation, is it not possible that an illegitimate entrepreneur may yield to a $100 million temptation simply by pirating a drug runner for the value of her cargo?

Several types of vessels are being used to smuggle marijuana and cocaine from Colombia to the United States. Predominately they are fishing vessels, including shrimpers, lobster boats, and swordfish boats, sixty to eighty feet in length and with a speed of up to twelve knots.[25] The second type vessel is a coastal freighter, up to three hundred feet in length. On such vessels it is even easier than on fishing craft to hide contraband cargo, under layers of legitimate freight or ice or fish. Third, there are pleasure craft, usually in the forty- to sixty-foot range. Although such vessels are occasionally gutted to make space for large cargoes of compacted marijuana, more frequently they are used for cocaine shipments, concealed in stanchions, life preservers, dinghys' fuel tanks, and the many nooks and crannies of a typical yacht, which gives no outward appearance of being a drug runner—to the untrained eye. Fourth, there are the large freighters, tankers, and liners, on which passengers or crew may smuggle valuable but compact loads of cocaine. Ultimately and most importantly there are the shuttle or contact boats, extremely fast powerboats that can outrun any Coast Guard cutter. Smugglers appear to prefer Cigarette-type boats, with top speeds of over fifty-five miles per hour for standard-version thirty-five- and forty-one-foot boats. Racing versions of these vessels have obtained speeds close to ninety miles per hour.[26] Their function is indispensable to mother ship operations, by which one of the larger vessels conveys a large shipment to a point at sea outside the jurisdiction of the United States but near enough to its shores, to permit off-loading to the swift and smaller shuttles, or contact boats, which then run their share of the cargo into any one of thousands of inlets or onto any of the beaches on our shorelines.

Mother ships and shuttles are well equipped with navigational and communications gear, in many instances superior to that of maritime law-enforcement agencies. Communications among the smugglers are superb. The operations are extremely well organized. Rendezvous points or off-loading spots can be changed at an instant's notice, depending on the smugglers' own counterintelligence of Coast Guard operations. Nevertheless, big seizures of contraband continue to be made in the nation's southern waters, and in the narcotics ocean. In December 1983, the cutter *Dallas,* based at Governor's Island, New York, returned to that base triumphantly from a tour of duty in the Caribbean, with a record seizure of more than $3 million worth of marijuana (fifty-one tons) and a seizure of six vessels and fifty-one smugglers. The *Dallas* had concentrated on the Caribbean choke points—the bottlenecks.[27]

Customs, too, in 1982 had made a record seizure, of cocaine

—680 pounds of it—worth $20.4 million *wholesale*—on the two-hundred-foot Panamanian ship *Mar Azul,* berthed at Miami. The illegitimate cargo had been concealed in twenty-gallon polyethylene containers.[28] By now hundreds of vessels have been forfeited to the U.S. government, by court decree, for having been the means by which drug contraband was transported to the United States. Federal law-enforcement agencies have augmented their equipment and their fleets (especially Customs) by those forfeitures. More recently, the states have increasingly used their forfeiture laws, either to supplement their marine police forces, or to provide additional revenue for maritime law enforcement. Thus, during the two years from October 1980 to November 1982, the city of Fort Lauderdale added $3,346,825 to its coffers through the seizure of eighty-nine vehicles, twenty vessels, two planes, cash, and other items, forfeited under the Florida Contraband Forfeiture Act.[29]

Whole new legitimate industries have grown up around the forfeitures: There are, first, the auctioneers and brokers of forfeited smuggling vessels. Here are two advertisements that appeared in popular periodicals:[30]

EX-DRUG
BOATS—PLANES

Seized by U.S. Government Drug Enforcement agencies, Customs, Coast Guard and other Federal, State and Local agencies are continually being auctioned off nationwide at BARGAIN PRICES! Workboats, Speedboats, Light and Transport Aircraft, Yachts, Sportfish, Freighters, etc. DON'T MISS THESE OPPORTUNITIES. KEEP IN-FORMED! **NOW PUBLISHED EVERY 2 WEEKS PLUS SPECIAL BULLETINS.** "ADDITIONAL INFOPAK COVERS PAST SALE PRICES, PROCEDURES, DEPOSITS, ETC. 1 YEAR SUBSCRIPTION (24 ISSUES) WITH FREE INFOPAK $35.00, SIX MONTH TRIAL $17.50, OR ONLY $5.00 FOR INFOPAK AND SAMPLE ISSUE. SATISFAC-TION GUARANTEED. ACT NOW. For MasterCard/VISA orders call toll free 0-000-000-0000 or in Florida (000) 000-0000 or mail check to: (Florida residents add 5% sales tax.)

[Address deleted]

Potential purchasers would be well advised to check the quality of any seized drug vessel they may wish to purchase at auction. Seized vessels may have been in federal custody for up to five years—without maintenance. In such a period, a $30,000 yacht could easily be reduced to a $5,000 hulk. Hundreds of vessels tied up at federal storage sites are literally rotting, with inadequately financed maintenance programs, at a considerable loss to the federal and state governments.[31]

Another new industry spawned by the drug boat seizures is that of ship refurbishers. Several yards are specializing in bringing deteriorated vessels up to snuff, or equipping them for special purposes. Thus, Dana Marine Service, of St. Petersburg, Florida, buys and refurbishes seized drug vessels and, at a break-even rate, these vessels are then acquired by a charity, the Pan American Development Foundation, which sends the vessels to poor Latin American countries. The same vessels that had earlier brought Latin American drugs to North America now provide North American assistance to Latin America, bringing health care, food for the needy, or vocational training. One of the vessels recently refurbished under this Boats for Development program is a sixty-seven-foot freighter, once a drug runner, now a supplier of food for Miskito Indian refugees from Nicaragua and Honduras. The food is being distributed by the United Nations' high commissioner for refugees.[32]

Our friends of the Coast Guard were always delighted to share with us their personal experiences in the drug war at sea:

One of the cutters had radioed a suspect vessel to heave to. She complied. It was a dark night, and the cutter kept the vessel under surveillance on the radar screen, pending radioed permission from the government of the flag state, whose pennant she was flying. Before permission was received, the guardsman working the radar could not believe his eyes: The blip indicated the vessel was rapidly disintegrating, until only a tiny speck was left. The cutter's searchlight convinced the incredulous sailors that where the fishing trawler had been, only a tiny rubber dinghy, with the crew aboard, was left. The crew had scuttled their vessel and destroyed most of the evidence. Alas, bales of compacted pot have a habit of bobbing to the surface. There was enough evidence left to convict the smugglers.

The *Steadfast*'s chief bosun, a veteran of many boardings, told us of one boarding he'll never forget, and an offer almost too good to resist: "Chief," said the skipper of the vessel on which he, as the chief boarding officer, had just perceived a full cargo of pot, "you didn't see a thing on this shrimper, and we'll make it worth your while. What's your pay now? And your retirement? Forget it! We'll pay you enough to retire from the Coast Guard right now—and send your kids through college!" The chief preferred active Coast Guard duty. The smugglers are now inactive at Leavenworth Federal Penitentiary.

Most of the crew's stories center around the naïveté of many of the drug runners, like that of the three college kids on the gleaming yacht belonging to one of them, a young woman. They had a ton and a half of pot aboard. Anticipating swift release on bail, they grinned, smiled, and laughed—all the way to the federal penitentiary, where they are now. Their vessel was forfeited and sold at auction.

And then there is the case of the nasty Savannah, Georgia, sailors, plus a Colombian, busted with pot on a shrimping vessel, who ribbed the cutter's crew about the Coast Guard life of drudgery versus the free life of smugglers, promising the Coast Guardsmen to greet them dockside at St. Pete, only to realize that a smuggler's life isn't all that free when they found themselves in Fortaleza Prison, San Juan, Puerto Rico. And here is another story from our gravel-voiced chief: "Those bums [on a vessel about to be busted] says to me: 'What right do you have to take this vessel?' So I says: 'Now, you bums listen to me, *Congress* tells me in 1790, when I catch you bums smuggling contraband into the U.S.A., I seizes you, you crumbs!'"

The cutter *Vigilant* was chasing a doper who refused to stop.

The *Vigilant* fired a warning shot across the bow, but the doper's skipper was observed calmly sipping his coffee. After the *Vigilant* fired round after round into the doper's stern—her skipper still sipping coffee—it was finally possible to board and seize her. She was sent to port with a prize crew. When days later the *Vigilant* docked at her home port, the doper skipper stood on the pier and invited the boarding party for drinks. They declined—and had a party of their own.

Some—too many—get away. The success of the defense at sea against the drug war attacks on our shores is partial at best. This is bound to be the case when a service, Coast Guard or Customs, is designed for a normal measure of peacetime routine duty and finds itself confronted with an enormous, unexpected assignment.

The drug onslaught has put an extraordinary strain on American law enforcement in general and the maritime services in particular. Yet, after the experience of Prohibition, we should have been better prepared and responded more vigorously than we did—especially in fighting, subverting, and crushing the forces of organized crime that are responsible for our plight. Due to our negligence, we permitted organized crime, the Mafia, to establish itself during Prohibition. Our bungling incompetence now facilitates the creation of a new crime organization: the cocaine cartel, with still other organizations growing up on its fringes.[33] And for the first time we are sharing this untoward experience with other nations; for cocaine, heroine, and marijuana are illegal just about anywhere. But the cartel will deliver to anyplace that can pay the market price. A dozen years ago, in lectures before Swedish, Swiss, German, and Italian law-enforcement executives and criminologists, we warned about the drug wave that would hit these affluent countries. Our words were greeted with incredulity: "The cultural and socioeconomic conditions in Switzerland (or Sweden, etc.), are different," we were told. "It can't happen here!" Today we see those countries under a flood of narcotics imports, with a rise in addiction and an increase in street criminality. The average cocaine user spends from $436 to $820 per week on his habit. One of four cocaine users, in a recent survey, admitted to stealing to support that habit. And where do the other three obtain up to $820 per week?[34] Our law-enforcement agencies are ill prepared to deal with this onslaught. They are not programmed to deal with this extraordinary situation. Above all, the encounter with organized crime is completely new to them.

British Customs reported at year's end that $88 (£62.9) million worth of heroin and cocaine had been seized in 1983, the cocaine being South American, the heroin Southwestern Asian (especially Pakistani).[35] These figures were unheard of just a couple of years ago. The Canadian government reported an estimated record of $38 billion netted by organized crime during 1983, mostly from drug sales.[36] The drug war at sea (and in the air) is being forced on all the Customs services and the maritime police agencies of all countries that have achieved a standard of living under which their citizens have the means to buy. "The Drug War is more than local," editorialized *The New York Times.*[37]

Our good friends at the U.N. Division of Narcotic Drugs at Vienna U.N. headquarters have just come out with the world drug report: Heroin seizures for 1982 were the highest in history and 9.6 percent higher than in 1981. Heroin seizures were a record of 12 tons, up by 27 percent from 1981, and cannabis seizures set a record of 7,278 tons, up by 37.4 percent from 1981. Yet, the agency concedes, seizures represent only 10 percent of trade![38] Can anyone doubt the existence of a World War of Drugs? Can the world's maritime police forces fight it?

Let's now take a look at this problem.

4

Poseidon's Police

•

Roll on, thou deep and dark blue Ocean—roll;
Ten thousand fleets sweep over thee in vain;
Man marks the earth with ruin—his control
Stops with the shore;—upon the watery plain
The wrecks are all thy deed, nor doth remain
A shadow of man's ravage, save his own,—

Lord Byron,
Address to the Ocean

IT WAS ONE OF THOSE RARE days of rest within a diplomatic schedule on an overseas mission, involving the prevention of crime, just a few years ago. Would we like to do anything for the weekend? the Minister of Justice asked. Well, yes. Could we spend just a few hours at sea with any of the naval or Coast Guard vessels? There was puzzlement among our Costa Rican hosts—consultations, concern, consternation, communications —and then the answer: You see, Costa Rica has not had an army or a navy for well over a century, nor did it have much of a police force, for Costa Rica has been blessed with peace for a century and with one of the world's lowest crime rates.[1] But the Minister of Transport just confirmed that the country owns two little tugboats, one on the Pacific side, one on the Atlantic side. And you are most welcome to come aboard either, because once a month they have to test-run their engines, anyway.

The trip on the tug was ever so peaceful and relaxing, and about the most exciting event on our sojourn was spotting a family of giant sea turtles lazily drifting past the tug—and that was just six years ago. My, how things have changed! By the summer of 1983 Nicaraguan gunboats were increasingly invading the territorial waters of Costa Rica as the anti-Sandinista rebels had stepped up their maritime and land-based attacks on

Sandinistan targets in Nicaragua.[2] The heat was on—on Costa Rica! But that was not all: On June 1, 1983, U.S. Customs agents seized 1,065 pounds of cocaine on the Costa Rican freighter *Lion Heart,* docked at Dodge Island, Florida. This illicit cargo had a street value of $319 million.[3]

And seizure of the *Lion Heart* contraband was not an isolated incident. Just a few months later, Costa Rican authorities seized another 380 kilograms of cocaine, valued at $325 million on the street, in San José, where a Costa Rican, a Colombian, and a Venezuelan had established a transfer point disguised as a jeans and toy factory.[4] Costa Rica had been drawn into the ambit of the vast international narcotics smuggling, and the shadowy figure of Vesco, so recently expelled from Costa Rica, loomed ominously in the background.

Costa Rica responded. It extended its law-enforcement activities to salt water. It created its Coast Guard of nine cutters, ranging from 41 to 105 feet in length. The new force scored immediate successes. It seized arms, motorboats, land vehicles, and a light aircraft that had been used in violation of Costa Rica's territorial waters and traditional neutrality.[5] As we were sailing the *Contessa Maria II* down the East River in the summer of 1983, a flotilla of Point class Coast Guard cutters (83 feet in length) passed us in smart formation—only they did not fly the Coast Guard eagle. Brightly painted on the hull were the words "Garda Costa de Costa Rica," and their standard was the blue-white-red-white-blue of Costa Rica, known to sailors as international "C." They were en route to Limón, Costa Rica, to augment the fleet. Even traditionally pacific Costa Rica could no longer do without Poseidon's police.

The world's oceans and other waterways are being policed not by international but merely by national services, foremost the national navies. Indeed, many nations use their navy as their principal if not only patrol agency for protecting their shorelines and waterways and their maritime interests on the high seas. In many cases such naval policing is augmented by the activities of national or local water and harbor police forces or Customs services.[6] Normally the navies of the countries following this pattern are equipped with special service vessels for such tasks as fisheries protection, pollution control, border and coastal patrol, buoy tending, and rescue duties, or whatever other requirements national interests may impose (for example, protecting oil rigs in international waters). The list of these multipurpose navies includes some of the most powerful navies in the world, poised to exert or assume global or regional control of the high seas. Yet, included also are many national navies with no such ambition but solely concerned with protecting their local coastal and maritime interests.[7] A number of countries have taken the logical next step of calling their maritime forces "Coast Guard," or something equivalent thereto, thus making it quite clear what the task of this maritime service is: nonmilitary law enforcement and protective patrol.[8]

The world's remaining maritime nations maintain separate maritime police and patrol forces, more or less independent of the Ministry of Defense and of the naval command structure, frequently attached to Ministries of Interior, Commerce, Finance, or Transportation, to emphasize the essentially civilian nature of this service. These special maritime police services frequently have considerable fleets to accomplish their tasks. Particularly impressive are those of Canada (146 ships plus close to 300 fisheries patrol vessels), Greece (80 patrol vessels plus 20 vessels engaged in antismuggling operations), India (2 frigates and several offshore patrol vessels of 1,000 tons), Iran (26 cutters of 65-foot length), Italy (over 200 vessels in the Corpo della Capitanere di Porto, some 500 patrol vessels in the Guardia di Finanza), Japan (over 400 vessels, several in the range of 3,570 tons, and 11,000 personnel), Norway (likewise with vessels in the 3,000-ton range), and Venezuela (with 44 vessels). Above all, there is the U.S. Coast Guard, which has served as a model for many of the world's coast guards. Indeed, its cutter types can be seen sailing under the flags of many countries, and many foreign Coast Guard officers, petty officers, and rated personnel have been trained by the U.S. Coast Guard.[9]

Examination of the two leading fleet listings of the world, *Jane's Fighting Ships* and *Weyer's Warships of the World*, reveals interesting developments: the creation of national coast guard services for countries which have not had such a service in the past, and the enlargement of existing coast guard fleets, or the addition of seagoing coastal patrol vessels within national navies, all evidenced by a significant increase in the construction and production of coast guard vessels and naval coastal patrol boats, far outstripping the rate of increase for earlier periods.[10] What prompted this development? Gerhard Albrecht, of *Weyer's*, finds the reason in the actions of the Third United Nations Law of the Sea Conference, which began in 1973, and which in the 8th Session of 1979 had before it the so-called Informal Composite Negotiating Text (ICNT, rev. 1), which documented a resolve to create vast extensions of maritime jurisdictions. Coastal jurisdiction was to be extended to 12 nautical miles (from three), economic jurisdiction to 200 nautical miles, and continental shelf jurisdiction (of vast importance to mineral exploitation) to 350 miles, all measured from the coastline or islands that are part of the national territory. These extensions subjected national jurisdictions to one third of the once free oceans, covering 90 percent of the world's maritime trade. Who would have to patrol and to police human activity in such vast regions of the oceans and to protect national interests against encroachment by the vessels or activities of other nations? That is the task of the national coast guards and maritime police services, including the navies. Consequently, we are witnessing a rapid increase in coast guard services. Unhappily, as Mr. Albrecht rightly notes, this extension of national maritime jurisdictions and maritime police forces to patrol them will also increase the possibility of conflict among nations, surely a trend that appears to run counter to the traditional notion of freedom of the seas!

But there is another reason for the recent strengthening of coast guard services—the well-nigh universal increase in maritime criminality which this book is all about. Here is just a summary to demonstrate our point: the resurgence of piracy, the vast growth of maritime insurance fraud schemes, the theft of vessels, terrorism, and, above all, the smuggling of drugs, weapons, high-technology products, and commodities that are scarce in some countries and abundant elsewhere. As an indication of the vast increase in drug smuggling for the U.S.A. alone, the number of vessels seized by Customs for drug smuggling increased tenfold from 1975 to 1980, from 129 to 1,319, and seizures by the U.S. Coast Guard went up thirtyfold from 1973 to 1980 (from 6 to 149).[11] As for boat thefts, the U.S. National Crime Information Center listed 881 boats as stolen in 1970. By January 1982 the number of stolen boats on file had risen to 23,761.[12] For Florida alone, the value of boats (and motors) stolen rose from $6,240,046 in 1977 to $21,474,095 by 1981.[13] The "rising tide of marine fraud" has been conspicuously noted,

yet "Lloyd's says it has never tried to put together any estimate
of the total value of known frauds around the world, much less
the suspected ones."[14] Piracy proper, virtually extinct for better
than a century, is now affecting the lives, the property, and the
integrity of millions in Southeast Asia, West Africa, the eastern
Mediterranean, and the Caribbean. It is little wonder, then, that
marine police forces had to be strengthened to meet the rising
crime rate on the crests.

However, police forces all over the world spend just a fraction of their time combating crime or apprehending perpetrators. Most of police time and effort goes toward emergency and
"social" services and such routine public duties as providing
information and assistance, regulating traffic, and other necessary public services. And so it is with marine police agencies.
Thus the highly respected Japanese Maritime Safety Agency—
which recently has been considerably strengthened—is mainly
concerned with regulating a vastly expanded marine traffic in
Tokyo Bay and other congested waterways, where the danger of
collision and other accidents has vastly increased in recent years,
where supertankers, loaded with highly volatile cargo, are considered small if they displace a mere 100,000 tons deadweight.

The maneuverability of such giants is severely impeded by
their sheer mass, which requires miles to bring them to a dead
stop. Yet the harbors and bays traversed by these vessels are
crisscrossed by hydrofoil and air cushion boats traveling at the
speed of automobiles on superhighways. Recreational boating
has increased manifold, adding to the congestion. Only a highly
trained Coast Guard fleet, equipped with the most sophisticated
radar systems, VHF radios, and computers, not to mention a
wide variety of multipurpose vessels, can maintain safety under
those circumstances.[15]

The efficiency of the Japanese Maritime Safety Agency was
recently demonstrated in the case of the downed Korean Air
Lines Boeing 747 off the coast of Homatombetsu.[16] With such
pressing demands outside the field of crime prevention, only a
strong agency can afford not to neglect its crime-prevention
duties, which, in the case of Japan, extend largely to the prevention of smuggling, water pollution, and fisheries offenses—
crimes germane to the sea, yet hard to investigate because of the
special burdens the sea imposes on the investigator; since the
evidence sinks and drifts, perpetrators have an easy means of
escaping into the vastness of the ocean.[17]

Among the world's coast guards, the U.S. Coast Guard is the largest, the oldest, and the most renowned. If the U.S. Coast Guard were a national navy, it would be equaled or outranked in ship and personnel strength by perhaps only twelve national navies of the world: Brazil, China, France, Federal Republic of Germany, India, Indonesia, Italy, Japan, Spain, Turkey, U.S.S.R., and the United Kingdom—not counting America's own Navy. This service's 260 cutters and 600 other craft, staffed by nearly 40,000 officers, warrant officers and enlisted personnel, are a powerful force protecting and guarding the national shorelines and waterways—not against foreign attack (except in time of war), but against illicit encroachment of national laws and interests.

One of the oldest organized government services in the world, the U.S. Coast Guard was created by an Act of Congress in 1790, and one of the service's branches, the Lighthouse Service, antedates this Act by one year. Alexander Hamilton can be credited with having had the vision to prompt Congress into building the Coast Guard's first fleet of revenue "cutters," and the U.S. government honored his memory by naming one of the largest "cutters" after him and referring to all of its seagoing vessels as "cutters" ever since.

The U.S. Coast Guard's longtime attachment to the Department of the Treasury and now to the Department of Transportation (except in times of war, when it becomes part of the Navy under the Department of Defense) attests to this service's essentially civilian duties. Among them the law-enforcement function generally had received less emphasis than other maritime obligations, ranging from ensuring the safety of vessels to maintaining navigational markers. Its first significant deployment in law enforcement occurred during Prohibition, when this wet service was charged with keeping the country dry—a story so well told in Stephen H. Evans' book *The Black Ships*[18] and Commander Malcolm F. Willoughby's official history, *Rum War at Sea.*[19] The Coast Guard's second major deployment in maritime law enforcement was prompted by the maritime drug onslaught on America and a consequent escalation of maritime crime without precedent.

The "rum war," the era of Prohibition, tempted thousands of alcohol-carrying vessels from Europe, Canada, and the Caribbean to approach U.S. shorelines to sell their much-desired yet illegal cargo at a three-to-one profit margin. The small and aging vessels of the Coast Guard were no match for the "rum runners," whose fleets included transoceanic steamers, commercial sailing vessels with virtually limitless operating radius, high-speed coastal vessels, and armored craft capable of withstanding the Coast Guard's machine-gun fire.

Four years into Prohibition, President Coolidge and Congress responded to the rum runners' challenge and recommissioned twenty-five Navy destroyers, built between 1911 and 1916 and thus veterans of World War I and assigned them to the Coast Guard. The first of these vessels, the Coast Guard cutter *Henley,* put to sea in the summer of 1924 and patrolled the ocean for a 60-day turn (with rookies for a crew!), a period that would not have been attainable by vessels smaller than these destroyers with a displacement of 742 to 1,150 tons.[20] Vessels of this size nowadays would be classified as corvettes, or medium-endurance cutters, and they have surely proven their worth for law enforcement in extended ocean zones! The U.S. Coast Guard, and the coast guards of other seafaring nations with protective interests extending far out into the oceans, were henceforth to rely on corvette-sized ships, or even on ships classifiable as frigates (in terms of size, though not of armament). In a recent review of this trend toward the construction and acquisition of larger and larger patrol vessels, among six of the nations with particular need to reach far offshore or to stay at sea for prolonged periods of time (the U.S.A., Denmark, India, Ireland, Norway, and the U.K.), Lieutenant John G. Tuttle of the U.S. Coast Guard noted that the weight of these vessels ranges to over 3,000 tons, with lengths from 164 to 378 feet, range capabilities to 14,000 nautical miles, crews up to 164 officers and ratings, and with nearly all the vessels equipped with helicopters, which increase the vessels' range of observation considerably.[21]

The long-distance and extended-time obligations of the coast guards compared in Tuttle's study vary to some extent, as do the oceanographic conditions of the areas patrolled. Thus, the U.S. Coast Guard's high-endurance cutters of 3,050 tons, and medium-endurance cutters of 950 tons of the Reliance class, or of 1,780 tons in the brand-new "Bear" class, are engaged largely in ocean patrols to intercept oceangoing smugglers of drugs, arms, and aliens, in fisheries protection, and in general-purpose activities, taking them frequently into frigid zones and heavy weather and sea conditions.

Denmark's high-endurance vessels of the Huidbjorner class, 1,345 tons, and the Beskytteren class, 1,970 tons, are designed for some of the roughest ocean stretches in the world, the North Sea and the North Atlantic, where their duties extend largely to fisheries protection and search and rescue, often in conditions of pack or drift ice. A smaller, corvette-class-sized vessel, the Havornen, of 505 tons, is designed to operate primarily in Denmark's immediate territorial waters.

Ireland's patrol vessels are designed to cope particularly with IRA arms smuggling; India's fourteen frigates with smuggling in general, Norway's with the protection of its fishing zones, fleets, and its oil resources and installations (in very rough water), as are the U.K.'s patrol vessels, in the same waters and under the same conditions.[22]

To boost the capacity of frigates and corvettes patrolling large and treacherous stretches of the ocean, air arms have been added by many coast guards. In addition to helicopters aboard, land-based air wings have been established to assist the seaborne service. The U.S. Coast Guard's air service was expanded from a single pilot in 1916 to an effective and wide-ranging air service placed strategically at many bases around the country and operating a large variety of special-purpose aircraft that meet the unique demands of a service with obligations around the globe.[23] As the coast guard patrols of the various nations are moving farther and farther out into the once-free ocean zones where now national interests touch each other or even overlap, one might want to ask why the policing of such maritime interests, based on international maritime law, should be left solely to national services, with the great potential of coming to loggerheads. We cannot conclude this chapter without proposing restoration of ocean policing to the universal power of Poseidon.

Yes, we do need an international maritime police force composed of volunteers from the maritime police forces of the entire world. The vessels of this force should be frigates or corvettes donated by member states and crewed by multinational crews. Their duty would be to protect and police the oceans fairly, according to international law, to within the twelve-mile limit of each coastal state. To demonstrate the neutrality, impartiality, and universality of these vessels, they should fly the flag of the United Nations in lieu of a national flag. The precedent for this maritime use of the U.N. flag has been set by the five Greek transport vessels that ferried Yassir Arafat's remaining loyalists out of Lebanon.[24] Moreover, Article 93 of the United Nations Convention on the Law of the Sea specifically recognizes the right "of ships employed on the official service of the United Nations, its specialized agencies or the International Atomic Energy Agency" to fly the flag of the United Nations.[25] Just as the Red Cross flag has inspired universal respect for missions of aid and assistance, perhaps someday the U.N. flag will command similar respect for the cause of maintaining peace on the oceans.

5

Posse Comitatus—
The Navy Gets into the Act

•

So blow, ye stormy winds—
    And ye flames, ascend on high;
In easy, idle bed
    Let the slave and coward die!
But give me the driving keel,
    Clang of shields and flashing steel,—

Charles Mackey,
The Sea King's Burial

Posse Comitatus[1]

THE LITTLE OLD TUG'S NAME was not *Toot,* as our children learned
in one of their first picture books. Rather, it was *Recife.* She was
chugging north, in the southern Caribbean, when, to the dis-
belief of all aboard, she was ordered, by a voice out of the
heavens, to stand by. Little old *Recife* had run into a U.S. Navy
battle group headed by the nuclear-powered aircraft carrier
U.S.S. *Nimitz* (with enough planes and nuclear weapons aboard
to devastate a continent), nuclear powered guided-missile frigates, and the nuclear-powered cruiser U.S.S. *Mississippi,* from
which the standby order had emanated. It is unlikely that in the
face of such nuclear might the eleven-man crew of the tug was
inclined to offer resistance. They presently showed the Honduran flag; but instant communications with the Honduran embassy in Washington revealed that no such vessel existed in the
Honduran registry. Thus the vessel was considered stateless. A
U.S. Coast Guard boarding party promptly left the *Mississippi* in
a Navy whaleboat and boarded the vessel, while the cruiser's
50mm guns were trained on the *Recife.* Within minutes the
boarding party radioed back to their superior Coast Guard
officer on the *Mississippi:* "Charlie"—the code word for contra-

89

band aboard. Indeed, twenty-five tons of neatly packaged and stacked marijuana, marked "Product of Colombia," had been found aboard. The Coast Guard complement aboard the *Mississippi* had suspected that all along. A Navy E-26 Hawkeye early-warning aircraft from the carrier *Nimitz* had spotted the tug earlier that day just off Colombian waters.[2]

The eleven *Recife* crew members had made history. They were the first drug runners to have been intercepted by a U.S. Navy nuclear battle group, the first ever to have been arrested with the assistance of the U.S. Navy, and they had the dubious honor to be the first convicted on the basis of such an enviable arrest record, on January 27, 1983, in San Juan, Puerto Rico. A defense argument to the effect that Navy assistance to the Coast Guard was illegal, was dismissed by the federal trial judge.[3] The Coast Guard lieutenant commander who had assisted the prosecution called it "a significant ruling because this is the first case to go to trial."[4]

The case of the *Recife* was indeed the first of its kind in American history. But not the last. When two ninety-five-foot Coast Guard cutters were chasing an armed narcotics smuggler, the guided missile frigate U.S.S. *Sprague* stood by to provide firepower if needed and to replenish the cutters' fuel.[5] Other naval ships have rendered similar assistance of guarded standby, or even towing services for drug runners seized by Coast Guard cutters. In midsummer 1982, the guided missile frigate U.S.S. *Farragut* towed and escorted two heavily laden drug runners into San Juan, and the minesweeper U.S.S. *Fidelity* took a drug runner into Key West.[6] But the appearance of the Navy's nuclear might did not always cow drug runners into compliance with the demands of the law aboard the naval vessel—i.e., the Coast Guard law-enforcement team. On July 16, 1983, the guided missile cruiser U.S.S. *Kidd* encountered the seventy-foot merchant vessel *Ranger* 450 miles out in the Atlantic, off Miami. The *Ranger* pretended to be Honduran, but according to the Honduran government, she was not. She claimed that her cargo hold was empty, but she was riding low in the water. When the *Kidd* ordered her to stop engines and stand by for Coast Guard boarding, the *Ranger* tried to outrun the nuclear missile frigate! Atlantic Fleet Command and Coast Guard headquarters granted the *Kidd* permission to use disabling artillery fire. The *Ranger* was advised that the *Kidd* would start firing into the stern of the vessel, and the master was requested to move the crew forward.

The master defiantly radioed back that he would deploy the crew the way he saw fit.

Eighteen rounds from the *Kidd*'s .50-caliber machine gun tore holes into the stern of the *Ranger*. She came to a stop and was boarded by the Coast Guard's law-enforcement team. She carried twenty tons of marijuana destined for the American market. Thanks to the careful aim of the *Kidd*'s gun crew, nobody aboard the *Ranger* was injured. She was taken into tow by the Coast Guard buoy tender *Sagebrush* and hauled to San Juan for the trial of her captain and crew.[7]

By now it is accepted that the U.S. Navy's ships have become "boarding platforms" for civilian law-enforcement agencies, the U.S. Coast Guard, and the Customs Service, from which tactical law-enforcement teams (TACLETS), in accordance with law-enforcement billets, in nautical language, may be launched to board suspect vessels in the drug war at sea.

In March 1983, while on the Coast Guard cutter *Steadfast*'s bridge, traversing the Straits of Florida between the Florida Keys and Cuba, a squadron of supersonic fighters appeared out of nowhere and buzzed our vessel. We ducked, instinctively. "Ours or theirs?" somebody yelled. They were ours—Harrier jet fighters of the Marine Corps were teaming up with the Navy and the Coast Guard in the drug war. The air arms of the Navy and the Coast Guard have become important supplements to the forces on the surface of the ocean. In one of the first deployments of U.S. Navy attack planes in the drug war, their mere "buzzing" of a suspect vessel so scared the crew that they threw their entire cargo, tons of marijuana, overboard!

Operation Thunderbolt, from October 1 to December 16, 1981, was the first experiment in the deployment of naval aircraft in the drug war, although information gathered by naval aircraft had been made available to civil law-enforcement agencies since at least 1978. Thunderbolt saw the use of E-2C Hawkeye surveillance planes equipped with APS-125 radar early-warning systems. One such plane can cover the entire air space between the Bahamas and Florida. Operation Thunderbolt was a huge success, resulting in 97 drug-related arrests, 45 seized aircraft, and a large amount of confiscated drugs. One thousand pounds of cocaine, 26,000 pounds of marijuana, and 250 pounds of hashish oil were seized in the 77-day period the Hawkeyes were on the prowl over the ocean lanes around the Florida coast.[8] And of equal success were the Navy's P-3 Orion sub-hunting planes, with a radar capacity even greater than that of the Hawkeyes. The Orions are particularly capable of spotting vessel movement. In a trial period from November 8 to 30, 1982, the Orion flights resulted in the seizure of twenty-one tons of marijuana.[9]

It was as obvious during the rum war as it is during the drug war at sea that the Coast Guard, with a total budget of half the budget of a single nuclear aircraft carrier, is totally unequipped to assume the extraordinary burdens of an entire war at sea, above and beyond its normal law-enforcement and other functions. Why then was the Navy not previously called upon to aid its little sister?

In 1877 Congress, to curb post-Civil War government abuses, especially in the former Confederate States, passed the Posse Comitatus Act as a pure civil liberties-oriented measure. This Act, as it reads today, provides:

> Whoever, except in cases and under circumstances expressly authorized by the Constitution or Act of Congress, willfully uses any part of the Army or the Air Force as a posse comitatus or otherwise to execute the laws shall be fined not more than $10,000 or imprisoned not more than two years, or both.[10]

This law never applied to the Coast Guard, as a civil branch of the government—at least in peacetime—and a number of court decisions have so held.[11] Oddly enough, even though the Navy is not specifically mentioned in the statute, the courts have held it to be applicable to all of the armed services, including the Navy.[12] One commentator concluded that while the Act does not make it a criminal offense to deploy the Navy for civil law enforcement, the purpose of the Act was to include all the armed services.[13]

As early as 1977, with the drug war heating up, Congress discussed the potential for increased coordination among the Department of Defense components, the Coast Guard, and civil law-enforcement agencies in using their aircraft and ships. Congress, on the basis of a comptroller general's report, also considered the economies that could be realized from greater sharing of assets and of alternative and cost-beneficial uses of personnel and equipment.[14] Although most of the report's emphasis is on potentially greater cooperation and sharing of resources with respect to search and rescue, established as a national policy in 1954, the report also had some incisive comments on military cooperation in civil law enforcement, especially including marine environmental protection, the control of illegal entry of persons into the United States, and the interdiction of contraband (especially narcotics). The comptroller general took note of the already existing cooperative arrangement for piggybacking between the Customs Service and the Coast Guard in the Florida area, "which includes the stationing of Customs' personnel aboard Coast Guard ships for patrol missions and berthing of Customs' boats at Coast Guard facilities."[15] On the basis of the success of that type of piggybacking, it was only natural for the comptroller general to envisage a similar piggybacking arrangement between the Coast Guard and the Navy. But he had the old Posse Comitatus Act to deal with. Wrote he:

A 1976 opinion from the Department of Justice stated that recent court cases, when read together, made clear that the Posse Comitatus Act is only violated if military personnel take a *direct active role* in executing the law through activities such as investigation, search, arrest or pursuit. The test is whether military personnel subject citizens to the exercise of military power, which is regulatory . . . or compulsory in nature. The opinion further states that *indirect roles* by military personnel, such as the loan and maintenance of equipment, aerial photographic flights, training and other expert advice are too passive to be viewed as violations of the Act and are therefore lawful and proper.[16]

The stage had been set for a potential piggybacking arrangement between Coast Guard and Navy—perhaps a more seaworthy term would be porpoisebacking! Yet some doubts remained: "The specific form of authorized indirect assistance is uncertain."[17] Federal lawmen exercised restraint. Thus, when the FBI investigated the disappearance of Federal Judge John Wood on May 29, 1979, in San Antonio, Texas, and needed satellite photographs of the area of abduction, only pictures taken by civil authority (NASA) were scanned. Pictures taken by the Department of Defense, although their greater potential was recognized, were taboo![18] The President needed a clarifying interpretation of the Posse Comitatus Act. In August 1981, in an address before the International Association of Chiefs of Police, which we had addressed on a previous occasion, President Reagan promised to obtain that legislation.[19] On December 1, 1981, Congress obliged, impressed with the successful—albeit not yet legislatively sanctioned—demonstration under Operation Thunderbolt in the Caribbean,[20] by passing legislation that interpreted the Posse Comitatus Act to favor Navy assistance to the Coast Guard and Customs in the drug war at sea. The Act specifically allowed the use of information collected during military operations, the use of military equipment and facilities, the training of civilian law-enforcement officials by the military, and assistance by Department of Defense personnel, specifically reiterating the prohibition of direct participation by military personnel.[21] The President got what he needed to provide the Coast Guard with floating platforms, with intelligence, and, above all, with morale. The Code of Federal Regulation published the implementation provisions on April 7, 1982,[22] and on the same day, the Secretary of Defense released the good news to all U.S. Navy and Coast Guard ships and installations.[23] The war at sea against the predominant crime at sea had entered a new phase.

So, ye masters, mates and mariners, yachtsmen and boaters, next time ye see a U.S. naval vessel, be it the tiniest PBY or the mightiest nuclear aircraft carrier, know ye that they are there for your civilian protection against crime on the seas. And ye pirates, rovers and assailing thieves, ye dopers and druggies, now hear this: Tremble at the sight of every U.S. naval vessel; they be after ye!

What is remarkable is not that the Navy was finally enlisted in the drug war at sea, but rather the care and diligence with which this involvement of the Department of Defense had to be facilitated, through participation of Congress. Less democratic nations may not have any such difficulties to contend with, nor countries in which the naval forces are charged with law-enforcement duties on the high seas. There a simple executive order would have sufficed.

One of the first steps of this Navy-Coast Guard cooperation was the brightly and proudly printed "E" on the superstructure of the U.S. Coast Guard cutter *Steadfast*, which greeted us as we boarded her in St. Petersburg, Florida. She had just returned from the Guantánamo naval base in Cuba and achieved the mark of *E*xcellence in naval gunnery practice. She was ready for the war against crime at sea—a war that, unhappily, has not been without its casualties. The first five American servicemen enlisted in the drug war under the amended Posse Comitatus Act died when an Air Force helicopter, engaged in a drug control operation over the Atlantic, crashed near Nassau in the Bahamas. Four survivors were rescued by the destroyer U.S.S. *Koelsh.*[24]

6

Heading North

•

Twas Yesterday He made me and Tomorrow I shall die,
The tomb of the old sea rovers, where their bones comingled lie
An azure ribbon roaming in my course beneath the sky—

You're standing out of Boston, Gloucester, any Eastern Town—
The spray's akissing rigging and the rollers wash you down?
The tops'ls cracking like a gun?—It's time for you to bear
For the stream of purple bubbles and the glories waiting there.

Francis Alan Ford,
Song of the Gulf Stream

Between "Serpent's Mouth" and "Dragon's Mouth"

FORT KING GEORGE, TOBAGO, JANUARY 1, 1984

THE WALLS OF THE ANCIENT BUILDING in which we are writing these lines are a foot and a half thick, easily betraying the original purpose of the edifice. It was the commandant's headquarters and home in the days of conflict among the crowns of Britain, Spain, France, the Netherlands, and Sweden. On January 16, 1666, over three centuries ago, pirates took over the island from the Spanish crown for the first time. The English originally didn't pay too much attention to Tobago. That was to change in the eighteenth century. By the 1770s, the power constellation in the Caribbean had solidified. Matters had become more organized, interests more entrenched. The British occupied the island. George III, of the House of Hanover, felt impelled to order the construction of a fortress, promptly dubbed Fort King George. Yet this impregnable fortification, so history records, has changed hands many times. Just about the only attack it withstood was that by the American privateer *Oliver Cromwell* during the Revolutionary War. That proved how right George III had been in ordering the construction of the fortress: to check the revolutionary spirit in the Antilles, which was on the move between St. Croix in the north—where Alexander Hamilton, who was soon to play a major role in the Revolution against the crown, spent his youth—to Trinidad and Tobago in the south, where slaves rebelled against their masters, and the masters against their rulers, while each major power was endeavoring to take advantage of the turbulence by outsmarting every other.

The twelve- and eighteen-pounders, and even a huge mortar, gauged for twenty-eight hundred yards, are still poised on the ramparts, as if to repel the next enemy. With an accurate firepower of at least three miles (the distance that was to establish the limit for territorial waters), the long cannons could easily devastate any fleet trying to make and take Scarborough. Yet today's enemy cannot be discouraged by the ancient cannons marked GR, for George Rex, and cast by Bacon and Sons, in England. Today's enemy uses cunning and stealth. But hadn't it always been that way? Twice before, the fortress had been taken over by stealth. In 1790 the fiercely republican French soldiers captured their officers, loyal to Louis XV, and hanged them on the flagpole of the fortress; then they rampaged through the town and burned down much of Scarborough. In 1793, a British man-of-war anchored secretly on the other side of the island, and a slave, loyal to the British crown, led a detachment of Royal Marines across the mountains, right into the fortress, where the sleeping French garrison was taken by surprise.

We are on the island of Tobago, the smaller of the two islands that form the Republic of Trinidad and Tobago, a member nation of the Commonwealth of Nations, and southernmost of the island republics of the Caribbean chain. Three passages lead from the Caribbean to the open Atlantic past Trinidad and Tobago. The first lies between the "Spanish Main," the coast of Venezuela, with the enormous estuary of the great Orinoco River, and the island of Trinidad. This is the tightest passage, leading through the Gulf of Paria and the narrow stretch of water known to sailors as "Serpent's Mouth." It is exceedingly narrow and becomes ever harder to navigate because of the profusion of wellheads being established to trap the rich undersea oilfields in that area.

Since the passage was as tight as a serpent's mouth, full of teeth, or navigational hazards, even before oil derricks grew profusely like mushrooms in a swamp, it never had been popular with the Spanish conveyors of the plunder of South America, nor, therefore, with the pirates; nor, for that matter, with today's drug smugglers.

But then there is the passage between Trinidad on the south and Tobago on the north, a mere fifteen nautical miles wide, yet far wider than "Serpent's Mouth" and thus an ideal passage for the galleons of old to make it from the plunder-exporting ports of Santa Marta, Cartagena, and Barranquilla, Colombia, into the Atlantic and thence to Spain—hence the term "Galleon's Passage." To protect this vital passage, Spain had regarded possession of the islands of Trinidad and Tobago as cruicial. "Station ships" would be kept there to chase rovers and pirates and to secure safe passage for the Spanish galleons. Yet often the pirates proved more powerful than the princes. The guns on shore were more than once taken over by pirates, the crown's station ships more than once replaced by swift brigantines flying the skull and crossbones. Today "Galleon's Passage" has become a crucial thoroughfare for the new breed of criminals of the ocean, whose vessels are guided safely through the passage by the lighthouse atop Fort King George: "Fl 2 20s 14.1 in 29 M" are the specifications of the light, as marked on nautical chart 24402.

Gone are the galleons, the brigs of war, the station ships, and the pirates' brigantines. Law and order are represented solely by the seagoing patrol boat *Sea Spray*, of the Trinidad and Tobago police. From north to south the passage is traversed only by the Danish ferry *Gelting* and the Trinidad and Tobago ferry *Tobago*. But from east to west, the passage has witnessed an increase in traffic—rusty freighters from a hundred to three-hundred feet, riding low in the water, exit into the Atlantic; riding high, they return.

FORT JAMES, TOBAGO, JANUARY 2, 1984

This is Tobago, the island on which Daniel Defoe placed his beloved Robinson Crusoe and his companion, Friday. Defoe must have studied the map of the island carefully. His descriptions are quite accurate,[1] although the island was not nearly as uninhabited as Defoe made it out to be. As much as all sailors dread the fate of Robinson on Tobago, they equally dread the

Bermuda Triangle, and that stretches from Bermuda to Miami —to Tobago! Fort James, with its twelve- and eighteen-pounders, overlooks but certainly does not command that other and far wider passage into the Atlantic preferred by the legitimate and illegitimate sailors who want to head north to U.S. ports, or east to Europe and Africa—the opposite of the route once taken by the infamous slavers whose human cargoes are now the good people on these islands. It is also the passage that was preferred by hunters of World War II, the German U-boat wolf packs that, once having made it through this passage, found the Caribbean to be a virtual shooting gallery. This passage is so wide that sailors dubbed it "Dragon's Mouth," for surely a dragon has a wider mouth than a serpent! The northern end of the passage is marked by Grenada.

The lighthouse atop ancient Fort James guides the seafarer through "Dragon's Mouth." From the fort's ramparts we see small coastal freighters way out on the horizon, and—very occasionally—a Coast Guard cutter or a helicopter—sometimes American, sometimes Trinidadian and Tobagonian (marked "National Security"). In the bay below us an antique schooner lies at anchor, displaying the Dannebrog (the Danish flag) and badly in need of a coat of paint. The Trinidad and Tobago police boat *Sea Spray* is anchored nearby, not quite sure what to make of the situation.

The island which gave tobacco its name now lies in the midst of the stream of a new weed flow: marijuana. Add cocaine, add weapons and ammunitions. That is today's deadly cargo of the outlaws of the ocean, which the "Dragon's Mouth" spews.

Does the tide that sweeps the shores of Trinidad and Tobago have an impact on the calypso-loving people of these paradisiacal isles? Commissioner Randolph Burroughs, International Association of Chiefs of Police, is a man who can relax only when the strain is hardest. Then he becomes cool as a cucumber. Alert to what the neighboring State of Grenada has gone through— after an intense smuggle of arms and subversion—he is coping with the current trials and tribulations of Trinidad and Tobago. Today's paper for instance reported that an American yacht, the *Dorcas Sue,* intercepted by the *Sea Spray,* had been permitted to leave Trinidad and Tobago under armed escort. She had sought refuge here at a point other than a port of entry. The yacht was found to have been armed to the teeth with a submachine gun, rifles, pistols, and nine-thousand rounds of ammunition.[2]

It did not ease Commissioner Burroughs' mind when he learned that the American yacht had been on a church's missionary relief cruise to Guyana, a country targeted by revolutionaries. Armed foreign vessels in the Republic of Trinidad and Tobago are illegal. The importation of arms is also illegal. The *Dorcas Sue* was politely escorted out of the republic's waters, with her armament aboard. U.S. "Embassy Mum on 'Dorcas Sue' " reported the *Express,* [3] accompanied by a satirical cartoon. Especially in the aftermath of the Grenada massacre of government officials, arms controls are tight in the democratic islands.

The Bottleneck That Wasn't Corked

We have, of course, no way of knowing whether, sometime between 1977 and 1980, the cocaine cartel and the marijuana mob called a general staff meeting, somewhere down South, perhaps on the Guajira Peninsula, or in Medellín, Colombia. Perhaps it was on October 20, 1980, when Judge Cecilia Cartagena was gunned down in that city, having just returned from Miami, where she had received testimony implicating the Colombian biggies of the cocaine war.[4] If such a general staff meeting took place, a marine historian would have been called in for consultation. And the meeting would have gone something like this:

> *Don: Señores,* I have called you together in the common interest. You all know what is going on. Too many of our cargoes have been intercepted; too many vessels and mules have been lost. The U.S. Coast Guard has made things a bit tough on us. The Caribbean has become too hot—*muy caldo!* I have called you all to chart a new course. Let's listen to the marine historian.

> *Marine Historian: Señores,* your worthy predecessors in the trade had faced such a situation several times before, notably in the seventeenth century. Then the Spanish Garda Costa was established, and naval station ships were posted at the "choke points," the narrow outlets from the Caribbean to the Atlantic. And the British Royal Navy was roving all over the place. The pirates had to move their operations elsewhere, namely

North. Waters were much cooler there, *muy frio*. With all the
Navy strength concentrated in the Caribbean, the North was
left relatively unprotected. The piracy operations up North
were a breeze.

Don: That's all very well, but we are not pirates. We have to deliver
our goods to American shores.

Marine Historian: Right, and here is the analogy, with one difference: So far you have brought your goods mostly to Florida.
Well, that has become the hottest point of them all. Take them
North—the Carolinas and Georgia, Virginia and even farther
North, New England, from which the U.S. Coast Guard cutters
have been withdrawn in order to bottle up the "choke points."
And here is the difference: The Coast Guard did not bottle up
the Leeward passages—Galleon's Passage, Dragon's Mouth,
and the lesser passages slightly farther north.

Don: Are you sure? Why haven't they?

Marine Historian: That's very simple. You have been bringing all
the seaborne freight in through the Caribbean and the Bahamas chain of islands. Those are the closest routes. In fact, they
were the only routes your shrimpers and trawlers could travel.
They are not designed for the long haul, a thousand miles
longer, which leads through the Leeward passages. And since
your vessels did not and could not exist through those passages, the Coast Guard did not have to bottle them up. Besides, it would be a darn inconvenience for them. Their
medium-endurance cutters, being much farther away from
home ports, could spend much less patrol time there. They
would have to bring their largest cutters down, and even then,
surveillance would be haphazard in the myriad of Leeward
passages. Besides, if their big cutters are not working in New
England, that makes it that much easier for you to off-load
your cargoes at New England shores.

Don (not being a mariner): But you said yourself that our mule
ships couldn't make that long haul and endure the open ocean
and the frigid waters of the North Atlantic.

Marine Historian: That was exactly the pirates' problem. In the
Caribbean they sailed in fast and smaller vessels that could
outrun the Royal Navy. When they moved North, they used
large vessels. These had the advantage of carrying more loot,
more crew, and more artillery. My suggestion is: Switch to
larger vessels—coastal freighters up to three-hundred feet,

send them through Dragon's Mouth on the long haul to the North American shores, and there use smaller vessels simply for off-loading operations. That has worked exceedingly well during the days of American Prohibition. Up there, your mother ships and off-loaders can blend in beautifully with the enormous traffic of in- and outbound freighters, yachts, and the enormous trawler fleets fishing the Great and the Georgia Banks.

Once in the northern trade routes, any smuggler of the North can easily disguise his true nature and masquerade as a legitimate merchantman. Indeed, this is exactly what Kidd, Teach (Blackbeard), Quelch, Bonnet, and other pirate captains had done. For their conversion to legitimacy, they favored such places as Gardiner's Island, at the eastern exit of Long Island Sound, or the Isles of Shoals, off the New Hampshire and Maine coasts. There they would bury their treasures, buy their supplies and provisions, and exchange the skull and crossbones for the King's royal standard—albeit always only temporarily, for these islands afforded opportune bases from which to prey on legitimate trade,[5] just as these isles are ideal places to off-load illegitimate cargo.

There would have followed a long debate about the acquisition of such vessels, but it was agreed that hundreds of idle rust buckets of that size could be pressed into service, and even if they made only one successful run, the cost would be worth it. Of course, the number of reliable Colombian contact people needed in North America, especially in the new target areas, would have to be increased substantially to ensure off-loading and distribution of the cargo.

Naturally, we do not know whether such a meeting ever took place. Only a cartel member in good standing would know. But we did wonder, during our various meetings with officials in Washington, South Florida Task Force members in Miami, and others, why more attention was not being paid to the need for choking the Leeward passages and increasing patrols off our northern shores. After all, by that time some druggies had been intercepted in northern waters, though through 1981, drug runs to the more northerly ports had been minimal. But in 1982, the seizures increased dramatically.[6] The drug war at sea had reached New England full force, and the federal government had felt compelled to establish three more antismuggling task forces in New England, to counteract the dopers' move North in the wake of the success of the South Florida Task Force. One of these new task forces was established in Maine, one at Cape Cod (Operation Cranberry), and one in Rhode Island (Operation Little Rhody).[7] But by that time the entire East Coast had been affected. Drug landings and interceptions were reported from Georgia to Maine. Between 1979 and 1982, drug seizures in the Carolinas tripled, especially seizures of cocaine from Colombia, brought by air.[8] Farther up, Pennsylvania felt the pinch.[9]

Between 1979, when the Coast Guard made its first drug bust off the New Jersey shoreline, and 1983, the New Jersey shore was to see more action in maritime criminality than it had since Prohibition days. Drug seizures occurred mostly on coastal freighters, including recent seizures of the Panamanian registry *Sirope* east of Cape May,[10] and the British registry 151-foot freighter *Hetty*, seized by the Coast Guard cutter *Vigorous* off Atlantic City,[11] with drugs aboard worth millions of dollars on the street. Aboard the Coast Guard cutter *Cape Starr*, stationed at Atlantic City, a proud crew told us that they had been the first to intercept the *Hetty*.

Matters are no better in New York, where the nation's largest cocaine haul was made in December 1983, a record 1,600 pounds, with an estimated street value of $160 million,[12] while the city was still fighting its heroin imports (via Italy) by smashing a major heroin ring.[13] And still the drugs keep coming in. Observable from our home on the East River, three men in wet suits swam to the 400-foot Panamanian sugar freighter *Anadria* to remove a cargo of 442 pounds of cocaine and 14.5 pounds of Dilaudid pills. Seven Colombians were arrested in that operation.[14]

At the same time, the West Coast was being attacked. As millions of Americans witnessed on CBS's *60 Minutes,* the Coronado mob, recruited entirely from among the brightest graduates of a high school class—by their teacher—had brought in millions of dollars' worth of drugs from Mexico on short runs in extremely fast powerboats. The scheme worked extremely well until the mob was busted. But others are taking up the slack.[15] Seizures in the hundreds of pounds of cocaine no longer are a rarity on the West Coast.[16]

But it is New England that we should be primarily concerned

with, since its coastline and maritime traffic offer the most favorable opportunities for the drug runners from South America. Let us analyze the New England situation.

The Coves of Maritime New England: The Coke and Marijuana Surf

As early as April 1977, it had become apparent to some law-enforcement officers in New England that the northern ports had been targeted for drug drops, at least on a trial basis. As yet, no patterns appeared, and intelligence was sketchy, at best. Indeed, the first boarding of a suspect vessel went awry. She was the wrong boat.[17] But on June 30, 1977, 1.5 tons of marijuana were seized in a small Maine coastal community, and some twenty pounds were found on a 73-foot vessel, off Procasset. The vessel was seized: "Drug smuggling by sea, according to various law enforcement officials, is believed to be on the upswing in New England," reported the *New Bedford* (Mass.) *Standard Times* of June 30, 1977. By August 1977, documents and ledgers seized in a Rhode Island drug raid identified Florida Mafia associate Meyer Lansky and fugitive financier Vesco as being involved in the Rhode Island importation and distribution of drugs.[18] At the same time, seizures of drug cargoes and of vessels carrying these increased significantly. After a Colombian fishing vessel had mysteriously appeared off the Rhode Island coastline, the 55-foot cabin cruiser *Wildcat* was seized with drugs aboard,[19] and two days later the fishing boat *Dorchester.* It was surmised that these incidents were interrelated.

Still, the problem remained unclear until a year later, when a Colombian freighter hovered off the Massachusetts coast. She did not call on any Massachusetts port and disappeared as mysteriously as she had appeared in the first place. Anybody who has sailed the New England coast in September knows how easy it is to get and remain lost in the early fall fog banks. The Coast Guard searched for her in vain. Instead it found and seized a 41-foot ketch and two outboard motorboats, with a combined cargo of 4,850 pounds of marijuana, which had been off-loaded from the Colombian mother ship.[20] The appearance of Colombian mother ships in New England waters, the connection with local organized crime interests, and the use of local, innocuous-looking craft for off-loading operations made it quite clear that the Colombian crime families were probing the feasibility of using a 150-year-old precedent of maritime criminality. It seems the marine historian had made his point. Indeed, the seizures of 1978 and of all subsequent years substantiate this, increasingly so after establishment of the South Florida Task Force with its concentrated capacity to bottle up the southern drug routes. Consequently, substantial amounts of drugs continued to be found on New England yachts (including one on a delivery voyage, in Warham),[21] and one seized by the Coast Guard cutter *Duane,* with the not insubstantial amount of 20 tons of marijuana. Needless to say, this 55-foot sailing yacht was seized and the 14 persons aboard arrested.[22] Outside the sailing season the smugglers resorted to larger vessels for their off-loading operations, including the 135-foot tugboat *Tasker,* seized with a load of marijuana on December 14, 1978.[23]

By 1979, oceangoing drug distribution rings were well established all along the New England coastline. From time to time they were uncovered and smashed by local law-enforcement agencies—e.g., on July 16, 1979, in Orleans and Wellfleet, Massachusetts.

The year 1980 witnessed even greater seizures of Colombian pot in New England, including $25 million worth in Maine, resulting in 22 arrests, and the seizure of 34 tons on the 71-foot trawler *Jubilee,* intercepted off Halifax, Nova Scotia.[24] In September 1980, another Colombian mother ship was operating off Edgartown, Martha's Vineyard, with a reported load of 15,500 pounds,[25] according to the statement of 9 arrested persons who were apprehended in Martha's Vineyard while trying to smuggle $4 million worth of Colombian pot on the state-run ferryboat.[26] The year 1982, with the South Florida Task Force in full operation, provided a bumper crop of drug imports into New England. By now the drug-running operations had become so profitable that smuggling vessels were easily expendable if danger of capture ensued or was even only remote. When on October 1, 1982, a 41-foot Coast Guard patrol boat chased a 50-foot schooner, her crew ran her aground and set her ablaze. The patrol boat saved $2.5 million worth of pot—only to be burned once it had served its evidentiary purpose at trial.[27] On August 23, the Coast Guard succeeded in seizing several more vessels, including a 28-foot high-speed boat at Mattapoisett Harbor.

Ten persons from Florida were arrested, 4.5 tons of drugs, and 10 weapons with 1,000 rounds of ammunition were seized—to the discomfiture of the Coast Guard who, so far, had not encountered any armed resistance but now had to be prepared for it.[28] To the shock of Maine's Down Easters, the drug war had engulfed the elite. A former state liquor commissioner and father of a state senator had used his lobster dock to accommodate large Colombian fishing vessels, landing millions of dollars' worth of marijuana. The Colombian vessel *Indomable* and two powerboats were seized with $24 million worth of marijuana aboard. The ex-commissioner and a score of others were arrested.[29] At the moment of writing, the case was still in the courts. On September 13, 1983, a motion to suppress the evidence was made by the seventeen defense lawyers on the case.[30]

In November 1982, the Coast Guard cutter *Duane* succeeded in identifying and intercepting one of the big mother ships, the Panamanian-registered freighter *Biscayne Freeze,* carrying 60 tons of marijuana. The *Biscayne Freeze* refused to be boarded, and the Coast Guard cutter had to fire five artillery rounds across her bow before she heaved to. On board were 22 Colombian nationals, a Cuban, and a Spaniard.[31] Some of her illegal cargo had already been off-loaded on fishing vessels, including the *Tiki X,* of Panama City, Florida.[32] We shall turn our attention to the *Tiki X* shortly.

After the seizure of the *Biscayne Freeze* and the *Indomable* as she docked in Bremen, Maine, with her cargo of 30 tons of Colombian marijuana, *Time* magazine commented that these ships were "running pot where it's not so hot."[33] The Bolivian-Colombian master plan had been executed, not without losses, but the drugs were coming into New England, through "Dragon's Mouth."

By now New England's public and their officials had awakened to the crime wave that was pounding their shores. Serialized editorial reports appeared in the leading dailies. Alan Levin of the *New Bedford Standard Times* analyzed the situation well: "Florida gets tough, so smugglers steer toward New England ports." He noted the sharp increase in smuggling following the winter of 1981–82 and the impact it had on New Bedford. The accompanying map traced the smugglers' new routes and pinpointed the six crime organizations dominating the drug traffic. Ultimately that traffic depends on the good people of New England to haul the stuff ashore in their fishing vessels or pleasure boats and to unload it in coves or busy fishing ports.[34]

Peyton Fleming alerted the citizens of the Granite State to "the seacoast connection" by means of a three-part series in that stalwart of the fourth estate, *Foster's Daily Democrat.* However little there is of New Hampshire's shoreline, the adjoining, extensive shorelines of Massachusetts and Maine are of equal significance to New Hampshire.[35] There was pot aplenty in Portsmouth and cocaine in Concord, and it all came out of Colombia, whence the druggies had traveled the same route to the Isles of Shoals that had once been taken by Captain Kidd and Blackbeard.

Politicians responded at the federal level with the already mentioned new federal task forces, and on the state level with the creation of state strike forces, as in Massachusetts,[36] or new marine patrol forces, as in Rhode Island.[37]

The frigid waters of New England—*muy frio*—were heating up—*muy caldo.* By the summer of 1983 it was time for us to take a personal look at the waters around New England's shores. The *Contessa Maria II* set sail from New Rochelle, New York, heading east and north, as a research vessel. Somehow the waters and the airwaves to which we kept the VHF receiver tuned seemed not quite as innocent as they had been on previous voyages. We had, of course, simply become alert and observant. But then, things had also changed over the years, hadn't they? We were anxious to reach the New England ports between Portsmouth, New Hampshire, to the north, and New Bedford, Massachusetts, to the south, where several druggie trawlers had recently been seized.

We headed out of Long Island Sound, past Gardiner's Island and Captain Kidd's still buried treasure, through "The Race" into Block Island Sound, to Rhode Island Sound and into Buzzards Bay, through the Cape Cod Canal into Cape Cod Bay, thence into Massachusetts Bay, through the Gloucester Canal into the Bight of Maine, to the Isles of Shoals. The run north and east, outward bound, was intended to be for general observation, the trip back for more detailed study of a port yet to be selected.

In ports such as Newport, Rhode Island, and Marblehead, Massachusetts, we marveled at the ease with which any yacht could sneak in with a cargo of drugs, especially easily stashed cocaine; and we were impressed at the easy access to cocaine in New England's yachting centers. Indeed, Newport, formerly home of the America's Cup Races, is regarded as the Mecca of cocaine in the Northeast, especially during the racing season. In Gloucester it became obvious to us how easy it is for a drug-carrying fishing trawler to make it to port, amid legitimate hard-working fishing vessels. At the Isles of Shoals we realized how easy it must have been for the pirates of old to apply a coat of paint to their ships and switch from the skull and crossbones to the royal standard. But all such operations require some support on shore. Two and a half centuries ago there were enough corrupt officials in America's ports to provide succor, although for the Isles of Shoals it is reported that the small local populace did not cooperate with the pirates, except for a fellow named Philip Babb, who sympathized with the pirates and whose ghost can still be seen on the rocks of the isles—by those who believe in ghosts.

In Massachusetts Bay the VHF alerted us to a flurry of activities. The blue lights of Coast Guard vessels were flashing near Boston Harbor Light. They had rushed out there after an alert boater had spotted bales of marijuana adrift. "We just wanted to get it out of there so we didn't have every pleasure boater in the world out there finding bales," said a Coast Guard spokesman.[38] When we passed, the Coast Guard was busy scooping up 139 bales of high-grade Colombian pot off Nantasket Beach in Hull, Massachusetts.[39] They missed only a single bale, which was found on Hull Beach the next morning.[40]

We were as curious as the Coast Guard why a multimillion-dollar pot cargo would be jettisoned near Boston Harbor Light. Might it have been jettisoned in fright because of some approaching Coast Guard vessel? Might it have been dumped for pickup by contact boats? But why at Boston Harbor entrance, where the traffic is heaviest? A Coast Guard spokesman even conjectured that "the marijuana may have been put in the water as a diversion for a larger operation."[41] We got the explanation soon after. It appears that a few days earlier the fifty-one-foot ketch *Snowwhite*—a name much more appropriate for a cocaine smuggler than for a marijuana vessel—had been beached at Quincy, Massachusetts, obviously by accident. The crew had abandoned the Wilmington, Delaware, vessel, including the remainder of its contraband cargo. Another yacht, the *Christiania,* documented at the Virgin Islands and apparently part of the operation, hid inshore for a few days and then, in panic, jettisoned the remainder of the Colombian crop.[42] Everybody was happy with the seizure of pot on the *Snowwhite* except the Quincy police department, which faced the headache of guarding $9 million worth of evidence at a daily cost to the city of $1,500. A merciful judge provided the appropriate aspirin by letting Quincy burn the pot, except for a tiny sample to be used as evidence in subsequent proceedings.[43]

On July 14, 1983, fifty-seven bales of marijuana had washed ashore off Mishaum Point, in South Dartmouth, Massachusetts. A capsized twenty-two-foot powerboat was found adrift nearby. By September 22, 1983, the cost of guarding the pot had risen to $32,000—draining the budget of the Dartmouth, Massachusetts, police department.[44] By October 1983, Dartmouth had become really desperate. Its police budget was nearly depleted just guarding the pot! Why not just take it out on the ocean and cast it upon the waves, somebody suggested, like the biblical injunction "Cast your bread upon the water"? There was another biblical solution, the "burning bush" method. Or why not put it up for auction? The Mafia might buy it! "The 'Mafia' could not be reached for comment."[45] Three and a half months after the pot seizure and $55,000 in armed-guard expenses later, Massachusetts Superior Court granted permission to burn the pot. Guarding the pot had cost nearly 8 percent of Dartmouth's 1983 police budget.[46] The town felt very high when the pot was burned. In all fairness it should be mentioned that the Commonwealth of Massachusetts reimbursed the town for guarding the evidence that had been so attractive to would-be hijackers.[47] As for the maritime pot smugglers who had caused the headache in the first place, the Dartmouth chief of police announced in August, "Arrest likely in Mishaum pot find."[48] By October 1983 the media announced, "Nationwide alert is issued for pot suspect."[49] As of this writing, no arrests have been made.

Among all of New England's ports, New Bedford has been the most rambunctious, from the days of the pirates and slave runners, as we noted, through the Prohibition era, to today's drug war. With an unusual mixture of staid Yankee stock and adventurous Cape Verdean sailors and fishermen, there is no place on the New England shores with a population more given to the sea—or taken by it—than New Bedford. If you don't know the difference between trolling and seining, between long-line fishing and trawling, between crabbing and lobstering, or whaling and sail-fishing, or dragging and drugging, you can learn it at any of New Bedford's piers or seafood restaurants. The Yankee heritage has left New Bedford not only its Whaling Museum but also that fierce independence from established norms—including, from time to time, those of law and order. New Bedford had recently made the news again in the drug war at sea. Four vessels of the marijuana crime syndicate had been seized on short order, just prior to our arrival: The *Southern Star,* the *Four of Us, Charly's Pride,* and the *Tiki X.* New Bedford had once again assumed center stage in the battle of crime on the crests. We wondered how we would approach our self-imposed assignment in New Bedford. Which of these vessels would afford the greatest opportunity for investigating the crime wave that has hit this port beyond its hurricane wall?

The *Contessa Maria II* entered the channel of New Bedford/ Fairhaven, Massachusetts. It was an easy approach, for we simply followed in the wake of a U.S. Coast Guard cutter of the Point class, towing a fishing vessel into port. We docked at the Fairhaven Marine Co. wharf. Wasn't that the wharf at which one of those druggies had been seized?

One sleeps well after a hard run on a sailing ship. The next morning was glorious. There, across the harbor, were the Coast Guard cutters *Unimac* and *Bibb* decorated by "hash marks" on their superstructures, attesting to many successful apprehensions of druggies and seizures of their cargoes. And right next to us we spotted a trawler with a familiar name: *Tiki.* She bore a federal impoundment notice dated April 24, 1979. Ah, but she is the *Tiki XI,* and we are interested in the *Tiki X,* seized much more recently as a drug runner! But a *Tiki* she was.

The morning edition of the *New Bedford Standard-Times* brought us the welcome news that the *Tiki X* trial was to start that day. We were in court. This was to be our case.

7

The *Tiki* X

•

The Owl and the Pussy-Cat went to sea
in a beautiful pea-green boat;
They took some honey and plenty of money
wrapped up in a five-pound note.

Edward Lear,
The Owl and the Pussy-Cat

NEW BEDFORD SUPERIOR COURT SITS in an ornate courthouse of the federal period, adorned by Tuscan columns. The grandeur of the architecture is slightly marred by falling stucco and rotting timber. This house of justice saw its grandest era at another time, when Daniel Webster and Lizzy Borden were the objects of attention of the courthouse crowd and of the nation at large.[1] Today it is an endless procession of drug runners and stickup artists which passes through the courthouse, and there is indeed a connection between the activities of the two types.

"Oyez, Oyez, Oyez, will everyone rise." And thus starts the *Tiki* X trial before the Honorable Chris Byron, judge of the Superior Court. The public had first learned of the *Tiki* X on November 5, 1982, when Fairhaven, Massachusetts, police had seized sixty-one thousand pounds of marijuana, then worth an estimated $30 million, at Mullins' Wharf, which faces New Bedford on the other side of the harbor basin. The bales of marijuana had reportedly been unloaded from the fishing trawler *Tiki* X, which, as she was exiting New Bedford Harbor into Buzzards Bay, was promptly intercepted by a Coast Guard cutter. The *Tiki* X was seized and hauled back to New Bedford. The Tiki fishing fleet, operating out of southern United States ports, allegedly had been heavily engaged in drug trafficking. For New

110

Bedford this was by far the biggest maritime crime case in years. Twenty-six defendants were arrested, though most were released on $2,500 bail, except the alleged truck drivers, whose bail had been set at $250,000 and $100,000, respectively.[2] The prosecution decided to split the massive group of defendants into two, to make trial easier. Thirteen were included in the first group, although the trial opened against only twelve.

From the outset, the trial was plagued by problems. During the four days of jury selection, 130 of the veniremen (and -women) had been excused for one reason or another, and only 14 of 16 needed jurors had been seated (16 is inclusive of 4 alternates). Judge Byron ordered a "roundup of people" at the shopping mall. Fifty shoppers were seized by Superior Court marshals; others scattered in fright and fled into nearby stores. The 50 veniremen so rounded up were packed into a stuffy bus for transport to the courthouse. "What is this? Are we in Russia?" one of the shanghaied would-be jurors asked.[3] Only 11 of the 50 bodies secured in such an unorthodox way of summoning jurors remained as likely candidates after questioning.[4] Eight days into the jury selection process and after a parade of 232 potential jurors, the trial judge gave up trying to find number 16 and satisfied himself with 15. But not everyone tried to get off the jury. At least one party, a reporter, tried to get his wife on the jury for better news coverage! This led to motions for mistrial by the defense, which also referred to the carnival atmosphere of the jury selection process. In anticipation of a defense motion for mistrial on the basis of prejudicial publicity, we surmise, one of the defense attorneys offered the trial judge a T-shirt, allegedly purchased in Fairhaven, with the imprint "Save the Bales" and a picture of the *Tiki X.* His Honor graciously declined the offer.[5] The disconsolate jurors, meanwhile, engaged in small talk, complained about their chores back home that wouldn't get done, and commiserated about their $14 a day jurors' fee.[6] New Bedford's citizens were upset about the whole jury impaneling process. Isn't there a better, a more organized, a more rule-of-law-oriented way?[7]

Once impaneled, the jurors' first duty was to inspect Mullins' Wharf, where the incident had occurred, and the entire Fairhaven waterfront. Certain spots were specifically pointed out to them without explanation. That led to further mistrial motions by the defense. Overruled.[8] Next came the view of the bales and bales of seized marijuana, 250 times as much as had been placed before them in the courtroom—"enough to buy 300 nice homes in Dartmouth!"[9] Then came the facts.

The two lonely prosecutors did not appear overawed by their seven opponents, high-powered counsel from Massachusetts and Miami, where all the experience of the past had been. But then, the prosecution had incontrovertible evidence. The arresting officers testified without a quiver in their voices. A magnetic little model of the *Tiki X* was being moved on a metal chart off New Bedford-Fairhaven Harbor from Buzzards Bay, right to Mullins' Wharf. And the marine police officer testified how he had cautiously pursued the *Tiki X* on her route. A two-hour watch of the waterfront had followed. Tractor-trailers were observed backing to the wharf. Twenty-six men unloaded the cargo from the *Tiki X* and into the trailors.[10] Defense counsel probed the testimony; questions of identification and police procedure in handling evidentiary items loomed large.[11] The prosecution parried all thrusts and even brought out that one of the defendants had admitted to having been paid $500 to act as lookout, equipped with a walkie-talkie at Mullins' Wharf gate.[12] Obviously he hadn't merited his fee.

As the trial proceeded, the defendants got more and more fidgety. They looked like ordinary fellow citizens of New Bedford, of New England, only a bit better dressed (for courtroom appearance) than the rest of the fellows you would normally meet at the State Pier or Mullins' Wharf. Some of their faces showed the marks of the sea and the burns of wind and weather. New Bedford's citizens watched in awe, sometimes via television right out of the courtroom. What was taking place here was not *Star Wars*. It was hometown and home people in a drama that showed how $100,000 can tempt the master of any trawler, and $5,000 any hand, to bring in and unload a cargo of drugs that had come all the way from the jungles of Bolivia, via Colombia, through a sea in which men of war had their 76mm guns trained on the bearers of deadly contraband.

Defense counsel never referred to "marijuana." "Herbs" is what it was to the defense.[13] In a last-ditch motion, the defense sought to have an expert called to testify that the "herbs" seized were not the statutorily covered *Cannabis sativa L.* but perhaps some other kind of cannabis not within the sweep of the statute. The motion was overruled.[14]

There was unrest among the defendants. Amid further defense wrangling, one of the twelve defendants who had gone to trial pleaded guilty in a "mystery hearing."[15] Now there were eleven. A week further into the trial, two additional defendants had accepted a plea bargain, while the debate about the various species of cannabis—and whether they all were covered by the statute—continued.[16] Now there were nine. The occasional absence of lawyers impeded the expeditious conduct of the trial of the remaining defendants, on charges of illegal possession of more than a hundred thousand pounds of marijuana with intent to distribute.[17]

As the defense geared up for the final argument—not having called a single witness, except the expert whose appearance was denied—a further defendant dropped out, apparently on a guilty plea.[18] Now there were eight. As the defense was summing up, emphasizing that much of the evidence was circumstantial, two further defendants copped a plea.[19] Now there were six. Seven weeks into the trial, the case went to the jury. In the meantime the judge, who had earlier fined himself $100 for being late to court, fined one of the defense lawyers $100 for tardiness.[20] Alas, another tardy person could not be fined—one of the remaining defendants had disappeared, and a bench warrant for his arrest was issued.[21] Now there were five.

On September 13, 1983, the *Tiki X* jury came in with a verdict of guilty for the five remaining defendants. Some of the bail money now released went for lawyers' fees. God knows whether it was drug money.[22] While the five awaited sentencing, the district attorney, whose assistants had brought the case to a successful conclusion, issued a "declaration of war" on the maritime drug criminals and vowed to bring the remaining eleven defendants to trial swiftly. (One had fled to Colombia, one had died.)[23] The district attorney called his war strategy the " 'scorched earth' drug war," although details were unclear as of the time of the announcement, especially due to the difficulty, we presume, of scorching the earth of the ocean.

Considering the latest abscondence, four defendants showed up for sentencing. Three were dealt stiff sentences in commonwealth prison, while one was given a jail term. Arguments by the defense that one of the convicts had a heart condition and another had to support two ex-wives did not appear to have moved the judge.[24] The prosecution readied its case against the additional eleven defendants, and their counsels were filing pretrial motions. Further information about the *Tiki X* affair leaked out. The Mullins' Wharf area had been rumored to be a drug-importing haven for a long time. Police had staked out the area for five months. One of the traffickers had even supplied the county jail with drugs, and a jail guard had in the meantime been charged in that case.

But clouds were forming out of the distant Commonwealth Supreme Court. In an unrelated case, on October 13, 1983, that Supreme Court declared the statute under which the *Tiki X* defendants had been convicted "void for vagueness." The law was no law. Had the defendants been convicted of a crime under a nonexistent law?[25] The statute, it appears, does not provide for mandatory prison terms, but rather for prison *or* a fine! The prosecution found the news "incredibly distressing"; defense saw the opportunity for at least a reduction of the sentence to two years or less under another, constitutional statute; while the Feds were probably licking their chops at the prospect of trying the same defendants under a federal conspiracy statute with maximum sentences of ten and fifteen years.[26] To put it mildly, the court, the defense, the prosecution, and the defendants found themselves in a mess. What about those who had copped a plea to violation of a statute that was now probably unconstitutional? Let alone those who had been sentenced? Or did the ruling of unconstitutionality apply only to a part of the statute not directly involved in the *Tiki X* trial?[27] In mid-December, Massachusetts' governor signed a new, clarifying law providing for mandatory prison sentences for drug smugglers.[28] But surely that law, being *ex post facto*, could not validate the sentences already imposed under the old and vague legislation! Meanwhile, lawyers for the defendants charged in the cases of the other three seized vessels sought clarification of the constitutional issues before going to trial.[29] While lawyers were waiting for a clarification, counsel for the sentenced *Tiki X* defendants moved in Bristol County Circuit Court to have the sentences vacated, as having been imposed under an unconstitutional statute.[30] As we are saying good-bye to New Bedford, the trial judge is pondering that motion.

It was now a year after the *Tiki X* was seized by the Coast Guard. The vessel was forfeited to the Commonwealth of Massachusetts and rotting on a guarded dock in New Bedford. The forfeiture proceeding was cake. The Florida owner of the vessel, although he steadfastly denied any knowledge of the vessel's drug operation, should have known, with due diligence, that the vessel was being used illegitimately.[31] A vessel in the frigid waters of New England, without maintenance and not in mothballs, deteriorates fast. On November 16, 1983, she was put up for auction.[32] By December 2, 1983, the auction had been canceled because the equipment and specifications of all four vessels put up for auction, the *Tiki X* being one of them, had been mixed up due to incredible bungling. Lots of bids had been received, and bidding had been complicated by various liens pending against the vessels.[33] By St. Nicholas Day in 1983, the New Bedford district attorney's office was expecting new advertisements for bids to go out shortly. There were now forty interested buyers, and the minimum bid for the *Tiki X* was to be $60,000—a steal for a swordfishing vessel![34] On December 28, 1983, finally, the *Tiki X* was sold at auction for the minimum bid of $60,000, subject to other claims against the vessel. The other seized fishing vessels went for higher bids. But after the auction it was discovered that the vessels had been vandalized over Christmas. "We're doing criminal law around here," not boat handling, was the explanation of the district attorney on whose authority the vessels had been seized and detained.[35]

Our patient readers will recall the anxiety of the South Dartmouth police department about recouping the enormous loss it anticipated for guarding seized pot. Fairhaven was to find itself in the same boat (or pot, as the case may be). It took a special act of the Massachusetts legislature to compensate Fairhaven for $43,869.92 of police overtime pay for guarding the *Tiki X* pot. We don't know whether the Fairhaven police chief had a tear in his eye when he received the commonwealth's check on October 4, 1983. It still left the Fairhaven police department with $15,000 in out-of-pocket expenses for guarding the pot.[36]

We shall have to leave the *Tiki X* case at this point. Heaven only knows when the case will come to a conclusion. What started out as a clean and clear-cut law-enforcement action by local police and the U.S. Coast Guard had become quagmired in a legal morass. "Law," Jerome Frank said, "is the science of inefficiency." If there was any doubt about the wisdom of this remark, the *Tiki X* case has laid it to rest.

But the science of inefficiency is cutting much deeper than its inability to bring the *Tiki X* case to a just conclusion. And the tide keeps rolling in: On January 20, 1984, local and federal agents seized the 90-foot trawler *Melinda Lee* in Fairhaven. This New Bedford-based trawler had unloaded a cargo of marijuana, as determined by an analysis of ample residue in her hold.[37] On December 11, 1983, the New Bedford-based Coast Guard cutter *Unimac* seized the Haitian 154-foot freighter *Adina* with a cargo of pot, street-valued at $25 million, 250 miles east of Cape Cod. Simultaneously, nine heavily armed men were arrested in Rockland, Maine; they were poised to receive the *Adina*'s cargo.[38]

The story of the *Tiki X* is only part of the story of the ancient whaling town of New Bedford in this modern age of crime on the crests. For New Bedford, the *Tiki X* case is only a recent chapter in a history that has witnessed men of the sea lured by temptations that a cruel, criminal sea would offer to the weak, the gullible, and the unscrupulous, from the days of Stamp Act smuggling, through the days of piracy, to alien smuggling and the rum war, to the days of the drug war at sea. Yet New Bedford's families have also supplied the nation with those honest sailors who harvest the bounty of the ocean, who convey cargo to and from our shores, and who man the vessels that fight crime on the ocean.

Let us take a final look at the weak and the gullible. To gain an impression of the impact that the drug war at sea has on a New England seafaring community such as New Bedford, we took note of the related events in the community itself. While the *Contessa Maria II* was still in port in New Bedford:

- Chelsea, Massachusetts, police arrested two Colombian nationals with 35 pounds of cocaine[39]
- In North Attleboro, Massachusetts, state troopers and their dog Max, a Rottweiler, captured two suspects with $2 million worth of cocaine[40]
- 103 pounds of marijuana were removed from a pot-worshiping couple[41]
- "Illicit drug lab raided in Bourne, Wareham"[42]
- "Drug suspect fled Cuba in '80 flotilla, police say"[43]
- "14 arrested in city drug raid—Police seize $200,000 in suspected heroin"[44]
- "The New England Connection: Noose tightens on drug sales"[45]

- "Fairhaven, New Bedford men arrested on heroin charges"[46]
- "Two-week investigation leads to two drug arrests"[47]

But the news kept coming in long after the *Contessa Maria II* had left port:

- "Two charged in heroin bust on route 140"[48]
- "Fairhaven police seize heroin, arrest 2"[49]
- "Police escapee dealt drugs, lived in luxury home before capture"[50]
- "Police arrest city men, seize heroin"[51]
- "Island drug ring suspect acquitted" (at least that much was nonnegative news!)[52]
- "Middleboro drug raid nets $8,000, 10 suspects"[53]
- "Cocaine, heroin found in car; three city men arrested"[54]
- "Pot farm found in brewery cellar"[55]
- "Fairhaven man arrested, marijuana seized"[56]
- "N.H. drug raids net a ton of pot, $8M in cocaine"[57]
- "Fisherman helped police in drug bust"[58]
- "Cordless phone broadcasts drug suspect's dealings"[59]
- "Crime keeps area police busy"[60]
- "Acushnet police seize marijuana, cocaine, arrest woman"[61]

This sampling of a few months' news items in the New Bedford community gives us an inkling of the impact the drug war at sea has on a small American port city, documenting the defeats we suffer for every drug runner not intercepted by the Coast Guard on the high seas. In fairness, it should be added that the commonwealth and the community, from the governor down to the last parent of New Bedford, among whose children drugs sales are routine and drinking is widespread, have rallied to fight the dope tide, and the media fully reflected this response.[62]

But basic economics tell us that the supply of drugs is being kept up, and if the demand for drugs persists and even increases, and if the profit margin for smugglers remains enormous, the problem will increase. Already New Bedford and its sister ports on the New England coast take on the aura that Key West was beginning to show a few years back, with drug runners becoming folk heroes, and Robin Hoods—as exemplified by the *Tiki X*

T-shirts. But if the situation gets worse, we shall also witness in New England the ugliness of gun battles among drug runners (they are armed already), with a spillover effect on the legitimate fishermen and yachtsmen of New England, whose vessels may become as armed as those of the southern ports. Violent criminality is bound to increase. When drugs, violence, and lawlessness made it undesirable to visit southern Florida, tourism shifted to the North.[63] Drugs have kept creeping up our shorelines, with violence in the wake.

We cannot leave New Bedford-Fairhaven, communities we have truly embraced through personal encounter and through continuing newspaper association, with the remaining three seized fishing vessels just rotting at the piers. We must bid farewell to the 75-foot swordfishing vessel *Southern Star,* the 65-footer *Four of Us,* and *Charly's Pride.* In a series of well-prepared raids, following months of intensive undercover operations by local police and the Bristol County Drug Task Force, these notorious drug runners had been seized on the New Bedford-Fairhaven waterfront, while unloading marijuana, or, in the case of *Charly's Pride,* having done so.[64] The *Southern Star* operation almost went awry, since the drug runners had schemed to draw the police's attention away from the off-loading operation at the Green and Wood Pier by setting the 129-year-old home of the Cape Verdean Benevolent Association ablaze. It was the second case of arson of that building since 1979, and a third case was to be committed a few weeks later.[65]

All three vessels hailed from elsewhere, though the Delaware corporation that owned *Charly's Pride* listed a local man as its top executive officer.[66] All three were swordfishing vessels. *Charly's Pride* had an ingeniously installed secret compartment to hide drugs, right aft of the bow. The unloading of the *Four of Us* at the Fairhaven Marine dock had taken seven and a half hours. Police had to remove tons of ice and fish to reach the drug cargo. When the U.S. Coast Guard cutter *Taney* had earlier inspected the vessel, the secret compartment had not been found, but the *Taney* had wisely escorted the vessel to port. In the case of the *Four of Us,* the police had no such heavy burdens to carry; the arrests were made after the druggies and their helpers had unloaded most of the cargo.

We need not pursue in any detail the legal obstacle course that followed these spectacular seizures. Of course, the suspects were charged and arraigned, and they pleaded innocent.[67] The vessels were forfeited,[68] but they shared with *Tiki X* the same frustration of a bungled auction, and ultimately a sale after having been vandalized. The pot seized on these vessels on the New Bedford-Fairhaven waterfront had gone up in smoke after having accumulated a whopper of a tab for SWAT-team security guarding.[69] All of the defendants are still awaiting trial under an unconstitutional statute.

But there has been at least one positive development up North. Under a law the President had signed into force in 1983, the so-called Kingpin Law, the U.S. Drug Enforcement Agency and federal prosecutors started moving against the big fish of New England's seaborne narcotics traffickers. On August 15, 1983, the U.S. attorney in Boston announced the first two indictments under that law.[70] Said the DEA's spokesman: "When we seize a boat and get the splashy 15 to 20 ton seizure that's really not the business of drug enforcement. . . . Now we've got the top level organizers. . . ."[71] By fall, thirty-four more people were indicted under the same statute, including long-time reputed New England crime bosses.[72] The federal Kingpin Law appears to work: In indictments unsealed simultaneously in Atlanta, Los Angeles, Miami, and Little Rock, Arkansas, in January 1984, fifty-three defendants were charged as kingpins in narcotics trafficking—"the largest cocaine trafficking ring in the nation's history"[73]—and thirteen more defendants were indicted as kingpins on the same day in Manhattan.[74] Federal officials called it "the beginning of a new era." And for the first time, the label "kingpin" was pinned on fugitive financier and alleged drug trader Robert Vesco ten years after his flight, still with uncertain whereabouts.[75] Might there be a kingpin indictment brewing against him? If all the big fish are caught, can the little fish survive? Or will they, too, grow up? The U.S. Attorney General certainly left no doubt that the Reagan administration was going all out after the big fish, but he was fair enough to concede that it had been his predecessor several administrations earlier, Robert F. Kennedy, who had instituted that policy. Under his administration of the Department of Justice, federal convictions of leading crime figures had risen from 45 in 1960 to 546 in 1964![76]

8

Hailing, Boarding, Searching, Seizing

•

Across the swiffling waves
    they went,
the gumly bark yoked to and fro;
The jupple crew on pleasure bent,
Galored, "This is a go!"

Anonymous,
The Cruise of the "P.C."

THE *Contessa Maria II* WAS COMING in from the Atlantic and sailing the Ambrose Channel toward New York Harbor. We had acquired a "friend"—a Cape class Coast Guard cutter was following us at a respectful distance. She didn't know what we were doing, but we knew what she was doing. She was radioing EPIC for the scuttlebutt, if any, on our vessel. That'll take twenty minutes at most. Meanwhile, we were hoping that we would be boarded, not only for the sheer excitement of it, but also because we wanted some firsthand impressions about this little cutter's law-enforcement procedures, and above all, some good photographs.

What we were witnessing was, of course, an exercise of the "right of approach" of a U.S. government vessel. No further action followed, simply because the requirements for further action were not met, although, as we shall explain shortly, the marine police forces have acquired great latitude in their powers to board vessels.

As our friend of the Cape class veered off, her crew was obviously disappointed that they had found no cause to board us, and we were equally disappointed at not having been boarded. Yet the maritime community is divided over the issue of boarding. The first items in the yachting magazines sounded

120

angry over the broad extension of the Coast Guard's boarding powers.[1] A rather cool and objective account of the boarding of a yacht by the Coast Guard cutter *Sorrel,* with good hints as to what to do (basically have papers ready and hold fenders out!),[2] drew a few angry readers' responses. Wrote a Canadian: "Have you Yanks lost your courage, your Bill of Rights, or what?"[3] An American called the procedure "heavy-handed" and "draconian."[4] He referred to the Coast Guard skipper's inquiry to the yacht about to be boarded "Are you racing?" and saw some interesting implications in that question. Certainly, being in a race cannot automatically immunize a suspect vessel from search, otherwise ocean racer Zimmerli, whose sloop *Evolution* sailed in the Southern Ocean Racing Conference (SORC), could never have been indicted for drug smuggling—the race would have been too good![5] At a meeting with their congressmen in December 1983, New Bedford fishermen complained bitterly about Coast Guard procedures during boardings, such as "the nitpicking in the inspections" and the carrying of automatic weapons by boarding parties.[6]

There is much misunderstanding in the maritime community about the law governing the boarding of vessels and about search and seizure by maritime police agencies. That is the more understandable since the law itself is confusing. Hardly any two U.S. courts of appeals have reached the same conclusions, and the U.S. Supreme Court has rarely pronounced itself on these issues, which are vital to the maritime community and crucial in controlling crime at sea. After our various references to boardings, searches, seizures, and, indeed, the exercise of law-enforcement powers on the waterways in general, it is time to take a closer look at the state of the law.

The case that led to the uproar among American mariners was that of the *Henry Morgan II.* On March 6, 1980, this forty-foot yacht was cruising the Calcasieu River Ship Channel between the Gulf of Mexico and Lake Charles, Louisiana, eighteen miles inland. The ship had markings of Swiss registry, although she actually carried French documentation. Acting on an informant's tip, Customs and police officers boarded the vessel, saw fifty-eight hundred pounds of marijuana in plain view, and arrested the two crew members. Long after those two crew members had been deported, the case reached the U.S. Supreme Court because of a conflict among the various U.S. courts of appeals regarding the law in question. It was agreed that the law officers had no "probable cause" for a search and seizure, as required by the Fourth Amendment to the U.S. Constitution. The officers' stated purpose was simply to check the vessel's documentation. Boarding for that purpose was authorized by a federal statute that provides:

> Any officer of the Customs may at any time go on board any vessel or vehicle at any place in the United States or within the Customs waters or, as he may be authorized, within a Customs-enforcement area established under the Anti-Smuggling Act, or at any other authorized place, without as well as within his district, and examine the manifest and other documents and papers and examine, inspect, and search the vessel or vehicle and every part thereof and any person, trunk, package, or cargo on board, and to this end may hail and stop such vessel or vehicle, and use all necessary force to compel compliance.[7]

In a six-to-three decision the Supreme Court found the execution of that statute reasonable and thus constitutional, even absent any suspicion of wrongdoing by the vessel's crew.[8] The Court's three dissenters objected vehemently, likening a vessel to a home that cannot be entered and searched without probable cause. We must interpret the decision with caution. It did not involve a *search.* It involved the right to board. No search took place, since the contraband was in plain view. Moreover, the ruling appears to apply only to inland water zones, not the territorial sea or any other part of the ocean.[9] The Coast Guard responded swiftly to the welcome news from the high tribunal: It beefed up its patrols in the inland zones by thirty-foot surf rescue boats.[10]

The statute that provides the Coast Guard with its law-enforcement powers is not dissimilar to the Customs statute involved in the case of the *Henry Morgan II.* It provides, in part:

> The Coast Guard may make inquiries, examinations, inspections, searches, seizures, and arrests upon the high seas and waters over which the United States has jurisdiction, for the prevention, detection, and suppression of violations of laws of the United States. For such purposes, commissioned, warrant, and petty officers may at any time go on board of any vessel subject to the jurisdiction, or to the operation of any law of the United States,

address inquiries to those on board, examine the ship's documents
and papers, and examine, inspect and search the vessel and use all
necessary force to compel compliance. . . .[11]

For a contemporary interpretation of that statute, we shall
have to turn to the decisions of the U.S. courts of appeals. Those
of the Fifth Circuit Court of Appeals are particularly relevant
since, ultimately, most major maritime search-and-seizure questions of the drug war at sea arise in our southern waters and
wind up in that court. That court's *en banc* (all justices sitting)
decision in *United States* v. *Williams* attempted to make order of
the chaos of maritime search and seizure, including, as the court
admitted, its own "muddled" precedents. The decision goes far
beyond the narrow facts of the case and is virtually an attempt
to provide a treatise or a piece of legislation—a set of landmarks,
as it were—by which to guide the conduct of law enforcers at sea.
The *Williams* case arose out of a Coast Guard boarding of a
Panamanian vessel in international waters. The Coast Guard
had tagged the vessel as a drug smuggling suspect. Some of her
crew had been making signals toward the cutter. One crew member jumped overboard and swam to the cutter. He complained
about working conditions and announced that there was "dirty
business" aboard the vessel. The cutter commander secured the
permission of the Panamanian government to board her. The
cutter's boarding party inspected the cargo hold for the ship's
identification number—as customary—and found a large quantity of marijuana. The question of the legality of boarding not
being an issue, since the government of the flag state, Panama,
had consented, the court now elaborated on the law of search
and seizure in detail.[12]

The court's analysis of the law of search and seizure on the
waters is not quite as comprehensive as it appears to be. There
are some interesting omissions: First, the court did not specify
the standard for a Customs search in the contiguous zone. The
court, in a footnote, hinted that probable cause and reasonable
suspicion were unnecessary, but it did not squarely reject these
standards or adopt some lesser standard of cause.[13] Second, it
did not specifically deal with the search of United States and
foreign vessels in foreign territorial or contiguous waters. To
be sure, the language of the opinion is broad enough to cover
such searches and seizures. But the opinion fails to pay any

special attention to the likely international consequences of our Coast Guard operating in foreign, sovereign waters, especially against foreign ships. One of the Fifth Circuit's earlier panel decisions had approved a search and seizure by the U.S. Coast Guard of an American ship in Haitian territorial waters,[14] a decision that most legal commentators found "difficult to accept."[15]

A fortiori, the power of unbridled search of a foreign vessel and a seizure therein, in foreign waters, is troublesome. Yet the Fifth Circuit Court seems to sanction it. That, however, exceeds the power granted the Coast Guard by its enabling legislation, the famous 14 U.S.C. §89(a). It also seems to violate international law.[16] Indeed, U.S. Coast Guard vessels may not even seize American ships in foreign territorial water absent coastal state permission. Such a violation, however, is a dispute between the two governments and would call for bilateral adjustment.[17]

Third, in approving U.S. jurisdiction over foreign vessels on the high seas, the Fifth Circuit Court failed to reconcile its opinions with notions of customary international law, recognized by Article 6 of the Convention on the High Seas, that a foreign country has exclusive jurisdiction over its vessels in international waters.[18] The Fifth Circuit Court circumvented this rule by invoking Article 23 of the Convention on the High Seas, which prohibits the boarding of a foreign merchant ship except where there is reasonable grounds for suspecting:

(a) That the ship is engaged in piracy; or
(b) That the ship is engaged in the slave trade; or
(c) That, though flying a foreign flag or refusing to show its flag, the ship is, in reality, of the same nationality as the warship.[19]

The *Williams* opinion seems to rely on subparagraph (c) of this article for its conclusion.[20] Yet the ship on which Mr. Williams was arrested was not suspected of being an American vessel. Indeed, through government contacts, the ship had been confirmed to be of Panamanian registry and thus was not stateless.[21] Nor was the ship suspected of involvement in piracy within subparagraph (1)(b). Drug trafficking does not fit squarely within the definition of piracy as contained in the Convention on the High Seas.[22] Nevertheless, the court views the search and seizure as having the "sanction of history" without pausing to explain the historical basis, if any, for treating drug trafficking as piracy.

Fourth and perhaps most troublesome of all is the court's failure to treat as separate concepts a warship's right (1) to approach another vessel and (2) to board and search (or visit) that vessel. Early on, the U.S. Supreme Court had recognized that the right of visitation and search, unlike the right of approach, does not exist during peacetime.[23] A panel of the Fifth Circuit approved the approach by a Coast Guard cutter in sailing up to an unidentified vessel to ascertain her nationality.[24] Yet a subsequent boarding of the vessel was held proper in that case because the Coast Guard had justifiably suspected that the seized vessel was attempting to conceal her identity and activities.[25] The Fifth Circuit saw an analogy and regarded Article 22 of the Convention on the High Seas to be a codification of the "right of approach or the right of visitation."[26] But the right of approach is unlike the right of visitation, since it is far less of an intrusion. But an intrusion it is, and therefore it is subject to constitutional limitations.

For the happy yachtsman and the armchair world navigator, our following ballad will provide much guidance:

OF SEARCH AND SEIZURE ON YOUR BOAT
WHEREVER SHE MAY BE AFLOAT

A Sailor's Guide as of 1984

In Inland Waters

> If inland waterways you sail
> the Coast Guard any time may hail
> you, even without cause,
> may board you and may make you pause
> to show your documents and gear.
> But more than that you need not fear,
> unless there's reason to suspect
> that crime aboard they may detect.
> When that is true, then search they may
> through fore and aft, all night, all day.

In Territorial Waters

When you are out, three miles all told,
the Coast Guard even may be bold
enough to make you hold
your vessel for a brief detention
and even board you for prevention
of smuggling crimes, especially dope,
which you won't have aboard, we hope.
They'll stop you cold in any season
and board you without further reason.
Regardless of the vessel's flag
They search you and will haul you back
if dope they find in any measure
and you will forfeit ship and treasure.

In the Contiguous Zone

If in contiguous zones you are,
from land it is just twelve miles far,
no matter what a flag you flew
the Coast Guard orders you heave to
when they suspect with some sound reason
that crime aboard is then in season.
Yet if on board they think is pot,
they make you stop right on the spot.
They'll board you for much lesser proof;
Heave to, drop sail, and be aloof.

On the High Seas

When on the open sea you cruise,
and if the Stars and Stripes you use,
it's probable cause the Guardsmen need
which to a boarding then may lead
to check on whether Uncle Sam
has suffered from a fiscal scam.
For ships of foreign registry,
the rules are tough, they're telling me.
While hail they may you out at sea,
and board you if you so agree,
or if your country will accord
a right to them that they may board.
But if aboard that foreign boat
conspiracy there is afloat
of crime to flaunt our codes and laws,

the Coast Guard may, on proper cause,
board and inspect that suspect ship
and ascertain her charted trip
to safeguard our land and shore.
There's too much dope, we need no more.

Stateless Vessels

And if you're stateless or display
the Jolly Roger on your stay
the Coast Guard may at any time
board, and investigate your crime.
For pirates have no rights at sea.
They are the sailor's enemy.

What if the Coast Guard does not abide by these standards? There is a short answer and a long one. The short answer is that any contraband or evidence of crime seized on a vessel in violation of these standards may be excluded in court. In most cases that means the defendant will go free. This has been the U.S. Supreme Court's major means of compelling law-enforcement agencies to abide by the law. Yet there is a longer answer. The "exclusionary rule" is not always that important to law enforcers. For one thing, a vessel that carries contraband may be subject to forfeiture anyway. For another, maritime law-enforcement agencies may be more interested in getting violating vessels out of the sea lanes and the contraband destroyed than in sending a smuggler to prison—or back to his home country, in the case of the many aliens involved in narcotics smuggling. To feed them in our prisons is even more costly than to ship them back home at taxpayers' expense, so the reasoning goes.

But the U.S. Supreme Court's insistence on abiding by standards of law, especially by the Constitution, definitely has had a wholesome impact on the maritime law-enforcement agencies of America. It has led to an upgrading of training programs for law-enforcement billets. Law-enforcement agencies sworn to enforce the law have been made conscious of *all* the laws, including those that restrict their powers. A truly professional law-enforcement agency takes professional pride in executing all laws. Our experience with the United States Coast Guard has certainly convinced us of that service's total commitment in this regard.

PART III

Pirates, Rovers, and Assailing Thieves

"I want to see the captain—hear?"
So screamed the woman in his ear.
"That can't be done," she was advised, "so go!"
"No one can see him, ever, *no*!"

The woman with extreme upset:
"Well, then, you give him this and that!"
She spat and spat and soiled the railing.
"World" was the vessel's name a-sailing.

Christian Morgenstern
(Mueller translation), *Ship "World"*

9

Piracy: The Jolly Roger Flies Again

•

We pounce on the ship that is our prey
like an arrow dispatched from the bow;
the cannons bellow and the muskets bay,
our grapplings hit high and low.
The victims' pennant is sinking fast
loud sounds our victory yell:
Hail to the sea, the stormy sea vast
long live our piracy spell.
And after the cannon's very last blast
we cheerfully muster for hell.

The mythical song of
Störtebecker's pirates
(Mueller translation)

This country has a long and precious tradition of
turning to the sea for food, commerce, and
recreation—and even escape, if you will.
Unfortunately, there is another, equally long
tradition that casts a pall over our enjoyment of the
oceans, that of piracy and murder on the high seas.

Congressman John M. Murphy[1]

Caribbean Corsairs

ON JULY 31, 1980, Illinois State Representative Harry ("Bus") Yourell and his son were cruising in their twenty-six-foot cabin cruiser, the *Shark III*, near Pipe Cay in the Exuma chain of the Bahamas. Dodging heavy winds and looking for a protective cove, they spotted a tall mast. As they approached what turned out to be the *Kalia III,* they found that she was adrift. Her dinghy was in the water, and a human body was draped over the gunwales. A bloody seat cushion lay over the *Kalia III*'s side. The *Shark III* approached the *Kalia III* with great caution, and young Yourell covered his father's boarding of the sloop with a shotgun at the ready. What the Illinois legislator saw on the sloop was grisly: Caked blood all over, spent cartridges, shotgun marks in the hull. Bus Yourell recorded the scene with both his still and movie cameras and then radioed a nearby yacht club. He got the Bahamian police to fly over the bloody derelict and to take more photographs, but it was not until a day or two later that a patrol boat of the Bahamian defense force finally arrived. By that time the dinghy was empty; probably sharks had done what comes to them naturally. The *Kalia III* was towed to port. By that time American family members of the *Kalia III* crew arrived and examined the vessel on which, by now, most of the evidence of value to detectives had been thoroughly destroyed by curious onlookers. The family found that the hidden cash aboard was gone, as were the owners' shotgun and handgun. The blood stained, torn, and ruined items of personal belongings were indeed those of the owners, Bill and Patty Kamerer, whose last entry in their logbook, dated July 25 at 5:00 P.M., read: "Sailed all day. Moored at Pipe Cay." The full-moon symbol for the day on their wall calendar had been enhanced as "a happy face—two dots and a smile."[2] Legislator Yourell exerted himself above and beyond the call of duty to get to the bottom of the mystery, but he hit dead ends wherever he tried. The Kamerers' children are yet waiting for an explanation. Bahamian authorities even denied that there had ever been a body (or even two, according to one Bahamian police officer early during the investigation). No bodies, no crime, no mystery: an incident that never happened? So nothing to worry about for yachtsmen in the Bahamas! But the Bahamians insisted on a $3,000 salvage fee for the *Kalia III.*

In Miami we discussed the *Kalia III* incident with Carl Hiaasen of the *Miami Herald,* who wrote the authoritative exposé on the occurrence. And naturally, Coast Guard officers at headquarters and in the Seventh District were eager to share their views with us on the much-publicized incident. (To their regret, the crimes took place inside the territorial waters of another sovereignty.) We also obtained the views of our chargé d'affaires in the Bahamas. He informed us that a Bahamian drug runner, the gun-toting owner of a Scarab-class speedboat, had boasted to others of having "ripped off" the *Kalia III*, and apparently he had flaunted Mrs. Kamerer's gold chain to prove his boast. The *Kalia III* case had caught both the Bahamian authorities and the U.S. embassy unaware. This kind of thing just couldn't happen! Hadn't the days of piracy ended years ago?

Bahamian authorities and the U.S. embassy cooperated far more effectively in subsequent cases—e.g., that of a sixty-two-year-old retired Pan Am pilot, Lawrence Halloway, whose thirty-seven-foot cruiser *Whip Ray* was boarded by three men at Joulter's Cay, off the northern tip of Andros Island, Bahamas. When the oldest of these intruders held a knife to Halloway's throat, Mrs. Halloway appeared in the companionway with a .45-caliber pistol. This startled the attacker long enough for Halloway to free himself and grab the pistol out of his wife's hands. He shot his attacker, and when the two younger intruders tried to overpower him, he fired again, fatally wounding them. There were threats of revenge on the part of the three pirates' villagers, but the Bahamian authorities, under the watchful eyes —and with the cooperation—of our embassy, swiftly cleared the Halloways, ruling the shootings self-defense. "The speed with which Halloway was cleared is another reassuring sign that Bahamian leaders have a more realistic grasp on the piracy problem," wrote *Yachting* magazine.[3]

But this was neither the end, nor, indeed, the beginning of the resurgence of piracy in the Caribbean. It was simply verification that once again we live in an era of piracy. Let us turn for proof to the Coast Guard's "summary of cases in which evidence of hijacking or an actual hijacking existed."[4]

> *Case 1.* U.S. registry yacht IMAMOU, 40-foot motor sailer departed Cartagena, Colombia in May 1973 for San Blas Islands of Mexico with two Americans and two foreign crewmen on board. Vessel was reported overdue at San Blas Islands and search of Caribbean commenced. Vessel reportedly called at Kingston, Jamaica in July for one night with only two crewmen aboard. Vessel located Pointe-à-Pitre, Guadeloupe, 28 January 1974. U.S. owner/operator and other American not on vessel. Two French-born men with known drug involvement claim Americans "gave" vessel to them. Following named men currently

being held by French authorities for possible piracy and unlawful possession of a vessel.

[Suspects' names and characteristics omitted.]

No trace of two missing Americans has been found by U.S. or private investigators; FBI case No. 45-1599 applies.

Case 2. U.S. registry yacht NINA, 40-foot motor sailer en route Tampa, Florida from Progresso, Mexico with American owner/operator and elderly friend. Hired two Americans in Mexico as crew for return trip (father and 16 year old son). Midway on trip on June 1971 crew member produced pistol and directed vessel to change course for Central America. During course of initial hijacking 42 year old hijacker suffered heart attack and medically evacuated along with son to New Orleans, LA, by Coast Guard helicopter and transferred to F.B.I. custody. The hijackers were identified as:

[Suspects' names and characteristics omitted.]

Case 3. U.S. registry yacht KAMALII, 75-foot motor sailer with three-man American professional racing crew on board was hijacked at gunpoint by three armed men at a berth in Honolulu harbor on 6 August 1971. The vessel put to sea undetected and headed southwest until approximately 140 miles from Honolulu on 7 August where hijackers put crew overboard in rubber raft and set them adrift without food or water. Later on the evening of August 7 the raft was spotted by an Italian freighter and the men taken aboard. The freighter's master radioed the story to the Coast Guard in Honolulu. Subsequently, Coast Guard aircraft located the fleeting yacht and the Cutter CAPE CORWIN overhauled the KAMALII and arrested the hijackers who were delivered into F.B.I. custody at Honolulu. The hijackers were identified as:

[Suspects' names and characteristics omitted.]

Case 4. The 45-foot Colombian sloop HEDONIST was seen getting underway from its moorings at Marina Del Rey near Los Angeles on 26 October 1973. This departure, noted by a number of persons, was notable because it was well known at the marina that the yacht's owner, Normal Finkbine, who lived aboard, did not have the expertise to sail the vessel alone and had made no plans to do so insofar as was known by his associates. Six months later, GARY DUNCAN, age 25, a drug addict and drifter who had been picked up by Los Angeles police on a minor charge, stated that in exchange for immunity he would clear up a murder. After gaining immunity, Duncan stated that he and RUSSELL WEISSE, another addict, hijacked the HEDONIST by coming aboard and forcing Finkbine at gun point to get the yacht underway. Once at sea, they killed Finkbine, dumped his weighted body overboard in the San Pedro Channel and took the yacht to Ventura, California, where they forged a bill of sale and other papers and sold the yacht for $47,500. The yacht was recovered, WEISSE arrested and eventually convicted for murder and grand theft. DUNCAN was sentenced to a lesser charge of assault and accessory to murder.

Case 5. The 33-foot charter sports fisherman SPOOK was hijacked at gunpoint on 21 July near Dry Tortugas by a couple and their two children and forced to take the hijackers to Havana, Cuba. The Cuban government took the hijacker and his family into custody, and, after providing fuel, released the SPOOK to return to Key West. The hijackers had chartered the SPOOK for an excursion to Dry Tortugas and once clear of Key West, both adults produced weapons and took control of the vessel. There is no known drug involvement, but the motivation behind the hijacking remains obscure. Those involved were:

[Suspects' names and characteristics omitted.]

Case 6. The 38-foot ketch SEAWIND, with its owners Mr. and Mrs. Malcome Graham, Jr., failed to make a preplanned radio contact with an amateur radio operator in Hilo, Hawaii after making regular contact from their moorings at Palmyra Island until 28 August 1974. On several previous radio contacts Malcome Graham had voiced suspicion of a couple aboard the yacht IOLA who called at Palmyra Island but on the last radio contact on 27 August expressed relief that the IOLA was sailing the next day for Fanning Island. After waiting three weeks the ham operator on Hilo reported the SEAWIND as missing to the Coast Guard and an extensive communication search of the Pacific was in progress when a yacht meeting the description of SEAWIND, but bearing the name LOKAHI, sailed into Honolulu's Ala Wai yacht harbor on 28 October 1974. An off duty Coast Guardsman sighted the craft and becoming suspicious called for a boarding party. When Coast Guardsmen and a F.B.I. agent closed to board, a man jumped overboard and swam toward shore while a woman attempted to row ashore in the yacht's dinghy. The woman was apprehended and identified as Stephanie STERNS, a convicted drug trafficker and the man who evaded capture was identified as Buck Duane WALKER, alias "Roy A. Allen," a convicted drug trafficker, bank robber and escaped Federal prisoner. WALKER was subsequently arrested on the Island of Hawaii and both STEARNS [sic] and WALKER have been charged with grand theft but have not been charged with murder or hijacking as no trace of the Grahams have [sic] been found and insufficient evidence exists to substantiate the latter charges.

Case 7. The U.S. registered fishing vessel EASY RIDER was anchored approximately 25 miles southwest of Morgan City, Louisiana, on January 12, 1980 when Crewman Robin Stansbury armed himself with a .22 caliber rifle and pistol and demanded at gunpoint that the Captain return to Brownsville, Texas, the homeport of the EASY RIDER. The Captain complied with Stansbury's demands and the EASY

RIDER proceeded toward the Texas Gulf Coast. The Captain was able to report the hijacking to the Coast Guard by radio. Stansbury then forcibly confined the Captain and the other crewman in the ice hold until the evening. Stansbury fired upon a Coast Guard aircraft and the Cutter POINT NOWELL who were dispatched to the scene to investigate a reported hijacking. The POINT NOWELL pursued the EASY RIDER throughout the night. On the morning of January 13, 1980, the EASY RIDER crew regained control of the vessel. Stansbury was placed under arrest and returned to Freeport, Texas.

[Suspect's characteristics omitted.]

Piracy, hijacking, or yachtjacking had been reborn, and not just in the traditional piracy beat of the ancient buccaneers. It reared its ugly skull on both coasts. Said Congressman Murphy, chairman of the Sub-committee on Merchant Marine and Fisheries:

Over the past six years, I have investigated and considered closely the modern-day version of high seas associated crimes. During my service as chairman of this subcommittee in the 93rd Congress, we began to study a suspicious pattern of boat and crew disappearances. In 1972 and 1973 we found that 611 privately owned yachts, cabin cruisers and motor vessels—496 sailing in the Caribbean and 115 off the West coast—had vanished. Most had given no distress signal and left no evidence of shipwreck and no trace of the passengers or crew. Rather than subscribing to the sensational Bermuda Triangle theory, the subcommittee explored a new possibility. We knew countless yachts were arriving on U.S. shores and covertly disgorging their cargoes of marijuana, hashish, cocaine, and heroin. Where did these boats come from, and how did the small-time criminals hired to do the actual transporting afford the luxury yachts which concealed their illegal mission?
　　When in 1974 this subcommittee and certain Coast Guard officials first explored this theory—that yachts used for recreation on the seas were being hijacked or stolen for use in criminal, drug-related enterprises—few people gave it much credence. Since 1974, this subcommittee has held comprehensive hearings both here in Washington and in southern coastal locations to ascertain exactly what is transpiring on the seas and what we and

the Coast Guard can do to stop maritime drug running. We have concluded that large numbers of yacht-jacking/yacht thieving and/or drug smuggling criminals operate between Latin America and our coasts.[5]

It was again the inveterate investigative reporter Carl Hiassen who went to the bottom of our " troubled waters."[6] In 1982 the U.S. Coast Guard compiled a list of 44 American vessels that were victimized by brigands or had mysteriously disappeared since 1971 under circumstances rendering it likely that they were the victims of yachtjacking; 175 persons aboard these vessels are "missing at sea."[7] Congressman Murphy's subcommittee established the profile for these vessels:

- The vessel is capable of carrying a hefty cargo for long distances.
- There are one or more crewmen involved with cloudy pasts.
- The boat's owner is carrying a large sum of money or cache of valuables aboard.
- The vessel is outfitted for a long voyage.
- The boat left its final departure point without being seen.[8]

According to the Coast Guard's hijacking expert, Commander Jack Streeper, all of these boats fit the profile outlined by Congressman Murphy and compiled by the Federal Drug Enforcement Administration.[9] One such vessel was the yacht *Pirate Lady*. Yachtsmen and sailors all over the Caribbean were familiar with the big poster:

$25,000 Reward

For information that conclusively establishes
the fate of Capt. Tony Letuso, his companion
David Diecidun, and the Yacht "Pirate Lady."[10]

She had indeed become a pirate's lady, yet her poster was not to be the last one to be hung in Caribbean ports! Above all, it appeared that many of the incidents involving hijacked or presumably hijacked vessels were somehow drug-related. Thus, some perhaps, had become involuntary witnesses of a major drug operation, some may have been mistaken for drug runners by hijackers intent on ripping off drug runners, and some of the vessels may simply have been pirated for their value as future drug runners, perhaps to be scuttled after a single voyage.

In an unusual gesture, in 1977 the Coast Guard issued a warning to American yachtsman bound for the Caribbean, especially for Bahamian waters,[11] and such respected publications as the *Yachtsman's Guide to the Bahamas*[12] and *Yachting World*[13] cautioned recreational sailors about the danger of being hijacked in the Bahamas, the Caribbean, and the Gulf of Mexico. Don Street's article in *Yachting World* "The Pirates of Paradise," heavily documented with the personal experiences of a respected yacht skipper and augmented by case reports,[14] and similar cautionary articles,[15] found a mixed reception in the yachting community. A number of readers simply wanted more information about as serious a matter as this, with some six people disappearing per week, and they wondered about arming themselves, to which the editors of *Yachting World* replied:

- Expect trouble if you flash large amounts of money or jewelry.
- Expect trouble if you neglect to make regular radio schedules and reports.
- Expect bigger trouble if you carry firearms.[16]

Yet more than one Coast Guard officer assured us he wouldn't take a yacht anywhere near the affected waters without a .38 or even a submachine gun. Indeed, that was the reaction of boat owners, who from here on invested heavily in security and alarm systems—anything better than thumbtacks on the deck at night, and firearms, preferably the corrosionproof type.[17] One need only compare the number of exhibitors' stands for security equipment at the National Boat Show of today with those of five years ago to realize how the piracy resurgence has affected the American maritime community. Curiously, however, some letters to the editors of yachting magazines coming mostly from charter boat interests disputed the existence of an epidemic of piracy.[18] Some letter writers considered a bare-boat crew (charters) a far greater menace than pirates. To have a truly trouble-free sailing excursion in the Caribbean, one letter writer suggested you simply follow these guidelines:

1. Prevention is better than cure. Sail only to known safe ports and check there with experienced yachtsmen about local conditions. ("Safe ports": Georgetown, Barbados; Port de France, Martinique; English Harbour, Antigua.)
2. Treat local people and customs with respect.
3. Engage a trusted local crewman (e.g., from Begnia) as the best insurance policy.[19]

Don Street himself had advised simply to stay out of the trouble zone. "Draw a line from the western side of the Gulf of Maracaibo to Mona Island and a line from there to Charlestown, South Carolina and stay East of this line."[20] Two years ago this probably was an accurate demarcation of the drug-war zone, although it left the hapless yachtsman with very little sailing territory in the Caribbean, the Gulf of Mexico, and the Bahamas. But as we have demonstrated earlier, this line of demarcation of the drug ocean no longer holds. The druggies have chosen passages farther south than Mona, and the entire Caribbean is affected. But in one respect Street's warning still holds: "It is insane for any yachtsman to approach the Colombian coast, as the country is the starting point for massive drug smuggling."[21]

One should, moreover, consider that not all acts of piracy in the Caribbean are drug-related. One report tells of a gun-toting German serving thirty months in a Martinique jail for commandeering two American yachts. It is known that he was involved in the hijacking of at least two other ships—all four were stolen for resale.[22]

As for pirates themselves, Coast Guard Captain Marshall Phillips has compiled a profile of the typical yachtjacker, based on known cases and evidence: He is a youth between twenty-one and thirty-two years old and has a narcotics record. He is rootless, but often intelligent and personable enough to charm his way onto a vessel. Once out to sea, he turns into a cold-blooded killer. As Captain Lawrence Kindbom, head of the Coast Guard's Washington, D.C., operations center, adds: "It doesn't make sense to leave the original crew alive."[23]

And where are we now? Our friends in the Coast Guard assured us, during the winter of 1982–83, that the Caribbean piracy problem had climaxed a year and a half earlier, putting that climax in about the summer of 1981. That is probably correct. Indeed, the number of reported hijackings of yachts in the Caribbean has decreased considerably. There are several reasons for this relative restoration of the safety of craft, especially pleasure craft, in the Caribbean. The task force is in place, U.S. Coast Guard presence and vigilance have been significantly increased, as we explained, and yachtsmen themselves have become more cautious, prudent, vigilant, *and armed.* But above all, the wild, free-for-all drug trade of the late 1970s has been replaced by an organized syndicate using "chartered" freighters and trawlers for their operations. Druggies no longer need the hijacked yachts on which they once depended. Perhaps American yachtsmen should be grateful to the cocaine cartel? But it would be premature to announce the exit of Blackbeard's kin from the Caribbean. The Schmahl and Schmahl files, to which we shall turn shortly, are still too crowded with more recent reports of shipjacking and piracy.[24] And right here, in the Republic of Trinidad and Tobago, while we are writing these lines, a cabin cruiser has been forcefully taken from its mooring and abducted to Venezuela.[25]

Piracy: Where the Slave Route Commenced—West Africa

"Vi ska stoppa sjörövarna" (We shall end piracy) announced Swedish Prime Minister Olof Palme on a state visit to Nigeria in 1983.[26] Had piracy become the principal topic of discussion between the Swedish and the then head of government of Nigeria? Sweden and Nigeria have massive trade relations. Sweden is as much dependent on Nigeria's oil, tropical products, and raw materials as Nigeria needs Sweden's machinery. The trouble with the trade relations was that the cargoes didn't get through—because of piracy! "Piracy?" The distrusting eyes of Stockholmers looked at *Aftonbladet's* "Extra" poster at their local newsstands. Piracy by Swedes? The "Extra" poster of February 15, 1983, announced: *"Svenska Pirater Kapade Fartyg!"* (Swedish Pirates Seize Vessel!)[27] But the trouble was not Sweden, it was West Africa; more particularly Nigeria. Of course, Sweden and the other Scandinavian countries, as primary seafaring nations and as traders with Africa, were particularly affected.

The coasts of West Africa have suffered from lawlessness for centuries, and it was not the Africans who created that condition in the first place. It was the slavers of Europe and America who brought pillage, kidnapping, rape, and murder to these shores. Pirates, bent on reaping an even quicker profit, would rip off the slavers. Corruption induced among local chieftains by slave traders became enigmatic to Africa's West Coast. The heavy hand of history rests on that coast now. Nigeria's oil wealth, Sierra Leone's diamond wealth, and the Ivory Coast's agricultural success have created a purchasing power far exceeding previous experiences. Ships are arriving in great numbers from ports all over the world, bringing the bounty of industrialized economies. The ports, however, were not equipped for the import/export demands of these rapidly developing countries. Neither the physical facilities nor the staff capacity were available to handle the sudden enormous trade. Long delays would occur. Delays of ships in port mean loss of income to the line. To cut down on delays, bribes had to be offered for preferential docking rights. That fouled up matters even more. Docking facilities being as limited as they are, many ships were bound to be delayed. And these delays were now being exploited by the new breed of harbor pirates!

As one report put it:

> One ship was recently attacked 12 times in a five-day period. The port, one of the busiest in Africa, never has fewer than 50 ships at anchor at one time, and it is estimated that every freighter that has called here regularly in the last few years has been attacked at least once.[28]

As the frequency and ferocity of incidents have increased, so have the official protests and demands for protection;[29] yet piracy

> has reached such an outrageous level that shipping agents representing lines from the United States, Europe and the Far East are concerned that their maritime unions might boycott the port.[30]

The government of Nigeria acted incompetently in the deteriorating situation. Neither a curb on nighttime movement of fishing vessels,[31] nor the establishment of a committee to study port security,[32] nor the stationing of some sixty soldiers at the entrance to the piers[33] did much to curb the piracy of the ships anchored in the roadstead.

> When a committee of the shipping trade groups of the Nigerian Chamber of Commerce and Industry asked the police to begin an anti-pirate patrol, it was told by the inspector general of police that the police did not have the means to do it.[34]

Help was not forthcoming from the Nigerian government. The shipping lines, contractually bound to convey cargo to Lagos, had to resort to self-help. Some took the risky measure of arming the officers of their vessels. Others, relying on insurance, advised their captains to yield when necessary to protect the lives of officers and crew. The most ingenious response was that of the Norwegian Karlander Line, which hired men from Nigeria's Hausa tribe, known for their ferocity, to stand guard at anchorage in Lagos and to shoot with bows and arrows at attackers.[35] But soon the pirates found out which of the Norwegian ships had bowmen aboard and promptly attacked those that didn't.[36] One tanker crew was so frightened after the first attack and ransacking of their ship that to a man they asked to sign off in the next harbor.[37]

Masters of vessels and ships' agents soon suspected collusion between the pirates and port and Customs officials, since pirates appeared to have accurate information on all "the ships and the flags they are flying and what kind of cargo they have."[38] As the captain of the West German freighter *Hartford Express* reported to his country's embassy in Lagos, "The aimed proceeding of the pirates implied that they had been in possession of the stowage plan, which must have been given to them by someone on shore."[39]

The pirates of Nigeria, and their accessories ashore, are acting out an age-old scenario. "It's our time to get rich and even. This is our opportunity!" The early American pirates used galleons, schooners, and brigantines. Today's Nigerian pirates are using dugouts with Mercury outboards.[40] There is excitement for the local youth in this kind of adventure, as they swoop down from their hideouts, storm ships, and loot their cargoes. And there is large and fast profit: "Within hours the booty finds its way into the Lagos shops and streets, where it is hawked by women and children at black market prices.''[41]

But pilferage of the cargo or of the crew's possession is not the pirates' only goal and bounty. Entire ships simply disappear. On January 21, 1978, *The New York Times* reported that the Panamanian-registry freighter *Chief S. B. Bakare*, with $4.2 million worth of Japanese cargo aboard, had vanished off the coast of Nigeria. A ship of 12,000 tons and her entire crew![42]

The life of international civil servants can be very frustrating. Engaged in the United Nations effort to promote economic and social development and to prevent crime, which so frequently goes hand in hand with that development, time and again we had occasion to caution heads of government and senior officials that developing countries will go bankrupt if they cannot curb the crime rate, and that governments will fall over the issue of economic corruption right there in the ports of the capitals!

On old year's night—or New Year's Eve—in 1983, Major General Mohammed Buhari of the Nigerian Army, in yet another coup, assumed all governmental powers over Nigeria, deposed President Shehu Shagari, and announced that all former officials would be charged with corruption. Several hundred former officials, upon reporting to police stations as requested, were arrested, their homes extensively searched, and records confiscated. Only seven former officials remain on the wanted list as of this moment.[43]

When are the leaders of some of the Third World countries going to realize that it doesn't have to be that way? There are other Third World countries—e.g., in the Persian Gulf—where the unloading of cargo proceeds in a very civilized, planned manner. Radio contact with ships on the high seas confirms the hour of docking and unloading. Graft does not have to enter the picture! The ports can be safe. The maritime crime rate is low. And the Persian Gulf states aim to keep it that way. At the crime prevention conference held at the Arab Security Studies and Training Center at Riyadh, Saudi Arabia, in January 1984, Prince Ahmad ibn Abdul Aziz, Saudi Vice Minister of the Interior, informed us that a joint security agreement among the Gulf states was about to be concluded.[44] At the same time, Norway was advising the Saudis further with respect to port and cargo processing developments to ensure speed and safety in the ports of that country.[45] Unhappily, the war between two of the Gulf states poses threats of a different sort.

Piracy: Levantine Style

The tramp steamer *Betty*, thirty years old and rusting, worth less than $500,000, was owned by a Greek shipping company in Cyprus. She flew the Greek flag when, on August 10, 1979, she left the Yugoslav port of Rijeka with $9 million worth of iron, timber, and ceramic tiles consigned to importers in Saudi Arabia and Jordan. Experiencing mechanical problems at sea, she headed for the island of Pylos, off the mainland of Greece, where she spent a few days undergoing repairs. While at Pylos, where aeons ago Odysseus' son Telemakhos had visited with Menelaos, she was sold to another Greek company that was registered in Panama and given a new name, the *Five Star*. Down came the Greek flag; up went the Panamanian flag, under which she went back to sea on September 1. A few days later (or at least such was the ship's last recorded radio message), the *Five Star* experienced further mechanical problems, near the island of Crete. In fact, the ship docked a day or so later at the Lebanese port of Aquamarina, fifteen miles north of Beirut, where her cargo was unloaded with a speed not normally to be found in Levantine ports and sold at a discount. The Lebanese government, such as it was, had been tipped off that there was something fishy about the *Five Star*. Troops were dispatched to seize her at dockside. But when the troops got there, the dock was deserted. The *Five Star* had given them the slip. Nothing was heard about her until about a month later when, while at sea in the Mediterranean, she was sold again, *sans* cargo, to a Spanish firm. She was registered in Spain and given the name *Ares*. Down came the Panamanian flag, up went the Spanish flag. This "Spaniard" was ultimately seized by Greek authorities at the port of Piraeus. Clearly visible under coats of paint on her bow were her previous names—some that nobody had even known her to have had—*Malaya, Black Eagle, Betty,* and *Five Star*.[46] We suppose that in the part of the world that invented Odysseus, odes like that of the *Betty* are taken only with a shrug of the shoulder. Said one Lebanese official: "We have other problems in this country. You expect us to spend our time worrying about a little smuggling?"[47] But the problem was not so little anymore. By 1979, the *Betty*'s ode had been repeated at least fifty times.[48] Perhaps in deference to Homer—who not only wrote the *Odyssey* but also, in it, recorded the existence of piracy[49]—the world dubbed these modern ships and cargo disappearances piracy. The modern pirates simply have different weapons in their hands: ball-point pens and radio buttons. But they do not mind the deployment of forces of arms, especially since many of the diverted cargoes consist of armament and munitions. In fact, a Beirut lawyer active and successful in tracing diverted ships and cargoes, lives under constant threat of death, and the Tunisian government had to send commandos into the port of Sidon, Lebanon, in July 1978 to recapture a vessel in pirates' hands and sail her back to Tunis.[50]

In a later chapter we will turn to the nightmares of marine insurance fraud that are often connected with the new form of Levantine piracy. Here we shall simply note the plight of honest Third World countries waiting for consigned cargo so urgently needed for development—cargo that will never arrive. Whether the Greek government likes it or not, by virtue of the sheer multitude of Greek-owned vessels in that part of the world, Greece is one of the most affected countries. So is Lebanon, simply because her ports are virtually without security, virtually without law, and virtually without effective Customs controls.

In an effort "to protect the good name of the Greek marine,"[51] the country's government has begun efforts at toughening its laws to deter piracy. Intended as a pro-active attempt at preventing this crime from becoming a problem, Merchant Marine Minister Emmanuel Kefaloyiannis is aggressively promoting "a new bill that, among other things, would make unauthorized cargo diversion or its appropriation subject to criminal rather than as now, civil procedures."[52]

Recently, while explaining his position, Mr. Kefaloyiannis said:

> . . . that even though most incidents in which cargo carried on Greek ships failed to reach its destinations were attributable to dishonest characters—in the main not Greek—the situation is now beginning to affect Greece's good relations with the Arab world.[53]

If these crimes were permitted to continue without preventive action, the minister reasoned, Greece would suffer both political and economic damage:

It must be emphasized that the insurers of Greek ships carrying general cargo are considering imposing higher premiums, which would mean that the already unfavorable position of Greek shipping, as a result of the international shipping crisis, would become still more unfavorable.[54]

By way of challenging the need for these new piracy laws, one critic, in an address to the Maritime Law League of Greece, pointed out:

... of 37 cases of alleged cargo fraud under investigation by the Merchant Marine Ministry, only one-fifth involved Greek-flag ships, and not even one of the accused owners was a member of the Union of Greek Shipowners.[55]

Still, the problem of piracy is "as old as Nelson, and older," and the Union of Greek Shipowners reports that it is "not closing its eyes to the problem." Accordingly, the Union,

... in its determination to defend the good reputation of Greek shipping . . . is cooperating with the underwriters and salvage associations internationally, has engaged a specialized British detective to help investigate all allegations, and is preparing its contribution to action in IMCO [now IMO] and other international organizations.[56]

There are, of course, several things wrong with this line of argumentation. It is true that the Greek flag may be flown on only one fifth of the fifty or more disappeared vessels with cargoes worth at least $150 million, but from all that appears, the ownership of the vessels, whether flying the Panamanian or Spanish flags, was largely Greek.

Although the Greek government and shippers disagree over the proper response to piracy, both appear intent on taking steps to protect their cargoes and reputations. In light of that country's position as one of the leading shipping nations of the world,[57] this concern is not exaggerated. As for the proposed legislation, the last report available gave it little chance of survival.[58] The Union of Greek Shipowners argued vehemently against the draft bill, pointing out that none of the shipowners identified as being involved in Levantine piracy is a member of the Union.[59] That is sort of like arguing against letting preachers preach against sin, since all the sinners are members of other congregations, or of none at all.

But Greece is trying to put its maritime house in order, and latest reports indicate a leveling off of piracy incidents. Perhaps the newly formed IMO's actions have contributed to greater security. As for Lebanon, her ships, shippers, and agents, the situation remains incredibly bad and has no chance of improving until the Lebanese settle their most pressing problems and until their invited and uninvited friends let them settle those problems. Lebanese officials "admit privately that there is little they can do."[60]

The Saudi government took the only step feasible for the protection of its own interests shortly after our visit with Saudi Arabia's national director of security. Or was it because they saw the Danish Maersk Line advertisement printed side by side with various articles on Levantine piracy? These ads announce regularly scheduled service to the Gulf state ports. Danish vessels do not have the habit of disappearing with their cargoes. Late in 1979, the Saudi government, frustrated over the loss of their goods, declared an unprecedented boycott of Lebanon's products and shippers. At the same time, the Gulf states, especially Saudi Arabia, Oman, and Kuwait, beefed up their maritime security forces. We had occasion to cruise on several patrol vessels of the Kuwaiti marine police forces. We must hand it to the Kuwait marine police, they are doing a superb job! Kuwait's ports and sea lanes are safer from crime (though not from the impact of the neighboring Gulf war) than ever. Oman's Sindbad, if he were still sailing in those waters, would no longer have to worry about pirates. And the Great Mogul's ships, if they were still plying those sea lanes, would not have to worry about English, American, Dutch, or French pirates, either. However, if Sindbad's reincarnation would leave the Gulf region heading east —as he did—he would have to worry, still.

In Sindbad's Wake: Piracy in Asian Waters

Sindbad did sail again as centuries before. Oman was the vessel's flag state and port of construction. She was built exactly like the first *Sohar,* out of the same materials, and according to the same construction plans. Only three things were aboard that the first Sindbad had not had: a radio, firearms (to make it through Southeast Asia's old-new pirate waters), and—may the Prophet forgive them—Scotch! Not for consumption, but as presents for corrupt Indian Customs officers. Everything went as expected, all items came in handy and in the manner anticipated, but the firearms were thrown overboard as the ship entered China's great Yangtse. That river is now free of pirates!

We are, of course, describing the sea lanes between the Strait of Hormuz at the southwestern end, and the South China Sea at the eastern end—the great trading region crisscrossed by Arab dhows long before Spanish galleons reached the Philippines, long before the British and Dutch East India companies imposed their will on the region and created great Western-dependent empires in Asia, with concentration on the ancient spice routes in the Strait of Malacca, between Malaysia and Indonesia, the waters off Borneo, Sumatra, and the southern Philippines, tropical islands in the Gulf of Siam, the Phillip Channel near Singapore, the Sula Sea, and the waters of "Noman's Sea" off the Thai provinces of Trat and Chanthaburi, as well as way south, around Mindanao. The pirates' cutlass is now gone. It has been supplanted by M-79 grenade launchers, hand grenades, machine guns, and even antitank guns. The unhappy Vietnam War has left enough armament to keep the pirates going for some time![61]

During 1981,

- The 90,900-deadweight ton Shell Co. tanker *Mammoth Monarch* was boarded while proceeding through the Phillip Channel at 12 knots on September 2. The pirates made off with money and property.
- Earlier, the 30,000-dwt. Mobil tanker *Corsicana* was boarded in the same area while traveling at 15 knots. The pirates threatened the crew at knifepoint before escaping with money from the ship's safe.
- The 21,000-dwt. BP tanker *British Beech* also reported a similar happening in the Phillip Channel.
- Last year an Australian master was shot and killed by pirates who boarded his ship in the Philippines. He was Capt. Arthur Dyason, master of the container-ship *Oriental Ambassador* of the Orient Overseas Container Line, which

operates a regular service between Australia and the region.[62]

The pirates are not choosy. They will attack anything that floats:
supertankers, container ships, passenger ferries, sailing yachts,
fishing trawlers, and rickety refugee craft.

But it is not just on the high seas that the pirates strike; they
also attack right in the roadsteads and harbors. In the port of
Singapore, the world's fourth busiest harbor, ships of all sizes
have experienced problems with what has been labeled "cases
of piracy by destitute fishermen."[63] As with other Southeast
Asian pirates, the Singapore marauders are said to strike primarily at night in small boats driven by powerful outboard motors.
After pulling alongside their prey, they board the victim ship,
using ropes with grappling hooks. Once on board, crew and
passengers are robbed of cash, equipment, electronic gear, and
even bicycles, and cargo is pilfered.[64] What distinguishes the
Singapore pirates is their willingness to attack even large oceangoing vessels (including large Shell, Mobil, and BP oil tankers).[65]

Even Manila Bay has become a pirates' area of operations.
We traversed the bay from Manila to Corregidor, over to Ba-
taan, where once Americans and Filipinos fought the Japanese
invaders, lost, and reconquered. Our Philippine patrol vessel
crossed the path of many a man-of-war of the U.S. Seventh Fleet,
stationed at Subic Bay. We rounded many islets and passed over
the sunken hulks of Admiral de Cervera's Spanish fleet sunk by
Admiral Dewey in the Battle of Manila Bay. Dewey's words to
the captain of the *Olympia* (now peacefully docked forever at
Penn's Landing in Philadelphia) seemed to ring over the waters:
"Fire when ready, Mr. Gridsley!" Yet even now that is the area
"where pirates approach anchored cargo ships and, taking advantage of skeleton crews, pilfer goods waiting to be unloaded."[66]

Piracy in Southeast Asia was a way of life when Sindbad
crisscrossed these waters. It became a dedication during the
sixteenth century, when English, Spanish, Portuguese, and
Dutch traders began to operate extensively in this area, destroying the ancient and established trade routes and reducing the
indigenous Southeast Asian traders to poverty. As one writer
has explained:

Muslim Malays had been the main carriers on all these routes. They had to learn to live by other means. And that meant piracy. It came to be regarded as an honourable profession—a patriotic one. It was a God-given crusade against the white barbarians. Progressively excluded from legitimate trade by European colonial powers the Muslim sea-warriors of the Sulu chain, Western Mindanao and North Borneo made plunder a profession in the 18th century.[67]

The socioeconomic conditions, the prevalence of strife and conflict, nourish piracy in Southeast Asia. Unless these conditions are successfully addressed, piracy will persist, as in Malaysian waters, where an incident of piracy occurs an average of every two weeks. The hot spot is that old pirates' lair the Strait of Malacca. There piracy often is blamed on Thai fishermen who apparently feel it is easier and more profitable to steal fish than to catch them. Malaysian fishermen reportedly now carry valuables on board—cigarettes, food, and money—which they offer as tribute for safe passage.[68]

In the Philippines, though the north has its share of buccaneering, piracy is concentrated in the south, around Mindanao. The Philippine Defense Ministry puts the blame on the Moro National Liberation Front (MNLF) guerrillas, said to be supplied and trained in Malaysia. Malaysia, of course, denies these charges and reports to have evidence "that Philippine armed forces personnel have become pirates and have been harassing our people, especially fishermen, and coastal ships."[69]

It is difficult to pin blame for a condition that has grown very much out of hand. Take the Phillip Channel, where both Singapore and Indonesia claim that the other has responsibility, simply because the channel is joint and has the highest incidence of piracy in Southeast Asia. Add thereto the scuttlebut about naval vessels and marine police patrol boats "moonlighting" as raiders of fishing vessels and coastal freighters![70] The tiny Republic of Singapore understandably claims that it cannot bear the expense of securing the vast sea lanes around its shores.[71] Yet international zoning regulations mandate the use of the Phillip Channel for the world's shipping in that area. Might it be asking for too much to propose the establishment of an international marine patrol to secure safe passage through the Phillip Channel[72] and through similar international maritime thoroughfares technically belonging to small countries that cannot ensure their safety?

While it is endemic to the entire region, piracy appears to have reached its most severe proportions in the waters off the coast of Thailand. That country has reported as many as two hundred incidents of "commercial piracy" per year, about half of which occur near the Cambodian border. Although the Thai government has mounted vigorous operations against the pirates, fishermen complain that there are too few government patrol boats to provide adequate protection. As a result, many fishermen have begun to arm themselves for self-defense. Alas, the pirates are usually better armed!

According to marine police sources, the pirates who raid Thai fishermen and shipping invariably operate at night. Using boats converted from fishing trawlers, the pirates prefer to attack smaller craft, which they often seize and later sell. As in the rest of Southeast Asia, piracy in Thailand is blamed on neighboring nations by authorities who suspect that collusion exists between the marauders and the Cambodians.[73] Regardless of who is to blame, the Thai government has promised its fishermen that it will attempt to improve their protection.[74]

Ironically, while the Thai fishermen are being victimized by Cambodian pirates, they are themselves being increasingly blamed for brutal maritime raids upon Vietnamese refugees. Since the conclusion of the last (we hope the *last*) Vietnam War, an almost endless stream of dissatisfied and disfranchised Vietnamese have attempted to flee their country by crossing the Gulf of Siam into Thailand or Malaysia. At differing times this flight of refugees has varied between as many as sixty-five thousand per month to a more recent four thousand.[75] Unfortunately, once they have put to sea, usually in underpowered boats crammed with people, the abuses they encounter exceed those in their homeland.

During the late 1970s, in the ornate chamber of the United Nations Economic and Social Council in New York, the report on the refugee situation, delivered by the United Nations' high commissioner for refugees—then Prince Aga Khan—would normally precede the report on the world crime situation, by Mueller, as chief of the United Nations' Crime Prevention and Criminal Justice Branch. The wait in the wings until the high commissioner's report had ended afforded Mueller a unique but sad opportunity to listen to an account of the worst of the crimes committed on the high seas. Yet not once did the august body see fit to provide the United Nations' Crime Prevention and Criminal Justice Branch with authority to step in and provide solutions. The connection between refugees and crime was simply not understood by the delegates.

No high commissioner's report has been as realistic as the story of Nguyen Tien Hoa, a South Vietnamese refugee who testified at the U.S. embassy in Kuala Lumpur, Malaysia. This was the ordeal as recounted by the embassy:

> The pirates took all of the young men aboard one of their vessels and conducted a body search, robbing them of all their valuables. Then the crews of all four pirate ships, totaling around 50 men with 15 firearms, came aboard the refugee boat to rape the women. Following the above events, which lasted about two hours, the pirates took all of the women and children aboard one of their own boats. They then removed from the refugee boat all of the engine's fuel and oil and threw all the food and water aboard into the sea.
>
> After having transferred all their male victims back to the refugee boat, they then tried to sink the refugee boat by ramming it. . . .
>
> Sometime later, totally exhausted, he crawled back aboard the refugee boat. He claimed that he saw no immediate evidence that anyone else was alive, either on the boat or in the water.[76]

The account of Mr. Hoa's flight from Vietnam is tragic, yet it recounts only one of hundreds of thousands of tragedies. On April 4, 1979, Boat 0105 left Kien Giang, Vietnam, with 380 people from 66 families aboard. Within days they too were set upon by pirates, who robbed them of their belongings and then repeatedly raped the women and female children on board. This, however, would turn out to be only the first of 23 separate attacks against boat 0105 by "Thai fishermen-turned-pirates." On December 31, 1979, 70 Vietnamese refugees were killed by pirates, some of whom repeatedly raped the surviving women and children.[77] During mid-December of the same year, another 80 refugees were killed in an assault near Ko Kra Island.[78] The list of similar abuses could go on indefinitely. It has been estimated that as many as one of every two refugee boats is attacked at least once by pirates while at sea.[79]

The plight of the refugees pirated, pillaged, murdered, and

raped appeals to any human being's sense of justice. Why can governments defiantly proclaiming a 200-mile zone around their waters for purposes of economic exploitation, not assume the responsibility for policing these zones to protect human life and dignity? And where is the international community while all this carnage is happening? At one point the United Nations' high commissioner for refugees became so alarmed over what he described as "undescribable acts of moral and physical degradation" that he appealed to Secretary General Kurt Waldheim for action. Waldheim, however, did little, believing that "the problem is largely one for the Thai and Malaysian Governments to solve, since most of the assaults take place inside their territorial waters."[80]

Not to be deterred, the United Nations' refugee agency next urged the United States to use its influence to persuade Thailand to crack down on the pirates. Saying that Washington does not want to antagonize the Thais, the United States declined and limited its response to supplying, through the high commissioner, one fast patrol boat. Malaysia reportedly rejected similar assistance, so as not to compromise its independence.[81]

"The main problem," according to one Thai official, "is we don't have enough boats, and the boats we do have are not fast enough. There is certainly concern, but we are limited in what we can do."[82] But another official, a key naval officer, declared, "Why should we try to protect refugees? We don't want them to come here."[83] Added to that

> . . . is a growing suspicion that the fishermen have the authorities' tacit approval to operate as a kind of savage, freelance coast guard. "Thai fishermen know that if they help these people they get punished," said one officer of an international aid agency. "And if the refugees don't come, the authorities are happy. So this gives the pirates a kind of carte blanche."[84]

The likelihood of a United Nations effort to curb piracy is still on the horizon.[85] Pending an international solution and weary of the haphazard attempts of locally concerned governments, can the mighty United States Asian fleet, the Seventh, provide any interim solution? This fleet has provided succor on occasion and rescued refugees from a fate worse than death, but attacks on pirates by the nuclear force appear a bit farfetched,[86] yet maybe not more so than the case of posse comitatus assistance to the Coast Guard in drug smuggling situations.

When governments fail, private initiative normally takes over. Passing merchant ships must be credited for their efforts to provide assistance and rescue.[87] Private initiative was also expressed when one of the oil companies (we were unable to determine which one) reportedly commissioned one of its own patrol vessels to guide its tankers through the pirate-infested sea lanes. But the noblest effort of all was the commissioning of the S.S. *Cap Anamur* by a group of West German physicians determined to assist the pirate-victimized boat people of Southeast Asia.[88] The *Cap Anamur's* sole mission was to patrol the affected waters of Southeast Asia, to rescue pirated boat people, and to save others from being victimized—by decisive yet unarmed action, as by having the ship's helicopter buzz a piracy in operation. We are sorry to have to report that our efforts to make contact with the West German relief organization sponsoring the vessel proved to no avail. It appears the *Cap Anamur* is no longer in service.

As the Sindbad II voyage led the *Sohar* through the pirate-infested waters of Southeast Asia, the voyagers were heartbroken when they encountered a tiny, rickety craft bearing eighteen Vietnamese refugees in search of a haven and of an escape from the human sharks of the South China Sea. The Sindbad voyagers did what was expected of any fellow sailor.[89] They resupplied the vessel, aided the refugees, and secured their passage to a safe port.

Faced with the incapacity of national governments, and of the international community as represented by the United Nations, the commercial fleets that are obligated to traverse the pirate-infested waters of Southeast Asia have resorted to self-help measures of their own. As early as 1973, the Mobil Shipping and Transportation Company issued a "Confidential" memorandum "To Masters of All Vessels," warning them of impending "hijacking" problems—though none had occurred yet. Detailed instructions were provided about "critical areas subject to attack," and measures to be taken in order to prevent such attacks or, if they occurred, to save the lives of those aboard, as well as the ship and her cargo. The Chamber of Shipping of the United Kingdom issued circulars to all its members about the dangers brewing in Asian waters, and providing guidelines for the masters of vessels. By 1975 the General Council of British Shipping had specific intelligence about planned attacks and issued detailed directives to masters for purposes of avoiding disasters, warning, however, that the directives should be safely locked, and their contents be made available only to officers directly responsible for security. In 1976 the British Department of Trade issued to all masters its detailed and confidential memorandum on the *Protection of Shipping Against Sabotage and Terrorism*. The fact that in subsequent piracies against large vessels in Asian waters few lives were lost, and that, indeed, relatively few piracies of super-sized vessels were successful, is in no small part attributable to the precautionary measures taken by the marine industry. By the time the attack on the *Corsicana* occurred—which we mentioned earlier—Mobil and other operators of tanker fleets had a well-established system for preventing and dealing with acts of piracy. But is it the task of shippers and mariners to assume the risk of piracy in the world's major sea lanes, and to combat the attackers with floodlights, foam monitors, and fire hoses? Where is the world community? Where is the Law of the Sea? Who is there to enforce it? Mobil and Shell, the International Shipping Federation Ltd., the Chamber of Shipping of the United Kingdom, the General Council of British Shipping, and other industry agencies are continuing to issue their directives to masters—more refined after each piracy incident—but the pirates are as resourceful as their victims, and piracy will continue—until there is law enforcement on the international sea lanes.

"Political" Piracy

"Political" piracy is a contradiction in terms. Piracy *jure gentium,* in the traditional connotation, was committed for private gain, *lucri causa.* Yet the term "piracy" has recently been applied to politically motivated acts condoned or supported by governments. For example, the seizure by Cambodian naval forces of the American merchant ship *Mayaguez* in May 1975, was labeled by President Ford as an act of piracy.[90] When the Israeli government intervened in a dispute involving the Israeli cargo ship *Persimonecore* in June 1976, it was accused by the American owner of the cargo of "an act of 'international irresponsibility' amounting to piracy."[91] And when, in May 1980, the Cuban government defended the sinking by a Cuban jet fighter of a Bahamian patrol boat investigating Cuban trawlers in Bahamian territorial waters, they did so with the explanation that they believed the patrol boat to be a "pirate ship attacking one of their vessels."[92]

A truly clear-cut case of politically motivated piracy occurred in September 1975, when a band of heavily armed Filipino bandits attacked and seized a Japanese freighter with twenty-seven persons aboard. The attackers, forty members of the Moro National Liberation Front, quickly established a two-day deadline and demanded a ransom of $133,000 for the return of the ship.[93] Fortunately, this incident ended peacefully when a fleet of eleven Philippine Navy ships made a sufficiently forceful response to provoke the pirates' surrender.[94] Although this may be but one isolated incident, we would do well to remember that we live in a world where terrorism has become a way of life.

By now our readers will know that this chapter is being finished in the West Indies. As if to provide us with a concluding sentence for "piracy"—especially politically motivated piracy—the news services are reporting this item:

Mystery boat under attack.

Caria-Reuters states that the sailing vessel *New Zealand* announced by ship-to-shore radio that she was being shot at. The vessel was close to Havana, which is edgy about spies, saboteurs, and insurgents. The U.S. Coast Guard could take no action, since the reported position of the *New Zealand* put her in Cuban waters.[95]

As we are leaving our "listening post" in the Leeward Islands, we can only conclude: The problem of maritime criminality, and piracy above all, will not be solved except by concerted international action, for pirates are terrorists. . . .

10

Where Land and Law End:
Terrorism at Sea

•

And, sick of prey, yet howling on for more,
Vomitest they wrecks on its inhospitable shore!
Treacherous in calm, and terrible in storm,
    Who shall put forth on thee,
    Unfathomable sea?

Percy Bysshe Shelley,
Unfathomable Sea

ON JUNE 3, 1983, THE YACHTS WERE gathering in the harbor of
Beaufort, North Carolina, to compete for a state championship
Performance Handicap Racing Fleet (PHRF) regatta. But the
starting gun was not to be fired. The harbor and downtown
waterfront had to be evacuated because a man on a cabin cruiser
threatened to blow up the vessel if police persisted in serving
him a warrant. Two Coast Guard patrol boats, later joined by the
cutter *Point Martin,* closed in but kept a respectable distance.
The harbor swarmed with SWAT teams, police, and Coast
Guard personnel. Police Chief Marvin Knox commented: "If
there was as much [dynamite] as was said to be here, it would
have made a mess on the waterfront."[1] After initial failures to
negotiate, a newspaper reporter and a Coast Guardsman finally
talked the terrorist, one Ojuveno Fonimechele, of Mecca, Saudi
Arabia, into surrendering.

We call Fonimechele a "terrorist." Indeed, under the accepted definition of the American Law Institute's Model Penal
Code, as adopted in a majority of American states:

> A person is guilty of a felony of the third degree if he threatens
> to commit any crime of violence with purpose to terrorize another
> or to cause evacuation of a building, place of assembly, or facility

158

of public transportation, or otherwise to cause serious public inconvenience, or in reckless disregard of the risk of causing such terror or inconvenience.[2]

When this provision was drafted in 1960 it was a novelty in American law, and no amount of imagination could have foreseen the magnitude of terrorism that was to follow on land, in the air, and on the sea. Nor were the international dimensions of terrorism anticipated by the drafters of the code, although there had at least been one international effort to deal with terrorism as a world phenomenon. In 1937 the League of Nations had drafted its Convention for the Prevention and Punishment of Terrorism. This instrument extended to "criminal acts against a state and intended or calculated to create a state of terror in the minds of particular persons or the general public," and it included all acts causing the death of or bodily injury to heads of state or government, their spouses, and other public figures, or attempts to do so, or causing damage to public property, or endangering the lives of the public or dealing with arms or ammunition for the commission of any of these offenses in any state.[3] Under this definition, which never became effective since only one country ratified the convention, and under the American Law Institute's definition, Fonimecliele is a terrorist.

Let us probe the concept of terrorism and how it may apply to seaborne activities.[4] It appears that writers on the subject choose their own definitions. The differences generally turn on such issues as whether a coercive threat against the state is a necessary ingredient, or whether state terrorism (e.g., repressive governmental action against population groups) is to be included, or whether distinctions should be made between national or international terrorism.[5] The latter point has an important bearing on the question of who may bring a terrorist to trial. If ever an international court of criminal justice were to be established, as we have proposed elsewhere,[6] such a court would have jurisdiction over international—but not national—acts of terrorism.

As a practical matter, most acts of seaborne terrorism are international in nature, not just because of the internationality of the high seas and the commerce they carry, but also because terrorism is, for the most part, an organizational crime, and most of the terrorist organizations are international in character, through membership, financial and other support objectives, or affiliation.

In most countries, "terrorism" itself cannot be found as a crime in the penal codes, but the variegated crimes that terrorists commit, such as murder, extortion, destruction of property, and mayhem, are well defined crimes under the laws of all countries. For our purposes, then, terrorism is the accomplishment of a criminal purpose by criminal means and through employment of massive and pervasive threats and measures that strike fear and panic in those affected and in large circles beyond them.

The pirates of old were terrorists. Not only did they seize ships and all persons and property aboard, not only did they murder, rob, and rape, but they also did so by creating fear and panic among their intended victims and seafarers everywhere. When a pirate ship approached a merchant vessel, the dreaded skull and crossbones, the Jolly Roger, or similar flags were flown from the mainmast. All the pirates were topside, dressed in fear-inspiring, grotesque outfits. They would make a deafening noise, with drums, trumpets, the rattling of chains, cutlasses and sabers, firing guns and pistols, emitting fierce battle cries. When the victims were frightened, the battle and plunder were half won.

Among today's terrorists, none is regarded with greater awe and disdain than the infamous Carlos, "The Jackal," of Venezuela, né Illich Ramirez Sanchez. Among his exploits was the 1975 kidnapping of the oil ministers of eleven OPEC countries, assembled at their headquarters in Vienna, whence they were flown across the Mediterranean—in a commandeered plane—to Algiers, where once upon a time U.S. Marines fought the Barbary Coast pirates. But Carlos' accomplishments are many, due to his ability to create and maintain contact with the world's most prominent terrorist groups, to coordinate their planning, training, and actions, yet always to slip out of the traps set for him by his pursuers. Until the world's crime prevention efforts are as well organized as those of Carlos', "The Jackal from Caracas," terrorism on land and water will continue.

In September 1980, delegations of the national governments of the world gathered in Caracas, Venezuela, for the Sixth United Nations Congress on the Prevention of Crime and the Treatment of Offenders. The meeting took place in the same congress center in which, a few years earlier, the Second United

Nations Law of the Sea Conference had been peacefully conducted. As executive secretary, Mueller was responsible for the preparation and the smooth functioning of the Crime Prevention Congress, at which the member states of the United Nations would review the successes and failures of their efforts to prevent crime in their countries and would decide on the course to be taken for the next five years. On the agenda was, among others, the interconnected, worldwide spread of crime affecting the economy of nations, including crime in boardrooms, the traffic in narcotics, terrorism in its various forms, as well as international cooperation to apprehend and deal with the now mobile lot of international criminals. The government of Australia had originally agreed to host this mammoth gathering of the world's crime prevention experts. But pressures involving the PLO participation, and related considerations, had prompted the Australian government to back out. Oil-rich Venezuela stepped into the breach and generously offered the magnificent facilities of the international congress building in Caracas as the site of the Congress. The task of coordinating the preparations for the Crime Prevention Congress was not easy. It required shuttling among New York headquarters, Vienna (where part of the staff had been transferred), Rome (where the research institute was located), and Caracas, not to mention a host of capitals, from Moscow to Tokyo, Warsaw to Cairo, Berlin to Manila, San José to Addis Ababa.

No sooner had the Italian delegation checked into the Caracas Hilton when Mueller was summoned to the suite of the head of the delegation, who calmly told him: "I have just received a threat on my life! The voice on the phone said, 'You will not leave Caracas alive!' " Mueller knew that the speaker was not given to hysterics. As head of the Italian criminal justice system, he had been through a lot. For five days he had been held hostage by the Red Brigades in Rome; his bodyguards had been gunned down; his car had been blown to smithereens. He had never faltered. Indeed, he had doubled his efforts, and had succeeded in breaking the backbone of the Red Brigades in Italy. Or had he? Never feeling safe in Italy, always driving in an armored car, always armed, always accompanied by bodyguards, he had looked forward to "safe" Venezuela. And now this!

Mueller assured him that he would take immediate action to protect his life and went to his own suite to make the necessary phone calls. As he was about to pick up the phone, it rang. He picked it up and an obviously disguised voice said in Spanish: "The end is near. None of you will leave alive."

What a fantastic plan! First the oil ministers, now the entire world's governments' experts on crime prevention! Those who fight world terrorism were to be the target of the world's terrorists! The end of the story need not be told in this book. Suffice it to say that the threats continued, that they came from within the hotel, that at one point even some officers of the state security forces could not be trusted, that the United Nations security experts, who had been immediately flown in from New York to Caracas, were disarmed at the airport—a first in United Nations History—and that SWAT teams armed with submachine guns had to be placed around the conference building and in front of every door. A peaceful gathering of the world peace organization was turned into an armed camp. The congress concluded successfully, contrary to the terrorists' plans.

Liners

Terrorists choose their objects carefully. Some of the most desirable objects are on that far larger part of the world's surface called oceans. Take a luxury liner. She is bound to carry some of the world's leading citizens, enormous wealth, but more than that, national pride and prestige of the country of the flag. Ernest Lehman told the story well in his 1977 novel *The French Atlantic Affair.* A group of disillusioned, laid-off, high-tech American adventurers seizes the pride of the French merchant marine, dubbed the *Marseille.* The ship is wired to explode—unless $35 million in gold bullion are delivered. The plan seems perfect; of course, it fails.[7] But we do not need fiction to make the point. We have the facts of a plan that did not fail.

The 20,907-ton Portuguese luxury liner *Santa Maria,* five-year-old flagship of Portugal's liner fleet, had crossed the Atlantic from Lisbon and had called on Caracas' port, La Guaira, the first stop on its Caribbean cruise. Additional passengers came aboard—seventy-one, to be exact, although not all had paid the fare; some were stowaways. In the middle of the death watch, at 2:00 A.M., on January 22, 1961, with all passengers asleep, while the ship was cruising near Curaçao, N.A., the group of seventy-one revealed itself as a well-trained band of insurgents and seized control of all strategic points of the ship in a brief struggle with resisting crew members. The third officer was killed; other officers and crew members were wounded. The captain was imprisoned aboard. The insurgents were well prepared for their piracy. Their armament included machine guns and other automatic weapons. Piracy—hijacking of an ocean liner!—in the same waters where such notorious pirates as Captain Edward Teach (Blackbeard) and John (Long Ben) Avery had plied their infamous trade centuries earlier!

As yet the world knew nothing of the events aboard the *Santa Maria*, which calmly followed the route traversed by another *Santa Maria*. But it was not Christopher Columbus who now commanded the *Santa Maria*, it was Senhor Henrique Malta Galvao, an ardent foe of Portuguese dictator Salazar, with a carefully selected troop of Portuguese freedom fighters and anti-Franco Spaniards who determined the destiny of the ship, its 962 passengers, and its 300 crew members.

The ship called at the island of St. Lucia, however briefly, to discharge the wounded. Before any authorities realized the seizure of the *Santa Maria*, she had disappeared in the wide expanses of the Atlantic. By the time that Galvao radioed the seizure of the ship to the world, she could have been anywhere in an ocean expanse of 2.2 million square miles, with her speed of 20 knots. Galvao's message to the world, and especially to President Salazar, was loud and clear: The *Santa Maria* was the first liberated territory of Portugal. If any attempt were made to seize the ship, she would be scuttled and lives would be lost.

A classical case of piracy in ancient piratical waters? No! Piracy requires a seizure for private gain. This was a political hijacking. Terrorism? Absolutely! The threat of a scuttled superliner, the potential death of a thousand people!

An unheard-of flurry of diplomatic and military activities ensued among Presidents Salazar, of Portugal, Kennedy of the U.S.A., and the outgoing and incoming presidents of Brazil. The chiefs of the navies of the U.S.A., Portugal, Brazil, Venezuela, the Netherlands, and the United Kingdom stuck their heads together. A U.S. fleet composed of the destroyers *Vogelsang, Wilson, Domato,* and *Gearing* (dispatched at top speed from Freetown, Sierra Leone), the oilers *Canisteo* and *Mispilion,* and the nuclear submarine *Seawolf,* as well as a sizable air wing, joined by naval vessels from all other nearby and concerned countries, commenced to track down the *Santa Maria*. It took sixty-three hours to find her, en route to Africa. And if it had not been for a Danish freighter that spotted the luxury liner with its distinct, sleek features, and its yellow, green, and white funnel, the naval search might have lasted even longer.

Ultimately the vessel backtracked to a point off Recife, Brazil, where negotiations between American admirals (dress uniform white and gold braid) and Galvao were held, with a powerless fleet standing by. The negotiations were successful. The *Santa Maria* was sailed into Recife, where the passengers and crew were released, and Galvao and his men were granted exile. But the repercussions of the *Santa Maria* incident were lasting: Galvao won his point. The Portuguese government of Salazar ultimately fell; the Portuguese colonies won independence. A victory for terrorism had been won, and the impotence of conventional naval strategies to deal with it had been demonstrated.[8]

Perhaps Galvao never seriously considered scuttling the ship or killing the passengers to remonstrate against dictatorship. But from the perspective of those hundreds of passengers aboard, what difference did it make? Terrorism had gone to sea with the *Santa Maria* almost five hundred years after the first *Santa Maria* had traversed these same waters, in search of a new world.

Passenger liners have continued to occupy terrorists' fascination. No less a ship than the *Queen Elizabeth II*, or *QE II*, was to become the ambition of terrorist objectives. During the era when Egypt and Libya were to consolidate their countries and already had created a joint military command structure, the Libyan head of state, Colonel Muammar Qaddafi, is reported to have ordered an Egyptian submarine to torpedo the *QE II*, then on a voyage in the Mediterranean, with a scheduled stop in Haifa, Israel, as part of Israel's twenty-fifth anniversary as a state. "President Anwar Sadat of Egypt, however, upon receiving word of the Libyan dictator's orders to the submarine, instantly recalled the vessel, avoiding a disaster that would have led to a major conflict."[9]

It was during a major world conflict that a superliner, no less glorious than the *Queen Elizabeth II*, is likely to have been the target of criminals of the water—saboteurs, in this case: " 'What palace, what triumphal way, what memorial have we built to perpetuate our civilization, as the cathedrals perpetuate that of the Middle Ages, the castles of the Loire that of the Renaissance, and Versailles that of the age of Louis XIV?'—the only answer was *The Normandie!*"[10] One of the grandest ladies ever to have crossed the Atlantic, this extravagantly luxurious and fast French liner was being converted to serve as a troop carrier when, on February 9, 1942, she went ablaze and, pumped full of fire-fighting water, capsized at her pier in New York Harbor. According to conventional wisdom, it was a spark from a welder's torch that set ablaze a bundle of kapok-filled life preservers, followed by incredible bungling by the workmen and the fire fighters, that occasioned the loss. Wagging tongues attributed the disaster to Nazi sabotage, as the *Hindenburg* Zeppelin disaster a few years earlier had been attributed to anti-Nazi sabotage. If Mafia sources are to be believed, the *Normandie* went down as a Mafia-created lesson in labor relations, after which management and government gave in and secured a smooth functioning of longshoremen services in America's war-strained ports.[11]

But another passenger liner was actually sunk while in service: On March 4, 1973, the Greek cruise liner *Sanya,* with 250 American tourists aboard and bound for Haifa, was sunk by a limpet mine in Beirut Harbor, Lebanon, for which the Black September Organization, a particularly militant offshoot of the PLO, claimed credit.[12] And even while we are in the process of research on terrorism against liners, the U.S. Coast Guard informs us of a bomb threat on a cruise liner docked in Miami! It is January 1983!

In today's world of terrorism, there is no such thing as a liner free from potential terrorism, though we would prefer to have it happen only on *Love Boat,* on the tube.

Tankers and Supertankers

From a terrorist's perspective there are objects at sea that hold a far greater potential for terrorism and thus, accomplishment of dissident ideals than liners: supertankers, for example. In his novel *The Devil's Alternative,* that master of international intrigue and suspense, Frederick Forsyth, places us on a supertanker—the world's largest, with a capacity of one million tons of crude oil. An obscure group of Ukrainian freedom fighters hijacks the vessel at its anchorage in the North Sea while she is awaiting the Europort Maas pilot. Unless the group's conditions are met, the crude oil will be discharged, causing the destruction of the entire North Sea ecology. "Because supertankers could be taken as easily as piggy banks, a captain and his crew of twenty-nine might die like rats in a swirl of oil and water."[13] Tankers, and supertankers in particular, are "floating bombs" that are inherently vulnerable because they are basically unprotected and thus are natural targets for those bent on terrorism.[14] The PLO is reported to have threatened repeatedly to sink a super-tanker in the Strait of Hormuz, between the Persian Gulf and the Gulf of Oman.[15] We have cruised the tanker lanes of the Persian Gulf in Kuwaiti patrol boats and become convinced that the multitude of tankers, the paucity of patrol craft, and the narrow-ness of the waterways render such a plan feasible and a conse-quent catastrophe likely, although, for the moment, the war between Iraq and Iran is creating more havoc for the oil com-merce and ecology of that region than any terrorist act could accomplish. But then, there are tankers and tankers, and the most explosive of the lot seem to be the LNGC's, the liquefied natural gas carriers, transporting natural gas chilled to $-260°F$ and thus reduced to one six-hundredth its original volume. Peter van der Linde called his book on LNGC's *Time Bomb,* and he makes a convincing case about the potential of vast catas-trophes that inhere in these large vessels, especially since they sail and dock with as little protection as ordinary tankers.[16] Saboteurs could manage to sign on as crew, they could board such a vessel while at anchorage with her Jacob's ladder down, or they could be picked up as apparent shipwreck survivors whom any passing vessel is obligated to rescue. The point of interception is easily predictable. LNGC's travel fixed and pre-dictable routes. Once in the hands of terrorists, they do indeed become time bombs capable of destroying a great part of the metropolitan area of New York, Baltimore, or Boston. Gas es-caping from a sabotaged and ruptured tank, or vented, could cover many square miles, causing death by asphyxiation. If the gas were to ignite, a fire storm would result that could cause the death of hundreds of thousands of people, and billions of dol-lars in property damages.[17] However, the fire-storm scenario is disputed by some scientists who argue that the explosiveness of liquefied natural gas vapor, even when high explosives are used, is not yet scientifically confirmed.[18] But Cleveland experienced a liquefied natural gas disaster on October 2, 1944, when 1.2 million gallons of such gas escaped a ruptured tank, spread over part of the city, and ignited—causing the death of 130 persons and leaving 14,000 others homeless.[19]

Stationary Ocean Targets

In Alistair McLean's 1977 novel *Seawitch,* a Gulf of Mexico oil rig becomes the target of an international intrigue in which Americans and Russians, Venezuelans and Cubans all play their roles. The oil rig ultimately disintegrates in an inferno set off by terrorists.[20] Six years later, on Friday, October 14, 1983, this drama was played out in real life. While Contadora countries, including Mexico and Venezuela, were desperately trying to bring peace to troubled Central American countries, while Cuba and the Soviet Union were shipping sophisticated arms to the Sandinista government of Nicaragua, and while the U.S.A. was supporting the anti-Sandinista rebels with weapons, waterborne terrorists (or freedom fighters, depending on one's point of view) blew up an underwater pipeline carrying crude oil from an offshore tanker unloading facility three miles out in the Gulf of Mexico, to an Exxon refinery on shore, virtually halting crude-oil imports to Nicaragua.[21]

Stationary targets inviting terrorist attacks include offshore crude-oil loading and unloading facilities as well as oil rigs that pump the lifeblood of industrial society from Davy Jones's locker. Over two thousand offshore oil-drilling platforms of various designs, including jackups, submersibles, and semi-submersibles, can be found all over the world's oceans. Their number is increasing with the expansion of national economic zones to two hundred miles beyond the shoreline. After all, oil is easy money for a sagging national economy. Each one of these platforms pumps from a cluster of wells. The output is enormous. The disaster that results from an ignition and explosion is potentially tremendous; the flow of oil and the spread of burning oil may last for months, as the world has witnessed in the Gulf of Mexico, where a well has been burning out of control for years, and in the Persian Gulf, where war action has caused widespread damage. So far, none of the Texas tower disasters appears to have been due to an act of terrorism, but sabotage can easily be accomplished by explosives carried in an indistinguishable launch or fishing vessel, or by a remote-controlled ramming.[22] The terrorist attack on the crude-oil off-loading and refining facilities in Nicaragua simply is an overture to more damaging acts of terrorism against stationary ocean targets.

The vulnerability of oil rigs was demonstrated on February 14–15, 1982, when the semisubmersible rig *Ocean Ranger*—the size of a football field—sank with the loss of 84 crewmen in the Hibernia fields, 165 miles east of Newfoundland. Better crew training and adherence to safety procedures could have saved the rig, the U.S. Coast Guard ruled.[23] But only a few countries have taken special precautions to protect their offshore oil rigs against sabotage. Norway is one of the few that has given special protective duties to her Coast Guard in this regard.

The age of terrorism is becoming ever more visible around stationary marine targets. A day or so after Christmas 1983, 3¼-by-3½-foot concrete blocks were placed at the entrance to the General Dynamics shipyard in Quincy, Massachusetts, after receipt of several bomb threats. At the time, the Navy had a submarine tender undergoing repairs in the yard.[24]

Among the world's most vulnerable stationary maritime objects, the great canals take top ranking, especially the three giants: the Panama Canal, the Suez Canal, and the Kiel Canal. We visited all three.

Panama, February 4, 1984: We are standing at the Panama Canal. Two hundred thirteen years ago, "Sir" Henry Morgan, one of the most notorious of English pirates, marched his band of merry rogues into the old Ciudad de Panama, singing, "There'll be a hot time in the old town tonight." They promptly proved their point by sacking the city and burning it to the ground. The ruins still stand where Morgan's men scorched them. Thereafter the Spaniards moved the city to more defensible grounds, the Casco Viejo (Old Compound). This is still the heart of Panama City, and there you can view the famous Golden Altar that Morgan had been after but that the citizens had concealed—just in time.[25]

We doubt that it has become harder over the centuries to create havoc in Panama, whose main attraction is the Panama

Canal, which you have to traverse from northwest to southeast to get from east to west. Few maritime objects in the world could be more attractive to international terrorists than this waterway, which connects the Atlantic with the Pacific sea trade, at the rate of over thirteen thousand blue-water ships annually since 1914, when the American freighter *Ancon* made the first transit.

At Miraflores locks we passed the happily smiling gatekeepers, who paid no attention to our briefcase. They paid even less attention to a couple following us, pushing a baby buggy. Briefcase or buggy could have been dumped into the lock—"accidentally"—right next to the gate, with a time bomb! A terrorist's dream! No surer way to draw attention to a cause, or to blackmail Panama, the U.S.A., or the international community into a concession. Easier yet, a bomb concealed on a tanker traversing the canal could create even more havoc.

The Twenty-fourth Congress of the Inter-American Bar Association convened here today, under the patronage of Vice President Illueca, who is also president of the current 35th U.N. General Assembly.[26] The focus is, *inter alia,* on the protection of the Panama Canal against terrorist attacks. Two newspaper articles preceded this Congress: *"La Seguridad y Defensa del Canal en el año 2000"* (The Security and Defense of the Canal in the Year 2000)[27] and *"¿Qué es el Costo de la Seguridad y Defensa del Canal de Panamá?"* (What is the Cost of the Security and Defense of the Panama Canal?)[28] The author of these articles presented his learned thesis before the delegates of the Inter-American Bar Association. The canal, with its 565 square kilometers of vulnerable territory, initially appears to be indefensible. Surely this must have been in the mind of President Carter when he signed the canal treaty that provided for the turnover of the waterway, in stages, to Panamanian sovereignty by the year 2000. To him, too, the canal was indefensible against potential—specifically Panamanian nationalist—terrorism. And the articles' author continues to speak in those terms, namely, potential terrorism by saboteurs—Cuban, or, in any event, Communist. But do Cubans in particular, or Communists in general, have any interest in destroying the canal? That is not to say that the canal is not vulnerable to terrorist attack. On the contrary, the ditch is vulnerable, but probably primarily to potential attacks by the lunatic fringe of terrorists intent on holding the world (not Panama

and/or the U.S.A. specifically) hostage, for concessions, or publicity, or both. It is, as Lebanon has taught us, the age of the
rebirth of the "assassin," or hashashin (in Arabic), and it attests
to the close connection between the use of hashish—inducing a
state of ephemeral frenzy—and a desire to risk one's life for a
"just" assassination or attack. The assassin's reward is the promise of an eternal, beautiful life in the hereafter.[29] Most likely, if
an attack on the Panama Canal occurs, it will be staged by this
lunatic fringe type of terrorists who will want to hold the world
hostage at any price. Panamanian Law 20[30] and training of the
Panamanian defense forces can go a long way toward the protection of the canal against terrorism, but, despite a potential
Panamanian expenditure of $423.3 million annually for the pro-
tection of the canal,[31] all of us are still potential maritime hostages.

By the end of the meeting, the press announced that President Ricard de la Espriella of Panama, had resigned, and Vice
President Jorge Illueca had succeeded him.[32] We don't suppose that it had anything to do with our briefcase at Miraflores
lock.

The situation is not much different with respect to the Suez
Canal and the Kiel Canal. At the Suez Canal we visited the
intricate general control system, which provides superb navigational safety, but virtually no protection against terrorism. The
1956 Israeli-Egyptian war has demonstrated how easy it is to
block the canal with a few sunken vessels. While the Kiel Canal
fared better during World War II, it is as vulnerable to terrorism
today as its sister canals.

Let us be precise on that: While superliners have been the
targets of terrorists, no oil tanker, supertanker, LNGC, Texas
tower, or canal has yet been used as a terrorist target. But the
ease with which a tanker can be taken over by an act of piracy
has been demonstrated by the pirates of Asia. "It is only a matter
of time," wrote Neil C. Livingstone in *The War Against Terrorism*,
published in 1982, "before terrorists or insurgents strike at one
of the so-called catastrophic targets, and when it happens, man-
kind will only then begin to grasp the real meaning of terror."[33]
And we predict it will happen, for the destruction of an object
far more catastrophic than that of any LNGC has already been
targeted by a band of conspirators, as we shall demonstrate
forthwith.

Naval Vessels as Targets

We are writing this on October 22, 1983, the day on which the *New York Post* announced in bold headlines: "Rush Marines to Grenada—U.S. diverts carrier, 2,000 troops." *The New York Times* is full of reports about the intra-Marxist rebellion in the tiny island State of Grenada that cost its President and seventeen others their lives. With some six hundred American medical students and many other Americans on the island—and, of course, considering the strategic significance of Grenada within the Caribbean power constellation—the U.S. government felt compelled to divert a ten-ship nuclear carrier task force from its station off Lebanon to the new trouble spot.[34]

The incident calls to memory another U.S. Caribbean venture. In 1898, the island of Cuba was in turmoil. Dissidents and revolutionaries were in command of most of the island. Atrocities were alleged. The Spanish colonial government, controlling only a few ports and urban areas, could not guarantee the lives of Europeans or Americans. "Finally affairs in the Cuban capital grew so threatening that our Consul General, Fitzhugh Lee, asked that a warship be sent. The battleship *Maine*, then at Key West waiting for an emergency call, was sent to Havana, arriving there January 25, 1898."[35] On February 15, 1898, a mysterious explosion shook the *Maine*. The ship's ammunition stores blew up in a secondary explosion and she sank, with a loss of 266 of her crew of 353. A court-martial established that the hull had been pierced by an underwater mine. The act was regarded as one of terrorism or sabotage, not of war, since no state of war existed between Spain and the United States. Nor was it ever ascertained who was responsible for bringing the mine into contact with the battleship. What was remembered is the battle cry "Remember the *Maine*!" on which party politics and national destiny were to be based for a generation or more.[36]

During World War II attacks by partisans against men-of-war were to continue, at least during wartime. Mueller remembers an attack by the Danish underground against the German heavy cruiser *Lützow* (pocket battleship *Deutschland*) while she was berthed at Lange Linie in Copenhagen. A truck manned by guerrillas of the Danish underground sped past the warehouses on the wharf at which this ship of the line was docked. The partisans threw packets of explosives onto the warehouse roof, whence they rolled off, right onto the deck of the *Lützow*. But that was, by the standards of the Danish underground, an act of war, not an act of terrorism (although the German admirality at that time was of quite an opposite opinion). What does matter is that naval vessels are natural objects of attack by any group opposed to whatever it is that these vessels stand for.

During the past few decades a number of successful counter-governmental attacks against naval vessels have taken place. Some were quasi acts of war, including the sinking of a U.S. aircraft carrier in the Saigon River in 1962. In August 1981, a group of Iranian exiles loyal to the deposed Shah and opposed to the Khomeini regime, captured an Iranian gunboat off the coast of Spain. In October 1981, Basque insurgents bombed a Spanish destroyer at dockside in Santander, Spain. In November 1981, insurgents attached a bomb to the hull of the British oceanographic ship *Hecate* berthed in Nantes, France. The bomb was discovered and disarmed, timely, due to the watchfulness of the French Navy.[37]

The surprise to exceed all expectations had occurred in 1978, when a group of ill-defined dissidents hatched a plan to seize the U.S. submarine *Trepang,* a nuclear-powered vessel equipped with nuclear-tipped ballistic missiles, at New London, Connecticut. The plotters were an assortment of revolutionaries, dropouts, and adventurers, including a former crew member of the *Trepang.* The plan was simple: The terrorists were to blow up the *Trepang*'s tender, thereby diverting attention from their principal object. They were then to board the *Trepang,* kill her crew, and sail her out of New London. We can assure our readers that sailing any vessel out of New London, whether the U.S.S. *Trepang* or the *Contessa Maria II,* on a dark night or a foggy day, is no mean task! Once out at sea, a nuclear-tipped missile was to be fired on an East Coast city, and then demands were to be made. There also was a hazy plan to sell the *Trepang* to an undisclosed buyer.[38] By now, history will have told our readers that the plan did not succeed. The fact is that the plotters, after an elaborate FBI investigation, were arrested, indicted, and tried in federal court and now are serving sentences for "unlawfully conspiring and agreeing to steal and purloin a thing of value from the United States. To wit, the U.S.S. *Trepang,* a United States Navy Nuclear Submarine."

By a successful act of terrorism against a naval vessel, the terrorists can accomplish two objectives: One, the disablement of the vessel, so as to reduce the capacity of the government whose flag she flies to deploy her as an instrument for implementing policy. Two, and perhaps more important, the destruction of a naval vessel deals a policy blow at the government it serves. The incident of the *Maine* is a superb example for the accomplishment of both goals. The *Trepang* incident, if successful, could have accomplished both goals as well—yet with far greater loss of life.

The navies of this world are very much alert to attacks against their floating and stationary forces. Heavy ships, wherever they are located, have well-trained security personnel. Smaller vessels and installations lacking such expertise and manpower are somewhat more vulnerable. But systems are operative to guard against acts of sabotage and terrorism. Routine protective measures include the following:

- Watches and patrols continuously throughout the ship
- Checks on classified material stowage
- Alertness for any signs of sabotage
- Control of the physical security of magazines
- Sounding of liquid storage tanks
- Surveillance re watertight integrity
- Deployment of picket boats around the ship to detect or deter approaches by swimmers
- Intermittent and random discharge of hand grenades
- Turning over the ship's propeller to scare away frogmen
- Moving the ship's rudder (for the same reason)
- Activating the ship's sonar (for the same reason)[39]

Even the deployment of dolphins is being explored to protect naval vessels against acts of sabotage and terrorism.[40] And next time you see Coast Guard cutters escorting the nuclear-powered aircraft carrier U.S.S. *Enterprise,* or any other capital ship, into San Francisco Harbor, or any other American port, you will know that this is not just an escort of honor. The potential of sabotage and terrorism is real.[41]

Assassinations

How easy it is to sabotage a vessel or to assassinate a VIP has been amply demonstrated by the IRA:

There was a green-and-white fishing boat, the *Shadow V,* moored off Mullaghmore, in the Irish Republic. The boat had no permanent guard, although the constabulary checked out the little vessel from time to time, for the vessel belonged to Earl Mountbatten, hero of World War II, last viceroy of India, first sea lord of the British Navy, admiral of the fleet, cousin of Queen Elizabeth II and uncle of Prince Phillip. As had been his wont for thirty years, Earl Mountbatten spent the summer of 1979 at his Irish home, taking the *Shadow* out for fishing expeditions. On August 27, 1979, the *Shadow* made it only a few hundred yards seaward from its mooring. A witness reported: "The boat was there one minute and the next minute it was like a lot of matchsticks floating on the water."[42] The dead included Mountbatten, a fourteen-year-old grandson, and a fifteen-year-old passenger. Four other persons, including Mountbatten's daughter, Lady Brabourne, were maimed. The IRA, in a news release from Belfast, claimed responsibility for the assassination and vowed to continue the "noble struggle to drive the British Intruders out of our native land."[43]

That the Mountbatten operation can be replicated in the U.S.A., by whatever group—and there are about a hundred potentials[44]—for whatever motive, was clearly demonstrated in January 1984. At 3:30 A.M., scuba divers entered the Potomac River on the Virginia side, penetrated heavy dock security at the Washington Navy Yard, on the Anacostia River, swam to the presidential yacht *Sequoia,* and attached an explosive to the hull —only it was a dud, and the whole exercise was a private initiative to demonstrate the weakness of the security system. Had it not been a mere demonstration, we might have lost another President as well as additional high-ranking officials.[45]

In the U.S.A., the Coast Guard bears the brunt of protective operations against terrorism and sabotage on the waterways. In collaboration with the International Association of Chiefs of Police, the Coast Guard has been running training exercises involving the breadth of terrorist activities on the water, under the direction of the project leader of the Coast Guard's Counterterrorist Action Task Force, Intelligence and Security Division.[46]

Among all the security tasks, one looms particularly large: The summer of 1984 will have seen the Summer Olympics, with all its sailing events at the massive Los Angeles-Long Beach Harbor complex. We remember the massacre of Israel's Olympics team during the 1972 Summer Olympics in Munich, Germany, with a loss of nine lives. Matters have not improved in those twelve years! A terrorist attack could occur from or at any of the stationary or floating objects near the Olympics. It might be directed against the athletes, the attending dignitaries, kings, queens, or other heads of state. The old hotel ship *Queen Mary*, a gracefully aging superliner, herself might be attacked. So could any of the sailing fleets, events, or accommodations. It appears, however, that the Coast Guard is ready and prepared, with a commitment of 450 personnel, and 115 vessels of all types, including a 400-foot icebreaker, 7 cutters, 21 41-foot patrol boats, 2 32-foot patrol craft, 3 high-speed Spectras, 45 rigid-hull inflatables, 37 auxiliary craft of various types, and an air wing of helicopters. Not since the Cuban boat people operation has the Coast Guard assembled such a force at any one trouble spot, not to mention the massive assistance the Coast Guard will receive from other federal, state, and local law-enforcement agencies.[47] Nevertheless, the government of Israel expressed its grave concern.[48] Time will tell whether the concern is justified, and by the time this book is in print, we shall know whether the Coast Guard's precautions were justified and adequate.

It is now October 23, 1983. Earlier in this chapter we referred to the 1898 sabotage of the U.S.S. *Maine* and to the news reports about the carrier task force's steaming up to Grenada. We wondered whether a *Maine*-style incident would be repeated. Not quite—but the radio news promptly reported a kamikaze-style attack on a U.S. Marine emplacement in Beirut. By now 240 lives are lost, almost as many as on the *Maine*. Another terrorist success, this time on a stationary Marine target established to keep the peace.

How then do we protect our oceans and waterways against terrorism, sabotage, and every other conceivable carnage? The divine eternal peace envisaged in Genesis was not achievable then, according to the same source, and appears as unlikely of achievement now as then, despite the emergence of the United Nations. Obviously, the resolution of the world's hotbed controversies, in the spirit of conciliation for which the U.N. stands, would go a long way toward ensuring *pacem in maribus.* With resort to conciliation, more than half of the incidents recounted in this chapter might have been without a cause worth fighting for, i.e., they would not have been. But what can we do until even that state of minimal bliss is achieved?

There are two types of solutions: national and international. Let us talk about national solutions first, for they are easier to achieve, although their outreach is limited by jurisdictional bounds. We already referred to the Coast Guard's well-rehearsed, well-supported eternal vigilance, and that is the function of all of the world's maritime law-enforcement agencies. But the navies themselves are subjects of law enforcement on the high seas and not just their objects of protection. As for the United States, the post-Revolutionary War Navy, established by the Naval Act of 1794, was indeed an antiterrorist navy, whose six initial frigates were slated to subdue the Barbary Coast pirates off Algiers, Morocco, Tunis, and Tripoli to protect peaceful American commerce in the Mediterranean.

Students of maritime terrorism tell us that today's maritime terrorism is more likely to strike ships at port, whether through bombings with limpet mines, hijackings, or other attacks.[49] Naval forces all over the world have developed their own systems of dealing with this type of portside attack against naval and merchant vessels. The U.S. Navy has its SEAL (sea-air-land) teams, successors to its famed World War II underwater demolition teams. Obviously, vigilance must be adjusted to vulnerability,[50] and it is equally obvious that vigilance must be cost-beneficial. If the maritime life of the nation were to be geared wholly toward security, stagnation of commerce would result. One must take calculated risks. That the national approach to dealing with terrorism holds a considerable potential is demonstrated by the drastic decline in airplane hijackings following the institution of airport and on-board security measures. But this same example also demonstrates the success of the second approach, the international approach: The more or less tacit agreement by Cuba to prosecute hijackers of aircraft abducted to Cuba has contributed considerably toward the decline in attempted hijackings to Cuba. Might it therefore not be possible to guarantee the safety of the oceans against terrorists and saboteurs by international collaboration, conventions, or treaties? So far the world has made relatively little progress in this regard, although three conventions against the terrorist threat to international aviation have been concluded and appear to be effective. A convention for the protection of diplomats and internationally protected persons likewise is in force and appears to be somewhat effective. Other draft conventions aimed at terrorism are still "at sea." The sea itself is still waiting for its antiterrorist convention.[51] Perhaps we should return to Caracas or Montego Bay, but this time the maritime lawyers should join hands with maritime crime preventers.

11

Tempting Tides:
Corruption

•

"It seems a shame" the walrus said,
"To play them such a trick.
After we've brought them out so far,
and made them trot so quick!"

Lewis Carroll,
The Walrus and the Carpenter

DECEMBER 11, 1976. DEPUTIES WERE CALLED to investigate four suspicious boats anchored without lights in a deep-water channel. They found a marijuana off-loading operation in full swing, with nearly 12 tons already stacked on the beach. Twelve Latin men were arrested; only one was convicted. The defense attorney argued that his clients were simply clam-digging when they inadvertently came upon the marijuana. Moreover, there had been a problem with a discrepancy in the evidence report. A clerk had written that all 398 bales were destroyed by court order, when in reality several bales had been retained for evidence. The state attorney blamed the police for inefficiency; the police blamed the state attorney for knowing about the erroneous report and yet not changing it before the trial.

May 23, 1977. A patrolling sheriff's sergeant noticed that there was a lock missing from a private gate. While checking the property, he was met with gunfire, shouts of "police," and frantic activity. A seizure was made of a lobster boat, two shrimp boats, a van, three trucks, a car, two guns, a semi-automatic rifle, and 919 bales of marijuana. Eleven suspects were found in a nearby swamp. An assistant state attorney, having had a negotiated plea rejected by the judge as too light, dropped the charges against all the accused smugglers, stating that the case

was too weak to prove that each suspect was, in fact, in possession of the contraband.

September 18, 1977. Marine patrol officers stopped a vessel for a registration check. There being no papers on board, one of the officers asked the captain, "What do you have on board?" "Marijuana," called out one of the crew. The hold was loaded with 12 tons of it. The captain and a crew member were arrested and convicted by a jury of possession of "more than 100 pounds" of marijuana. The captain got a five-year sentence, the crew member three years. Eleven months later the federal Court of Appeals in Miami reversed the convictions because the registration check was "improper." Both smugglers were released.

May 30, 1978. Another check, this one on a trimaran's registration papers, yielded a stash of 1,200 bales of Jamaican marijuana. Again, a negotiated plea—guilty by the captain to a felony possession charge in exchange for a $3,000 fine—was rejected by the judge as too lenient. The assistant state attorney then dropped all felony charges against the captain and filed a misdemeanor charge against him in county court. The captain agreed to forfeit his sailboat. He received probation. Another defendant got five years' probation and a $3,000 fine. The 38-foot sailboat still remains in a Key West marina. She is among the many seized vessels up for sale.

January 29, 1980. Key West police raided a waterfront home in an affluent neighborhood where circuit court judges, a former sheriff, and a county judge all live on the same street. Three thousand pounds of marijuana were confiscated. No arrests were made.

The study reporting these and many similar cases also included a computer analysis of arrest and trial records of 19,888 felony and misdemeanor arrests in Monroe County, Florida (including Key West) between 1977 and 1979. The data show that while statewide the proportion of felony-drug cases dropped by prosecutors was 45.2 percent, the proportion in Monroe County was 74 percent. Further, for all felonies and misdemeanors in the county, 48 percent of the drug cases and 28 percent of the nondrug cases were dropped.[1] According to the investigation, "almost every multi-ton marijuana smuggling case prosecuted by the Monroe State Attorney's Office since 1976 has been botched, lost or plea-bargained to misdemeanors, according to court records. In some cases, suspects caught with many tons of pot were permitted to plead guilty to possession of less than 20 grams and pay a modest fine. . . .[2] Among the well-known figures linked to recent Key West pot smuggling busts are two high-ranking firefighters, a Monroe County Sheriff's detective, a county commission candidate, a brother of the county attorney, the son-in-law of a circuit judge, and a former city building director, once a prominent city contractor."[3] Indeed, four veterans of the Monroe County police force are facing federal trial on charges of acting as hired lookouts for smugglers.

According to a recent investigation into the "smuggling industry" in Key West, Florida, "law enforcement agencies are unwilling or unable to stop it, prosecutors don't prosecute it and the islanders have nonchalantly accepted it as a 'legitimate illegitimate business.' "[4] Accused smugglers rarely go to trial and seldom go to jail. The story of Key West is a story of what can happen when a vast underworld market in forbidden goods with its attendant "fast bucks" reaches out its tentacles to co-opt even those who have been sworn to uphold law and order. The very people who have been engaged by the state to enforce its mandates are made vulnerable to corruption, to protection for payoff, and to bribery by virtue of that authority. The spoils are great, the risks often minimal. These are the fertile conditions for the growth of greed and avarice.

In the case of Key West, a whole community has been tainted and tempted by a network of illegal opportunities. Those tempting tides that have risen so high in the eighties are like tides everywhere—they are eternal. And the history of North America certainly demonstrates the point. Although the smugglers' loot may have changed from bales of muslin, calicoes, elephants' tusks, opium, and slaves[5] to marijuana, cocaine, and heroin, the business maxim stays the same: Tempt government officials into cooperation and collusion. During colonial times, pirates, to ply their trade free from government interference, or even with government protection, so ingratiated themselves with the highest government officials that they were regular guests in the finest homes, regarded simply as gentlemen outlaws.[6] After all, they did enable the gentry to grace their tables with exquisite silver and china, to drape their windows with elegant silk brocade, to sip Madeira wines, and more importantly, to subvert the Navigation Acts, which forbade the colonists from buying or selling products that had not been shipped through England in English ships.[7]

Among the array of corrupt colonial administrators, Benjamin Fletcher, governor of New York between 1692 and 1698, stands out. He was determined to create his own commercial center unencumbered by the King's restrictive laws and to build this power base with the help of the pirates whose company he admittedly preferred over that of the "plodding preachers and bureaucrats of the colonial council."[8] Fletcher's coffers swelled. A privateering commission went for £6,000. Ships were outfitted for pirates Coates, Tew, and Hoare, among others, in return for a cut of the enormous riches being brought back from the Red Sea, or the East Indies, or Madagascar. It was well known that New York City had become their home port.[9]

According to court records:

> His Excellency gives all due encouragement to these men, because they make all due acknowledgements to him; one Coates a captain of this honorable order presented his Excellency with his ship, which his Excellency sold for £800 and every one of the crew made him a suitable present of Arabian gold for his protection; one Captain Twoo who is gone to the Red Sea upon the same errand was before his departure highly caressed by his Excellency in his coach and six horses and presented him with a gold watch to engage him to make New York his port at his return. Twoo retaliated the kindness with a present of jewells.[10]

Fletcher was not the only colonial administrator to succumb to the tempting tides. Chidley Brooke, the royal collector of Customs, could be "bought off" by ships entering the harbor;[11] Frederick Philipse, a twenty-year member of the New York City Council, supplied provisions to pirate ships;[12] Captain Giles Shelley maintained a flotilla of neat, fast sloops to receive cargoes off of New Jersey,[13] and even the officers of the Royal Navy stations ship *Richmond* were in on the take (a £700 bribe plus £100 per each crewman, for protection).[14] The famed pirate John Avery numbered among his "friends" some of colonial America's finest; Rhode Island Deputy Governor John Greene is known to have assisted him with supplies, horses, and donkeys. Some of Avery's men settled in Philadelphia, where one married Governor Markham's daughter.[15]

We are told that on one occasion Governor Bellomont of New York ordered the seizure of a vast amount of East India goods stored in the warehouses of Mayor Jonathan Selleck.

When Selleck was told to open his doors, he replied that a search warrant from the local justice of the peace was necessary. As it turned out, he, Selleck, was that official! And besides, the search really didn't matter because Connecticut Governor Fitz-John Winthrop testified that all the goods had been purchased many years ago by a deceased member of his family![16]

Not to be left out of our discussion of bribery and corruption is that most infamous of all pirates, Blackbeard. It is said that "had the burghers of Charleston returned their loyalties to their old pirate friend, Edward Teach (Blackbeard) might have retired to some manorial estate on the delta, planted rice and harvested indigo, and have contributed his name to one of the grand geneologies of the aristocratic South."[17] But he fell out of favor over a hostage incident and sailed out of Charleston in a huff for his new base at Ocracoke Inlet, North Carolina, where he quickly set up "cordial" relations with Governor Charles Eden and his Customs chief, Tobias Knight, who also happened to be the judge of the Vice Admiralty Court—the very court responsible for declaring a ship "abandoned." Blackbeard just happened to have found one of the "abandoned" ships. Of course, both Governor Eden and Chief Knight shared in the cargo, one so rich that many began to doubt the extraordinary tale of its abandonment. The Customs chief was subsequently indicted by a provincial council. A letter was introduced as evidence. This letter had been found on Blackbeard's ship, *Revenge*. It was addressed to the pirate, in Knight's handwriting. It read:

My friend:
    If this finds you yet in harbor I would have you make the best of your way up as soon as possible your affairs will let you. I have something more to say to you than at present I can write; the bearer will tell you the end of our Indian war, and Ganet can tell you in part what I have to say to you, so referr you in some measure to him.
    I really think these men are heartily sorry at their difference with you and will be very willing to ask your pardon; if I may advise, be friends again, it's better than falling out among yourselves.
    I expect the Governor this night or tomorrow, who I believe would be likewise glad to see you before you go, I have not time to add save my hearty respects to you, and am your real friend.

And servant,
T. Knight[18]

At the trial the key witnesses against Knight were slaves, whose testimony was not admissible in southern courts. He was acquitted.

The past has provided us with ample evidence that the lucre of the sea is no less attractive than the lucre of the land. It is little surprise, then, that when once again the illicit sea trade became particularly lucrative, the potential of corruption loomed large: Prohibition! In the 1920s the tides proved particularly tempting. This time the illicit trade was in alcohol. Those who plied that trade at an extraordinarily high profit margin were in a position to offer rewards to the officials charged with combating the illicit trade. The rum runners tried to bribe everybody, from front-line Customs and Coast Guard personnel to the judiciary. And, as in the past, the heavy conscience of those who yielded to corruption was somewhat eased by the widely held notion that Prohibition itself was immoral or at least unpopular, just as the contraband of the Stamp Act era was deemed morally untainted.

It is not known how many of the front-line Prohibition fighters actually did yield, but the number is far smaller than is popularly believed. According to the official history of the Coast Guard's rum war, the "runners" would make their bribe offers as a matter of course, but usually unsuccessfully.[19] The bigger problem was with judges who were so exceedingly unsympathetic to the Coast Guard's and Customs' evidence as to raise suspicion of having been bought out. To top it all, the rum runners made it their business to besmirch the integrity of Coast Guard officers by filing unfounded charges in local courts, accusing the officers of larceny of part of the illicit cargo, of personal belongings, and of sextants and compasses following a seizure.[20] Such charges normally made the headlines, and a sympathetic public would nod their heads: Of course these tempting tides would corrupt. As a matter of routine these cases were transferred to federal courts, where they would die for want of evidence.

There was bound to be corruption during the era of golden opportunities when America was still on the gold standard and booze was worth its price in gold. History tells us "that contact boats passed through the Golden Gate at certain hours when a particular official on duty found it profitable to be unobserving."[21] The "Golden Gate story" may be apocryphal, but it is illustrative.

A generation later the tempting tides swelled to heights un-

heard of since the days of piracy. Whereas the profit margin of
the rum runners had been three to one, the profit margin of the
drug runners is anywhere from three hundred to three thousand
to one or more. The drug runners cannot operate without corruption. As criminologists, we are used to the "dark figure" of
criminality, by which we mean the real amount of criminal activity as contrasted with the far smaller part that surfaces. The tip
of the iceberg is said to measure a tenth of its real substance.
When it comes to the crimes of bribery and corruption, the tip
of the iceberg may be as little as one one-thousandth. The real
figure will never be known, but examples abound to illustrate
the titillating temptation to compromise and the range and
scope of that temptation. Take the case of a naïve youngster in
the Coast Guard:

On June 20, 1982, during a routine patrol in the Gulf of
Alaska, the 378-foot Coast Guard cutter *Boutwell* seized the *Orca,*
a 39-foot sloop, with its crew of three and its cargo of 3,100
pounds of marijuana. She was put under tow for the return trip
to Kodiak. Two days under way, the cutter's crew members
began to notice a series of mechanical breakdowns. Upon investigation they turned out to be sabotage. A 19-year-old Coast
Guardsman was formally charged with two counts of damaging
machinery, one count of damaging military property, one count
of conspiracy to endanger the cutter, and one count of attempting to steal the sailboat. The thwarted plan was to disable the
Boutwell and to sail off in the *Orca* with a cargo that would bring
an estimated $5 million on the street.[22]

At a somewhat higher level, a Coast Guard reserve lieutenant
stole and sold secret information on federal law-enforcement
efforts to arrest drug smugglers in South Florida. The plans
detailed the personnel, equipment, and whereabouts of Coast
Guard ships and planes in a joint effort by the Drug Enforcement Administration, the Coast Guard, and the Customs Service.[23]

In the public image, those who enforce the laws must be like
Caesar's wife—totally above suspicion. Much ado was made
about Coast Guard inspectors required to fly abroad to inspect
hull and engine safety of American vessels in foreign ports at the
expense of the shipping lines.[24] Even more fuss was raised about
Coast Guard inspectors' accepting tickets for sports events from
maritime companies. Are they violating the Code of Federal

U.S. Coast Guard

WMEC 623, the U.S.C.G. cutter *Steadfast*, of the Reliance class—the true work horses for law enforcement on the oceans. This was the vessel on which the authors joined a "combat mission" against drug runners.

A law-enforcement team about to enter port launch, to board suspect vessel. Note gun at the ready.

Mueller and Adler

Mueller and Adler

The launch casts off from *Steadfast* en route to board a suspect drug runner.

Sea routes favored by drug smugglers.

The swordfishing vessels *Four of Us* and *Charly's Pride.* Secret compartments in the bow were installed to conceal drug cargoes. After seizure, the vessels were rotting in New Bedford. They have since been sold at auction, but some of their gear had been stolen.

The rusty fishing trawler *Tiki X* was seized in Buzzard's Bay for having un-loaded $30 million worth of marijuana in Fairhaven, Massachusetts. The fishing gear aboard is just for show and largely useless. Her interest was limited to "square groupers," namely bales of pot.

Marge Westgate and the Fairhaven *Advocate*

It took Fairhaven, Massachusetts, police seven and a half hours to remove tons of ice and fish before the "square groupers," bales of marijuana, were located.

Marge Westgate and the Fairhaven *Advocate*

The pot from the *Four of Us.* It went up in smoke after costing Fairhaven a whopper of a tab in SWAT-team security.

South China Sea and surrounding countries—scene of modern-day pirate attacks .

Twentieth-century piracy victims. One of the rickety craft, crammed with refugees, which made it to Indonesia across the South China Sea. Many others are scuttled by the pirates after rapes and murders.

A massive one-year effort, in 1982, to rid the South China Sea of the pirate plague had only limited success. Thai Patrol Boat 110 (a former U.S. Navy P.G.S. of one hundred tons) and a spotter plane in action.

United Nations Environmental Program

When the authors sailed in Washington State waters, around the Olympic Peninsula back in the 1950s, water pollution was not a problem. Today, criminal abuse of the watery environment has made these waterways unsafe for man and beast.

United Nations Environmental Program

A Danish fishing port—but it could be any port. Disregarding laws against polluting the waterways, man has turned once-clean ports into sewers.

Courtesy of Schmahl and Schmahl

Insurance fraud on the high seas. An explosion has ripped the bow off the freighter *Eva Maria* en route to Mexico.

Mueller and Adler

Marina bulletin-board posters of the 1980s:"Security Afloat,""Swedish Pirates Seize Vessel," "$1,000.00 Reward," or even "$5,000.00 Reward" for any information leading to the recovery of stolen vessels.

Regulations, which states that Coast Guard personnel are not allowed to solicit or accept anything of monetary value? It is not uncommon for these tickets to be offered to officials responsible for checking the hulls and engines of vessels for safety and for ordering necessary repairs. The companies in question claim that tickets are made available to anyone who claims them, whether employees of the company or Coast Guardsmen.[25] But the Plimsoll line is clearly passed when anyone entrusted with the enforcement of our laws—in this case an official of the Drug Enforcement Administration—embezzles funds of the agency and thus commits an offense, even though not directly related to the laws he has been entrusted to enforce. Caesar, who so efficiently dealt with pirates, may demand that his wife remain above suspicion, especially since he claims progeny of the gods, of whom Neptune, or Poseidon, was one.

The wash of the tempting tides has also reached the beaches of local law enforcement. For some the temptation is irresistible. One Joseph Price, for example, an agent with the Customs service for 20 years, assigned to the Vice President's South Florida Task Force, was arrested in Miami on September 23, 1983, for an attempt to sell 10 pounds of hashish oil.[26] On a grander scale, a former North Miami policeman was found guilty of conspiring to trade two airplanes for 400 pounds of marijuana in April 1983. The former police officer, who had become an attorney, appears to have been heavily involved in drug transactions and faced disbarment as well.[27]

Most disturbingly, when the drug onslaught on the New England coast reached its height in the summer of 1983, when seizures of vessels and contraband increased, and when all law-enforcement agencies geared up to combat that onslaught, a disconcerting event occurred at the state police barracks in Middleboro, Massachusetts. Two pounds of cocaine with a stated wholesale value of more than $50,000 disappeared from those barracks, where they had been held as evidence. Consternation was followed by an investigation. A witness in the case of the missing cocaine disappeared.[28] Soon the missing cocaine was reevaluated as being in the neighborhood of $500,000. Sixteen officers at the barracks had to take lie-detector tests. They all passed.[29]

Soon thereafter more than two hundred uniformed troopers who had access to the evidence room were questioned.[30] Five months into the investigation, a Plymouth County grand jury was confronted with evidence linking a state trooper to the theft and other efforts to deal in narcotics.[31] One day later, on October 4, 1983, a grand jury indicted the seventeen-year veteran state trooper for the theft, the third law-enforcement officer within a two-year period to face drug-related charges. A state police lieutenant had earlier pleaded guilty to accessoryship to the theft from the state police barracks, with intention to sell, of 3,400 pounds of marijuana.[32] The lieutenant involved is now serving a four- to ten-year sentence.[33] A month later, in an unrelated case, two civilians pleaded guilty to possession and attempted sale of 2.2 pounds of cocaine, allegedly taken by the state trooper. Their sentence: five to ten years each in Walpole State Prison.[34]

The coke caper at the Middleboro barracks demonstrates two points: (1) the enormous temptation posed by the narcotics war, to which a given percentage of the officialdom involved in fighting that war is bound to yield; and also (2) the integrity of the overwhelming majority of the officials. Were it otherwise the American system of justice could not get to the bottom of corruption in the effort to weed it out. We can only hope that the criminal-justice forces of the greater part of the world share the devotion to duty and abhorrence of corruption expressed by Article VII of the United Nations Code of Conduct for Law-Enforcement Officials, in the drafting of which we had a leading hand and that was adopted by the General Assembly at the United Nations in December 1977 by consensus.[35]

All over the country prosecutors and judges have been confronted with the lucrative fruits of maritime law enforcement. Temptations have been met, and resisted for the most part. Our own records, however, contain a number of cases of prosecutors and judges suspected of having yielded to the tempting tides, but usually (although not always) the cases were dismissed or the defendants acquitted. On May 21, 1983, "A former District Attorney was sentenced to five years in prison for helping protect a marijuana-smuggling operation in a coastal Alabama county where he was prosecutor for 22 years. The Government had charged that James Hendrix, who served as Baldwin County Prosecutor in 1959–81, was paid $20,000 to protect the smuggling operation by keeping law officers away from a landing strip."[36]

What is true about the governmental administrators of the United States in this era of the drug onslaught may not necessarily be true of the governmental services of some of the countries of the Caribbean basin from and through which the illicit cargo finds its way into the United States. It is only too obvious that suspicion should fall on the government of any country in *mare narcoticum* (the drug ocean), by which we mean the Caribbean Sea and the Gulf of Mexico, separated only by the Yucatán Channel. The two countries flanking that channel are Mexico and Cuba. Mexico, which occupies a vast portion of the Gulf and part of the Caribbean shoreline, has been singularly cooperative with the U.S. government in controlling the drug traffic, and there is little if any evidence of corruption linking Mexican officials with the drug traffic destined for the United States. Aspersions have frequently been cast against Cuba, a country with a government toward which the U.S. government assuredly harbors no friendly, neighborly feelings. In a speech before Cuban ex-patriots—some of whom had been linked to drug smuggling into the United States—President Reagan bluntly accused the government of Fidel Castro of involvement in the illicit drug trade that flows through Miami, citing "strong evidence." Castro promptly responded with a denial, stating "Cuba has systematically combatted international drug traffic."[37] In our own patrol circumnavigation of Cuba we encountered no evidence of any direct or indirect Cuban involvement, and as researchers we would appreciate release of any governmental information on Cuban implication. Yet we are impressed about the sincerity with which knowledgeable American officials, including Coast Guard officers, keep referring to a "Cuban connection." Might it be the Vesco link? We shall revert to this phenomenon shortly.

There is another country, the Bahamas, which, by sheer geography, is intimately tied to the drug war simply because its islands stretch from a northern latitude almost parallel to Cape Canaveral to a southern latitude corresponding to the Yucatán Peninsula of Mexico. The Bahamas, thus, constitute the outermost barrier of the drug ocean in that part of the Western Hemisphere. In a previous chapter we referred to individual instances of corruption by Bahamian officers. But a formal case against Bahamian leaders will yet have to be made. NBC News, in a program aired in September 1983, reported that payments of up to $100,000 a month had been made to top Bahamian officials, including Prime Minister Lynden O. Pindling, to secure their acquiescence in illicit drug transfers. Speaking in Miami on September 14, 1983, Mr. Pindling, accompanied by his Attorney General, Paul L. Adderley, vehemently denied the charges: "My faith in your democracy has been shaken,"[38] he said. *The New York Times* article reporting on the incident was fair enough to point out that the Bahamas consist of seven hundred islands, not counting islets, stretching for five hundred miles, policed by a mere two thousand officers and by a tiny fleet of eight seagoing vessels, the ninth one having been blown to smithereens by Cuban attack bombers. Indeed, during our own patrols in Bahamian waters, we found Her Majesty's Bahamian defense forces most cooperative, and the sight of a U.S. Coast Guard helicopter had greeted us on our arrival on Grand Bahama, surely a sign of good neighborly cooperation. *The New York Times* news story, not surprisingly, had referred to the ominous presence of the illusive Vesco and his minions on Norman Cay. Might *there* be the source of corruption? The pressure on Prime Minister Pindling continued throughout the fall of 1983. By early 1984 a royal commission had been appointed to investigate NBC's allegations against the Pindling government. The commission is composed of prestigious jurists and law-enforcement officials from various Commonwealth countries. Its chairman indicated that the committee would do its job "fearlessly, regardless of consequences."[39] We fear, nevertheless, that the shadow of Vesco hovers just over the horizon.

At approximately the same latitude as the most southerly of the Bahamian islands, separated by the Caicos Passage, are the British-controlled Turks and Caicos Islands. When Governor Christopher Turner assumed office there, he commented about the drug trafficking in those islands, surely with the eyes of officialdom closed. "We are doing as much damage to America now, as if we were bombarding them with missiles."[40] He left no doubt in his statement that things would change.

The westernmost shorelines of the drug ocean are formed by Mexico, and by the countries of Belize, Guatemala, Honduras, and Nicaragua, countries involved in the turmoil of revolution, rebellion, insurgency, and counterinsurgency. The drug traffic does not appear to be their principal concern. (We shall return to discussion of these countries in connection with the traffic in arms and with terrorism.) The southern border of the drug ocean is formed by Costa Rica, Panama, Colombia, and Venezuela. We have not come across a single incident of drug traffic facilitating corruption in traditionally democratic and pacific Costa Rica, nor in stable Panama, nor in democratic and oil-rich (though financially strapped) Venezuela. Their problems are different, by and large, although, as we have noted, these three friendly nations could not help but become involved in the drug traffic, particularly Panama, which as a flag-of-convenience nation freely grants its maritime sovereignty to all comers.

That leaves us with Colombia, on the southern shores. Colombia's vast involvement in the drug traffic has been recorded in an earlier chapter. The question looms large: How is it possible that drugs worth billions of dollars on the streets of New York can be loaded so freely in the Caribbean ports of Colombia —Cartagena, Barranquilla, Santa Marta, and others, plus uncounted inlets and beaches? After all, the production, transfer, importation, and exportation is illegal in Colombia, a signatory to the various international narcotics conventions. But then we have heard frequent comments by Colombians that the problem of drug consumption is ours, not theirs.

A case against drug involvement and corruption at high government levels will yet have to be made. The local level is another matter. When Schmahl and Schmahl, the famous American marine surveyors, undertook on behalf of an American insurance company to reclaim a fishing trawler stolen in the United States and abandoned after drug runs in Colombia, they were forced to pay sums nearly totaling the value of the vessel to the harbor captain, the police commandant, and other officials for protection. They were confronted with a $65,000 fee by a politically connected local attorney for legal services, which in the United States would have amounted to $500. And Schmahl and Schmahl's agent, after release of the vessel by local authorities, discovered that while the exorbitantly expensive police protection had been in force, the vessel had been stripped of block and tackle, radio, compass, sextant, and other navigational equipment. A compass was needed so that the new crew, flown in from the United States, could safely take the vessel to sea. A compass was found in a local pawnshop for $600. It turned out to be the same compass that had been purloined from the vessel; its original U.S. price, installed, was $250. When Schmahl and

Schmahl's agent complained to the police commandant, he was advised, "Shut up, get yourself out, and get your trawler out." The agent's report concluded: This report "will serve to spotlight the incredibly corrupt and crime-ridden atmosphere which permeates the lifestyle of that bizarre country."[41] As if to emphasize the report's conclusion, one of Schmahl and Schmahl's agents, resident in Colombia, was found in a ditch along a Colombian road with a bullet wound in his head. The remaining resident agent's home was fire-bombed, and an assassination attempt had been made against him. No wonder, then, that Coast Guard officers have persistently advised us and other yachtsmen: "Keep out of Colombian waters."

Yet there is a country south of Colombia that plays a far greater role in the waves of corruption that create the tempting tides. For decades, Bolivia had enjoyed the doubtful blessings of a right-wing military dictatorship. It also enjoyed a climate most conducive to the production of the highest grade of cocaine and marijuana. Of course, Bolivia, too, was signatory to the international conventions on narcotics control prohibiting the production and export of narcotic drugs. Yet here we are at the source: This country is a vast plantation that was run by pistol-packing generals and their Nazi and neo-Nazi thugs directing, supervising, and organizing the production and transportation of the drugs demanded by the North American market. That story deserved particular attention, which we gave in chapter two.

A quick glance at the as yet unmentioned countries engulfed by the outer perimeter of the narcotics ocean is now in order. Take Jamaica. As related earlier, we were on a mission to this paradisiacal island in the northern part of the Caribbean Sea. The country was in deep financial trouble, and a law-enforcement crisis had developed. Warring factions were fighting pitched battles for turf. And where did the arms come from with which these battles were fought? The planes and vessels that had ferried Jamaica's high-grade ganja (marijuana) to U.S. shores were returning with weapons. The tiny Jamaican maritime police force and the few planes at the disposition of the commissioner of police were no match for the smugglers' vast maritime and air fleets, the latter taking off from makeshift jungle clearings. Obviously this trade could not have been carried on without local corruption. Yet the highest governmental level remained clear of suspicion.

And then there are the British-controlled Cayman Islands, conjuring up the vision of specks of land in the northern reaches of the Caribbean, separated from Jamaica by the Bartlett Deep, and lined from one land's end to the other by air-conditioned branch banks of every conceivable banking enterprise of Canada and the rest of the world. We doubt that drugs are touching the shores of the Caymans. But is the incredible wealth that flows through the Cayman bank branches anything but a huge financial launderette receiving dirty bucks and delivering clean cash?

It is impossible to comment here on all the islands that so recently have gained independence and swelled the membership list of the United Nations. But inasmuch as we are writing this chapter on Christmas Eve 1983 at Fort King George, Tobago, we want to end it with the Christmas message of the Trinidad and Tobago commissioner of police. Well aware that with the Coast Guard's bottling up of the more northern passages from the Caribbean to the Atlantic, the drug runners would now have to exit through the southernmost passages, past Trinidad and Tobago, through the Dragon's Mouth and Galleon Passage, the commissioner said to his troops:

> On the horizon there lies a situation that could possibly reach the Service and eventually tarnish its reputation. The increasing trend of drug trafficking brings with it an international situation, whereby certain individuals would endeavour to tempt you through monetary means, so that you would close an eye to their illicit trade.
>
> My advice to you, therefore, is to be watchful of certain elements in the society who would be endeavouring clandestinely to "use" you. Do not be led into temptation by the spawn of money by these illicit traders.[42]

12

Vanishing Vessels: Marine Insurance Fraud

•

> The fisherman has curious eyes,
> They make you feel so queer,
> As if they had seen many things,
> of wonder and of fear.
>
> Abbie Farwell Brown,
> *The Fisherman*

Touching the Adventures and Perils,
which we, the said Underwriters,
are contented to bear and take upon us,
they are of the Seas, Men-of-War,
Fire, Lightning, Earthquake, Enemies,
Pirates, Rovers, Assailing Thieves,
Jettisons, Letters of Mart and Counter-Mart,
Surprisals, Takings at Sea, Arrests, Restraints
and Detainments of all Kings, Princes and People,
of what nation, condition or quality so ever,
Barratry of the Master and Mariners
and of all other like Perils, Losses and Misfortunes
that have or shall come to the Hurt,
Detriment or Damage of the said Vessel, etc.
or any part thereof;
excepting, however, such of the foregoing Perils
as may be excluded by provisions elsewhere
in the Policy or by endorsement.

Ancient perils clause of Lloyd's hull insurance policy[1]

By 1978, the *Eva Maria* was an aging tramp steamer, German-owned, Liberian-registered, with German officers and a motley crew from all lands, insured in America, with a mixed

192

cargo for North American ports. Plowing through the Atlantic on her way to Mexico, a violent explosion shook the entire vessel, disintegrating the bow. It was clear within minutes that the vessel could not be kept afloat. The captain ordered "Abandon ship." The ship sank fast, going over the port stern. The first mate had the presence of mind to record the event with his camera from one of the *Eva Maria*'s lifeboats.

What had happened? Schmahl and Schmahl, the marine surveyors of Fort Lauderdale, with an enviable record of having solved hundreds of major marine mysteries, was called in on the case. The sinking was obviously suspicious, yet the evidence lay in Davy Jones's locker. This is the problem with marine insurance investigations. Where landlubbing insurance investigators can measure tire track marks, survey body damage, and inspect the insured object, or what is left of it, marine insurance investigators normally can rely only on circumstantial evidence. It is that which makes marine insurance fraud such an attractive business for those who buy and operate rust buckets and leaky tubs, risking the lives of those who operate them.

The ancient Lloyd's of London's marine insurance policy provides us with the text of the perils clause found in modern marine insurance contracts, including that of the American Institute Time (Hulls) form of policy. The perils described constitute extraordinary risks for shipowners, charterers, masters, and mariners. In normal times of international peace, few worry about being encountered by pirates, rovers, or assailing thieves, and few shipowners expect barratry of the masters and mariners. Consequently, the premiums on marine insurance policies are reasonable, facilitating the transport of goods and persons on the high seas at affordable rates. When, however, the perils are suddenly increased at unheard-of rates, the very industry which, through its insurance, facilitates peaceful commerce on the oceans may be threatened with extinction. We are living through such times now, when, as demonstrated in this book, the perils of the sea have not just edged up a bit but have increased manifold.

The perils clause quoted at the beginning of this chapter covers insurance of the ship itself—her hull, machinery, and tackle. There is another type of marine insurance, which provides indemnity for loss of cargo. Obviously, both types of insurance contracts protect only the innocent insured against the losses specified in the policy. They never protect an insured in the case of fraud that he himself perpetrates against the insurer. We shall return to these matters later in this chapter.

Yes, the *Eva Maria* case was solved. She had been carrying in her forward hold blasting caps destined for Mexican mining enterprises, and it was established that a saboteur had driven metal spikes into the crates containing the caps. This manipulation was calculated to create friction which, with the increased pitch and roll of the ship in the Atlantic, inevitably had to lead to the explosion of that cargo.

We are sitting in the office of Horace W. Schmahl, president of Schmahl and Schmahl, a former OSS officer whose World War II experience has made him familiar with sabotage. The files of his firm are filled with hundreds of cases of shrimpers, trawlers, swordfishing boats, tugboats, barges, freighters, and special-purpose vessels reported lost at sea. One hundred twenty-eight of these files are active, offering a hope of solution. The values involved are vast, and very often the United States government has provided or insured part of the funding for the vessel; when Schmahl and Schmahl get called in on such cases, they represent both the insurer and the U.S. government.

The challenges posed to the marine insurance investigator by the criminals of the sea are boundless. Let us look at Schmahl and Schmahl's files:

The Case of the Bahamian Landing Craft

A Dominican firm had purchased a sugar mill to be dismantled in the Bahamas and transported to the Dominican Republic for installation. Horace Schmahl inspected the vessel that was to carry the dismantled parts of the mill, a rundown but still seaworthy World War II U.S. Navy landing craft. He supervised the bolting down of this cargo in a manner calculated to prevent the various parts from damaging each other on the high seas. In the captain's decrepit cabin Mr. Schmahl extracted a promise that no other cargo was to be carried on the vessel on that run. The captain had barely given his assurance when the door opened and the mate walked in, ignoring the visitor, and announced to the captain, "Captain, the five hundred steel drums arrived and we got plenty of space for the pot." Under the circumstances, Mr. Schmahl remained at the pier until the vessel actually left, without drums and pot. But as he sat in his light plane flying over Freeport Harbor on his way back to Fort Lauderdale, he saw the landing craft making a U-turn back to the dock it had just left. Nothing was heard from the vessel for some time while she made her way through the vast expanse of the islands of the Bahamas. Somewhere near the Florida shores it must have off-loaded its illegitimate pot cargo. The next that was heard of the vessel was a message to the effect that it had foundered near Jacmel, Haiti, on the southern shores of the island of Hispaniola. Schmahl's agent flew to Jacmel and found the vessel beached and abandoned by master and crew. The sugar mill was still aboard, as were the steel drums that had been loaded in violation of contract. Negotiations with the local governor to obtain release of the vessel proved difficult. As it turned out, the governor had personally seized the ship and cargo. In effect, the original purchasers of the sugar mill had to buy it a second time, along with the landing craft. Of course, there was the additional expense of pulling the ship back into deep water and providing her with a crew for the remainder of the voyage to the Dominican Republic.

The Case of the Fishing Vessel **Amy Michele**

The *Amy Michele* is a fishing vessel of eighty feet, insured by the Peninsular Fire Insurance Co. for $305,000. Her owner reported her as overdue in November 1980. She had last been seen shortly before the unloading of a catch of nineteen tons of bonita and tuna for pet food. Then the vessel, her skipper and crew of seven from Boise, Idaho, and the live-aboard girlfriend of one of the crew members, disappeared from sight. Schmahl and Schmahl was called into the case and immediately distributed its reward poster all over the Caribbean, offering, to begin with, $1,000 for any information leading to the discovery of the vessel. The firm learned that the captain and crew, although hailing from Boise, were actually experienced fishermen operating entirely on their own, having virtually no contact with the owners. The captain was responsible for hiring the crew and maintaining and operating the vessel. Captain and crew received 60 percent of the profits; the insured owners, 40 percent.

Schmahl and Schmahl learned that the live-aboard girlfriend had been put ashore in Panama, and one crew member in the Cayman Islands. Both were now back in Boise but refused to talk. At this point, suspicion that the vessel had been subverted for illegitimate trade had become great indeed. The vessel was spotted on November 19, 1980, in Colón, Panama. She left there on November 20 but, according to the records of the canal authorities, she did not pass through the canal. Schmahl and Schmahl did establish that the vessel had made several runs with arms and ammunitions destined for insurgents fighting the government of El Salvador. On December 22 she had been seen at San Cristóbal, Panama, a notorious arms smuggling port. On the basis of evidence gathered up to this point, the U.S. attorney in March 1981 obtained an indictment from an Alabama federal grand jury against Captain Larry M. Crews, charging him with barratry under U.S. Code Title 18, Article 66. Barratry, as an insurable peril, is constituted by any "unlawful, fraudulent, or dishonest act of the master, mariners, or other carriers, or of gross misconduct, or very gross and culpable negligence, contrary in either case, to their duty to the owner, and that might be prejudicial to him or to others interested in the voyage or adventure."[2]

As the facts further developed on January 8, 1981, the vessel had been seen in Miami. It was suspected that she had brought in a drug cargo. All appropriate U.S. agencies were alerted to the phantom vessel, which had left her legitimate calling and had joined the outlaw fleet of the drug ocean. Panamanian authorities were notified as well, but that country, with its vast paper fleet and its extremely limited resources, could be of little help. It was recommended that the name of the master of the ship be deleted from the record of documentation. Oddly enough, the insured, an Alabama firm, did nothing to follow up on the recommendations, including the recommendation to take steps for reclaiming the vessel from Colombia, where she was ultimately located. Captain Crews was no longer in charge of the vessel. It appears that one Ian Johnston had taken over possession through theft or piracy and continued using her in illegitimate trade. Captain Crews was found back in the United States and arrested in Tampa, Florida. Piracy charges were filed against Ian Johnston. He remains a fugitive.

We need not repeat the experience that Schmahl and

Schmahl agents had in Colombia in their ultimately successful efforts to reclaim the vessel. On June 2, 1981, at 4:45 P.M., the pickup crew that had sailed the *Amy Michele* back from Colombia docked her at her pier at Bayou La Batre, Alabama, after an incredible seven months of barratry and piracy. The Peninsular Fire Insurance Co. was not out $305,000.

Following the *Amy Michele* case, it was found necessary to use code references for all vessels, persons, officials, and places in all communications going to or referring to Caribbean contacts. Yes, it has gotten that bad. As for Captain Larry Crews, it was subsequently determined that he had a long felony record, which included a charge of skyjacking. Is it possible that the owners would entrust their vessel, innocently—ignorantly—to a chronic felon? It is rumored that Crews had $100,000 stashed away in a safe-deposit box in Tampa. The FBI and the insurance company are interested.

When the Peninsular Fire Insurance Co. refused to pay the insured under the barratry provision for the losses they had suffered in connection with the temporary loss and retrieval of the vessel, the insured filed a civil claim in federal court against the insurer. The insurer was adamant about its refusal to pay, since the insured, both in hiring the captain and in its failure to follow up on the recommendation for deregistering the captain and reclaiming the vessel, had been negligent. The suit was ultimately settled out of court to the satisfaction of both parties.

The Case of the Fishing Vessel **Sundowner**

This sixty-seven-foot fishing vessel, insured by the Stonewall Insurance Co., was docked at her Florida Gulf Coast port. Her skipper was enjoined from using the vessel by virtue of his drug-run reputation. The vessel was reported missing in June 1981. Intelligence information reported her as having left the port of Cartagena several times in May 1981 with cargoes of contraband. Then, oddly enough, the boat was reported as having burned and sunk off Carrabelle, Florida. When the police officer who had prepared the original report on the burning of the *Sundowner* was approached, he most unfortunately could not find a single copy of the report. Further investigation by marine fraud investigators led to rumors that that same officer had agreed to buy a $26,000 share in the *Sundowner.* So, what really happened to the *Sundowner?* The thieving master confided that he had made up the story of the burning of the vessel off Carrabelle and that she was really sunk by gunfire from the Colombian Navy when she left Cartagena with another cargo of contraband and refused the naval vessel's order "Heave to." A letter from Schmahl and Schmahl of April 12, 1983, to the Colombian naval attaché in Washington has remained unanswered. For all that we know, the vessel has either been taken over by the Colombian underworld (some of the original crew claim to have been held for ransom), or it is being operated with or without involvement of the original owners in the twilight zone of the drug ocean. She was last reported seen near the mouths of the Orinoco River, Venezuela, off the islands of Trinidad and Tobago.

The Case of the Yacht Great Escape III

The yacht *Great Escape III,* a forty-foot Marine Trader trawler, built by the same yard as our *Contessa Maria II,* was owned by a couple, both high-school teachers. At the time she disappeared from the face of the ocean, she had been on charter through Yachts International, a yacht brokerage firm. Five days after the charter expired on February 15, 1983, the charterer called from Nassau, Bahamas, and informed Yachts International that the vessel had foundered at Samana Cay, an uninhabited island twenty miles north-northeast of Nassau, off the northeastern point of Ackins Island, that the skipper had experienced steering problems, and that while he was belowdecks working on the steering mechanism, the ship foundered and washed up. The Bahama Sea Air Rescue Service flew its planes over Samana Cay. There was no trace of the ship in the shallow waters of the cay. Being familiar with that part of the ocean ourselves, we cannot imagine how, at Samana Cay, a forty-foot vessel can disappear without a trace unless during a hurricane, and none was passing over Samana Cay during February 1983. Indeed, we were in those waters at about that time. The *Great Escape III* was subsequently reported seen in Montego Bay, Jamaica. Investigation established that of the four persons reported to have been on her when she foundered, only two had actually been aboard. But it is hard to establish the facts. The charterer is a fugitive from justice. He disappeared one day after Horace Schmahl notified him of his intention to interview him. The present market value of $125,000 for the yacht is, of course, not payable if the loss of the vessel was a mere theft as distinguished from a take-over by "assailing thieves."

As tempting as it is to explore further and display the fascinating cases of crime on the crests of consequence to insurers, we must restrain ourselves so as to maintain manageable dimensions. Basically, these cases from the drug ocean are all variations of the same theme. They are efforts to record and collect for a loss that has never taken place, usually in an attempt by the owner, insurer, charterer, master, crew, or others to use the vessel in the enormously profitable, illegitimate trade of the clandestine drug and arms fleet of the narcotics ocean.

Therefore, we shall refrain from commenting on the "Murder by MasterCard" case; the case of the cryptographer killed by a steward in his cabin on a Bahamian cruise liner; the case of the cabin cruiser *One Time Around,* scuttled with gunfire at the waterline (entailing divorce proceedings, cut short only by the murder-conspiracy conviction of one of the parties); the case of the fishing vessel *Sapelo Gal,* reported stolen in 1981, seized by the Coast Guard a few days later with a cargo of pot (those cases are so dreadfully routine by now!); the case of the infamous *Laurelyn,* rumored to be in and out of Barranquilla, Colombia, a town which in such an eerie way appears to be connected with the power structure of Apalachicola, Florida; or the vessel *Shrimp Chase I.* But perhaps we should complete our report with the tale of a 67-foot shrimper seized by the U.S. Coast Guard on July 9, 1980, 32 miles west of Cedar Cay, with 106 pounds of marijuana aboard. The vessel, appraised at $221,000, was sold at auction for the benefit of the United States for $10,000. The owners had lost in their bid to regain the vessel, having charged the master with barratry. The law is clear: Claimants must prove by a preponderance of the evidence that they made all reasonable efforts to prevent the proscribed use of the vessel. The owners had not met that burden, claiming the captain had been a good captain. Although it was established that the owners, during the precise time of the drug haul, had been visiting Singapore, the captain apparently had hired a crew that was anything but reputable, thus casting doubt on the master himself and putting in question the exercise of reasonable care on the part of the owners.

We concluded our visit with Schmahl and Schmahl and family, including daughter Captain Patty Schmahl, at the backyard of the family home, with its dock at which a seagoing cabin cruiser is moored. Horace Schmahl (LL.B., Harvard) was musing about the past and the present: "A big explosion occurred next door and my neighbor, his garments fully ablaze, jumped into his swimming pool to douse the flames. He had bought his house for three hundred thousand dollars in cash. He is currently under indictment for running a cocaine laboratory. And then there are the large cabin cruisers which keep us awake all night passing by our house. Annoyed, I put my searchlight on one of them and a voice from the flying bridge shouted, 'Turn it off or I'll blow your brains out!' One of the captains had apparently missed his usual channel. The boat ran at high speed with a Coast Guard launch close behind. Well, that bridge was just about six feet too low for her. It sheered the superstructure right off. All you could see the next morning was the debris and bales of marijuana all over the canal.

"But the event," he continued, "which really drives home to you and to myself how much we have become engulfed in maritime criminality, involves one of my own people, a simple little fellow from a Caribbean country. He had heard that I had wanted to get rid of the firm's five K cars in a trade-in for new automobiles, and he approached me, asking, 'Boss, will you let me steal those cars?' My puzzlement urged him to explain. 'You see, boss, those Bahamian shrimpers that bring the dope to the dredging company port usually take a stolen car or two back to the Bahamas, and I can get a good price for any car stolen within twenty-four hours!' "

(The dredging company port is a private harbor facility apart from the Port Everglades public port facilities, and therefore it is subject to little if any Customs patrol. It is, incidentally, the same company that had built the airstrip on Grenada that was used in the U.S. Marine invasion of that island. The contract for the construction of the Grenada airstrip had been arranged by one Vesco, now reported to be living in Cuba.)

Concluded Horace Schmahl, "Things weren't nearly as bad when my grandpappy served as a Confederate naval officer under Robert E. Lee."

Our recitation of cases from the files of Schmahl and Schmahl, mostly cases from that part of the world we have dubbed the narcotics ocean, should not lead to the hasty conclusion that matters are the same everywhere. They are, and they aren't. *Mar narcoticum* provides us with the far greatest number of vessels involved in the effort to defraud the marine insurance industry and to enhance the fleets of smugglers and pirates, but the oceans of the rest of the globe provide the cases involving sheer tonnage of destruction.

In recent years, several factors have combined to cause a marked increase in the incidence of maritime fraud. A rapid expansion of trade in the ill-prepared, developing ports of Nigeria and the Arab countries of the Middle East means that ships discharging their cargoes were forced to wait weeks, perhaps months, for an unloading dock. Shippers and charterers, unable to withstand the costs of these extended layovers, often were forced to move on to less crowded ports where they could quickly unload, thus freeing the ship to take on new cargo. It didn't take long before the less honest traders turned this necessity into a criminal invention—instead of simply unloading the cargo for future transfer, why not sell it, especially in a country where laws were known to be ineffective. Lebanon was such a country. According to a report in *Barron's:*

> The vanishing of ships and cargoes after entering ports from Tripoli to Beirut, where Palestinian Syrian or Christian Phalangist factions would buy cargoes with no questions asked, became a huge problem with the collapse of Lebanese government authority during the seven years of Palestine Liberation Organization occupation. Indeed, Saudi Arabia, after one swindle too many, rocked the waters of the Middle Eastern maritime trade by refusing to deal with companies whose ships called at Lebanon (on several occasions when cargo owners have flown to Beirut to try to prevent their goods from being unloaded from a vessel diverted to a Lebanese port, docksides and courtrooms have been invaded by men with Kalashniko assault rifles, staking their own claim to cargo and ship).[3]

Reverberations of the rapid expansion of world trade along with the increasing complexities of international transactions were soon felt in the Far East, too, where growing numbers of ships involving millions of dollars' worth of cargo were "sinking" in the South China Sea. Indeed, one investigator found that one of these "scuttled" ships was in fact ferrying refugees from

Vietnam, where he also came upon a black market for the luxury goods that had "gone down" with the "sunken vessel."[4] Things got so bad that a special Far East region investigation team was set up by the London-headquartered Salvage Association to look into the mysterious "problems" of a firm in Hong Kong, which had the misfortune of losing one third of its vessels over a two-year period; of the Chinese smuggler who was seen often in Djakarta and Bangkok long after he "died" of cancer while dodging an arrest warrant; and of an old rust bucket, ostensibly laden with luxury cargo, that refused to sink even though her "empty" holds were full of holes.[5]

At the same time that dry cargo demands were increasing, the oil glut created miseries among the world's tanker fleet. In October 1975, 400 tankers were rusting away at anchorage in Norwegian fjords, idle because of dwindling business. Yet contracts for the construction of new supertankers could not be canceled fast enough. Christine Onassis christened the *Olympic Bravery* in October 1975, a ship of 275,000 tons capacity. Thirty-five miles into her maiden voyage the ship rolled over and joined the ever-increasing fleet resting on the bottom of the ocean. She was a dead loss, and Lloyd's of London paid $50 million to the owners of the Onassis group. *Time* magazine headlined its report on the disaster. "Maritime Disaster, or Is It?" Even rusting at anchor in a Norwegian fjord, the ship would have cost its owners $20,000 a day in maintenance, insurance, interest, and amortization.[6]

Half of the world's idle supertankers are available for "cheap" deals, with few credential checks. There are increasing complexities of international trade in moving dry cargo. Add to this the fact that there is an extremely low probability of getting caught, or if caught, of ever being punished and you have the makings of a growing maritime fraud business. Imagine the incredible intricacies of a case involving any given product sold in country A to a buyer in country B, who makes credit arrangements at a bank in country C, with the product loaded on board a ship registered in country D, and with a master from country E. The ship sinks off the coast of country F, while her "sunken" cargo appears in country G. And this listing of nationalities does not even account for the dozen or two dozen countries from which the sailors hail who might have to be summoned as potential witnesses. This is not an atypical fraud case. The question is: Where is the venue? Which country can dispose of the case? No doubt, had the master gone back to country A after the scuttling, he would have faced prosecution. Or perhaps if he had landed in the country of the original buyer, he would have been subject to its criminal law. On the other hand, would country G, where the goods finally wound up, be willing to go through the expense of such a complicated investigation, and, if so, do the local officials have the ability to handle such a sophisticated inquiry? Or would the ship's flag state be responsible—in this case the flag being one of "convenience"? And if any one of these countries *should* compile enough evidence against an offender, a person outside their jurisdiction, then how arduous will extradition proceedings be? Besides the legal entanglements, there has been a laxity by insurers themselves, who often find it cheaper in the long run to make good on the claim, fraudulent though it may be, without going through months or maybe years of expensive investigations involving police officers, marine police forces, and lawyers from a plethora of countries.

It is little wonder, then, that maritime fraud, a high profit/ low risk offense, shows a steady rise from an average of about three per month (reported) in 1979[7] to over ten per month in 1981,[8] with a direct loss per incident of approximately $5 million. And these figures represent only the tip of the iceberg. As we have just indicated, most of these illegal operations never make their way into the public records.

To grasp the full implications of marine insurance fraud, let us take a more detailed look at specific types of crimes subsumed under this heading. Eric Ellen and Donald Campbell make a good case against the commonly used division of marine frauds into the "hull" and "cargo" cases, because typical situations entail an overlapping of those two categories. We agree, and we have decided to adopt their classifications of documentary frauds, frauds in connection with charters, scuttling, and cargo thefts.[9] (Even in this categorization, any single crime typically contains overlapping elements.) Documentary fraud involves buying and selling goods where one or more of the documents in the complex chain of transactions—among buyer, seller, shipowner, charterer, agent, banker, insurer, or Customs authorities —have been falsified. These cases may involve overinsurance of cargo, false invoices, phony packing lists and certificates of non-blacklisted vessels, or manipulation of survey reports. There are trumped-up certificates of origin—for example, a ship was actually unloading potatoes in Luanda, Angola, on the same day that other documents showed her being loaded with frozen chickens in Tampa, Florida, some eight thousand miles away.[10] Country-of-origin papers have particular significance given the fact that many countries either have preferential duty rates in favor of certain other countries or completely ban products from others.

The most crucial document in the maritime trade is the bill of lading, which attests to the fact that a given cargo has been securely loaded on a given vessel to be transported to a stated destination. By this document the master acknowledges receipt of the cargo and promises to bring it safely to the consignee, and the shipper acknowledges that the amount and quality of the cargo is that agreed upon with the buyer. The bill of lading and other certificates are presented to a bank against documentary credit. If these appear to conform to the terms of the contract, the banks are obliged to make payment. It is neither required nor customary for banks to verify the authenticity (including signatures) of the trading documents. Nor are they responsible for checking the credentials of the beneficiaries—it is assumed that these investigations were made by the buyer before making a contract with the seller. There appears to be no end to the sophistication of financial manipulations. Nigerian banks in 1979 were forced to stop making their payment instructions by Telex to banks around the world. Someone had learned how to hook into the Telex link and to use inside information to direct banks in far-off places to make payment on fraudulent documents. The size of the losses has not yet been determined, but the point is clear: As the complexity of modern-day transactions grows, so, too, does the ingenuity of the racketeers.[11]

A century ago, trust in one's partner in a maritime commercial transaction might have been justified. But the sad fact is that in today's "rip-off" world such trust is frequently misplaced, and the prudent mariner, shipper, insurer, or banker should be cautious enough to check and double-check all those with whom he is doing business, and particularly as regards the verification of all documents involved—for, after all, there are Lagos Lilly and her counterparts elsewhere. As anyone engaged in the African maritime trade will tell you, for a mere pittance Lagos Lilly will produce any document the cheat may want. She can provide bills of lading or certificates of insurance. In fact, she helps to keep marine insurance frauds in business.[12]

The Case of the Angolan Groundnuts[13]

In 1976 the Angolan government contacted a Portuguese merchant, Manuel José Pires, manager of an exporting firm, Rimalpi of Lisbon, to arrange for a shipment of groundnuts. The price was U.S. $6,844,200. The Bank of Angola opened credit with the Union Bank of Switzerland, with instructions to make payment to Pires upon receipt of the bills of lading, certificates of origin, weight, quantity, quality, and packing, and an insurance policy, among other documents. Pires arranged for shipment with Doraldo Perreira Lima, head of Lima Navigation Limited, a Hamburg-based shipping company registered in Bermuda, using Greek-owned vessels on time charter—for this shipment, the *Pistis* and the *Saronicos Gulf.* The requisite documents were presented attesting that both ships had taken on their cargo of groundnuts at Beira, Mozambique. The bank paid Lima on April 18. If the bank officers were to have checked Lloyd's list, the fraudulent scheme would have ended, for on the same day of the alleged loading in Beira, the *Pistis* was in dry dock in Greece and the *Saronicos Gulf* was sitting in the port of Luanda. Meanwhile, Angola awaited the shipment. It was not until May 4 that the master of the *Pistis,* Georgios Mavrommatis, was instructed to pick up a cargo of groundnut cake (not groundnuts as ordered) at Banjul, Senegal, but to misrepresent the loading port as Beira. Four months later, on August 30, the *Pistis* finally reached Luanda, where port officials discovered the altered documents and the useless cargo. And what had happened to the *Saronicos Gulf?* It was not until mid-August that she loaded her cargo, again groundnut cake, not groundnuts, 3,000 tons at Banjul and 2,885 tons at Dakar, Senegal. The master, Christos Terzoglou, was given similar instructions: Change the bill of lading. He refused. The vessel reached Lobito, Angola, on September 30, where the deception was immediately uncovered.

Both ships suffered the same fate—guards were posted, and locks were put in the radio rooms. Troops secured the ships to the pier, where they have been sitting as hostages since 1977.

The Angolan court handed down a judgment against Pires, Lima, the Swiss bank, and the owners of the seized vessels. Lima and Pires disappeared and have not been heard from since.

The Angolan groundnuts incident is, unhappily, only one of an increasing number of swindles being perpetrated against Third World countries, which are easy prey for the sharpies of the industrialized world due to the lack of a trained business and professional class in these countries. This was so well demonstrated by the working paper of the United Nations Secretariat for the Sixth United Nations Congress on the Prevention of Crime and Treatment of Offenders, which dealt specifically with the multifarious schemes used by experienced business organizations of developed countries against the usually naïve governments of newly independent countries.[14] Angola was victimized not only by the groundnuts deal but also within a very short time by two other losses—in a fraudulent $600,000 palm oil case, and in a fraudulent $1,575,000 meat deal. In all three instances the buyer was attracted by a "bargain" either on goods or transport —a "bargain" that had social and economic consequences costing a whole lot more than the price of the products.

Some countries fall prey to fraudulent schemes not as buyers but as sellers. Take Costa Rica, for example. One of the most famous swindlers of them all, Emil Savundra, in 1959 "bought" six thousand tons of coffee, one tenth of Costa Rica's crop that year, but never paid a cent. Somehow he managed to convince the Costa Rican officials involved in the purchase that currency regulations precluded payment for half a year. By this time the racketeers had used the proceeds from their sale to finance even bigger fraudulent activities.

Cargo Fraud

Files of insurance companies are replete with yet another type of fraud—the "disappearance" of the whole or a part of a ship's cargo. Typically these cases involve the disappearance of the vessel as well, either by scuttling or faked scuttling, actually perpetrated by fast change of name and flag. The insurer thus becomes liable for both cargo and hull, and the insured walks off with yet another bonus—proceeds from the clandestine sale of the goods to some third party.

The Tomato Paste Case[15]

In 1977 the Greek-owned and -registered M.V. *Mariner* was chartered to transport 110,000 cartons of tomato paste, valued at U.S. $1,300,200, from Greece to Libya. Immediately before departure from Greece she was sold to a Panamanian outfit, the owners agreeing to honor the charter intact. Mysterious extensions of estimated time of arrival led the shippers to send out an alert to Interpol, the International Criminal Police organization at St. Cloud, Paris, and to various Greek government agencies, and Lloyd's Intelligence Service. Meanwhile, in mid-January, word came in that a vessel, one *Tarina T.*, had unloaded 110,000 cartons of tomato paste at Bissau, in Guinea-Bissau, West Africa. Two months later a United Kingdom loss investigator was dispatched to Bissau, where he found a somewhat less than friendly reception from local authorities. A government commission of inquiry refused to allow the investigator to present his evidence and closed the case in favor of the local importer, who had already arranged for 35,000 cases to be distributed in Bissau and the other 75,000 to be reloaded for export to Conakry, Guinea, on board the *Gale,* which had already sailed under the names *Mariner, Arine I, Aloha, Marina K.,* and *Tarina T.* By the time the U.K. investigator caught up with her in Conakry, he found that she was discharging her cargo under yet another name—this time the *Daler.* With the aid of a Libyan chargé d'affaires, Customs officers stopped the unloading, awaiting further details on the case. As it turned out, a Swiss firm, acting in good faith, had been offered a shipment of tomato paste at a bargain price. Satisfied with the standard credential and document checks, they had bought the cargo and then made a deal to sell it to a purchasing agency in Guinea. When the fraud was discovered, the Swiss agency canceled its contract with the Guinea importers, suggesting that they pay $862,500, the agreed-upon price, to the Libyan insurance company. Given the duration of the product's wholesomeness and the expense of chartering a ship to transport it to Libya, this was deemed the most feasible plan. There were still 35,000 cartons in Bissau that had to be dealt with.

Scuttling

In his memorable novel *The Strode Venturer*, Hammond Innes tells an heroic tale of a master whose vessel was abandoned by her crew in distress. She nevertheless pursued her course like a ghost ship, with only the master aboard, and he was unconscious. From a fall? A blow? The ship foundered in the Minkies, that pile of rocks off the coast of France in the English Channel. Yet it was the master who came under suspicion for having endeavored to scuttle the old rust bucket of which he had taken command only recently. After all, had he not lost a ship before? Master story teller Innes solves the mystery with the help of the crew of a small salvage vessel. It was the owners who had condemned the vessel to a watery grave, hoping to collect not only for the loss of a cargo that had been sold to the government of China before the master had taken control of the vessel, but also for the vessel itself. After all, of what use is an old rust bucket?

Most scuttling frauds are committed by shipowners, and generally they are not the "blue chips" of the industry. Ships are not all that different from automobiles. Imagine the average owner of an eight-year-old car, or of a twenty-five-year-old ship, who experiences mechanical failures with greater and greater frequency. The manufacturer has long stopped producing the appropriate spare parts for the car. The owner has to scrounge for replacements at junkyards, a task even more difficult for shipowners, whose vessels usually are not manufactured serially. The resale value, or even the junk value, of the car, or the vessel, is minimal. What hope there must be that the car or vessel will be totaled in an accident, with the other guy at fault! The prudent carowner or shipowner has calculated his depreciation and obsolescence and will be ready to finance the acquisition of a new vehicle or vessel. The fly-by-night/drive-by-night/sail-by-night owner will succumb to the temptation of fraud. If all has been well planned, the underwriter will pay far more than the junkyard, or the ship's breaker. Ideally, the underwriter will even pay for the loss of cargo—which may have existed only on paper.

The Case of the Supertanker Salem

On a warm January day in 1980, the supertanker *Salem* (214,000 tons), off the coast of Senegal, was ripped apart by a series of mysterious explosions. She sank swiftly, carrying her cargo of 193,000 tons of crude oil with her. Or did she?

Fortunately, no lives were lost. Officers and crew soon after arrived healthy and with all their suitcases packed, at their pre-registered hotel rooms in Senegal, whence they dispersed to the four corners of the earth. This sinking could have caused a major environmental disaster. Indeed, it should have created the oil slick of the century! But no oil slick ever floated off the West African shores, and questions began to arise. Barbara Conway, author of *The Piracy Business*, found the answers: The *Salem*'s name had been painted over. Under a false name she deviated from her course, unloaded her crude at Shell Oil's own Durban, South Africa, facilities, and there sold her cargo for $43.5 million to Sasol, a South African oil company. The proceeds vanished smoothly in Swiss and Italian bank accounts. Sasol had been happy to get the cargo and asked no questions, since OPEC had placed an oil embargo on South Africa for its apartheid policies. The aging *Salem*, then called the *South Sun*, had been purchased for close to $12 million. Mr. Soudan, her Lebanese-American owner, residing in Texas, and his Dutch and German business associates had insured her hull for $24 million, her cargo for $60 million. The ship, built in Sweden, had been flying the Liberian flag of convenience. Her unlicensed captain was Greek (at the time under investigation for another alleged fraud), the crew Tunisian and Greek. She carried Kuwaiti oil for Pontoil, an Italian firm, which sold it in transit to Shell International. The conclusion of this nightmarish entanglement was that Sasol agreed to pay Shell $30.5 million in compensation for the oil it had purchased from the swindlers. Mr. Soudan has changed his phone number four times, has not been available for comment, and has not pressed a claim with Lloyd's of London for the insurance on his vessel. But presumably he is some $40 million richer.

There is no use denying that the battle at sea between saints and sinners, between saviors and sinkers on today's oceans is being fought on unequal terms. While the sinners have resorted to Exocet missiles, the saints are fighting with three-pounders. But the unevenness of the battle is more conspicuous in communications than it is in armament. The war against the boardroom pirates and pushbutton outlaws of the sea is being waged, in essence, with the tools of the early 1800s. There is, in short, no organized command structure in the battle against the outlaws of the ocean, and nowhere is this more apparent than in the domain of insurance fraud.

Where is the organized resistance? On the governmental level it has become quite apparent that individual nations, on their own, are virtually powerless in combatting the international gangsters of the seas. Let us look at the traditional nongovernmental organizations that have waged the struggle against marine frauds and related saltwater criminality on an international level. There are, to begin with, the interlocking organizations that derive from Lloyd's of London, including Lloyd's Registry of Shipping and the Salvage Association. Neither their heritage nor their contemporary value should be demeaned, but their capacity to command cooperation in the investigation of maritime criminality is limited. In the same category we find the venerable and highly esteemed Baltic Exchange, the Protection and Indemnity Clubs, and, since 1919, the International Chamber of Commerce. Next there are organizations ranked either as intergovernmental organizations (for example, Interpol) or as nongovernmental organizations in consultative status with the United Nations (the International Association of Chiefs of Police, the International Association of Airport and Seaport Police, and other international organizations of law-enforcement officials). Although these organizations have been successful in fostering a universal approach to solving problems of law enforcement, their capacity involving cases of fraud and other criminality on the ocean is limited. They have neither sovereignty nor jurisdiction.

That leaves us with the international organizations that, as part of the United Nations family, have received certain charter responsibilities in this area. Let us mention the U.N. Conference on Trade and Development (UNCTAD), the U.N. Conference on International Trade Law (UNCITRAL), the U.N. Crime Prevention and Criminal Justice Branch, and the International Court of Justice at The Hague. Although all these United Nations agencies have had contact in one way or another with the problems that concern us here, such contacts have mainly been peripheral. While Mueller was head of the U.N. Crime Prevention and Criminal Justice Branch, he would have loved to have seized upon the issue of international marine insurance frauds, which at that time were (and still are) so costly to the countries of the Third World. Alas, a General Assembly mandate to that effect simply was not there, and the work of the branch could barely mention these issues.

Fortunately, in 1983, the International Maritime Organization (IMO), successor to the London-based intergovernmental Maritime Consultative Organization, became a full-fledged member of the United Nations family. Here at last is the potential capacity of the organized world community to deal with maritime fraud on a worldwide scale. The IMO would do well to examine the experience of all the other organizations in dealing with the prevention of maritime fraud, and we are referring particularly to the work of the International Chamber of Commerce through its International Maritime Bureau.[16]

The recommendations of that organization are of course detailed, resting on a multitude of experiences, but they boil down to a demand for the exercise of greater prudence by shippers, underwriters, banks, and agents in checking out the integrity of those with whom they are dealing, the seaworthiness of their vessels, and the reputation of the masters in command. But we would not stop there. As long as any one of the parties involved in a maritime transaction has to depend on correspondence with a multitude of agencies—governmental, intergovernmental, national, international, private, and public—to be assured of the integrity of his counterparts and thus of the safe delivery of his goods on the sea lanes, the chances of failure are great because the loopholes for the unscrupulous are large. Ultimately, then, what is needed for the oceans of this world, the pond of today's global village, is a universal registry of shipping and maritime transactions that, thanks to the availability of computers, should prove an entirely feasible task. Whether it be the IMO or some other universal agency under the aegis of the U.N. remains to be seen. Steps in this direction are being taken. Above all, what the maritime community needs is training of the masters and shippers of the world's oceans to sensitize them to the dangers of maritime fraud and to co-opt them for the new life of tranquil commerce on the oceans. We trust that the World Maritime University, recently created in Malmö by the United Nations and the Government of Sweden, will play a large role in this regard.[17]

13

Street Crimes of
the Ocean Lanes

•

In spite of rock and tempest roar,
in spite of false lights on the shore
sail on, nor fear to breast the sea!
Our hearts, our hopes, are all with thee.

Henry Wadsworth Longfellow,
The Ship of State

ON DECEMBER 13, 1981, SHOTS RANG OUT on the German yacht
Appollonia, headed for the Caribbean on the high Atlantic. The
owner of the vessel, Herbert Klein, and his girlfriend Gabriella
Haupt were dead, and a passenger, Michael Wunsch, was seriously wounded. There never had been any doubt about the
perpetrator. Paul Termann, forty-four years old, had fired the
shots. One year after the homicide, Termann was sentenced by
a court in Bremen to life imprisonment, having been convicted
of two counts of murder and one count of attempted murder.
His girlfriend Dorothy Permin received a three-year sentence as
an accessory. It is amazing that Termann had succeeded in getting the vessel into Bridgetown, Barbados, following the homicides. He was not an experienced sailor. For that matter, there
was no experienced sailor among the six that left Germany in the
first place on the *Appollonia.*

Of course, one could treat the case as ordinary homicides.
But ordinary homicides they were not. They were homicides on
the high seas, tainted by all the characteristics that go with living
together in a confined space, bobbing, pitching, and rolling,
subjected to the stresses of interpersonal relationships. Worse
yet, what makes most homicides on the high seas difficult for the
prosecution is the evidence itself, which by the time the vessel
reaches port has long been obliterated by the sharks.

212

Termann's only defense was that he had been driven to firing the shots in desperation, virtually a case of self-defense, but at least warranting a reduction of the charges to manslaughter, so his counsel argued. Whether that was so depended on the evidence of a single person capable of testifying. Termann and Permin tried to establish that by virtue of the wind and weather conditions of the ocean it would have been impossible for Termann to have planned and perpetrated the execution in the manner alleged. For that reason their defense counsel had requested that an expert be called at the trial to testify about the motions of the vessel, the intensity of which motions might be determined on the basis of the direction and strength of the wind and on the characteristics of the sails the vessel was carrying. The trial court had denied that motion.

Hearing Termann's appeal in landlocked Berlin, the Supreme Court, three of whose members appear to have had sailing or yachting experience, confirmed the judgment of the trial court below. And that confirmed the prosecution's theory that Termann committed murder in order to acquire the ship. Does this amount to ruling that the special conditions of the sea are not different from those that affect crime on land? Can it be assumed that trial and appellate judges are as familiar with the ways of the waves as they are with the solidity of the soil? Does it mean that the evidentiary pecularities of shipboard criminality require no special consideration?[1] And we have not even mentioned the special difficulties encountered in bringing a perpetrator of a crime on the high seas to justice in the first place, whether in the courts of the next port or those of his home country or of the country of the flag!

In their book *Strange Crimes at Sea*, Louise B. Davidson and Eddie Doherty discuss the passing of yesteryear's crimes at sea, by which they mean offenses by and against seamen. They attribute that decline to the invention of the wireless—which ties the captain to the owners and to authorities—as well as to the captain's loss of control over the propulsion of the vessel with a switch from sail to motors. Crimes at sea "still happen, but the horrors of the past no longer assail us. We have no replicas of the dreadful homicides of the past."[2] We can think of additional reasons for the decline of crimes by and against seamen that might have occurred, such as the shortening of time at sea with the advent of steam and diesel and the opening of canals, increased ship speed, increased comfort of crew, and computerization of navigation, but above all, through greater professionalization of the maritime trade and industry. Captains and mates no longer are the bullies depicted in *Mutiny on the Bounty.*

While we have reason enough to believe that, indeed, certain types of crime by and against seamen may have gone down, there are other maritime crimes, as we have documented in earlier chapters, that show enormous increases—the seaborne narcotics trade, the smuggling of aliens (indeed, the smuggling of anything worth shipping), piracy, terrorism, and maritime fraud. About the only area of sea criminality about which neither we nor anyone else has any reliable indicator is what we have termed the "street criminality" of the ocean lanes. By this we mean the common-law offenses or code crimes that fill the typical police roster, crimes common to land and sea. Among these we have included offenses against the person, particularly homicides, morals offenses, and offenses against property such as burglary, larceny, and related offenses. Last, we shall briefly discuss offenses peculiar to masters, mates, and mariners, whether as perpetrators or as victims.

Death on the Deep

Although we know little about any trend in maritime homicides (largely because neither the FBI's Uniform Crime Reports[3] nor any other national crime statistics, nor consequently the United Nations World Crime Survey[4] draw any distinction between maritime and land-based homicides), contemporary occurrences convince us that the type and ferocity of today's shipboard homicides may not differ much from those of the past. Witness the Termann case with which we started this chapter, or the many atrocious homicides committed in relation with piracy (discussed in another chapter). Nor has mass murder on shipboard changed much over the years, certainly not in the half century spanned by the *Morro Castle* sinking in September 1934 and the bloodbath aboard the 58-foot purse-seiner *Investor,* to which we shall turn shortly.

As the world well knows, the luxury liner *Morro Castle,* on a return gambling trip from Havana, Cuba, to New York, sent out an SOS. The ship was ablaze in a gale, 134 lives were lost, and she had to be beached near Convention Hall, Asbury Park, New

Jersey, to save the remaining lives. But her captain was dead before the disaster. Shortly before his death from a poisoned steak dinner, he was said to have exclaimed: "I'm going to get them or they'll get me. . . ." Mystery still surrounds this perhaps most famous of all homicides with consequent mass murder on the high seas. The three books already published on the *Morro Castle* disaster have only contributed to the mystery. (We understand that a fourth book, which may at last solve the mystery, is in press.) All investigators agree that the ship's radio operator, Rogers, was deeply involved. Rogers subsequently spent nearly four years in Trenton State Prison, where he died in 1958. His last conviction was for murder in the first degree for killing two persons. One of his pastimes had been setting fires. The *Morro Castle* herself, a liner of 11,500 tons built at Newport News, Virginia, had anything but an untarnished reputation. The ship had been used for running drugs, said to be hidden in one of the elevator shafts, with the elevator sabotaged and thus out of commission. She had reputedly brought illegal Chinese immigrants from Cuba to the United States, and she had, in general, been known as a "floating gin mill." Strike action and crew rumblings had been common.[5]

In 1983, Deborah and Larry Race celebrated their fourteenth wedding anniversary by dining at a Ft. Lauderdale restaurant followed by an evening cruise aboard their twenty-one-foot boat the *Jenny Lee*. At some point during the evening the boat stalled, water beginning to fill the bilge. According to Race, his wife panicked and jumped into an inflatable raft. He jumped overboard, pushing the raft toward shore, until his hands numbed and the raft drifted into the darkness. The next day Deborah's body washed ashore. The county attorney, in describing what he called the "perfect murder," argued that Race, an avid diver, went back to the *Jenny Lee*, put on his air tank, and returned to the raft under water, puncturing it with his knife. Other facts surfaced at the trial: Seven months earlier Race had taken out a $108,000 life insurance policy on his wife. The marriage was supposedly unhappy, and he was in the midst of having one of several affairs. An eight-woman, four-man jury found him guilty of first-degree murder. He is serving a life sentence.[6]

On Labor Day in 1982 a man described as white, in his early twenties, about five feet ten, of medium build, with straight

brown hair and a sallow, pockmarked complexion, and wearing
glasses with rectangular lenses, crossed over two of the fishing
vessels docked in Craig, Alaska, and killed all eight people
aboard the third vessel, the *Investor,* including the owner from
Blaine, Washington, his pregnant wife, five-year-old daughter,
four-year-old son, and four young sailors. He navigated the
Investor to a nearby cove, where he ultimately set fire to the
vessel, leading to its total destruction and the incineration of
the victims and all other evidence. He calmly rowed ashore,
offered his skiff to anyone who might want to take a closer look
at the burning vessel, and disappeared without a trace. No vessel
or airline leaving the area saw a man of that description. American and Canadian police dragnets failed to come up with any
clue. The motive as well is totally mysterious. The *Investor* had
not been engaged in any drug runs. Her owner-skipper had no
known enemies and was well reputed. Fire and sea had swal-
lowed the evidence.[7]

But from time to time the evidence may remain within reach
of law enforcement—namely, when the vessel bearing evidence
of a homicide is sunk in shallow waters. On September 27, 1983,
Boston police scuba divers raised a twenty-six-foot cabin cruiser
the *Malafemmina* (Evil Woman), in order to find evidence pertaining to the disappearance and potential murder on that vessel
of a Harvard graduate student in 1981. The owner of the boat
was the prime suspect. As of the moment of this writing, the case
is not yet closed.[8] And then there are the cases of homicide
occasioned by the dereliction of duty by the master, as exemplified by the "*Sadie and Edgar* incident," which occurred near
Atlantic City on January 28, 1976. This sixty-foot schooner was
shipwrecked in frigid waters, icy winds, and rough seas. Anyone
who has sailed the Jersey shores between Sandy Hook and Cape
May knows how nasty and unpredictable the wind and weather
on that stretch of the ocean are, even in summer and fall, let
alone winter. The vessel was lost. Her master saved himself, his
wife, two crewmen, and his dog Hap in their eleven-foot wooden
lifeboat. The three remaining crew members hung on to lines
attached to the lifeboat. These three died, and the captain was
charged with manslaughter. Surviving crew members testified
that the master had refused to throw his dog overboard to create
space in the skiff for one more human life to be saved. Allegedly

he had also refused to permit rotation between those in the skiff and those in the water.[9]

Every American law student is exposed to two cases that establish the defense of a master or mariner against the charge of homicide committed against passenger or crew in a situation of *necessity*. In *Regina* v. *Dudley and Stevens,*[10] three shipwrecked sailors had been adrift in an open boat in the doldrums of the equatorial Atlantic. Their predicament had lasted for weeks. They had neither food nor water. They were delirious and the end appeared near, especially for the cabin boy, who was about to expire. In phantasmagoric exasperation, Dudley and Stevens killed the cabin boy and ate his flesh. This enabled them to survive for another few days until they were rescued by a passing vessel. The Court of Kings Bench convicted them of manslaughter: Innocent human life must never be taken even to save one's own life, and even under the most dire necessity. Yet, the manslaughter conviction was justified because, in their psychological and emotional condition, the two sailors were in fact incapable of harboring that malignity of heart the common law requires as malice aforethought for murder.

There is an American precedent which is somewhat kinder to mariners in distress. The American packet *William Brown* was cn route from Liverpool to Philadelphia with a shipload of 65 Scottish and Irish immigrants when she struck an iceberg on April 19, 1841, 250 miles southeast of Race, Newfoundland. She sank rapidly in a howling nor'easter. The captain and some sailors manned the jolly boat, with one passenger aboard. The first mate and eight sailors manned the longboat, filling it with thirty-two passengers. Even while the longboat was shoving off, they saw the *William Brown* go down, with the remaining passengers screaming, praying, and disappearing in the waves. The jolly boat, under the command of the captain, was never seen again. The first mate managed to keep the longboat afloat, but the seas and the wind grew worse. The sea cock plug was lost, and the boat took on more and more water. The crew bailed as much as they could. The first mate shouted to his fellow sailors, "This work won't do. Help me, God. Men, go to work." Finally, the sailors obeyed, throwing a number of passengers overboard, being careful not to separate husband from wife, or mother from child. By such action the longboat was saved, and all still aboard were rescued by a passing vessel.

Holmes, one of the sailors, was tried on a murder charge and found guilty of manslaughter, but only because, as the court said, he had failed to exercise his duties toward passengers by throwing some of them overboard indiscriminately rather than by casting lots. This ruling has been much debated by lawyers and sailors alike.[11] Had the judges of the court been present when the longboat was tossed about among the icy waters of the North Atlantic, in a screaming gale, trying to avoid collision with icebergs, they might have been less sanguine about the requirement of drawing lots. But at least some good came out of the decision. Unlike English law, American law recognizes the defense of necessity in taking of innocent lives on the high seas under extreme conditions and subject to certain limitations, particularly the paramount duty of masters and mariners toward their passengers, to whom they are bound by a contract of safe carriage at sea. It appears that English law requires self-sacrificial heroism at sea, while American law gives in to some extent to the human survival instinct. Yet true heroism at sea has its own examples. We remember but cannot document the case of two American survivors at sea in the Pacific. One was clinging to a life preserver, yet he had lost his legs. The other was not wounded but had no life preserver. The wounded man gave his life preserver to his buddy with the words, "Take it, matie, you'll need it. It won't do me any good."

The Slave Trade

Captain Quogg, a onetime whaling captain, regarded "blubber" and "black ivory" as simply cargo with which to make a profit. He was also an ardent admirer of the Confederacy and hated the Union's antislavery war. It was after Fort Sumter had fallen that he took his ship, the New Bedford whaler *Butler,* on a slavery mission to Africa in clear violation of the 1820 slave importation prohibition. On the way back from Africa, a man-of-war approached his vessel, which was clearly recognizable as a slave-running ship. He brought his cargo of miserable and barely surviving Africans topside, tied them all to the anchor chain, and threatened to let the anchor go, killing them all and destroying all the evidence, unless the man-of-war disappeared. It did. The slaves were taken to their holds again, where many of them died. Their bodies were thrown overboard. Many of the sailors died as well. Quogg sold his cargo in Havana and then went on a whaling trip in order to return to New England with blubber. But the ship's mate, Farrington, who had deserted the ship in horror over its slavery trip, had gotten to Boston first. Captain Quogg and the owner of the vessel *Skinner* were tried and sentenced, albeit to a mere five years in prison.

Strange as it may seem, during the very same War Between the States, there was a second vessel, the *Erie,* whose skipper, Nathaniel Gordon, tried to run a cargo of eight hundred African captives into a West Indian slave port. The ship was intercepted by a Union naval vessel. Gordon was brought to trial in New York and couldn't believe the sentence he received: Death by hanging on February 7, 1862. After all, hadn't Quogg gotten away with a mere five years? Gordon's appeal to the U.S. Court of Appeals having failed, he took poison to beat the gallows. But he was revived. It took eighty marines from the Brooklyn Navy Yard to restrain the crowd who wanted to lynch him. He was finally hanged on February 22, 1862.[12] Thus ended the slave trade in North America. But despite the Paris Peace Conference of 1814–15, the Congress of Vienna of 1815, the Treaty of London 1841, the British abolition of slavery in 1833, the American abolition of slavery in 1863, the many antislavery conventions concluded by 1926, and the many U.N. conventions on the subject, the slave trade continued to be practiced within memory in certain parts of the world.[13]

But the most nefarious slave trade of our time was that practiced by the government of Nazi Germany, involving the transportation of millions of enslaved humans from one concentration camp to another to work under the most brutal conditions or to die in a death camp. That last massive incident of slave trade ended in the Baltic Sea when two vessels, filled to capacity with concentration camp inmates, were bombed by Allied bombardiers who did not know the nature of the human cargo aboard. We have referred to this story elsewhere in this book.[14]

Up to this point our samples may have shown that the oceans are particularly capable of being abused for the most serious crimes against life, human dignity, and humanity itself. By the same token, the experience of Mueller in the service of a water police force has taught that the waters can equally be abused for forms of petty criminality. In 1945, a Liberty ship had docked at the port of Kiel, and a call came over the radio, "Send a bus, I already counted twenty-four prostitutes going aboard, and I'm still counting." We wondered exactly how many crew members were aboard that Liberty ship, but the practice of ladies of easy virtue visiting sailors aboard ships in port is as ancient as sailing itself. Adler encountered a new version of the *dolce vita* of shipboard on a yacht docked next to us in a small New England port. She was a charter vessel of sorts, but then the outrageously steep charter fees seemed strange. We soon found out from the locals that the ship came equipped with easy ladies of the sea, and they were not mermaids. Credit cards were honored, and the receipts would show clearly and cleanly that it had just been a yacht charter, perhaps even a corporate meeting or business conference. Here too, the sea tends to hide at least some of the evidence.

The period of floating bars off the American Atlantic coast in Prohibition times ended only with the repeal of the Volstead Act. And the floating gambling casinos, or moonlight gambling cruises ended for America only when New Jersey legalized casino gambling in Atlantic City, thus making it easy for gamblers of the vast eastern population centers to find a nearby outlet on land for their drives. But even now a handful of people insist on making "book" aboard, as demonstrated by the case of the four New Jersey men recently arrested on the *Dolly J*, tied to a New Jersey dock.[15] On a grander scale we have seen floating gambling casinos in several parts of the world, especially in Asian waters where land-based gambling is illegal but where a truly floating crap game is beyond the reach of the law. Usually, however, the law tries to curb fun and games as much on the water as on land. To the chagrin of high-ranking U.S. Army Corps of Engineers officers, their friends, and a group of United Nations diplomats, aboard the 124-foot drift collector *Hayward*, on a merrymaking excursion celebrating the Brooklyn Bridge Centennial, the vessel collided with a 42-foot ketch. According to the press reports, the *Hayward* committed a hit-and-run offense by proceeding without stopping to inquire whether the vessel she had damaged required assistance. The last we heard was that a settlement had been proposed.[16]

Party cruises may run afoul of the licensing laws, as when, in summer of 1983, the yacht *Miss Northampton*, carrying a fundraising party commemorating Prohibition-era President Calvin Coolidge, was intercepted by Massachusetts Marine Police, and charges were placed for purveying liquor without a license. To top it all, the captain had no "ticket" (license).[17] Unhappily, drunk sailing can lead to as much if not more tragedy as drunk driving. In July 1983, four people died in a collision of two power boats near the Annapolis Harbor entrance. All the people had consumed a considerable amount of alcohol right before the accident. A month later, an off-duty police officer was killed on the Potomac River when his small cruiser crossed the bow of a dinner cruise ship. An autopsy showed an unusually high concentration of alcohol in his blood.[18] Laws against drunk boating are being more strictly enforced, and jurisdictions not yet having such laws are adding them. Of the state laws "prohibiting operation of a vessel while intoxicated, 39 have no defined blood alcohol concentration to determine intoxication, and 40 have no mechanical testing requirement."[19] As for this crime, what we have said for the rest of street criminality of the waterways is equally true: There are no credible national statistics available on the link between drinking and boating accidents. The Coast Guard feels that a skipper suffers sufficient impairment of his capacity to operate his vessel at a blood/alcohol level of .35 percent. The New York Bureau of Marine and Recreational Vehicles is supporting a new drunk-boating statute, much the same as that which covers operators of motor vehicles and snowmobiles. It calls for a Breathalyzer test, establishes a blood/alcohol limit of .10 percent, and provides for penalties of $250 or fifteen days in jail for the first offense, $250 to $500 or thirty days in jail for the second offense within a three-year period, and $500 or more or ninety days in jail for a third violation within five years. At the federal level a bill has been introduced making operating a boat while intoxicated a federal crime, carrying a fine of up to $5,000.[20]

When we started the research on this chapter and suggested that all criminality on land had its counterpart at sea, we didn't really expect to find such a ludicrous demonstration of our point as the case of the owner and crew of the lobster boat *Honi-dew*, who were arrested by the Massachusetts Department of Marine Fisheries on a charge of—of all things—possessing two untagged deer.[21]

Vanishing Vessels

At about 9:00 P.M. on September 13, 1982, the forty-seven-foot classic schooner *Toddywax* disappeared from her mooring in fog-covered Rhode Island Sound. She was known to many from her frequent appearances in regattas. Built in 1924, she had remained in the Ashton family ever since. The owners alerted the Coast Guard, posted a $10,000 reward, and mounted their own search of neighboring waters in a hired Cessna. Various leads took them up to Cuttyhunk, Massachusetts, where a boat resembling the *Toddywax* had been reported fast aground with an inexperienced crew of three hippie types, two men and one woman. They had hailed a passerby and inquired about tidal conditions. There were other tips, one substantial enough to take owner Ashton on another aerial search (this time off the Florida coast); another to Williamsburg, Virginia; and another back up to Cuttyhunk to check some remnants of a blown-up boat spotted by some fishermen. All false alarms. To date, the whereabouts of the sixty-year-old pride of the Ashton family remains a mystery.[22]

Closer to home, there's the story of Captain Jim, who some years back had a ship near ours at a City Island marina. He was a helpful fellow, always willing to fix your outboard or adjust your shrouds. He tried to make a comeback in the marine industry and put all his assets into the purchase of a decommissioned forty-one-foot Coast Guard patrol boat. That was to be the beginning of his new business. One morning the ex-Coast Guard boat was gone, vanished from the face of the sea. Jim could only surmise that someone wanted the diesel engines of the cutter and had scuttled the boat in Long Island Sound after extracting the parts.

Ours was a happy marina—although not without its problems, for this is where New York City and New England meet. There are the lobster restaurants, New England style, and the yards at which some of the earlier America's Cup defenders had been built, yet there is also a spillover from New York City's crimebound culture.

Not long after Captain Jim's problems—two weeks, perhaps —our outboard motor disappeared. Could it have fallen overboard? Unlikely. And it certainly had not been removed by the big, fat rats that frequented those docks, attracted no doubt by the delicacies in the bins of the nearby restaurants. Just a few days later, as we slept in our sloop *Contessa Maria I*, we were shocked into consciousness: Our boat was adrift on Long Island Sound. The docking lines had been cut. We could only surmise that whoever had taken the motor had returned for more. We couldn't help but think that they had come back for the *Contessa,* realizing only after she was torn from her cleats that there were people on board the blacked-out boat.

Only a few years ago thefts of boats and boating equipment were uncommon. The reason is simple: There were relatively few boats and relatively few people capable of handling them. All that has changed. Today quiet, tucked-away harbors as well as big city docks experience enormous losses, with a conservative estimate of the dollar value stolen annually put at over $60 million.[23] Due to the absence of a centralized statistical data base, the lack of uniform state titling and licensing laws, hull identification numbers that are easily removed, and confusion by boat owners as to the proper reporting agency for stolen boats, we may never find out the real size of the problem. But we do know that it has risen rapidly and steadily over the past decade. Figures from the National Crime Information Center (see Table 1) demonstrate the yearly increase of stolen boats between 1970 and 1980.[24]

TABLE 1

Stolen Boats on File

1/1970	881
1/1971	2,470
1/1972	4,555
1/1973	6,889
1/1974	8,385
1/1975	11,483
1/1976	11,981
1/1977	12,396
1/1978	15,559
1/1979	17,865
1/1980	21,277

Yet another indicator is the growing use of the NCIC Boat File by law-enforcement agencies. There had only been 4,313 inquiries in 1970 but 341,059 in 1981.[25]

In Florida alone the value of stolen boats and motors more than tripled, from 6 million to 21 million over a four-year period.[26] A recent survey of 3 percent of the boat owners in New York City's five boroughs found that 36 percent of the respondents had been victims of marine theft within the past five years. (It is interesting to note that only 51 percent of the victims had reported the crimes to the police.)[27] The statistics are sketchy, but the point is clear: The problem is massive.

The question naturally arises why there is this steady and steep increase in the theft of vessels. America has gone once before through a period of a steep and steady rise in thefts of a transportation and recreational vehicle—the automobile. The analogy between vehicles of the land and vessels of the sea appears reasonable. We therefore looked at the figures which one of America's most famous criminologists, Jerome Hall, had assembled to correlate the growth of the car industry and the parallel growth of car theft criminality.[28] He analyzed a consistent rise in theft from the time in 1895 when there were four automobiles in the United States to 1950, when there were over 40 million, and concluded that "sheer quantity is the first factor that makes possible their large scale theft."[29] And so it is with boats. Americans have become a nation of boat owners, and boat-handling skills are widespread. Moreover, today's pleasure crafts are small vessels, for the most part left unattended at night, unlike yesterday's yachts, which were large and always had crew aboard. Also, today's boats carry a plethora of easily removable expensive electronic gear, which fetch high prices among fences.

Besides the sheer increase in the number of boats and boat equipment which raises the number of opportunities for theft, there are other reasons for the enormous rise. As we have documented in other chapters, many vessels are stolen for quickie drug runs and are then either scuttled or abandoned; others are "stolen" by their own masters, who want to get rid of the boat while the insurance company makes good on the "loss." Add to this a maritime law-enforcement system simply not able to keep up with the new demands for protection. While the number of maritime police personnel has remained basically constant, the problems have continued to grow. What is particularly significant is the drain on law-enforcement time occasioned by the increasing deployment of personnel in fighting the drug war at sea. When you are out chasing crooks, you cannot guard the front and back doors of your house! Marine thefts in ports were bound to increase as the drug war at sea accelerated.

And who are the thieves and rip-off artists of the waterways? There are, above all, those connected with organized crime. Just as you can place an order with your local Mafioso for delivery of a Mercedes 300 within forty-eight hours—cheap and hot—so you can place an order for the vessel of your choice, whether sail or motor. It will be found and speedily delivered with numbers, names, and hull color changed to suit your taste and so as to make the vessel unrecognizable. The second group of thieves are those who act *lucri causa* (for their own personal benefit). Among them may be the fisherman who needs a new boat, the unscrupulous sailor who can't buy the yacht he wants, or maybe just a fellow who needs a new diesel for his workboat, who then steals the vessel of another, removes the engine, and scuttles the stolen vessel. There is a third group of thieves. One might also call them contract thieves (like the first group), who will "steal" a boat at the request of the owner, who can then collect a handsome insurance settlement. Strictly speaking, such cases do not constitute larceny. They are insurance frauds, pure and simple. Next, there is a group of boat thieves who also would not qualify as such under the common law of larceny, for they lack the *animus furandi* (the intention to deprive the owner permanently of his vessel). They are the waterways' counterpart to the joyriding juvenile delinquents of the highways. For example, "The captain was too short to see over the wheel without standing on a chair. The first mate was three inches shorter. That didn't deter the two boys from stealing a ferry at Cumberland Island, Georgia, and heading for Miami."[30] The twelve-year-old captain and thirteen-year-old navigator ran aground in rough seas ten miles out of home port.

Thus far, marine theft has been a high profit/low risk business with a recovery rate of stolen boats and equipment running under 30 percent.[31] State and local law-enforcement agencies are just beginning to rise to the challenge. Brochures on "security afloat" have been widely distributed, motion pictures and lectures are presented to boaters, and the establishment of a nationwide tracking system is being considered to supplement the National Crime Information Center boat file. Police departments that in the past have treated marine thefts as minor problems are beginning to realize their magnitude. Unveiling a computer program listing of all the twenty-five thousand boats registered in Rhode Island by hull registration and engine numbers, Assistant Rhode Island Attorney General told a group of officers from Maine, New Hampshire, Massachusetts, and Rhode Island: "The public is unaware that we have a most sinister boat theft problem. . . . We have to pull together really fast and come out hitting really hard. . . . We're not going to charge them with just larceny. We'll charge them with violation of the tax laws, filing false reports, conspiracy to commit larceny. We'll use the habitual offender statute, subpoena them for grand jury testimony, and investigate for drugs."[32]

In New York State, where boats are commonly stolen for resale to Canada, no registration decals are required, and about one third of the boats remain unregistered. Some officials claim that only a new titling and registration law could help marine police in their enforcement efforts.[33] While the legislature works toward this end, the Police Harbor Unit of New York City added as crime fighters four new thirty-foot aluminum-hulled launches to its fleet of six fifty-two-foot launches used primarily for rescue and patrol.[34]

At the federal level, new rules require boat manufacturers to put a second, concealed hull identification number on all models built after August 1984. Along with improved identification standards, the House Coast Guard subcommittee pushed for financial assistance to be made to the states through boat fuel taxes to help them develop better law-enforcement programs. A uniform boat titling system for all states is considered crucial to any massive antitheft effort.[35] After all, as Hall has demonstrated, not until after the requirement of automobile registration did the number of auto thefts decrease dramatically.[36] Although forty-five states have some kind of boat titling or registration law, we have a long way to go before we reach a nationally uniform standard that would allow a swift identification of every boat.[37]

The private sector has reacted more rapidly than the government, as evidenced by the growth of a multimillion-dollar marine safety industry, visibly present at all boat shows. Few private boats are without some security device, ranging from the age-old scattering of tacks in the would-be path of the light-footed predator, to sophisticated burglar alarms that come in the form of sirens, shrill bells, or even a powerful voice that shouts, "Burglar! Burglar! Burglar!,"[38] to high-powered arsenals of semi-automatic rifles. Writing in *Sail*, one yachtsman reports that "in Suva, Fiji, what I really wanted was a pack of Dobermans on deck. Granted, the presence of such startling hounds might have inhibited me from ever venturing topside—but so might the organized gangs that were raiding the boats around us. Some boats had been hit twice in their owner's absence. Companionway locks had been ripped apart with crowbars, and everything removable had been stripped from below."[39]

Marine insurance companies, various boaters' associations, and countless articles in yachting magazines remind us that above all, we should take commonsense precautions not very different from those we take every day to protect our households. How many of us would store an extra set of keys under the front-door mat? Why, then, do we attach our boat keys to the inside of an unbolted locker, or worse yet, hide them under one of the extra gasoline cans in the cockpit? Thieves don't have to "break in." They know as well as the rest of the boating community about the commonly used "hiding" places. And yet one wonders why burglars bother to use keys in the first place. Who needs to open the companionway when typically hatches can be raised with the gentle shove of a crowbar? And then again, crooks don't even have to bother going belowdecks —most of us are prone to leave expensive, easily removed equipment topside, in full view, thereby giving easy access to anyone who wants to lay hands on it.[40] Besides ordinary crime-prevention measures, it's a good idea to make sure your hull numbers are permanently displayed, to take your title papers along when you leave the ship unmanned, to photograph your vessel for future identification, to mark all equipment, and to make frequent visits to your vessel at different times of the day to discourage some would-be thief who may be watching your habits.[41]

Pilfered Packets

Almost every year between the end of the summer and the Christmas season, there was scheduled to be a joyous event for the children—the arrival of the boxes and crates from Europe, where part of the summer had been spent. The boxes could re-create the magic of the summer, for they contained not only personal belongings too bulky for air passenger luggage but also the souvenirs and mementos of the summer and the good

European candy. Each time, upon arrival at the warehouse on the docks of Brooklyn, Manhattan, or Port Newark, the disappointment would be equally as great. No matter what new and improved methods we had adopted, the boxes were broken, the contents had been pilfered. Every time we cursed the sailors or longshoremen who had committed the outrage.

Ever since the invention of the "packet," shippers between European and American ports have deplored the pilferage and have wracked their brains to prevent the dissipation of a good part of the cargo at each loading, unloading, and transportation in between. Yet by the 1930s petty pilferage of cargo had become so much an accepted risk of shipment that the longshoremen of Hamburg, to mention just one of dozens of ports, were permitted to carry a bag of a size not to exceed certain dimensions, in which they were allowed to carry home with them the spillage on dock or deck that normally occurred in the unloading process. At the free-port gate, the longshoremen would have to open their bag and display the contents: a pound of beans, a handful of cacao powder, or whatever. They were allowed to keep it. If there was no natural spillage, one could easily create one. A burlap bag dropped from a hoist at considerable height is bound to burst. A wooden box skillfully dropped from the shoulder of a longshoreman so that one of its corners hits the steel deck at just the right angle splits apart.

By the 1950s the art of pilfering had been perfected to such an extent that locked and sealed crates would be systematically opened, searched, and vandalized. There appeared to be no protection — until somebody invented the idea of container-ized freight. Containers are secure enclosures of a standard size, a long version or a short version, either one capable of being easily trucked on any highway or easily stacked on a container ship. They are sealed by the shipper, and the consignee will not accept the cargo unless the seal is unbroken. Containerization booked manifold successes. The shipbuilding industry boomed. Container ships were designed and built, while the old break-bulk carriers declined and largely went out of business. New port facilities were constructed in Southampton and Baltimore, in Bremen and Port Newark and just about every other major port, while the once-crowded, crummy, now decrepit break-bulk terminals folded, their piers rotting away. For a decade or more, shippers, masters, and consignees were delighted about the success of containerization. Pilferage was down to a fraction of its former magnitude. But the criminal mind is ever inventive. In a lecture on crime in the maritime industry, Jack Wilson, former assistant commissioner of New Scotland Yard and now with Security Investigation Services (SIS) of London, revealed the pilferers' new method: The supposedly impregnable seal can indeed be opened by the application of heat. The contents of the container can then be removed at leisure either while the container is at the warehouse, or while it is stacked on a vessel—although that may require some planning, since containers are stacked end to end, top to top, and side to side. After completion of the theft, the seal can be reconstituted, almost invisibly, by the application of Krazy Glue.[42]

But longshoremen and sailors, or thieves working in cooperation with them, should not be singled out for the recent emergence of container thefts. As Ellen and Campbell recently reported, unscrupulous shippers are engaging in malpractices, particularly in self/self shipments—i.e., where consignor and consignee are the same person or corporation. The methods are intricate and range all the way from underdeclaration of weight (to perpetrate a fraud), to failure to declare the hazardous nature of contents (which might invite catastrophe at sea), to violation of exchange control violations by conspiratorial action.[43]

What benefits the cargo thief most is the absence of an effective policing system. The Port Authority police officer whose attention we called to our broken crates dockside at Port Newark shrugged his shoulders and asked, "What do you want me to do about it?"[44]

Mariners as Victims and Victimizers

Mueller shall never forget the ashen face of the broken man who only hours before had been a proud if not cocky captain. The masters of the ferries in Kiel Sound that he had to patrol had always had a reputation for fast maneuvers—and self-assurance. Each one of the ferries could carry several hundred passengers and commuters with the regularity and frequency of a tramway. The ferries had to dock safely and swiftly to meet their schedules. For that reason, the ferryboat masters didn't like anybody crossing their bows and were averse even to cutting their speed for a fisherman dragging gear. There never had been an untoward incident, until that fateful day in 1946 when Mueller had to arrest the master of a ferryboat on two charges of manslaughter. The master had not cut his speed, trusting that the little trawler ahead of him would yield his right-of-way. The vessels collided; the fisherman and his son drowned.

Above all, masters and mariners are obliged to observe the rules of the road on water and the commands of good seamanship, whether imposed by statute or mere convention. Masters of vessels have a far greater responsibility in this regard than drivers of automobiles. Whereas automobile drivers risk the lives of a few and property in the thousands of dollars, masters are more likely to risk the lives of many and property in the millions of dollars. This was vividly demonstrated by the sinking of the tugboat *Morton S. Bouchard, Jr.* in Cape Cod Canal in April 1983. The tug was pulling a barge laden with sixty-three thousand barrels of gasoline through the canal on a towline the Coast Guard subsequently established to have been too long for proper control of the tow. The barge overtook the tug, capsizing it, spilling two thousand gallons of diesel fuel, and blocking the canal for five days. One crew member was severely injured. The result of the negligence as established by the Coast Guard might have been catastrophic.[45]

Every act of negligence at sea has potentially disastrous consequences. It cannot be our purpose in this book to detail the commands of good seamanship. Most of our readers may already be familiar with Chapman's *Piloting, Seamanship and Small Boat Handling,* [46] and professional sailors will long have internalized the rules of the road and standards of good seamanship. Violation of some of these is criminal by statute; violation of others is criminal if it results in death, injury, or property loss.

The New Jersey Code of Criminal Justice contains this cryptic provision under the title "Recklessly Endangering Another Person": "A person who purposely or knowingly does any act . . . which results in the loss or destruction of a vessel commits a crime of the third degree."[47] This statutory provision could conceivably become a doctrinal nightmare, because its title speaks of recklessness while its text does not, but requires an intention. The law presumably is directed at mariners and shore folk alike. But an additional provision is clearly intended to protect mariners. The paragraph punishes those who cause the loss or destruction of a vessel by "putting up a false light." This ancient provision was clearly directed against the wreckers of the Jersey shore from Cape May in the South to Sandy Hook in the North, who made their living causing shipwrecks by displaying misleading shore lights. Similar provisions found in the code books of many states and lands have put an end to the nefarious practice. The Conches of Key West were so much affected by the law that they resorted to other means of livelihood—smuggling.

The cruelty of the sea and the hazards and temptations of the seafaring trade have caused most seafaring nations to pass special legislation to both protect and restrain mariners at sea. Thus the ancient mariners' law that granted the master trial and appellate jurisdiction as well as executive power with regard to the infractions of sailors aboard his vessel, and that had fostered the reign of terror among many vessels of the eighteenth and nineteenth centuries, was curbed by such provisions as Title 18, Section 2191 of the U.S. Code, which makes any master a felon who "flogs, beats, wounds, or without justifiable cause, imprisons any of the crew of such vessel, or withholds from them suitable food and nourishment, or inflicts upon them any corporal or other cruel and unusual punishment."[48] Likewise curbed by contemporary legislation are the unholy practices of shanghaiing sailors or abandoning them abroad. By the same token, the duty of seamen to their master is codified, and anybody who incites seamen to revolt or mutiny is punishable under U.S. federal law and the laws of other seafaring nations.[49]

For those of our readers who may have been deceived by *Love Boat,* we want to conclude this chapter by pointing out that any crew member of a U.S. vessel who "during the voyage under promise of marriage, or by threats, or the exercise of authority, or solicitation or the making of gifts or presents, seduces and has illicit connections with any female passenger" is guilty of a felony and may be sent to prison for a year, or fined $1,000, or both![50] The perils of the sea are as finite and as infinite as the bottom of the ocean.

PART · IV

Smugglers, Spies, and Spoilers

The shattered water made a misty din;
  Great waves looked over others coming in,
And thought of doing something to the shore
  That water never did to land before.

Robert Frost,
Once by the Pacific

14

People for Profit: The Alien Smuggle

•

Give me your tired, your poor,
Your huddled masses yearning to breathe free,
The wretched refuse of your teeming shore,
Send these, the homeless, tempest-tost to me:
I lift my lamp beside the golden door!

> Emma Lazarus, *Colossus*
> The New Pedestal Inscribed
> in the Statute of Liberty

EARLY IN NOVEMBER 1981, the nation's wire services, papers, and radio stations focused on a drama then taking place on a beach near fashionable Fort Lauderdale: Thirty-three Haitian bodies were being washed ashore or plucked from the water. Thirty other Haitians managed to scramble ashore after their homemade thirty-foot wooden sailboat, *La Nativité,* was swamped in gale conditions. She capsized less than sixty yards from shore. Police were alerted when residents of the wealthy town of Hillsboro spotted crazed survivors drifting down the highway. Recovered bodies, battered and mutilated, lay strewn along the beach. A plastic-wrapped copy of the New Testament lay among them. The local medical examiner, through postmortems, found remnants of substantial meals in the victims' stomachs and concluded that the illegal would-be immigrants had been transported on a "mother ship" to the vicinity of Fort Lauderdale and then had been crammed into the rickety *La Nativité* for a landing.[1]

The trade in human lives belongs to the most sordid chapters in human history, whether it be "legal" or "illegal" slave traffic, or the modern transportation of aliens wishing to escape political oppression or economic malaise. The evidence indicates the

235

existence of a network or networks, operating with the open or tacit approval of some governments, overcoming the resistance of others, and capable of smuggling millions of political or economic refugees from country to country, usually by water route and normally under exploitation of the unfortunate victims, who must part with everything they own for a chance to be transported. Major points of origin for alien smuggling are: (1) Haiti, from where tens of thousands seek to reach the United States; (2) Cuba, whence the "Freedom Fleet" ferried 125,000 "Marielitos" into Florida ports; (3) Colombia, which at one time provided the United States with an army of shoplifters, trained at Colombian shoplifting schools, and now oozes drug traffickers into the country; (4) the Dominican Republic, which, although somewhat more prosperous than Haiti, shares Hispaniola's economic misery; (5) Bangladesh, ravaged by poverty and the effect of a disastrous war; (6) mainland China, among whose population millions have relatives in the United States; (7) and finally Pakistan, whose citizens seek reunion with their families already settled in England.

The ideal objective for most of the refugees is to reach the United States, that traditional haven for the wretched of the world. The closest staging area for that last jump to America's hallowed soil is Bimini, the foreign island closest to the coast of Florida. Traditionally, British-controlled Bimini, now part of the Commonwealth of the Bahamas, has been a sore spot for U.S. law enforcers, from the days of piracy through the era of Prohibition to the contemporary drug war. Luxury and the misery of crime have always marked life on the island, where the people-smuggling business has been a major source of income since the 1800s. As Ashley Saunders, a Bimini historian, put it: "If it wasn't Cubans, it was Haitians. If it wasn't Colombians, then Spaniards, Nicaraguans, Peruvians, Indians or Koreans. I've seen them all in my lifetime."[2]

It is estimated that more than two thousand aliens a month are smuggled into South Florida by over a dozen smuggling rings, each operating at a net profit of about $600,000 annually. Hundreds are entering with bogus Costa Rican passports, either forged or obtained under false pretenses.[3] The number of aliens apprehended by the South Florida Border Patrol and the INS are shown in Figure 1.

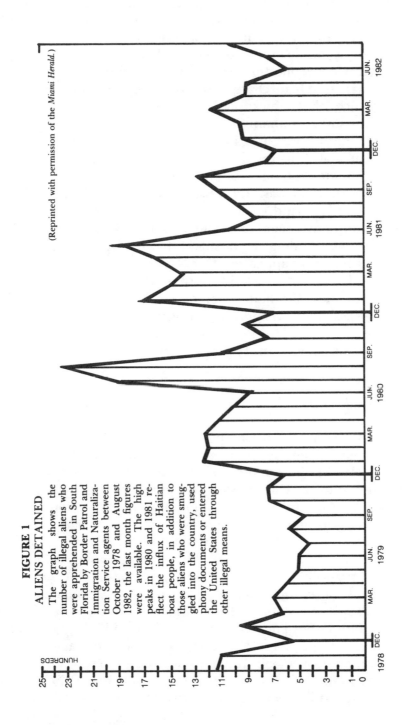

FIGURE 1
ALIENS DETAINED

The graph shows the number of illegal aliens who were apprehended in South Florida by Border Patrol and Immigration and Naturalization Service agents between October 1978 and August 1982, the last month figures were available. The high peaks in 1980 and 1981 reflect the influx of Haitian boat people, in addition to those aliens who were smuggled into the country, used phony documents or entered the United States through other illegal means.

(Reprinted with permission of the *Miami Herald*.)

Smugglers of aliens are among the most ruthless entrepreneurs of the sea. When there is the slightest peril to themselves, they prefer to dump their human cargo overboard, to
drown or to be devoured by sharks. Less vicious alien smugglers, after collecting their exorbitant fees (life savings, for the
most part), simply discharge the would-be immigrants on a remote beach of the pickup island under pretense that this is
American soil and Miami is just around the next cove.

The case of Rosa Ortez Fuentes, a forty-six-year-old Chilean,
is not unusual: Frustrated over trying to get a visa to join her
husband in the United States, she turned to a woman well known
in Freeport, Bahamas, for arranging an illegal entry. Rosa
phoned her husband each night along the way. On what was
supposed to have been the final day of the journey, a call came
from the agent telling the husband that his wife had arrived in
Miami. Rosa never appeared. Her Nassau tourist card indicated
a fifteen-day stay at the Holiday Inn on Paradise Island. Investigation revealed she had never checked in. Neither police in
Miami, Nassau, or Freeport, nor a private detective have found
any trace of Rosa. The alleged dealer in human cargo has also
mysteriously moved on. Her apartment was up for rent.[4]

The Haitians

Illegal entry of Haitians peaked in 1980–81. According to
figures taken from the Immigration and Naturalization Service
(see Table 2), the number of Haitians known to have been
smuggled into the United States during those years was 15,093
and 9,322, respectively,[5] a major jump from the previous years.[6]
And these are only official figures! Some of the Haitians fled
their country for political reasons, but most were economic refugees, trying to escape from a life of programmed economic
stagnation and hopelessness in the poorest nation of the Western Hemisphere. And when they arrived on U.S. soil, many had
a destination, a section of North Miami now known as "Little
Haiti." There they knew they could find food if they were hun-
gry, money to get started, a bank, an employment agency, and
a real-estate broker—all willing to deal with the thousands who
show up penniless. "Little Haiti" started back in 1977 when a
pioneering family opened a grocery store in a ramshackle build-

TABLE 2. HAITIAN FLOW

Month	1977 Actual	1978 Actual	1979 Actual	1980 Actual	1981 Actual
Jan.		12	8	577	769
Feb.		20	12	308	262
Mar.		35	38	1,401	530
Apr.		94	44	1,174	475
May	96	178	75	1,266	803
June		630	171	1,456	1,507
July		454	219	1,462	1,717
Aug.	77	206	223	1,731	978
Sept.	45	99	185	1,874	629
Oct.		17	637	2,280	306
Nov.	52	62	330	1,021	47
Dec.	4	8	580	543	46
	274	1,815	2,522	15,093	9,322

ing—a store where the then handful of Haitians could buy their dry mushrooms, peas, plantains, yuca, and other familiar items from back home. Business boomed. New arrivals even found a Creole-language radio program of community features plus educational broadcasts on American history. About twenty-five thousand now make "Little Haiti" their home.[7] But their number has stopped increasing. (We will return to this point later on.)

Not everyone who tried was lucky enough to reach "Little Haiti." On Christmas night in 1983, a refugee was crushed to death while jumping from a foundering boat during rescue operations of the cruise ship *Scandinavian Sun*. He was one of two dozen who had made their way in an eighteen-foot boat all the way to a point seventy-five miles northeast of the Miami shore.[8] In March 1982, twenty-one would-be immigrants went down with the *Esperancia* as she foundered and sank off Palm Beach County. In July 1981, half-crazed refugees dropped into the sea at the Florida Keys charged that during a reign of terror a voodoo-practicing crew either starved or cast overboard or hacked to death with machetes ninety-six victims. Survivors claimed there were over a hundred passengers jammed into the thirty-three-foot boat *Jesula*. In July 1980, a thirty-two-year-old male was thrown overboard by the crew of the *Dieu Qui Donne, 1,* claiming that he was possessed by evil spirits. In February 1980, five more Haitians drowned when their boat sank within twenty miles of Fort Lauderdale. In January 1980, smugglers pushed their human cargo into the surf near shore. One didn't survive. Her body washed up on the beach. In August of 1979, the captain of a twenty-eight-foot speedboat forced eighteen passengers to jump overboard at gunpoint. A mother and five of her children never made the South Palm Beach shore. In January 1979, eighteen Haitians disappeared after their eighteen-foot boat broke up off Andros Island on its way to South Florida. And in May 1979, six Haitian bodies were found on the beach of Paradise Island, a luxurious vacation and gambling spot off Nassau.[9] And then there are those who never even get a crack at that last lap of the route to the United States. Many an immigrant dream has ended in a nightmare in the Bahamas. There they come face to face with the rates of the unscrupulous smugglers, rising from $500 to $2,000 per would-be immigrant over a two-year period. The alternatives are horrifying: the fear of reprisal if they return home, and unwillingness by the Haitian government to allow those convicted of violating emigration laws back into the country. And so some twenty-five thousand sit in limbo, unable to obtain jobs because of work permit requirements. They fight for survival in homemade shacks sharing a communal water well and outhouse, waiting for the leaky tub that might reunite them with a husband or a child, separated somewhere along the haphazard route between Haiti and the United States. In the "transient" villages they sit huddled by a radio listening to South Florida newscasts—and their visions become clouded with reports of detention centers, violence, and unemployment. Many among them have simply given up. One of the early arrivals says that fate "will decide whether he remains or moves on. 'Maybe one of these days, God might bless me,' says Josive, 48, his skin roughened from exposure. 'I might move out. Maybe back to Haiti, maybe another place where life is better. One of these days.' "[10]

The era of mass illegal immigration of Haitians, but not of continued attempts to reach the United States, ended in the fall of 1982 when the United States revised its policy by (1) placing in detention centers those who managed to make it to our shores and (2) making an agreement with Haiti whereby U.S. Coast Guard cutters would assist the Haitian Navy. The cutters would be permitted to patrol waters around Hispaniola to intercept would-be immigrants to the United States and to escort inter- cepted vessels back to Port-au-Prince, the Haitian capital. In January 1984 alone, 266 Haitian boat people were diverted back to their homeland. Indeed, a veritable Coast Guard barrier has been set up along Haiti's north coast that includes the island of La Tortue, birthplace of the guild of the buccaneers in the 1500s and more recently the site of landings by Haitian revolutionaries and of fierce shore battles by them with the Haitian Army. Along with the agreement, the U.S. government obtained assurance from the government of Haiti that henceforth there would be no reprisal against or persecution of the returnees. In fact, U.S. embassy personnel have visited the villages of returnees to check that there had, indeed, been no problems. We, too, went by Land-Rover through tiny jungle settlements in remote parts of the country, studying the economic and political conditions that determine the life-style of the creative and friendly Haitian people. We saw the reasons why they might gamble away all they own to reach U.S. shores, in most cases to join family members there already. While villagers talked a bit about past reprisals against returnees, more recently no reprisals had been per- ceived.

There is little doubt that the Coast Guard policy has been successful in not just stopping the flow of illegal aliens into the United States, but also in terms of saving innumerable lives that would have been lost if the small, leaky, and overcrowded ves- sels had not been intercepted. In fact, we learned that one such vessel sank within an hour after Coast Guard interception. But the detention policy has had mixed results and also adverse reaction in America and elsewhere.[11] As to the mixed results, we learned from Haitians in Haiti of the rumor circulating among the populace that if an illegal Haitian immigrant would be inter- cepted by the Coast Guard or the INS, he would be thrown into the dreaded Krome Street Jail in Miami. If, on the other hand, he carried drugs, he would go to a federal prison with much better facilities and much better treatment. With good luck, he would ultimately stay in the United States anyway. Conse- quently, from there on some would-be immigrants carried small amounts of marijuana with them as their insurance of humane treatment!

The American detention policy vis-à-vis Haitians has riled

civil libertarians and federal judges alike.[12] It cannot be our purpose here to examine the variety of constitutional and procedural issues by which the detention policy was flawed. Suffice it to say that many bar groups rallied to the rescue of the Haitians, who almost universally had engendered the sympathy of the American public. By now most of these Haitians have been released from confinement. Unhappily, some still wait through the long, arduous appeal for political asylum. In protest, a hundred of them recently went on a hunger strike, calling for a "collective suicide."[13]

As usual, when one channel of illegal income dries up, it is soon replaced by another. The Coast Guard blockade around Haiti forced the people smugglers to adopt new methods of ferrying their cargo. They switched to little (sixty- to one-hundred-foot) dilapidated freighters. A vessel might come to the United States with a crew of twelve or more, making the return voyage with only three. The rest have prearranged to "jump ship" at one of the freight yards along the Miami River. The $1,000 fine imposed on masters for each vanishing head didn't seem to matter much. It was simply chalked up to business expenses and was more than covered by the exorbitant fees charged by the smugglers. In one three-month period alone, some $60,000 in fines were levied against Haitian traders in Miami, a noncontested amount paid promptly by cash.[14] More recently an ID card system was instituted by the U.S. government and on every return trip a captain has to give a strict accounting of each crew member. All those who come must also leave. So some captains have now resorted to equipping their vessels with concealed compartments. The aliens jump overboard before the ship docks at the Customs pier, quickly disappearing into Miami. Guests staying at one of the hotels bordering the Miami River were startled one day by the sight of dozens of Haitians swimming to shore from a small freighter and scrambling up the side of the building's premises.

The sixty-five-ton freighter *Elizabeth* was fined on three different visits—$1,000, $4,000, and $3,000. On one occasion, as she pulled away from the dock some dozen crew members stood on deck waving farewell to neighbors and to a Border Patrol inspector. Just around the bend they jumped onto shore and fled. Within minutes the Border Patrol was on board. A fine, of course, was paid, but the missing "crew" had already melted into Miami.[15]

The Cubans

In May 1980, Fidel Castro opened the emigration floodgates, and some 125,000 Cubans poured into the United States. The "Freedom Flotilla"—the name given to that motley fleet of some 2,000 lobster boats, shrimpers, leaky tubs, and pleasure craft—was haphazardly put together by Cuban Americans seeking to ferry their relatives out of Cuba while the open-door policy lasted. Many lives were lost in the process as unskilled boaters in less than safe craft attempted the three-hundred-mile round trip, Mariel, Cuba, to Florida and back, sometimes in heavy seas. Unscrupulous American captains, despite the exorbitant fees paid for their services, often grew impatient moored out in Mariel Bay for two to three weeks while Cuban authorities rounded up the charterer's relatives. A case in point:

The forty-three-foot lobster boat *Shortcut* was chartered by a group of Cuban Americans for $28,000. According to the captain, the arrangement included a wait of only three days at Mariel. But the days dragged on. After two weeks, he and his wife decided to head back to Key West and ordered their son and his friend to weigh anchor. But the Cuban Americans had other plans. They had been waiting for years to retrieve their families out of Castro's Cuba. They were not about to let a few days interfere. And so, armed with makeshift weapons— fishhooks, bottles, and a shovel—the "mutiny" began. The captain "charged piracy and said he ceded command."[16]

The boatlift, as it turned out, brought with it more than long-lost relatives, who made up only about 30 percent of the mass exodus. The remainder of the Marielitos leaving Cuba with the government's blessing were prison inmates, including hardened criminals, sadly afflicted mentally ill people, and political dissidents.[17] There were even two among them who had been wanted by the FBI for a decade, one on charges of air piracy and kidnapping, and the other on a charge of stealing a plane.[18] The Justice Department estimates that from four thousand to five thousand Marielitos have been detained in the federal penitentiary at Atlanta, in mental hospitals, and in state and local jails.[19] They have been characterized by the federal government as petty criminals, sexual deviants, antisocial personalities, and alcoholics. Releasing such people, government attorneys have argued, poses a real threat not only to society, but to these Cubans as well.[20] Lawyers working to protect the Cubans' rights, on the other hand, claim that the incarcerated refugees are "in a legal no-man's-land—not entitled to constitutional rights because they have not been admitted to this country, and not deportable for the same reason."[21] As of this writing, the legal battles involving the Mariel boatlift continue.

The Colombians

No group of alien smuggling entrepreneurs has challenged the patience and imagination of U.S. law-enforcement agencies, especially the INS, as much as the Colombians. As early as 1973, there existed what EPIC was later to call the Sandoval Pipeline. The Atlas Travel Agency of Sandoval Associates in Cali, Colombia, provided efficient transportation for Colombians into the United States. Tour guides would assist the travelers, who found their hotel rooms booked along the way. Taxis would be waiting at other prearranged points. It all seemed very cozy. The only hitch was that the Colombian travelers, whose heavy burdens Atlas carried on his shoulders, were illegal immigrants into the United States. They could pay Atlas's exorbitant fee, all right, and they carried plenty of cash. In fact, many had cocaine concealed on their bodies, for they were not only mules for the cocaine cartel but also the cartel's appointed resident agents in various cities in the United States. INS and DEA, in cooperation with Mexican authorities, shut down the operation. We were visiting Mexico City at that time and received a briefing from the Under Secretary of Justice on this nefarious trade through Mexico, which put the government of Mexico in a bad light just at the time when Mexico was successfully curbing marijuana imports into the United States. In Pacific Coast ports of Mexico, riding in a Mexican Drug Enforcement Administration jeep, we observed the zeal with which the Mexican agents were doing their share to plug the Sandoval Pipeline.

But Atlas merely shrugged and transferred his operations to the Bahamas. By the time we sat in the office of our chargé d'affaires there, Mr. Antippes, in 1983, even that new pipeline had been cut. As many as three hundred Colombians had been brought into the Bahamas, whence they were ferried by light plane or twenty-five- to thirty-foot cabin cruisers to America's shores. The skipper of one of the alien-smuggling cabin cruisers made an easy $60,000, at $600 to $700 a head, for the short run between Bimini and Fort Lauderdale. The risks were slight, and once caught, the penalty for the first offense was a peccadillo. But after his first conviction, he went out of business, because the second offense would have netted him five years per head of illegal alien cargo.

At the height of the Colombian smuggling operation through the Bahamas in 1981, our chargé d'affaires there interceded with the Bahamian government, and the open-door policy vis-à-vis Colombians was changed. Henceforth, Colombians needed a Bahamian visa. When Atlas's agent appeared with a handful of Colombian passports requesting the issuance of visas, it was the Bahamian immigration officer who shrugged his shoulders. But then, as we said, Atlas is resourceful. Later, during 1982 and 1983, Colombians would fly in directly, albeit illegally, to any one of the hundreds of airstrips in Florida that can accommodate light but long-distance aircraft flown by greedy American pilots.[22]

The Dominicans

The Dominican Republic shares the island of Hispaniola with Haiti. Economically better off than Haiti, the Dominican Republic is nevertheless one of the poorest countries of the Latin American region. Two of its exports are particularly noteworthy: (1) since Castro's takeover of Cuba, exquisite cigars, which can be imported into the United States quite legally, whereas Fidel's Havanas cannot; and (2) Dominican citizens, who cannot go to the United States legally except in the rare case when there is an immigrant or visitor's visa. Yet Dominicans by the thousands try to make it into the United States via the Mona Passage, which separates the Dominican Republic from the Commonwealth of Puerto Rico. Once having made it ashore in Puerto Rico, the next step is easy—a Pan Am ticket to New York or Miami with no border patrol. The trip across the Mona Passage could be purchased from Lobo del Mar, the "Sea Wolf," otherwise known as Juan José Santania Perez, also known as Juan Julio. INS agents credit him with an operation that during its years of activity has landed two hundred to three hundred Dominicans monthly in Puerto Rico. South Florida Task Force officers indicated that his ring also provided Dominican prostitutes for Puerto Rico and the U.S. mainland. Both the Dominican and the U.S. law-enforcement agencies are searching for him after he jumped bail in the Dominican Republic and escaped from jail in Puerto Rico. Dozens have charged that the "Sea Wolf" is responsible for the death of their missing relatives. As of the moment of this writing Lobo del Mar is still at large.[23] The most cruel of all crimes committed against would-be Dominican immigrants was the sinking, on September 5, 1980, of the *Regina Express* at her dock in Santo Domingo. The probably worthless vessel appears to have been scuttled with human cargo in her holds. The smugglers opened the water valves to silence the shouts of the drowning. A suit was filed in Dade County Circuit Court in 1981 against the ship's captain, a resident of Miami, for wrongful death. A Dominican Republic inquiry revealed that the people smugglers had routinely paid Dominican Customs agents $200 per head, and Dominican Navy guards $100 per head, for each would-be passenger permitted to board one of the smuggling vessels, whether the human cargo was delivered or not.[24]

The Bangladeshis

In the early and midseventies, so Mr. Antippes told us on our visit with him in Nassau, the social and political conditions had driven many Bangladeshis out of their country, then known as East Pakistan, and they sought their fortune in Western Europe, especially West Germany, which needed labor for an industry working at maximum capacity. Soon thereafter the West Germany economy slackened, and Bangladeshis and other immigrant workers who had been received with open arms were no longer welcome there. Most chose not to return to Bangladesh and tried the big jump to the United States. Under a recent reciprocal agreement between West Germany and the Bahamas, residents of West Germany, whether German citizens or not, could legally fly to the Bahamas. Once there—as so many other would-be immigrants before and since—the Bangladeshis would make their contacts in Bimini. But by 1982 the price for the short boat ride from Bimini to the mainland United States stood at $950 cash per person, as was learned when a U.S. Coast Guard cutter on August 13, 1982, intercepted the first vessel carrying Bangladeshi illegal immigrants en route to U.S. shores.

The trade in aliens by their fellow islanders is accepted by Bimini's population. In fact, it is regarded as a welcome boost for the local economy. According to recent reports, for each Bangladeshi captured by the Florida Marine Police, the INS, or the Coast Guard, many more make it through. Those who are caught are a headache to U.S. taxpayers, who have to pay the price of the deportation ticket back to Bangladesh, the country of origin.[25]

The Mainland Chinese

Biminians ask no questions about the nationality of the people they ferry to Miami, Fort Lauderdale, or points in between. Mainland Chinese have been among their recent human cargo. Theirs is a trek even longer than that of the Bangladeshis. The most hazardous part is the escape from mainland China on a junk or a "bum boat," hidden under vegetables, cattle, and household animals.[26] Once in Hong Kong, it takes contacts and money to obtain the documents that "prove" the would-be immigrant is a Hong Kong citizen. Once that obstacle has been overcome, the route to be taken is that pioneered by the Bangladeshis, as Commonwealth citizens, via London to Nassau, Bahamas, as "vacationers" on an excursion ticket, thence to Bimini and across to the States by cabin cruiser or speedboat.

Almost Like Dunkirk: The Pakistanis

"How busy was the beach near Boulogne in those days? Was it like Victoria Station?" "Not like Victoria Station, but maybe like 'St. Pancras.' " Or, to put it in maritime terms, it looked a lot like Dunkirk. Our visitor was referring to the "boatlift" in Britain in the late sixties. The Pakistanis were making their onslaught on Britain, and the story is well described in Timothy Green's *The Smugglers.*[27]

For £1,500 a Lahore travel agency would arrange the entire

trip, legally to Frankfurt, and from there to Boulogne. The overall fee included the £50 or £100 that the English head smugglers would charge for the ride to England, on decrepit cabin cruisers or fishing vessels, including one cabin cruiser named *Rahre,* which had been stolen in Marseille. When British maritime enforcement agencies clamped down, the smugglers took a longer route, as far west as Devon. One Rye, Sussex, fisherman boasted of having taken more than twenty Pakistanis across on his vessel *Carrick Lass* and claimed that once the beach at Boulogne was so crowded that he had picked up somebody else's human cargo by mistake.[28]

People emigrate from one place to another for a variety of reasons, but always to improve the situation they experienced at the place from which they emigrate. There is a consistent impact on the borders of any state to which emigrants may wish to turn in their quest. There were, in fact, a million aliens apprehended in 1983 alone, in their attempt to enter the United States.[29] Yet it is of the very essence of sovereignty that states may monitor their borders and shorelines to regulate the influx of immigrants seeking entrance. Among our own heritage we count those who were persecuted for religious, ethnic, or political reasons, those who wanted to improve their economic conditions, and those who wanted to be reunited with their families. America's first immigrants had no visas from the "Indians" who resided here. Yet those immigrants established a republic and imposed conditions on their successors for admission. The INS, the Border Patrol, and the Coast Guard are charged with implementing these immigration laws. During the past decade, which witnessed the enormous increase in maritime crime documented in this book, America also witnessed a vast increase of illegal immigration via the sea lanes. That, too, is a form of maritime criminality. Yet while those seeking illegal entry are of course guilty of violating federal criminal statutes, Americans generally offer them sympathy and certainly condemn those who profit by running the would-be immigrants to our shores and who do not hesitate to kill them for profit or self-service.

15

Security at Stake:
The Murky Waters of
Espionage and
Treasonous Trade

•

"The time has come," the walrus said,
   "to talk of many things;
Of shoes—and ships—and sealing wax—
   of cabbages and kings"

Lewis Carroll,
The Walrus and the Carpenter

Of Guns and Goons: The Smuggle of Arms

FORT KING GEORGE, TOBAGO, DECEMBER 1983

THE ANCIENT GUNS at Forts King George and James will forever remain silent. But there are new guns in Trinidad and Tobago! During the 1983 Christmas holidays Commissioner Randolph Burroughs and his troopers staged a raid in Trinidad and seized a virtual arsenal of weapons,[1] a commodity which has been seeping into Trinidad and Tobago in increasing numbers.

The local mass media have one preoccupation: the Grenada issue! Grenada, the "spice island," one of the happiest among the paradisiacal hideaways in the Caribbean, among the smallest of the world's independent countries, had become an arsenal. Its national route led from colonial fiefdom, to democratic independence, to socialist revolution, to murderous factionalism, to American gunboat diplomacy (via Caricon) to status quo. How did it happen? Sure, there was a revolutionary fervor, support

249

by socialist governments, even capitalist mob involvement (Vesco! mentioned elsewhere) and every other ingredient it takes to boil a tranquil country into turmoil. But the basic ingredient was *weapons*. And that is why Commissioner Burroughs and his counterparts in the neighboring republics are concerned about the illegitimate trade in arms.

While the entire world is the gun runner's sales district, the market is being controlled from a few hubs. A nightclub on the Rue de Char et Pain, in Brussels, was the "Gun Bourse" for decades, but Miami was not far behind. "End use" certificates are needed to buy and export arms legally. To the exporting country this is meant to be a guarantee that the weapons will not find their way to enemies of that state. Yet we have it on reliable authority that such certificates are easy to obtain through greedy counsel or officers, or forgers. And then there is the trader who doesn't care at all about quasilegalities. Employing pilots who lost their license, and masters who lost their ticket, willing to sail rust buckets without insurance, they will ship arms that have been busted, pilfered, surrendered, purloined, or stolen to anybody who buys, for cold cash.[2]

The destinations of the deadly and illegal cargo are dictated by current events. There always is Northern Ireland. An Irish Navy seizure a decade ago revealed the nature of the business. Five tons of weapons from Libya were seized on the S.S. *Claudia* destined for the provisional IRA. On board was Provo leader Joe Cahill![3] Another hot spot is the Middle East, where every faction in the Lebanese civil war uses ammunition at a fierce rate— though much of it is being provided officially by one or the other of the major powers behind that conflict. In the Far East weapons and ammunition have been in plentiful supply ever since the American pullout from Vietnam, so that the pirates of Thailand and the dissidents of Molucca or of Mindanao have had no cause for complaint. The stuff simply is shipped where needed.

The Caribbean is the focus of today's gun runners. There are twenty-six countries in the Caribbean basin, and their interests are even more diverse than those of the major powers hovering above the region. Soviet ships are suspected of bringing arms in vast quantity to Cuba and Nicaragua, whence they are distributed elsewhere. The Panama Canal has become a conduit for Soviet arms shipments. Between January 1, 1979, and December 31, 1982, 2,209 Soviet cargo ships traversed the Panama Canal. Let us take a closer look at one of them, the S.S. *Novostrov*. Her agents in Panama are Fernie and Company. In October 1983, she unloaded five large crates in the free port of Cristóbal, destined for Nicaragua. The captain certified that, inasmuch as Nicaragua was not on his itinerary, some other vessel would have to pick up the cargo. According to the documents, the boxes contained sanitary articles sent from Caracas, Venezuela, for the company of "Ferreteria Federico Lam" in Managua, Nicaragua. When newsmen examined the cargo they found mortars, rifles, machine guns, grenades, and other war material.[4] Yet neither U.S. nor Panamanian authorities have the right or the capacity to prevent arms shipments through the Canal, which under the Canal Treaty, is to be "permanently neutral." Whether coming through the Atlantic or through the Pacific, arms are pouring into the Caribbean countries. Grenada was a dramatic demonstration, but other countries are equally affected. Canadian police arrested eight people on Christmas Eve 1983 in a conspiracy to smuggle machine guns and grenade launchers to Guyana in an attempt to overthrow the government of Prime Minister Burnham.[5] Just before Christmas 1983, Soviet arms and ammunition were found on Antigua's outlying islands, and Dominica's Prime Minister, Eugenia Charles, was very much disturbed about the proximity of the arms to her country. And French authorities are highly aggravated about continuous bomb explosions in Guadeloupe![6] The lesson that Grenada has taught the Caribbean countries is that the arms trade is simply the more visible part of overall subversion that in turn is intimately linked to the vast resources provided by the narcotics trade. And now that the "Shining Path" Maoist guerrillas are operating—for the first time—in north-central Peru, center of that country's cocaine production, matters will get a lot worse before they get better![7]

The topic "The Problems of Caribbean Countries in Dealing with Subversion"[8] was the focal point of discussion in the Military Law Committee of the XXIVth Conference of the Inter-American Bar Association in Panama in February 1984, at which military brass from the concerned nations were very much in evidence. The planning of a Caribbean defense force was uppermost in their minds.[9] Meanwhile, the United States was setting up a substantial intelligence network to monitor the illegal arms trade on America's front portico.[10]

For sixty-two days the Cyprus-flag freighter *Cloud,* abandoned by her crew, had drifted through the Atlantic—like the

Flying Dutchman—with not a single living soul aboard. Un-manned, the *Cloud* had come two thirds of the way from near the Canary Islands, off the coast of Africa, to the coast of Venezuela. She was finally spotted by the Venezuelan freighter *Maracaibo*, whose captain circled the *Cloud* with suspicion and awe. He finally sent an armed boarding party to the *Cloud*. The boarding party found weapons and ammunition aboard—and evidence of an electric fire that had burned out and that apparently had caused her crew to abandon her in haste. A call for help to Caracas brought a boarding party of nine airborne *infantes* (ma-rines), who parachuted onto the deck of the *Cloud*. They found the ship full of TNT—five thousand wooden boxes full of it—in 122mm shells, a caliber used exclusively by Soviet forces.[11] Until seized by the Venezuelan *infantes*, the *Cloud* was a time bomb on the high seas, an embodiment of the secret and often illegitimate ocean trade in arms, explosives, and other means of destruction, the utmost destabilizer of peace on the ocean, and of the tranquillity of maritime—especially insular—nations.

The Not-So-"Innocent Passage": Maritime Espionage

Field Marshal Count Helmuth von Moltke, father of the great Prussian General Staff, is said to have smiled only twice in his life: the first time when he was informed that his mother-in-law had died, the second time when he was shown the fortifications of the Stockholm-Vaxholm fortress, which guards the last ap-proaches to the harbor of Sweden's capital, very much as the old batteries at Fort Totten and Throgs Neck Point stand sentry over the East River access to New York City.

The good ship *Christina,* a sloop of the Royal Swedish Yacht Club, skippered by Professor Jacob Sundberg, a specialist on terrorism and international law, and crewed by Christina Sund-berg, Adler and Mueller, passed Vaxholm, outward-bound into the archipelago of Stockholm. This once sleepy and peaceful sailing paradise is now crisscrossed by vessels of the Water Po-lice, the Coast Guard, and the Royal Navy. Something has hap-pened to disturb the tranquillity of these waters and the almost phlegmatic complacence of the Swedes. In October 1982, midget submarines, off-loaded from submarine mother ships, so it was reported, had invaded Swedish territorial waters. The subs were spotted by the Swedish Royal Navy, but all efforts to force them to the surface by traditional means of naval warfare failed. Why? These vessels, it turned out, were not conventional subs depending on buoyant maneuverability for their operations, but rather could move, caterpillarlike, on the bottom of the sea. Naval divers followed and photographed the underseas track marks, which led right past the Vaxholm fortress to the inner harbor where, undoubtedly, the sub crews had a spectacular view of Stockholm, right into the windows of the Royal Palace. We sailed through the maze of channels among hundreds of islands in the Stockholm archipelago. All vessels have a right to "innocent passage" through the territorial waters of other countries. Can a submerged submarine innocently get that deep into the Stockholm archipelago?

Over dinner we talked with Admiral Bror Stefenson, chairman of the Swedish Joint Chiefs of Staff, himself a former submariner. He takes a dim view of the alien exercises ("or do you suppose that it was the Navy of Liechtenstein that has been crawling around our naval bases?"). Such intrusions, after all, happen to be highly illegal under Chapter 19, Article 5 of the Swedish Penal Code.[12] They also violate what is most sacrosanct to Swedes: their traditional neutrality. These incursions into the Swedes' cherished tradition appear to have transcended all factionalism. Swedes have grown closer together. Somehow the bright blue flags with the yellow cross on Swedish yachts seem to have grown, too. Swedes are on the alert. The Navy has distributed to all seafaring Swedes and coastal residents fifty thousand copies of a guide booklet on spotting alien submarines, *Vara Objudna Besökare,*[13] with phone numbers to call if anyone sees a sub or periscope in the archipelagos. And the reports keep coming in. Between 1962 and 1982 there were 143 confirmed alien submarine intrusions into Swedish waters (40 in 1982 alone), including the embarrassing incident of a Soviet Whiskey class sub high on the rocks near the Karlskrona naval base. All these incidents were documented in great detail by a royal commission of inquiry, which published its report in April 1983.[14]

The creepy-peepy midget subs crawling and resting on the bottom of the sea are virtually indistinguishable from rocks and thus escape detection by traditional systems. By summer 1983, the Swedish admiralty got the orders to get tough. Under new regulations, the Swedish Navy is permitted to attack submarine intruders without prior warning, to bring them to the surface if

they are within the inner part of Swedish territorial waters between the islands along the coast and the mainland. Beyond
those limits—i.e., within the Swedish twelve-mile limit—the old
rule prevails, and the Royal Navy may force subs to the surface
only if they refuse orders to leave.[15] Yet, announcement of the
Swedish get-tough policy did not have any impact by itself. The
creepy-peepy subs kept crawling around in Sweden's archipelagos. During the summer of 1983 forty incursions by foreign submarines were detected. Although in April 1983 Sweden
had accused the U.S.S.R. directly for such violations, in a
strongly worded statement in September, Defense Minister
Anders Thunborg did not mention any foreign power specifically but added, "There shall be no doubt about Sweden's determination to prevent further violations."[16] By December 1983,
Thunborg used his fist to emphasize the point about Sweden's
determination. The defense ministry had photographic evidence of nuclear submarine invasions![17] By mid-February the
Royal Swedish Navy dropped—in earnest—ten depth charges in
the vicinity of the Karlskrona naval base and activated its minefields in the seabed around the base.[18] Around the Baltic the
story is told that upon graduation from the Soviet submarine
commanders' school, the graduation assignment consists of
making it into the Swedish archipelagos undetected, and prizes
of cases of Stolichnaya await the skippers with the greatest exploits.

But the explanation is not that easy, especially if one consid-
ers that neutral Sweden's submarine plight is shared by neighboring Norway on the northern NATO flank. U.S. Secretary of
Defense Caspar Weinberger reported in early June 1983 that
between 1969 and 1983, 250 possible submarine incursions of
Norwegian territorial waters had occurred.[19] As if to emphasize
the point, on June 29, 1983, a Norwegian frigate felt compelled
to fire six Tern missiles near Bodø, Norway, in a hunt for a
submarine intruder.[20]

While it might be surmised that the alien submarines are
probing the defenses of neutral Sweden or of NATO's northern
flank, the better guess is that the Soviet admiralty is exploring
safe underwater havens for its nuclear submarine fleet in case of
a nuclear conflict. Both sides to a potential nuclear conflict
figure that most land-based nuclear missiles will be wiped out in
the first confrontation. To destroy what is left of the earth after

such a nuclear holocaust requires hidden nuclear missile launchers, namely nuclear-powered submarines. Consequently, we are witnessing an ever-escalating drive to develop systems for the fail-safe, foolproof detection of enemy submarines. (The United States is spending an estimated $26.8 billion on that system in 1984!)[21] But we are also witnessing efforts to reach agreement among the superpowers aimed at preventing surprise attacks. Yet, the Soviet Union has been charged with seeking sanctuaries, including the Indian Ocean, where nuclear submarines would be free from antisubmarine warfare.[22] That is, of course, exactly the policy behind the probing of Sweden's archipelagos and Norway's fjords, both so close to the Soviet bases in Kronstadt and Liepāja, on the Baltic, or Murmansk, on the Barents Sea. After all, would the West want to bombard friendly Norway and neutral Sweden? Their coastal waters would provide sanctuaries for the Soviet nuclear submarine fleet in case of a conflict —if it can't be the Indian Ocean.

In June 1983, an American surveillance satellite took a surprisingly detailed photograph of a huge submarine under construction in Leningrad.[23] It appears that she is a transoceanic mother ship for creepy-peepy minisubs, capable of taking her crawling reconnoiterers to Cape Canaveral, Newport News, or Groton, Connecticut. Is it possible that some day they may be looking for nuclearproof sanctuaries for Soviet nuclear-missile subs in U.S. waters? It bears emphasizing that the Soviets have steadfastedly denied any incursions into Swedish waters, except the grounding of their submarine of the Whiskey class near Karlskrona, "due to navigational error," and have attributed the Swedish reaction to right wing hysteria.

The watery spy game, as old as it is, is just beginning to develop its potential. And it is crime on the ocean! Americans had been oblivious to the spy war at sea until that shocking January 22, 1968, when North Korean patrol boats seized the U.S.S. *Pueblo*, a reconnaissance vessel, off the coast of North Korea. Frantic efforts by captain and crew to destroy the intelligence-gathering equipment and documents proved only partially effective. The courageous captain and crew spent many months in North Korean captivity. But why should Americans have been surprised that their nation, any nation, would want to learn what other nations, with conflicting interests, were up to? The intelligence game at sea amounts to a sail in very murky waters indeed. Just as any nation wants to find out what other nations are doing, every nation will exercise every right to protect its neutrality, confidentiality, and information. Although espionage in territorial waters clearly violates the penal code of the coastal state, espionage outside the territorial waters is less clearly criminal, although the United States, among others, extends its conspiracy laws beyond the limit of its territorial waters. American submarine surveillance activities have been a standing feature of U.S. intelligence operations for decades, surfacing only when something goes wrong. Thus, in 1969–70, a U.S. nuclear submarine beached herself at low tide on the U.S.S.R.'s Pacific coast but was freed by the tide and left undetected. In March 1971 collisions occurred between U.S. and U.S.S.R. submarines off the coast of Murmansk and inside Vladivostok Harbor.[24]

It is hardly possible, nowadays, to have any U.S. fleet operate anywhere without a Soviet escort watching every move. Cape Canaveral has become a virtual floating grandstand for Soviet naval vessels watching U.S. spacecrafts being launched. Most of the intelligence ships had been armed with only the latest in electronic gadgetry. But that has changed recently. The Soviet naval vessel *Balzam* is equipped with surface-to-air missiles and a weapon similar to a 30mm Gatling gun. And she is one of the Soviet Navy's best-equipped spy ships, assigned to the American West Coast, and occasionally has been spotted outside U.S. territorial waters off Hawaii.[25] Her advantage seems to be that her firepower will keep her from becoming the Soviet Union's counterpart to the *Pueblo*.

For the time being, the hot spot of spy-ship operations remains the Korean peninsula, where sharply opposed ideologies confront each other in an aura of immense distrust. That is where the *Pueblo* was taken; that is where in June 1980 an armed North Korean spy ship was sunk by South Korean forces, with the loss of a great many lives; and that is where, on August 5, 1983, South Korean aircraft and sea patrol vessels sank another armed North Korean spy ship, with loss of lives[26]—heroes to their country, criminals under the law whose interests were violated. Suspicion falls not only on nations with directly opposed interests but also on neutrals, as the hapless sailors of the Japanese refrigerator ship *Fujisan Maru* found out during their detention in North Korea.[27] The tentacles of espionage in the murky waters on the fringes of the oceans, where passage is supposed to be safe when innocent, reach far indeed. There is an old German proverb, "Intelligence makes well and woe."

Exit: The Prime Minister

Culpam poena premit comes (Crime has punishment as burdensome companion) says the badge of the New South Wales police officers manning our boat. The New South Wales Police Force cruiser is rounding Bennelong Point, on which stands the magnificent structure of the Sydney Opera House, one of the modern wonders of the world, Joern Utzon's architectural masterpiece. Its superstructure juts into Sydney Harbor like a giant futuristic sailing vessel, sails full blown before the wind. The Sydney Opera House was to be the site of the Sixth United Nations Congress on the Prevention of Crime, at the invitation of the Prime Minister. Government delegations of the world were to debate the world's common crime problems in the halls where normally Richard Wagner's *Flying Dutchman* sails. The only thing the Opera House lacked was office and working space for our staff of 250 professional officers, and the President, Vice President, and reporters. Our plan was to charter a ship and dock her right next to the Opera House, with space enough for the entire staff, the printing presses, word processors, communications equipment, audio video studies, and whatnot. The problem was to find a suitable ship.

As the police cruiser picked up speed, the old aircraft carrier *Sydney* came into sight. She had been laid down in World War II but had not been commissioned until 1948, under the name *Terrible*. Having seen active duty off Korea, she was converted to a fast transport in 1962 and served during the early part of the Allies' operations in the Vietnam War. As a transport between Vietnam and Australia she became fondly known as the *Vung Tan Ferry*, carrying troops, the wounded, and an occasional load of contraband drugs to Australia. But then, in a conciliatory gesture toward China, the Australian Prime Minister pulled Australian troops out of Vietnam and terminated the *Vung Tan Ferry* service. She had been rusting in Sydney Harbor ever since. While available, examination proved that she could not be our ship. Her overall length of almost seven hundred feet would not permit her to dock at the Sydney Opera House. "Maybe you really don't want a floating U.N. headquarters in Sydney Harbor," one of the police brass suggested. "You diplomats are known for your drinking habits, and if somebody falls overboard, snap, the sharks will get him. Sydney Bay is famous for its sharks, and they are really all around Australia. Remember what happened to our Prime Minister!"

We remembered, all right. Prime Minister Harold Holt had gone swimming one fine day in 1967, and that was the last anyone had seen of him. Officially, the Prime Minister's mysterious disappearance was considered a drowning—until late 1983, that is, when English novelist Anthony Grey published his tale *The Prime Minister Was a Spy.* [28] Having pieced together bits of information, Grey offers the thesis that the Prime Minister had been an agent for the Nationalist Chinese government since the 1920s and that he later switched his loyalty to the government of the People's Republic of China. The drowning was a fake, concludes Anthony Grey. In fact, says Grey, Holt was received by Communist Chinese frogmen, off the Australian beach, who guided him to a waiting Chinese submarine for exit from Australia, barely ahead of the Australian counterintelligence agents assigned to the case. [29]

Our readers may wonder whether we ever found our floating headquarters for the U.N. Crime Prevention Congress. As it turned out, it was not necessary to find one. In 1979, within a few days after a tightly closcted meeting between Australia's Prime Minister and U.N. Secretary General Waldheim, Australia announced the withdrawal of its invitation, immediately followed by the invitation of the government of Austria to hold the congress in Vienna, as part of the move to transfer part of the U.N. headquarters, including the Crime Prevention and Criminal Justice Branch, from New York to Mr. Waldheim's home country, Austria. Although Vienna did not get to host the Sixth Crime Prevention Congress (Venezuela was chosen as the site of the Congress), Vienna did get the Crime Prevention and Criminal Justice Branch, which ultimately, gave us the great opportunity to sail with the congenial friends of the Burgenland Province water police on Neusiedler Lake, patrolling the border between Austria and Hungary, in search of the occasional refugee who needs assistance, or the occasional spy, who wants anything but assistance while making it across the freshwater Iron Curtain.

Meanwhile, Norway has had its Arne Treholt affair, a case of espionage by a high-placed Norwegian official arrested while carrying secret documents en route to Vienna. These documents, it was surmised, pertained to NATO's efforts to guard the prime shipping lanes along Norway's coastal waters "that Soviet warships from the Northern Kola peninsula would use in wartime."[30]

High-Tech Tacks on the Ocean Lanes: The Smuggle in Sensitive Technology

More vital than arms and as vital as strategic information is the technology with which nations chart and construct their destiny. There are technical advances in the West that the East does not have, and vice versa, and that means that years of research and billions in investment can be saved by either side if equipment could be gotten hold of—clandestinely. Why not by normal trade? Because the equipment could be advantageous militarily in this never-ending game of one-upmanship in world domination. We are not able to document the high-tech smuggle scheme on today's oceans; we can only illustrate it.

"Ever since World War II, the Soviet Union and its satellites have found it more economical to acquire Western technology than to develop their own. What's more, many of these experts believe, the Russians have siphoned off so much of that technology that America's already slim lead time in the production of sophisticated weapons systems has been seriously jeopardized."[31] Senator Sam Nunn of Georgia made his point forcefully when he concluded: "The Soviets have come to view our technology as their technology, to be obtained whenever they want it."[32] Operation Exodus resulted from such considerations. This operation was the Reagan administration's response to the drain of American high technology to countries of an adverse political persuasion. The objective was to spot "advance technology exports to make sure they are duly licensed."[33] "From its inception in October of 1981, through October of this year, Operation Exodus detained 4,275 foreign-bound shipments, resulting in 2,330 seizures of goods valued at $148.8 million . . . [resulting in] 221 indictments"[34] under the Arms Export Control Act or other federal statutes pertaining to the illegal export of high-technology items. For 1983 alone, 1,444 unlicensed shipments were seized by Customs officers, up from 765 in 1982![35]

The federal statutory restrictions on the export and the public release of information pertaining to high technology had their repercussions in Soviet strategy—namely the clamping down on the release of Soviet information of scientific value.[36] There are two issues in today's high-tech smuggle on the high seas. The first is premised on the fact that, basically, high-tech know-how is pretty well evenly dispersed among the nations of the world, so the more practical question is how to get the hardware to the right place at the shortest possible time under the most cost-beneficial terms. The best example is the "sugar-to-fuel" technology developed in the United States for converting cane sugar into fuel, which Fidel Castro wanted to acquire for his country to alleviate Cuba's endemic fuel shortage. None other than the elusive Robert L. Vesco, on the lam from U.S. authorities for innumerous frauds, offered help to beleaguered Cuba by promising to sell a sophisticated American mechanism for converting sugar cane to fuel. Alas, Mr. Vesco's American agents, caught red-handed in the exportation scheme, were indicted under the "Trading with the Enemy Act," and that ended that ploy.[37]

There is, however, a second issue. It is based on the premise that there still is a gap in technology among the major competing powers and that that gap basically points in one direction: Know-how is likely to flow from West to East: The East wishes to acquire Western high technology to cut its own budget on technology development. Yet we wonder whether most of the restrictions of the export of so-called high technology are really meant to secure the advantage in know-how and thus to widen the strategic-scientific gap, or whether they are simply a form of harassment vis-à-vis unfriendly nations. Let us look at the case of the three "patrol boats" seized by Commerce Department agents in Miami just prior to their export to Nicaragua on the Panamanian freighter *Carolyn* on December 9, 1983. According to informers, the boats were to have been used for "spying, smuggling, and gun running." That, however, does not constitute legal grounds for seizure. They were seized because of their sophisticated equipment in the high-tech category, under the Export Administration Act, which carries penalties of up to ten years in prison and fines of up to $250,000.[38] Yet these boats were a stock twenty-five-foot Boston Whaler, a twenty-five-foot

Mako 254, and a twenty-five-foot Robala, with two-hundred-horsepower Mercury engines, equipped with standard Japanese electronic boating gear, equipment found on any sport-fishing boat. The export transaction was straightforward. Apparently it was the radio direction finder, again a piece of standard equipment, that had been on the Commerce Department's list of items subject to special export license if to be shipped to Nicaragua.[39] That country shares with Libya a special place on the federal government's bad-boys list, as the Tencan Corporation of Chicago must have known when it sold $16 million worth of aircraft spare parts to Libya in sixty unlicensed shipments.[40]

In both of these cases defense counsel had argued that the statutes and regulations are so confusing that no reasonable trader can understand them or comply with them. Knowledgeable investigators of the exports control system agree. Overlapping statutes, conflicting authority among various governmental departments, contradictory policy objectives, disagreement among friendly nations, and frustration over the incapacity to influence the behavior of foreign governments by export controls have created a jungle in which survival is difficult, equally befuddling the regulated and the regulators.[41] But there is little doubt about the determination in the White House to stop "the massive hemorrhage of American technology to the Soviet Union," and that is exactly why President Reagan indefinitely extended the Export Administration Act of 1979, which had ended September 30, 1983.[42] The U.S. Customs Service beefed up its Operation Exodus, determined to let no sensitive equipment out of the country. The great computer caper is illustrative: A highly sophisticated computer system, capable of military and civilian use, the VAX 11/782, manufactured by Digital Equipment Corporation of Maynard, Massachusetts, had been licensed for export to South Africa. There is, of course, a general United Nations embargo on the sale of such equipment to South Africa, but neither the U.S.A. nor many other Western governments have taken that embargo seriously. But the embargo on the transfer of dual-use (military-civilian) equipment to the Soviet Union is taken seriously by the U.S.A.—though not necessarily by the other Western Allies. Thus, when it was learned that the computer was not really going to South Africa but was being routed to the Soviet Union, orders went out to stop the shipment immediately. Seven minutes before the departure of a Swedish container ship from Hamburg, West Germany, the sensitive cargo was located on that vessel. German Customs, at the request of U.S. authorities, unloaded the computer.[43] While the ship was sailing for Sweden, it was learned that not all computer parts had been taken off the vessel in Hamburg. No sooner had the ship docked in Hälsingborg, Sweden, when Swedish Customs officers seized the remaining boxes, because no Customs declaration had been received with the shipment.[44] But there was more to the computer than that. On November 24, 1983, Swedish Customs officials found a second shipment of American computer parts, officially destined for South Africa but actually headed for the U.S.S.R., in the port of Malmö, and seized the shipment.[45] A few days later Swedish Customs officials announced that their investigation had uncovered a regular computer-smuggling route, via Sweden and Finland, to the U.S.S.R.,[46] and a few days thereafter a shipment of U.S.-made computer parts destined clandestinely for the U.S.S.R. was seized by British Customs in London.[47]

The People's Republic of China, while accorded more cordial trade consideration than the Soviet Union by the United States, still falls under the ban of Operation Exodus. In a secret operation, $1 billion worth of equipment was to be shipped from the U.S.A. to China through Hong Kong. "If the Chinese got everything on that [shopping] list, they would be right behind us technologically," concluded the Customs Service officer who uncovered and stopped the transaction.[48]

But the exodus continues, as does Operation Exodus, a matching of wits, a war of nerves short of a shooting war but spanning the skies and the oceans of the world with bad guys and good guys earning their just and unjust desserts. Surely the valiant efforts of Customs officers all around the world to enforce their countries' laws on export and import restrictions deserve more than a mere mention; yet with all due respect, that is all we can accord them.[49] The field is too vast, and the conceptual borders among goods that move by air, by sea, and overland are too fuzzy to permit easy analysis. Smuggling in gold and silver, jewelry and watches, parrots and cheese, bull semen and automobiles, optical instruments and antiques is vast. Nor will it ever stop—as long as there is demand—in the face of legislated policy not to let it out or in, conditionally or unconditionally. However, as Customs officers are increasing their cooperation across international frontiers through such organizations as the Customs Cooperation Council[50] or the European Community's Customs Union,[51] the smugglers' risks are increasing. Perhaps it is only through regional and inter-regional cooperation that the oceans can be freed from smuggling. Certainly the world's limited experimentations point in that direction.

16

The Ocean Is
the Victim

•

The very deep did rot: O Christ!
That ever this should be!
Yea, slimy things did crawl with legs
Upon the slimy sea.

About, about, in reel and rout
The death fires danced at night;
The water, like a witch's oils,
Burnt green, and blue and white.

Samuel Taylor Coleridge,
The Rime of the Ancient Mariner

The Ultimate Melting Pot: Pollutants and Polluters

WE HAD BEEN SAILING for barely a day on the United States Coast
Guard cutter *Steadfast* when the captain called us to the bridge
to view a phenomenon common to the Atlantic but unknown to
us: a chain of sargassum seaweed stretching all the way to the
horizon and varying in width from 25 to 250 feet. And trapped
in the chain was the refuse of our civilization—oil spills, plastic
bottles, flotsam and jetsam of every description, tons of it.
Groupers and dolphins were feeding: "Poor bastards, they may
not survive the tummy aches," said a sailor.

We soon crossed the path of a tramp streamer, her name
painted over, the old name still recognizable. By her old name
she was a suspect vessel of the drug trade. We hailed her. The
grouchy master, from one of the islands of Germany, grudgingly
identified the vessel, her dubious nationality, her last port of
call, and her destination, adding: "The discharge you see on my
port side is clean sea water and not diesel. And now I have had
enough and will go to bed!" The master had been more con-

cerned about being cited for ocean pollution than for drug running. (He was, indeed, clean—this time.)

While the world's foremost marine scientists of GESAMP (Joint Group of Experts on the Scientific Aspects of Marine Pollution) of the United Nations expect the oceans to digest ocean pollution at the present rate of effusion, they are careful to point to the hot spots that are biologically dead or that are reaching that condition at an alarming rate.[1] There are United States waterways to which no yachtsman would take his vessel for fear that the hull might dissolve in the chemicals. In certain coastal waters and semi-enclosed seas, e.g., the Baltic, the Mediterranean, the Caribbean, alarm is, likewise, justified. From time to time, fish caught there is inedible. "We caught some mercury with traces of tuna" is a local joke no longer.

We can only marvel at the trust that some administrators place in the capacity of the oceans to recover from pollution. Seven of ten people in the world live within fifty miles of a coast, and half the cities with a population of over a million are situated near river mouths.[2] Open sewers flow into rivers, which in turn empty into oceans, not just at India's Malabar Coast but also in New York and New Jersey. New York City's sleek and gaily painted tankers (the *North River, Newtown Creek, Owl's Head, Bowery Bay,* and similar vessels operating under charter) of the Environmental Protection Administration fleet—proudly displaying the EPA symbol—pass down the East River at the rate of six a day, to dump their cargo of raw sewage into the Atlantic, barely off Ambrose Light. The charter fishing boats out of Sheepshead Bay, Sandy Hook, and Shark River, are anchored nearby—catching "mercury." And in Mauritius toxic industrial effluents have cut the fish catch by 10 percent. Oil pollution threatens Camoran beaches, and shorelines have been covered with mud and silt caused by poor cultivation of the soil by Madagascan nomads.[3]

For a year and a half, Exxon tankers have carried away fresh water from the Hudson River for use in running oil refineries and as drinking water at Aruba, off the Venezuelan coast. The tankers discharge their petroleum in Linden, New Jersey, take on saltwater ballast, go up the Hudson, jettison the ballast, and take on fresh water for the return trip. The riverkeepers are not pleased, but it appears that no law has been broken.[4] On a worldwide scale, every large freighter or tanker contributes about one ton of copper to the sea each year just from its paint.

For the United States alone it has been estimated that there are 270,000 sources generating hazardous waste, plus 10,000 transporters and 32,000 storage sites.[5]

At an ever-increasing pace, the oceans of the world are being victimized. More and more people live near them, eat from them, play on them, make their living from them, and use them as waste dumps. And by and large, the public remains unaware of any problems until they read in the newspapers that the local fishing catch is unfit for human consumption or that a massive oil slick is threatening their favored beaches. In March 1983, *The New York Times* reported that "a giant oil slick, said to cover an area the size of Belgium, is likely to hit the Persian Gulf State of Qatar!"[6] Seven thousand barrels of oil a day were spewing from damaged Iranian wells only six miles offshore, threatening to wipe out rich fishing areas. And just a few months later, in August 1983, the world's papers carried photographs of the 271,000-ton Spanish supertanker *Castillo de Bellver* burning and breaking up off the South African coast, with her 73 million gallons of crude oil threatening massive pollution of a 15-mile coastal sanctuary for bird and marine life. The five-year-old ship carrying her cargo from the Persian Gulf had erupted into flames about 80 miles from Cape Town. Her oil slick measured an estimated 540 miles. The explosion must have been immense. Farmers along the Atlantic shore reported that strong winds had carried a choking smog that covered their grain fields and vineyards with an oil film.[7] And there have been many other giant spills—among them an oil production platform blowout in California's Santa Barbara Channel (1969), the breakup of the *Argo Merchant* off Nantucket (1976), the 120,000 tons of oil released from the stranded *Torrey Canyon* (1967), and the tanker *Amoco-Cadiz* running aground off France, polluting an extensive area of its northwestern coastline (1979).[8] But these highly visible major catastrophes are not the principal sources of pollution. By far the largest source of oil pollution from ships results from normal tank cleaning operations, which routinely occur after a ship discharges her cargo and before she takes on a new one. In addition, there is the runoff from loading and discharging operations, which usually take place in port or near shore. The conditions can only worsen. Over the past twenty years the amount of oil transported rose 700 percent. Tanker fleets increased from 64 million deadweight tons in 1960 to 328 million deadweight tons in 1979. The capacity of tankers increased from 30,000 deadweight tons to over 500,000 deadweight tons.[9] A number of supertankers, and oil installations at which they take on their cargo, have been damaged by Iranian and Iraqi missiles, with devastating and lasting effects on the ecostructure of the entire region.

But oil is only one of the offenders against the seas, albeit the one that engenders most widespread awareness because of the mass publicity surrounding catastrophic incidents. Other public protests over the release of toxic wastes into the sea take place locally, usually following the actual or planned dumping of potent carcinogens in amounts exceeding the toleration point of neighboring communities. This happened after the decision to burn up to 300,000 metric tons of PCBs, DDT, and other chemical wastes in the Gulf of Mexico aboard two incinerator ships, one about two hundred miles off Corpus Christi, the other located near the Houston ship channel. In November 1983, some 2,000 protestors packed a public hearing in an effort to stop the full-scale burning of cancer-causing compounds before a thorough study could be made of the effects of the incineration technique. In December 1983, the Environmental Protection Agency announced its decision to issue permits for the operation.[10] Another scare erupted when residents of Dade County, Florida, became aware that a scrap metal plant had been illegally dumping PCBs into the ground just 150 yards from the Miami Canal, which flows toward the well field serving 500,000 residents. Although no trace has yet been found in the well field, the existence of PCBs in the canal bank is a major cause for concern.[11] The owner of the plant could not be contacted—the business phone was disconnected and the home phone number was unlisted.

On the other side of the Atlantic, in November 1983, a radioactive spill near one of the world's first atomic plants threatened the continued existence of Britain's nuclear industry. The plant, known as Windscale, routinely dumps more radioactivity down a pipeline into the Irish Sea than the rest of the world's atomic plants put together, and plans are in the making for a major extension. As the reprocessing center of nuclear waste from Japan, Spain, Sweden, the Netherlands, West Germany, Belgium, Italy, and Switzerland, it is often referred to as the "nuclear laundry."[12] Although the pipeline had discharged over a million gallons of radioactive waste *daily,* it was not until the November accident that a public outcry arose. With their beaches closed and their fish inedible, "Britons are beginning to view with a jaundiced eye their role as international nuclear garbage collector."[13] To date no decision has been made on whether to prosecute the plant owners.

Although dramatic events—blowouts, massive dumpings, giant spills, and the like—catch the public eye, there is by and large little scrutiny of the environmental stress on bodies of water, particularly those that are enclosed or semi-enclosed, by constant incursion over years, decades, or even centuries. For 4,000 years of recorded history, for example, European, Asian, and African civilizations have depended on the Mediterranean, a sea now washing 120 cities. In one decade the population of the 18 surrounding countries increased by 50 million. Some 100 million make a living from the sea, and 100 million vacation on its beaches annually. It is also a thoroughfare for over one third of the world's oil tankers. According to Dr. Tolba, executive director of the United Nations Environment Program (UNEP): "The Mediterranean, once a symbol of the sea's beneficial impact on man, has now become a symbol of man's destructive impact on it. The Mediterranean is under attack from land and sea, and from unsustainable demands of tourists who visit the area by the millions every year, from over-fishing—in short, from development that destroys."[14]

Although some seas have suffered centuries of abuse, others are more recent victims. The virtually landlocked Arabic or Persian Gulf, bordered by eight countries that enjoyed clean beaches for ages, is now considered one of the most endangered environments in the world.[15] Waste from booming industry, with investments of $20 million to $40 million per coastline kilometer, pollution from giant tankers (about 988,000 metric tons of oil are dumped each year), and refuse, 75 percent untreated, of a burgeoning coastal population are being dumped into a body of water where pollution remains unflushed by rain and fresh water.[16]

On a much smaller scale, bays, harbors, and shelf zones are consistently under environmental attack. The U.S. government plans to spend $1 million to identify polluters of Chesapeake Bay, once one of the nation's most productive fishing areas, which, according to the EPA, is so polluted "that only worms could survive."[17] Boston Harbor was recently scrutinized because of concern over sewage problems. During the first five months of 1983, 863 million gallons of brown polluted fluid were dumped into the harbor, raising the pollution level to such an extent that it "threatens the health, safety, and welfare of those using the Quincy area [near Boston] for recreation, is harmful to growing economic and tourist activities and already has endangered shellfish flats and eroded the fins of harbor flounder."[18] Long Island Sound has had its share of problems as well. Since March 1983, the U.S. Army Corps of Engineers dumped close to 200,000 cubic yards of silt into the new Western Long Island Sound III Dumping Site, located near Lloyd Harbor, to unclog the waterways of Mamaroneck Harbor. There are plans to dump 75,000 more cubic yards, taken from the badly silted Milton Harbor in Rye, New York, where the federal channel in that largely recreational harbor has not been dredged since 1976. Residents of the Lloyd Harbor area are concerned about what the metals and contaminants will do to their lobster industry. A suit has been filed in federal district court to stop all dumping at that site.[19]

Contamination: The Effects of Pollutants on Marine Life

> Water, water, every where,
> And all the boards did shrink;
> Water, water every where
> Nor any drop to drink.
>
> Samuel Taylor Coleridge,
> *The Rime of the Ancient Mariner*

Since 1976 the federal government has banned commercial fishing for striped bass along the three-hundred-mile Hudson River because of contamination by PCBs. Fishermen who make their living from the river claim that the PCB level has fallen below the danger point. But due to variability among individual fish, the New York State Department of Environmental Conservation refuses to reopen the Hudson River fishery. The president of the New York State Fishermen's Association claims otherwise—that the state is holding off the reopening not for public health reasons but to get a $20 million appropriation from Washington for dredging "hot spots." The battle rages. Meanwhile, the state maintains its warning: Don't eat more than one meal per month of Hudson River striped bass.[20] Tests of bluefish found off the New Jersey coast show that these, too, are contaminated with PCBs. Officials of that state's Department of Environmental Protection warned the public once again to limit intake of yet another fish. Moreover, children, nursing mothers, and pregnant women were advised not to eat any bluefish at all from this area.[21]

The Hudson River striped bass and the New Jersey bluefish stories are further complicated by the fact that these same fish, which have been banned from commercial fishing in New York and New Jersey, may well be migrating to Massachusetts, where they are considered the state's top game fish. Contamination levels are now being tested by the Massachusetts Health Department. Should the fish turn out to have dangerously high levels of toxic chemicals, a heavy blow would be dealt to the area's sports/fishing industry and to the many fishermen there who make their living from the sale of bass and blues.[22] As of now, however, both species continue to be caught for sport and eaten for pleasure.

Besides the human health problems created by the consumption of infected fish, biologists are worried about the effects that contaminants will have on future stocks.[23] Some believe that reproductive damage from PCBs and other toxins is responsible for the overall decline in certain species of fish, from the U.S. East Coast striped bass to the Baltic and Dutch Waddensea seals. Although the sudden death of large numbers of a given stock in any area alerts the public to pollution problems, the long-range but far greater difficulties due to reproductive damage are virtually overlooked except by scientists.

The pollution of a given area typically goes on for years, maybe decades, before anything is done about it. Toxic levels are measured and remeasured. But not until an area is *closed* and the livelihood of the fishermen disappears do the long court battles ensue—far too late for the local industries that depend on charter fishing and the sale of large catches. Take the case of two New Bedford firms that allegedly dumped PCBs directly into the harbor over a period of about thirty years. It was not until September 1979 that the state health department decided to close the inner and outer harbor after finding up to ten times the accepted level of PCBs in lobster samples. The fishing industry in that area remains dead pending the outcome of the U.S. Justice Department's landmark contamination suit (the first one filed by a government agency for damage to nonfederal property) claiming damages of millions of dollars for fish loss. Contamination is still present in the harbor's lobster, clam, eel, and flounder specimens. A drawn-out court battle is anticipated. It already took three years to try to quantify the problem, and it is expected that it will take close to another year to obtain the results of a $3.4 million EPA study. Only then can proposals for remedial action be made. It is virtually impossible to guess when the harbor might be successfully cleaned up—and the fishermen must wait,[24] as many before them have waited. Twelve years ago a small oil spill off Falmouth, Massachusetts, killed the local fish and shellfish. That area still remains closed—oil continuing to surface intermittently in the marshes.[25] Sporadically over the past five years, the Westport River shellfish beds have been closed due to pollution from area farms and septic tanks. The cost to fishermen has already climbed to $300,000. Now that the beds have reached "gross contamination" levels, the state agency responsible for the closure order is unable to give even an estimated date for lifting the ban.[26] It took almost twenty years for the once-tainted 1,372-acre clam beds along the shore at Barnegat, New Jersey, to be reopened.[27] But other polluted beds probably will remain closed permanently. Take, for example, the 20,000 acres of clam beds along Long Island's south shore. A three-year federally funded study estimated that it would cost $70 million over the next twenty years to clean up the area—an amount that the affected counties feel is simply not cost-effective.[28] Back in 1971, swordfish worth hundreds of thousands of dollars were confiscated from commercial fishermen because of high levels of mercury. Recent tests conducted in San Pedro, California, have once again—some dozen years later—found levels of mercury that have scientists concerned about the public health hazards of eating the fish. Health officials are awaiting results of further studies before deciding whether to pull the product off the market—with another loss of hundreds of thousands of dollars to fishermen.[29] Both marine environmental advocacy groups and government agencies continuously survey problem areas. For example, a two-year,

$225,000 study by the Oceanic Society of bottom life in the entire western end of Long Island Sound concluded that industrial discharges, sewage, runoff from highways, and spilled marine fuel that have been emptying into the inshore waters have left a sea bottom virtually devoid of marine life. More encouraging results came from a second study, this one done by Connecticut's Division of Agriculture. Their survey of the offshore waters of Long Island Sound found a much healthier environment for marine life and dozens of thriving species of fish and shellfish—but for how long?[30]

In another case, preliminary findings of an EPA project alleged that Dow Chemical Company discharges over forty toxic chemicals, among them a dangerous dioxin, into the Tittabawassee River in Michigan. (It is alleged that an earlier report in 1981 had been illegally censored by Dow.) The amount of poison in the river's fish pose a health hazard, but the exact risk is not yet known, so there is no outright ban on fishing as yet.[31]

And so the testing of polluted waters goes on, and warnings continue to be issued about rising toxic levels. But by and large very little is done about any given situation until it gets out of control or until it results in the serious illness or deaths of people known to have eaten tainted specimens from the polluted waters. For example, government administrators of Clarks Cove, Massachusetts, had been warning for many months that the local pollution level was rising beyond tolerable limits. But it was not until late 1983 when 19 New Yorkers became ill after eating tainted clams at a firemen's clambake that the cove was finally closed permanently.[32] For over three decades, up until 1968, mercury was discharged from a chemical plant into Minamata Bay, Japan. Again, nothing had been done to stop the polluters until a number of human deaths resulted from eating fish from those waters.[33] And most recently, in January 1984, contaminated Bangladesh shrimp were responsible for the death of 13 and serious illness of another 113 in the Netherlands.[34]

The Catch of the Day: Protection of the Species

No whale-hunting ship is more infamous than the *Sierra*—captained by a shady South African, flying a Cyprus flag, owned by a dubious Liechtenstein company, and probably supported by Japanese money. Infamous she is, since she defiles the name of the famous club, "Sierra," which stands for nature preservation. Five hundred fin whales fell prey to the *Sierra* in one year alone. Kills are made indiscriminately by methods geared to protect the meat, not the animal. Rather than dealing a quick death by explosives, *Sierra* slaughters drag on for hours while the whale slowly bleeds to death, his insides wrenched out as he fights the huge barbed spear in his belly. True to the custom of whales, the harpooned whale's mates will surface alongside him to help their stricken brother or sister. That is when the *Sierra*'s harpoons strike again and again, while the sea is red with blood and the air is filled with the sad sounds of bleeding, struggling whales.

The bloodbath inflicted on our fellow mammals—of the sea —prompted determined responses from many environmentalist groups, to whom the preservation of species is more important than industrial profit. UNEP is as concerned as are the private organizations, the Sierra Club, the Defenders of Wild Life, the Environmental Defense Fund, the World Wildlife Fund, the Friends of the Earth, and many others. But the patient path of negotiation and accommodation appeared to be too slow to some of the more militant wildlife advocates. Witness the sea battle off the coast of Portugal, in which the 210-foot trawler *Sea Shepherd*, crewed by maritime vigilantes from the Fund for Animals, pursued the pirate whaler *Sierra*.

The *Sea Shepherd* was on a mission to seek and destroy the *Sierra*. Off the coast of Portugal, the *Sea Shepherd* encountered the *Sierra*. The captain of the *Sea Shepherd* opened his throttle to twelve knots, ramming the *Sierra* with her one-hundred-ton concrete bow. The *Sierra*, suffering a big hole amidships, managed to make it into port before she sank. The incident appears not to have deterred her owner; he is reportedly building two more illegal whalers, the *Susan* and the *Theresa*, named after his daughters.[35] As much as conservationists may applaud the combat of the *Sea Shepherd* against her nefarious nemesis, the *Sierra*, this sea battle obviously runs counter to the quest for peace on the oceans. We can only repeat our earlier demand for an international maritime police force, capable of ensuring law compliance on the oceans, so that vigilantism on the high seas will become as obsolete as it is—for the most part—on dry land.

Fishing for fun affords as much pleasure as fishing for profit offers pain. Only the hardiest of men have been drawn to the life of a fisherman, where the sea is not the only enemy. There are the poachers to contend with, or the pirate fishermen who chase condemned species, and there are hostile governments seeking to protect their "territorial" sea or traditional fishing banks. Few fishermen ever sail unarmed. Every lobster boat, so we have been told, has its high-powered rifle, and, on some whalers, harpoon cannons have not just been trained on whales. Pollution, as we have just discussed above, is another enemy. And often fishermen view the law as yet another adversary. Catches are limited by laws that strive to preserve various species that appear to be on the decline. Just a few days before New York's new striped bass regulations went into effect, a local fisherman caught 150 striped bass near the Statue of Liberty, selling them for $1,400 at the Fulton Fish Market. Within a week he went out again, but under the new rules he had to throw back 108 of the 111 caught—they were less than 24 inches, the size at which striped bass can spawn. He didn't even have enough of a catch to throw back his last fish, which he does routinely for good luck at the end of every season.[36] All along the East Coast from Maine to Florida, states are asked to follow New York's lead. The emergency measures being adopted either by administrative fiat or by legislation will carry through the crisis period until egg production increases—it would have to go up threefold just to maintain the present striper population.[37]

But the striper is not the only species in trouble. To name a few, there are new offshore laws in mid-Atlantic states to protect declining summer flounder stocks,[38] to curb king mackerel catches in the Gulf of Mexico,[39] and to protect Alaska's red king crabs by shutting down fishing entirely in Bristol Bay, Kodiak, and Alaska Peninsula (perhaps until 1991).[40]

Nations zealously guard their waters against overfishing by strict laws against foreign encroachment. Just recently a Brazilian naval ship fired 30 rounds of her machine guns into a Florida-registered boat found illegally trawling for shrimp at Cape Orange, off the northern coast of Brazil. The crew of three had ignored an order to halt.[41] The U.S. government has likewise seized its share of illegal fishing vessels. One of the latest incidents involved the *Maria Michela*, a 249-foot vessel with a 35-man crew found trawling for squid about 70 miles southeast of Cape May, New Jersey. The case was turned over to federal marshals.[42]

Worldwide there is a vast disparity in penalties meted out for such violations. They range from long imprisonment (for example, in Peru and North Korea) to fines of over $50,000, plus confiscation of the boat (for example, in Guyana).[43] While nations fight to defend their turf, so too do neighboring fishermen. For example, Long Island Sound remains the center of a controversy between lobster groups, the pot lobstermen accusing the dragger fishermen of depleting the lobster population. The Massachusetts legislature is looking at a bill that would tighten up the present lobster law, imposing fines of $25 per lobster for the first violation, $50 per lobster for the second, and $100 per lobster for all subsequent violations.[44] And halfway across the country, local fishermen are asking for stringent limitations on the number of fishing licenses issued for Mississippi Sound. They claim that Vietnamese refugees who have settled along the Mississippi Gulf Coast are depleting the stock, resulting in economic hardships.[45]

Endangered species present yet another host of problems. Environmental vigilante groups take what they refer to as "ecological atrocities"[46] into their own hands—often at great risk. In July 1983, twenty-three activists in the Greenpeace movement staged a dramatic entrance into Soviet territory. Crossing the Bering Strait on their vessel *Rainbow Warrior,* they landed in a Siberian hamlet, where they scattered Russian-language anti-whaling treaties and tried to take photos of a whale-processing factory that operates in violation of international agreement. Six Americans and one Canadian were arrested. The *Rainbow Warrior* fled to Nome, Alaska, hotly pursued by a Soviet warship and helicopter. A few days later in an agreement with the U.S. State Department, a Soviet ship handed over the detained activists in a rendezvous with the *Rainbow Warrior* in the Bering Sea.[47] More recently, Greenpeace members have publicized the destruction of a thousand penguin eggs, which were destroyed in violation of an international treaty, when workers cleared an airstrip in France's Terre Adelie on the edge of Antarctica.[48] Meanwhile, the volunteers in their sister organization, Fund for Animals, have a second *Sea Shepherd* to replace the one that was impounded after the *Sierra* ramming incident. This time the seven-hundred-ton deep-water trawler, skippered by a thirty-two-year-old Canadian, is hunting ships leaving Halifax on seal expeditions.[49] Pressure groups make headlines when they head out to sea for such confrontations—but usually they take to more subtle means of species protection. Greenpeace, the Animal Welfare Institute, and the Humane Society of the United States, for example, closed ranks to stop Frionor Norsk Frossenfish A-L of Norway from processing and marketing whale meat. A campaign was mounted to persuade present and past Frionor customers not to buy products from any country which does not support whale conservation. With Long John Silver's Seafood Shoppes of Kentucky and the Friendly Ice Cream Corporation of Massachusetts withdrawing contracts worth $7 million from the Frionor processing plant in the United States, the parent company in Norway announced that it would be out of the whale meat business by 1986.[50]

Governments, too, keep a close eye on endangered species. Over a three-month period, the recently opened office of the U.S. Fish and Wildlife Service at Port Elizabeth, New Jersey, has confiscated almost $400,000 worth of banned products. One of the major hauls was an illegal shipment of 12,096 cans of soup made from sea turtles raised in the Cayman Islands and processed in Germany. Sea turtle products have been prohibited in the United States since 1979. They gain further protection under the convention on International Trade in Endangered Species, to which seventy-eight nations have become signatories.[51]

While the sea turtle, that amiable, lovable, and delicious creature of the sea gets much attention from protectionists, the whales get their greater share. And why not? Their incredible intelligence, their social behavior, and their capacity for communication make them close kin to the human. Like humans, whales can sing and express love. How more human an animal can be found in the ocean? The _Contessa Maria II_, out of the Isles of Shoals in Maine and New Hampshire, sailed among a whole family of them. They played around our ship and entertained us with their happy games, spouting off and whistling as they crossed our bow. Over the past decade, since the United Nations urged a moratorium, three hundred thousand whales have been killed. It was not until the summer of 1983 that the "save the whales" campaign scored a resounding victory. Member nations of the International Whaling Commission (IWC) voted twenty-five to seven for a five-year moratorium on commercial whaling, commencing in 1985. Unfortunately, the three nations that kill 90 percent of the whales—the Soviet Union, Japan, and Norway —opposed the draft resolution! Although IWC may have no enforcement power, individual governments do. Countries not complying with the regulations can be denied fishing rights within the two-hundred-mile national economic zones—a price most fishing nations cannot afford. Japan, for example, has a fishing industry worth ten times that of her whaling industry.[52] It appears that the nations of the world are, indeed, resigned to uphold the international resolution. Said the Agriculture Minister of seafaring Britain, host of the 1979 conference of the IWC: "I think the whale is a highly intelligent animal, and from everything I can tell, a jolly nice one as well."[53]

Safeguarding the Seas

When we first considered the inclusion of a chapter dealing with the protection of the maritime environment and its inhabitants—the fish, marine animals, and the amphibians—we were hesitant. After all, this book was to be concerned with crimes on the oceans. Yet it appears that little if any use is made of the criminal sanction in its traditional sense when it comes to the victimization of the ocean itself. Indeed, when the issue of the protection of the environment first surfaced in international discussion, at the U.N. Congress on the Environment, held at Stockholm, Sweden, in 1972, there was little call for resort to the criminal sanction. As delegates we even opposed resort to the criminal sanction for maritime environmental protection. It would have been too facile to subject fisheries offenses and marine pollution to these sanctions when it is perfectly clear that enforcement of such laws would have been a sham. Punishments under those circumstances are a placebo, detracting from the possible use of more effective measures of control. Yet nations since time immemorial have resorted to criminal penalties for pollution of the waters and the violation of fisheries laws in their own zones of effective control. Thus there are ample precedents for regarding the violation of these laws as crimes in the traditional sense. It appears, however, that such sanctions have had more success respecting the protection of marine life than they have had regarding pollution. As we pointed out, there exist innumerable problems in the criminalization of pollution offenses, not the least of which is the question of who pays the fine. If it is the company or political body that does the polluting, whether from a stationary or floating source, is it not ultimately the local citizenry who will have to bear the cost of either the fine, cleaning up the mess, or of installing antipollution devices? Such questions remain unanswered.[54] But the danger to the entire ocean environment that may result from ocean pollution —especially the deposit of nuclear waste—is one that justly concerns all humankind. Argentina has proposed creation of an international crime called geocide, consisting of the destruction of the world's ecosystem, or any substantial part thereof. But such an approach likewise has its problems. There is first of all the question of enforcing such a crime, internationally or nationally. A world criminal court is not yet in existence and barely on the horizon.[55] Second, there is the problem of defining and quantifying that crime. How much must the individual polluter contribute to the overall aura of existing pollution to be labeled a criminal?

For the time being, then, the United Nations Convention on the Law of the Sea reflects a realistic attitude based on the experience of maritime countries when it provides the following basic structure: With respect to the conservation and management of the living resources of the high seas, states have the duty to pass and enforce their own legislation within the area subject to their control. At the same time, states are obliged to collaborate "with each other in the conservation and management of living resources in the areas of the high seas."[56] We are happy to note that progress has been made regarding bilateral and regional efforts to protect marine life.

While in some areas international fishing conflicts continue unabated, especially between Japan and the U.S.S.R., the United States and Peru, and North Korea and South Korea, there are prospects for a more peaceful future. The United States and Mexico, for example, appear to be reaching some agreement over fishing zones after three years of frustrations that began with the seizure of twenty-four U.S. tuna boats in 1980 and the U.S. retaliation by an embargo on Mexican tuna products. As of August 10, 1983, Mexico had decided to issue a limited number of licenses to the Southern California tuna fleet and some other qualified vessels.[57] Other individual conflicts have begun to be settled, and regional compacts have been created (for example, among the members of the seven-country Organization of Eastern Caribbean States[58]) to draft laws covering regional cooperation and local responsibilities.

Navies traditionally have their fisheries protection vessels; some nations maintain special maritime services for that purpose (in the case of the United States, it is the U.S. Coast Guard); and some navies fulfill no function other than fisheries protection. A case in point is Iceland, a country that earns three fourths of its foreign exchange through fish exports. We have looked at the Icelandic government vessel *Thor* and her hardy men, who made history a few years ago when they braved the Royal Navy, which had come out to protect the British fishing fleet operating in waters claimed by Iceland. The *Thor* rammed several of the trawlers, intercepted a Royal Navy vessel, and bombarded her deck hands with—raw potatoes. Icelanders gained exclusive fishing rights to the North Atlantic waters surrounding their island in 1975. (It is interesting to note that although the poachers are gone, overfishing by local fishermen has resulted in the lowest cod catch in thirty-seven years.)[59]

When it comes to prevention, reduction, and control of pollution of the oceans, the U.N. Convention on the Law of the Seas takes an approach similar to that regarding fisheries. Above all, the signatory nations have bound themselves to adopt and enforce laws and regulations for the prevention and control of pollution, whether penal or regulatory, and whether emanating from land-based or floating sources, and this includes pollution by dumping. Coastal states, flag states, and port states are equally obligated. The scheme envisaged by the Law of the Sea Treaty calls for mutual assistance among states concerned, as well as further international agreements aimed at the harmonization of national, regional, and international law. The treaty does not rule out the use of criminal sanctions; on the contrary, enforcement rests largely on the imposition of fines under national legislation.[60]

Typifying the concept of international cooperation in the prevention of ocean pollution is UNEP's Regional Seas Program, agreed upon by the member states in 1974 under participation of 120 states, 14 bodies of the United Nations system, and 12 other international organizations. Accordingly, the world has been divided into ten regional seas programs:

- The Mediterranean Region (1975)
- The Red Sea Region (1976)
- The Kuwait Region (1978)
- The Wider Caribbean Region (1981)
- The West and Central African Region (1981)
- The East Asian Seas Region (1981)
- The Southeast Pacific Region (1981)
- The Southwest Pacific Region (1982)
- The East African Region (1984)
- The Southwest Atlantic Region (in the process of formation)

The regional action plans have benefited greatly from the experiences gathered by the 1974 Helsinki Convention on the Baltic Sea, whose resulting international treaty went into force in 1980, but dates back to negotiations commenced in 1968. This treaty contains provisions on land-based sources of pollution, ships, dumping, and an agreement to limit pollution from exploration and exploitation of the seabed resources, all resting on a strong empirical basis for decision-making. The regions have been very enthusiastic in drawing up their regional plans. Indeed, the West and Central African Region Program went so far as to grant its member states the "right of hot pursuit to go after oil tankers cleaning bilges in the ocean then making for the coastal waters of another country to avoid sanctions."[61] Indeed, "it is hard to think of another international forum where Libya will sit down with Israel, the U.S. with Cuba or Iran with Iraq, and agree on a common solution to their collective problems."[62] Unhappily, the Regional Seas Program is plagued by inevitable problems. There is lack of expertise and infrastructure in many of the developing countries, and consequently information on which to base action is scarce. There is next a paucity of resources. In most of the regions, governments simply have not provided the requisite finances for executing regional plans, and that may indicate the problem of priorities, which has been plaguing pollution control throughout history. A provision happily deleted in

1970 in the Japanese "Basic Law for Environment Pollution Control" exemplifies this conflict in countries undergoing rapid industrialization: "The conservation of life environment shall be balanced against the needs of economic development."[63]

It will be well to conclude this chapter with a glance at U.S. law pertaining to water pollution. There is, above all, the Water Pollution Control Act (the Clean Water Act) of 1972 and the Rivers and Harbors Act of 1899 (the Refuse Act). Both of these laws have led to a substantial number of prosecutions, resulting in heavy penalties (for example, $50,000 fine and two-year imprisonment).[64] The provisions of these laws were augmented by the provisions of the Toxic Substances Control Act (TSCA) of 1976 and the Resource Conservation and Recovery Act (RCRA) of 1976. The Clean Water Act was passed over the veto of President Nixon in light of vociferous public clamor for better pollution control.[65] The law prohibits the discharge of radiological chemical or biological warfare agents or high-level radioactive waste. It requires pretreatment of toxic substances before they are introduced into public treatment plants. Dumping in navigable waters must be done by special permit. Violations of the law are subject to criminal penalties—for willful or negligent offenses there is a fine of up to $25,000 per day of noncompliance and up to one year imprisonment for the first offense.[66]

There is every indication that the American law pertaining to the protection of marine life and the prevention of ocean pollution is meant to be serious. Despite its commitment to the drug war at sea, the U.S. Coast Guard has not neglected its duties in the enforcement of this legislation, and state and local police forces are equally serious about law enforcement in this regard. Environmental conservation officers on Long Island Sound have recently obtained an allocation of $125,000 for the purchase of seven new patrol boats,[67] and the Environmental Protection Agency has recently received a donation of two 230-ton 124.7-foot former German minesweepers as environmental patrol craft, each with a crew of 24. Anybody doubting the seriousness of marine environment offenses need only look at the engine room of the *Contessa Maria II* (or, indeed, of any other American vessel). There is prominently and permanently attached a plaque with the following text:

> ## WARNING
>
> *Discharge of Oil Prohibited*
>
> The Federal Water Pollution Control Act Prohibits the Discharge of Oil or Oily Waste Upon the Navigable Waters and Contiguous Zone of the United States, if Such Discharge Causes a Film or Sheen Upon, or Discoloration of, the Surface of the Water. Violators are Subjected to a Penalty of $5,000.

Failure to display this plaque is in itself a federal offense.

PART · V

Taming the Oceans

The Sea is still a great door
never opened. . . .

Lawrence Ferlinghetti

17

Lessons of History

•

They that go down to the sea in ships,
that do business in great waters; . . .
They mount up to the heaven, they go down again
    to the depths: their soul is melted because of trouble.
They reel to and fro, and stagger like a drunken man,
    and are at their wits' end.

Psalm 107: 23, 26, 27

Crimes at Sea in Ancient Times

IT WAS IN THE YEAR 81 B.C. that an aspiring young Roman politician, accompanied by his staff and servants, was cruising in the eastern Mediterranean en route to the island of Rhodes. Their vessel probably was a squat merchantman then in use, called a corbitar. The young politician had wanted to study rhetoric with Professor Apollonius Molon, on Rhodes, who had the reputation of being the greatest orator of his time. Even in those days, a politician's future depended very much on his oratorical skills, and Professor Molon could provide these. Near the island of Pharmacussa, the slow corbitar was spotted by a much faster naval-type vessel, which gained on her fast. To the Romans' dismay, their pursuer proved to be a pirate. The encounter was fierce and brief. Some of the Romans died in hand-to-hand combat; the others were taken prisoner. The pirate captain had the Romans' leader brought to his quarters and informed him that he would hold him for a ransom of twenty talents. At that the Roman laughed in the pirate's face. Didn't they know whom they had captured? The great Gaius Julius Caesar, of a family descended from the goddess Venus! "Raise your ransom demand to fifty talents!" That amounted to twelve thousand pieces of gold! The pirate captain gleefully obliged. Most of Caesar's men were sent ashore to borrow the amount from relatives and friends; only Caesar's physician and two valets remained with him on the pirate ship, manned by "Cilicians, about the most bloodthirsty people in the world." Plutarch tells us that Caesar treated his captors with the greatest disdain. He made them listen to his poems and speeches and called them barbarians whenever they failed to react properly. More than once he threatened that someday he would crucify them all.

No sooner had the twelve thousand gold pieces arrived and Caesar and his companions had been put ashore on the island of Miletus than he raised a private navy with heavily armed and swift vessels and manned by experienced fighting men. It did not take Ceasar very long to locate the pirate ship. A brief naval engagement ensued, and those pirates who did not die in combat were taken prisoner. Caesar kept his word: He crucified every one of them, yet he showed mercy to those who had treated him with respect. Caesar's mercy consisted in having them killed before being nailed to the cross. Obviously he recovered his twelve thousand gold pieces, but also all of the pirates' considerable loot and their vessel.

Plutarch commented: "The pirates . . . even at that time, controlled the seas with their large fleets of ships and innumerable smaller craft."[1] The power of Rome, whose armies had occupied or subdued most of the Mediterranean lands, was not up to the task of controlling crime on the seas. The continued warfare among the Mediterranean countries made it difficult to establish peace on the ocean. Yet merchant vessels with rich cargoes, and supply vessels with armament, were attractive to the outlaws of the sea. Corrupt governors often provided protection to the pirates' fleets. The gain was potentially vast, the investment small, and the risks minimal. The pirates had the advantage of geography—the countless islands of the eastern Mediterranean, with their many bays and inlets, which afforded safe harbor and escape. This classical phase of piracy, with all its characteristic hallmarks, was bound to continue until a semblance of order was restored in Rome's internal and external affairs. In 67 B.C., in a three-month campaign, Pompeius cleaned the pirates out of the Mediterranean. Ironically, Pompeius was the archrival of pirate victim Caesar. After Pompeius' success, a standing fleet enforced the uniform law of Rome. Crime on the seas was under control. The sea lanes remained relatively secure, but only for as long as the strength of Rome lasted, and not a day longer.

The piracy of the Roman era of history was by no means the first wave of Mediterranean piracy. In his *Odyssey,* Homer tells us of the "rovers" who, in about 1184 B.C., made the Mediterranean unsafe. Ulysses' son, Telemachus, nearly fell victim to a murder plot on the high seas. Said his mother, Penelope, with a sigh:

> And now murder is hatched on the high sea against his son, who sought news of his father in the holy land of Pylos and Lakedeimon.[2]

If it was tough for the Romans to bring crime on the sea under control, it must have been even harder for the Greeks, operating in the same waters, under the same geographic conditions that favored pirates, yet at a time when strife and conflict were so pronounced that central control was out of the question. And their vessels were far less seaworthy than the Romans'. The Greeks' triremes, with three banks of oars on each board, required a large crew, thus limiting their operating radius. The long-distance sailing vessels of the time—Ulysses' ship *Argo,* for example—were basically open vessels subject to the vagaries of wind and sea. Square-riggers with single masts, their maneuverability was limited. Their long voyages, with rich cargo or war booty, would lead them past the Aegean Islands, where the rovers and pirates had their lairs, with little need to go on long voyages.

Nor had the Greeks been the only ones to suffer these frustrations. On the southeastern shores of the Mediterranean the Phoenicians, forebears of many of today's Lebanese, went through the same experience. Their advanced mercantile system saw their ships all over the Aegean Sea, carrying grain and wine, oil and spices, textiles and glassware, metal products and jewelry, as early as 1000 B.C. Such wealth on the water was bound to attract pirates, and those Phoenicians who were too poor or too lazy to trade, or to create the goods to be traded, turned pirates and plagued their own countrymen. There was no machinery for control of the sea. It was every ship for herself.

History has a habit of hiding essential facts. We do not know what terminated the sea crime wave that had plagued the Greeks and the Phoenicians. Was it the Draconian laws, or the wise legislation of Solon, embraced by all Greeks? More likely it was the Athenian (or Attic) Maritime Confederation of 476 B.C., which resulted in the creation of a common Greek fleet for the defense of all isles and shores, a mighty fleet to which all city-states had to contribute vessels and crew under common command. Certainly history reports much less sea criminality after this great task-force approach for dealing with insecurity on the high seas. And a few generations later, during the time of Alexander the Great (reign 336–323 B.C.), the peace on the sea was extended even to the Asian seas.

In this brief review of maritime crime in antiquity, we have encountered the names of places that were to reappear in history. "The holy land of Pylos," of the *Odyssey*, was to be the place where, nearly two and a half millennia later, a tramp steamer named *Betty* was changed to be the *Five Star*, and a huge piracy —modern-style—commenced. And Phoenicia-Lebanon! Remember Chapter 9, "Piracy: The Jolly Roger Flies Again"?

So what does antiquity have to teach us? For crimes on the sea to flourish, you need a recipe not all that hard to concoct:

- Take a maritime geography which favors local outlaws and disfavors distant law enforcers
- Add the chance of enormous profit at little risk
- Mix it generously with strife, internal and external
- Avoid maritime law-enforcement capacity, and do not add common law!
- Corruption helps for spicing! Make it hot.

Merchant Marauders of the Middle Ages

The Prospect of Whitby is not your ordinary London pub. Tourists do not normally stop by. Nor does it seem to be an average neighborhood hangout. But it's always been there, sitting right on the Thames, and the tides swirl the riffraff of the river around the ancient walls that separate land from water. We sipped Pusser's Navy Rum, the Union Jack brightly emblazoned on the label. What would the pirates of old have guzzled at The Prospect of Whitby? This is the spot, en route to the place of execution, where the sentenced pirates had their last earthly stop for a wee drink before their heads would roll, or their bodies would hang, right on the edge of the water. In accordance with the custom of sea-bordering peoples, especially the Frisians, who had settled at the Thames a millennium earlier, execution had to take place below the high-water mark, presumably so that the returning tide would keep the soul of the executed from returning.[3] The corpses or impaled heads of the executed outlaws of the ocean would be prominently displayed at water's edge as a warning to wayward seafarers and as a landmark of sea law and sea lane.

This is England, spawned by the biggest wave of piracy of all time. In the eighth century a rambunctious lot of sailors with an intense drive to explore and to exploit started sailing their small, graceful, and immensely seaworthy craft (two of which may still be admired in Oslo and Schleswig) out of their lairs in the Baltic and North seas, seeking fortune and adventure. They sailed for five centuries. Coming from the North, they were of course called the "Northmen," or Norsemen, or Normans, or Vikings. And the latter term became virtually synonymous with pirates. Their fleets visited (and we use this term with its double meaning) the entirety of the continent of Europe. There being not much to take at sea, they plundered the lands. In A.D. 787, they landed their first marauding party in England. They next sacked the cities of the Frankian Empire. They would sail their vessels as far as river navigation would permit; then they went on horseback—plundering and devastating. Antwerp was sacked in 836, Rouen in 841, Nantes in 843, Paris and Hamburg in 845, and Bordeaux in 847. By 859 a Viking fleet was plying the Mediterranean, devastating the Rhône Valley and the Italian coastline. Pisa was attacked in 860. Between 881 and 886, the Vikings besieged or devastated Maastricht, Luttich, Aachen, Julich, Cologne, and Paris. During the tenth century they moved east and south, traversing the whole of Russia, from the Finnish Bay through Moscow all the way down to the Black Sea. Constantinople was besieged many times.

This was the biggest piracy of all time. And yet something very strange happened. Outlaws became in-laws. The ruins we studied in the old Swedish royal capital of Uppsala attest to it. Grave markers would say something like this: "Here rests Gunnar Gunnarson, who returned home to die on native soil, after

having served the Emperor in Constantinople as a loyal guardsman for twenty years." And the Vikings settled in the North of
France, where Rollo established a kingdom. His successor William the Conqueror invaded England in 1066, linking up with
his Norman-Viking cousins to establish what was to become the
empire that ruled the waves.

We are retelling well-known history, but we are doing so for
a reason. For five centuries piracy ruled the Western world—
even to North America, where Norman remnants still are recognizable. It was the ultimate triumph of crime on the crests, for
there was no effective resistance. Where was the law? Piracy was
the law! Yet the pirates became co-opted into the maelstrom of
human civilization. To continue maritime crime would have
been suicide and genocide. Instead, the new order of the Western world emerged—England and France, Russia and Sweden,
Norway and Denmark, Germany and Italy, after five centuries of
ocean lawlessness carried in the holds of graceful Viking ships.

The Middle Ages, that dark era of human history, was to
witness yet another upsurge of ocean criminality. The Vikings
had barely settled down when their descendants got the whiff of
tremendous profit—for little investment. By the twelfth century,
trade in the Baltic and North seas was booming. Regions and
cities had developed their indigenous capacities to produce and
to manufacture. The need arose to ship the goods produced at
place A to place C in exchange for the goods that place B wanted
to deliver to place A. A new type of vessel had been developed,
the "Kogge," a fortresslike vessel with a forecastle, ("fo'c'sle")
and an aftcastle, capable of carrying cargoes for great distances,
armed, and yet vulnerable to locally based vessels that could
outsail these heavy behemoths. The merchants of the Baltic and
North Sea ports took their licking. The Emperor of the "Holy
Roman Empire of the German Nation" (which was neither holy,
nor Roman, nor really an empire, and a German nation did not
exist) could not protect the merchants. Self-help was called for,
so under the dominance of the city of Lübeck, the Hanseatic
League was created in the twelfth century, with Hamburg and
Bremen as partners. London and Bergen (Norway) soon were
members, and ultimately all of the northern-European trading
cities (port or not) had joined, paying tribute into the league's
coffers to equip and maintain a powerful fleet that could repel
the pirates.

In 1979 we sat at dinner in Lübeck, yet the menu was of 1403: swan and boar, sturgeon and crayfish, and all the delicacies that the herb gardens of the Middle Ages could provide. From time to time Lübeck and the other Hanseatic League cities celebrate their victory over Störtebecker—the most notorious of the league's enemies—with a meal just like then! Störtebecker, having created havoc with the merchants' vessels, had finally been apprehended, but only because one of his men had betrayed him. Led to the place of execution, Störtebecker was granted the condemned man's customary last wish: "Yes, grant freedom to all of my condemned men, in line, that I shall pass after my head is severed." The judges agreed, with smirks on their faces. Störtebecker's head rolled—yet, erect and headless, he walked past the line of his pirates and collapsed just before he reached the last, the one who had betrayed him, so legend says.[4]

The Hanseatic League had conquered the maritime criminality of its time by a strong common commitment to law enforcement on the high seas. The league died a gradual death, not just for the want of pirates, but because the world's trade moved elsewhere: India and the New World!

London, whose "Steelyard" (or *Stahlhof,* as the Lübeckers called it) had been the mainstay of the medieval trade, now was gearing up to be the pivot of the maritime trade of the new era and of its accompanying criminality. And all the while the outlaws of the ocean went into London's Prospect of Whitby to wet their throat as long as they still had one.

Criminals of Colonial Commerce

Sails dropped at no-wake speed, the *Contessa Maria II* approached her anchorage among the Isles of Shoals, Maine or New Hampshire, as you wish (some are in Maine, some in New Hampshire). The water is clear and the air is crisp. "Two fathoms, drop anchor." Down goes the anchor at exactly the spot —we are sure!—where pirate captains such as Teach ("Blackbeard"), Quelch, Kidd, and Bonnet dropped their hooks. The *Mermaiden* reputedly was the first pirate vessel to have called at the islands, late in the seventeenth century. These isles, seven miles out of Portsmouth, New Hampshire, and Kittery, Maine, provided ideal anchorages for the pirates of the late seventeenth and early eighteenth centuries. It was about as far north as they cared to go, or had to go, to escape from their more favored hunting grounds, the West Indies, whenever it got too hot down there for their operations. Whenever a semblance of law enforcement would reign in the Caribbean, the pirates would either head east, for Africa, or come north. Theirs was no longer a local trade. They had become worldwide operators, which is just a way of saying that the world had expanded. The world no longer was a Mediterranean pond; it was a globe of mostly water with a few land masses sprinkled between, just to make navigation a bit easier. And the roving Vikings had pointed the way. For all we know, they too had called at the Isles of Shoals. "Vineland" they called the North American landmass, the land of wine, which is probably the biggest travel agency promotion fraud in history. (Although, by now, New Hampshire does produce wine of sorts.)

We were reminded of the Viking connection when, near the Isles of Shoals, we encountered a thirty-foot sailboat with a lone, bearded sailor aboard. The vessel came from the open Atlantic, flying the Swedish flag. Having Swedish guests aboard the *Contessa Maria II,* we set a small Swedish courtesy flag on our flagline and hailed her. The skipper waved and smiled, not at all surprised to see the flag of his country. Questions and answers were exchanged. Had he just crossed the Atlantic? *Jo!* Good crossing? *Jo!* Any problems? *Nej!* Nothing to it for a Viking.

The anchorages of the Isles of Shoals are well protected from view and weather by hills on all the isles. The bottom holds anchors easily, even of the substantial vessels the pirates brought here. In this anchorage the crews could apply a new coat of paint to their ships and switch from the skull and crossbones to the royal standard, pretending to be just another honest trader. They could bury their treasures here; some of them have since been found. But $250,000 worth still are reputedly there. Here the pirates could resupply their vessels by provisions brought over from the mainland, but they could also make profitable sorties from here, preying on the rich trade between New England and England or France, and especially the contraband trade coming in from the Caribbean: rum, sugar, molasses, and spices. The rum route had been well established, some of the leading citizens ashore were growing rich by it, and the pirates were simply looking for their share.

On the isles themselves the pirates did not find much sympathy or support among the "Shoalers," a close-mouthed, close-knit lot of fisherfolk. There was not much they could do about the presence of those heavily armed rogues in their waters except one thing: complain to the Royal Navy. That had results. Royal naval vessels increased their patrols and engaged the pirates. Several pirates were hanged in Boston and, by about 1725, the pirate spook at the northern point of the pirate trek had come to an end.[5] But now it was the smugglers who had to contend with the Royal Navy patrols. And any Rhode Islander can tell you proudly that it was that damn Royal Navy station ship of Providence, R.I., the frigate *Rose* (which you can still see there in full replica), that started Rhode Island's independence two months prematurely. Her vigorous antismuggling operations had antagonized the local merchants, who had grown rich through smuggling.[6]

What had given rise in the first place to what we call the colonial era of piracy? The credit should go to the French. The Spanish conquistadores had just started to loot the enormous wealth of Central and South America, and tales of treasure galore had been spreading all over Europe in those early years of the 1500s when the French decided to persecute their Protestant countrymen, the Huguenots. Many fled France. Some went to America. As early as 1510 French corsairs were marauding the coast from Nova Scotia to Brazil. In the West Indies we find some of them as early as 1530, under the leadership of Pierre le Grand (d'Escambuc) of Dieppe, engaged in local piracy. They settled on the island of La Tortue, an hour's sail north of the coast of Santo Domingo, now Haiti. From there they could control the passages through which the Spanish gold and silver galleons had to exit into the Atlantic.

On his third voyage to America, Columbus had to change course to avoid French pirates, corsairs, who had lain in wait for him off Cape St. Vincent, under the great French "sea heroes" Jean Bart and Surcouf (after whom the French Navy was later to name some of its proudest ships). Over the years these French developed a vessel type called *flibustier* or *flibots* (or, in English, "flyboats") because of the enormous speed they could reach. Hence these pirates were often referred to as *flibustiers*—from which we derived the term filibuster, adventurer. They were also referred to as buccaneers because, while inhabiting Santo

Domingo, they hunted cattle that had turned wild, dried the meat over boucans (open fire pits), and used the meat for trade. Since they smelled of the bucan fires, they naturally deserved the term buccaneers. By 1625 the buccaneers had formed a brotherhood on St. Kitts dedicated to plundering the Spanish commerce and based on extraordinarily democratic principles. The captain had authority only in combat. He was elected by the crew, and at all other times he lived with the crew—share and share alike.

The buccaneers had no shortage of recruits. Young men fleeing Europe's poverty, persecution, and misery flocked to the West Indies. Runaway African slaves and Arawak Indians, English prisoners bearing marks of branding, Dutch refugees from Spanish oppression—they all came and formed the enormous might of the largest piracy force since the Vikings. The Dutch among them built their own type of swift attack vessel, the *vrij buits*. The name stuck, and the pirates had acquired yet another name: freebooters.

The clumsy Spanish galleons were no match for the swift attack vessels. By 1536 the French corsair fleet probably numbered forty vessels. Yet French influence began to decline, without ever withering away. As late as the early nineteenth century, French pirate captains were operating in the Gulf of Mexico, and without the help of one of them, Jean Lafitte, General Andrew Jackson ("Old Hickory") might not have been able to win the Battle of New Orleans in 1815. For that great deed to the United States, President Madison pardoned Lafitte and his corsairs of all their acts of piracy.

The decline of French influence among the colonial pirates during the sixteenth century was due to the ascendancy of the English. Francis Drake, more than any other, must have inspired his countrymen. Armed with a commission from Queen Elizabeth, whose favorite he was, and ample financial backing by the Queen and powerful London interests, Drake set out ostensibly to explore and open the riches and the seaways of the world for the English crown. In fact, in 1572 he attacked the Spanish Main on the Atlantic side. On his trip around the world (1577–80) he raided the unprotected Spanish American West Coast in Chile, amassing enormous booty, which he increased by the capture of a Manila galleon. Back in England, he paid his backers 4,700 percent on their investment. Elizabeth knighted him. Perhaps this knighthood was warranted *ex post facto,* when, with the help of God, a hurricane, and Lord Howard of Effingham, Drake defeated the Spanish Armada in 1588 after he had made yet another profitable sortie to the Caribbean.

Other Englishmen joined the profitable trade of privateering, which differed little from piracy. Commissions to harass the Spaniards were freely granted to all comers, and especially Englishmen, by the Dutch, the Huguenots in France, and the English crown, which realized profit from such concessions during hard times. Indeed, the times were once again so hard that sailors by the thousands joined the free and potentially prosperous life of privateers and pirates.

It cannot be our purpose to recount the history of piracy. That has been done by others, ably and frequently. We are confining ourselves to an identification of its salient features in an effort to find out what it is that at different times in history, yet so often in the same regions, gives rise to virtual tidal waves of ocean criminality. And no region is more illustrative than the Caribbean, no period more demonstrative than that long colonial period from the early 1500s to the early 1800s. Not that this was an uninterrupted stretch of history. It has its distinct phases: the French phase, which we described, followed by a largely English phase, and an English and Yankee phase.

The first English phase began undoubtedly with Sir Francis Drake and included such later privateer-pirates as Sir Walter Raleigh, Thomas Cavendish, and Sir Henry Morgan, who, as we described earlier, sacked Panama City in 1671 (and Portobelo in 1668). This phase ended with the war of the Grand Alliance in 1689, which saw not only the establishment of a powerful naval-police force in the region but which also, in effect, gave freebooters a chance to become legitimate (again) as privateers, accountable to their governments.

But the Caribbean peace was of short duration. The European wars spilled over, and each new strife brought the opportunity for more privateering. The chance of vast profit tempted more privateers into piracy. The pirates did well for themselves: For a year or two under sail as a pirate, a sailor might earn the income of an earl, instead of a pound a year under the brutal and harsh conditions of the Royal Navy or the merchant fleet. Nor was it hard to hide greed behind the façade of morality: The Spaniards were papists, *they* were greedy and possessive, and brutal in exploiting the Incas and the Mayas and all the indigenous nations they had suppressed.

The Spaniards countered every move of the pirate-privateers. Their vessels now sailed in convoys, heavily escorted by carracks. Havana was their easternmost fortress-harbor. Here the incoming fleets would divide: Half the convoy would sail south to Cartagena di Indies (today's foremost drug exportation center); the other half would sail to Nombre de Dios or Portobelo. There they would unload the supplies for their forces, and load the plunder of the Americas for the Spanish court. On the Panamanian coastline they even received the plunder of the Philippines, carried in galleons all the way across the Pacific and then by land route to the Caribbean coast. At Havana the vessels coming from the various mainland ports would unite again for the convoy to Spain. That meant that the vessels were most vulnerable to attack while in the Caribbean. There the Spaniards had the ingenious idea of establishing a Coast Guard, *guarda costa*, with station ships at the choke points of the Windward Passage, and at the ports of the Spanish Main (the mainland). Piracy got to be more difficult in the West Indies. But word was spreading of fabulous riches to be had in the East Indies, the eastern coast of Africa, and the Arabian Sea.

Indeed, there were fabulous treasures afloat on the other side of the world, as enticing as those of the West Indies—if not more so. The English, the Dutch, and the Portuguese were competing for empires in Asia. The British East India Company (established in 1600 by Queen Elizabeth) and the Dutch East India Company had become empires. Their fleets and forces did pretty much the same as the Spaniards had been doing all along, in the Americas and the Philippines: exploiting the local wealth, establishing plantations, and ferrying the wealth back home. So far, during the seventeenth century, the armed merchant vessels of the trading companies had done quite well against the traditional pirates of the Indian Ocean. That was to change as soon as the Caribbean pirates transferred their operations to that part of the world where the Great Mogul of India ruled over a vast and wealthy Islamic empire. Charles II had granted the East India Company the right to grab land, property, and wealth from those whom they considered infidels wherever possible, and the Caribbean pirates now sailing these waters grabbed that wealth from the East India Company, if not from the Great

Mogul directly. The pirates would attack vessels when encountered alone, preferably when storm-crippled. They soon established their own bases of operation—on the small island of Ste. Marie, off Madagascar; then on Madagascar itself; then on the Malabar Coast between Bombay and Mangalore. John (Long Ben) Avery established a virtual pirate kingdom on Madagascar, run like a regular nation—with the wealth he obtained from the capture of the Great Mogul's personal ship, probably the greatest treasure ever to fall into pirates' hands. That was by no means John Avery's only exploit! Earlier he took over the ship *The Duke,* built in England and sold to Spain as a Coast Guard vessel. He turned *The Duke* into the opposition of the Coast Guard.

The English Caribbean pirates were speedily joined in the Indian Ocean by Yankee pirates. The ship *Resolution* and the Rhode Island-outfitted ship *John and Rebecca* soon were raiding the merchant vessels of Muscat. In a countermove, the Royal Navy sailed to Ste. Marie, offering pardons to the pirates. They found few takers. The business was too profitable. At a minimum the pirates could take a shipload full of slaves from Africa back to America. We have stood at hills in Africa where the villagers would point in the direction of the sea: That's where our brothers and sisters were taken by the slavers!

The Indian Ocean piracy was so profitable that it had an invigorating impact on the economy of the North American colonies. Governor Granfield of New Hampshire noted, in 1684, that every man on a returning Malabar Coast pirate vessel brought seven hundred pounds sterling in loot with him, and "Arab gold" had become common currency in New York.

In the meantime, the East India traders had armed themselves more heavily and were traveling in convoys, which was tough on the pirates. So many of them headed back to the Caribbean for a great new fling at New World piracy, the "Golden Age" of piracy, dating roughly from 1695 to 1725. After all, the "commerce" had to go on. The demand was there in the North American colonies, and since the Navigation Acts had made it impossible to bring in the riches of the world legitimately and at reasonable cost, smugglers and pirates had to fill the void. Elsewhere we have described the incredible greed and corruption in North America, among pro- and anti-English alike, that facilitated this unholy and bloody trade and that in-

volved even the Livingston family, for which one of the colleges
of our university is named.

This was the age of John (Long Ben) Avery, whose exploits
were to be portrayed in Ben Johnson's play *The Successful Pyrate,*
performed at Drury Lane Theatre, London, in 1713. And then
there was Samuel (Black) Bellamy, who, anxious to see his
fifteen-year-old girlfriend, supposedly ran a treasure-laden ship,
the *Whidah,* aground off Cape Cod. And there were William
Kidd; Thomas Tew; John Halsey, a Boston man (who had re-
solved to take on only "Moors"); Captains Condent (whose
exploits in Brazilian waters are known, but whose first name is
not) and Thomas White of Plymouth; William Fly; Thomas
Howard; Cornelius Lewis; David Williams; Samuel Burgess;
Nathaniel North of Bermuda; Thomas Murdock from New
Brunswick, New Jersey (our university's main campus!); Bar-
tholomew ("Black Bart") Roberts, who took four hundred ships;
and Edward Teach ("Blackbeard"), who, finally, on November
17, 1718, was killed in hand-to-hand combat by Lieutenant Robert Maynard of H.M.S. *Pearl.* And let us not forget those infamous two ladies of the piracy trade, Anne Bonny and Mary
Reed, of whom it is said that they excelled in all but one of the
most ancient professions, that one being medicine.

Why did they all choose piracy? At an annual profit of from
£1,500 to £4,000, compared to a wage of £1 a year, what greater
incentive? Even the governor of the East India Company earned
only £300 per annum, and his clerks, £5! As the laws stood, you
would hang for stealing a pound out of a man's pocket. So why
not steal a fortune?

But perhaps nobody stated the real reasons as well as pirate
Captain Samuel (Black) Bellamy, addressing those of a captured
merchantman who refused to join his pirate crew:

> Damn ye, you are a sneaky puppy, and so are all those who will
> submit to be governed by laws which rich men have made for their
> own security, for the cowardly whelps have not the courage other-
> wise to defend what they get by their knavery. But damn ye alto-
> gether. Damn them for a pack of crafty rascals, and you, who serve
> them, for a parcel of hen-hearted numbsculls. They vilify us, the
> scoundrels do, then there is only this difference, they rob the poor
> under cover of law, forsooth, and we plunder the rich under the
> protection of our own courage: had ye not better make one of us,
> than sneak after the arses of those villains for employment?[7]

After the Royal Navy had shut down pirate operations in Madagascar in 1716, they flourished again in the Caribbean, at least for a few more years, mostly Bahama-based. Indeed, Royal Navy vessels were not averse to reaping a share from pirate operations. Yet gradually the forces of law won the upper hand. Under Governors Bellamont and Nicholson, the ports of New York and New England were closed to the pirate trade. Honest administrators took over, the Navy became more and more professional, and a sense of international responsibility on the oceans took hold.

Of course, piracy was to linger in the Caribbean until well into the nineteenth century, but those latter-day pirates now stole potatoes and the first products of the industrial revolution. President Monroe sent the Navy down to put an end to the last vestiges of Caribbean sea crime. The Barbary Coast pirates of the early nineteenth century, along the North African shoreline, were similarly put down by the U.S. Navy, the forerunner of our Sixth Fleet; and "Old Ironside," the U.S.S. *Constitution,* played a leading role.

Except for brief outbursts here and there, it seemed piracy had ceased to exist except in the South China Sea and except for its resurgence in the twentieth century, amply described earlier in this book.

The Supercargos' Accounting

We feel like supercargos, the ships' officers responsible for the commercial concerns of the voyage, who make marks for the bales and casks being loaded and unloaded, adding it all up, and accounting to the entrepreneurs. The entrepreneurs? They're our readers. What does it all add up to?

By our accounting, there were three separate phases of crime on the sea in antiquity: the Greek, the Phoenician (overlapping), and the Roman. In the Dark Ages there were at least two big phases: the Viking era, and that of the time of the early Hanseatic League (not counting piracies during that time affecting the Indian Ocean and the Levantine). During the colonial era of history there was one huge stretch of ocean criminality, which, as we have noted earlier, can be conveniently divided into the first, the French phase; the second, the largely English phase; and the third, the English and Yankee phase, geographically stretching from the Caribbean to the Indian Ocean and back. The fourth era of sea crime, of the nineteenth and twentieth centuries, again has three major phases: the first, during the years of the early American republic; the second, during Prohibition; and the third, worldwide today (the second and third phases have been covered in other chapters).

As for the geography of crime on the ocean, the globe itself provides the limit, but the reappearance of piracy and other sea crimes in certain areas is remarkable: the (especially eastern) Mediterranean; the Baltic and North seas; the North American and Caribbean coastlines; and the Indian Ocean, from the eastern coast of Africa to the South China Sea. But it is not just geography that matters as far as sea criminality is concerned. Geography is only the facilitator in that it combines two elements: transit need on the one hand, and the opportunity to base and to shelter criminal attack vessels on the other. Criminality on the oceans requires much more than geography to flourish. And it is here that our brief historical survey may assist us:

During all eras of crime on the seas there was a vast economic incentive to turn outlaw and to prey on legitimate ocean commerce. Cargoes of unimaginable value were being transported: gold and wine, pearls and jewels, grain and drugs. To the extent that the import and export of such goods was legally restrained, that in itself provided an incentive to become an outlaw of the ocean. How much greater an incentive it is simply to take such a valuable cargo by force! Piracy comes into existence. For piracy truly to flourish, a corrupt officialdom and/or merchant class is needed, especially to "launder" ill-gotten gains. But above all, it requires a nonexistent or confused legal and enforcement system. During none of the eras of piracy here surveyed was there a congruence of law, an agreement on law enforcement. Indeed, all periods of sea criminality are marked by political and military strife, internally or externally. As soon as this strife is terminated, as soon as there is agreement on laws, standards, and enforcement, crime on the seas decreases.

In all periods of sea crime there were large, exploited, unemployed, dissatisfied population groups providing willing recruits for the hordes of criminals of the sea, at low risk, since law enforcement was minimal. Any moral qualms usually could be overcome by the argument that the values attacked were tainted, the result of exploitation. Sociopolitical disorganization constitutes a further contributing factor. How easy it has been, and still is, to slip into and out of legitimate and illegitimate trades of the sea! The biggest blame for the existence of sea criminality seems to lie with the laws themselves, the Navigation Acts, the Stamp Acts, the import-export laws. No, we are not going so far as to say that if we did not have laws against theft, there would be no crime of boat theft, or if there were no law against the importation of drugs, there would be no drug smuggling. Yet "rum running" ceased with the end of Prohibition. Nations have to make their choices!

Above all, all eras of high crime on the high seas are marked by a conflict of jurisdiction, an unresolved question as to who can and should intervene, and by a lack of operational capacity to do something about it. When the criminals of the sea have no one to fear, they can function unmolested. When their vessels are superior to those of the law enforcers, they will succeed.[8]

If you sailed New England waters in August 1983, as we did on the *Contessa Maria II,* and if you passed the waters off Marconi Beach, near Cape Cod, you might have spotted the seventy-five-foot *Vast Explorer 2* and the twenty-five-foot *Expedition Whidah* combing the ocean floor for what might be left of history— history being Captain Samuel (Black) Bellamy's private–slave–trade–treasury ship the *Whidah,* wrecked in a gale in 1717, toward the end of the "Golden Age" of piracy. There is supposed to be $80 million worth of gold on that three-hundred-ton ship, if she is still there. How close are we all to exploiting what history has left us?[9] Alas, Congress wisely proposes to protect the remnants of the exploiters from exploitation by modern pirates.[10] History, whether above or below the level of the sea, is national treasure, common human treasure.

18

Charting a Course for the Future

•

Gentle breath of yours my sails
Must fill, or else my project fails,
Which was to please. Now I want
Spirits to enforce, art to enchant;
And my ending is despair
Unless I be relieved by prayer;
which pierces so that it assaults
Mercy itself, and frees all faults.
As you from crimes would pardon'd be,
Let your indulgence set me free.

William Shakespeare,
from Prospero's Epilogue
in *The Tempest*

Crime on the oceans is a fact of contemporary life. It was equally a fact of life during earlier periods of history, and there probably was no time since humans made their first raft, or hollowed out trees to make their first boats, that the oceans were entirely free from crime. Yet boats and ships are meant to be instruments of salvation for humankind. If the Bible is to be believed, we all owe our survival to the grand vessel built by Noah, the Ark. And Moses, the recipient of the Ten Commandments, owes his life to survival in a tiny craft, as, according to Roman history, do Romulus and Remus, the founders of Rome. But since the oceans have been turned into crime scenes, and ships into instruments and objects of crime, and sailors have become criminals as well as victims, what can be done about it?

Let us explore a few strategies that the experiences of the past and the present appear to suggest.

302

Don't Go Near the Water!

"Don't go near the water!" Mueller remembers his mother's admonition well. But what is an adventuresome four-year-old to do when he sees the sparkling water of the river only a block from his home? Peasants would stalk their flatboats up and down the river, with feed or cattle aboard. Spring, when the river widened to three times its normal width, brought from the mountains the log rafts skillfully navigated around the river's bend by muscular and bearded lumberjacks and rafters. And summer would bring whole fleets of kayaks gaily decorated with pennants. Every once in a while you could see a little sailboat. And the biggest excitement was the occasional appearance of the river inspector in a small motorboat. A few miles down the river you could still see the docks from which the Hessian soldiers had embarked on flatboats for the trip to Bremerhaven and thence to America to fight for George III and against the "American rebellion."

Of course, Mueller did not heed his mother's injunction, and he went to the river's edge to float his turn-of-the-century scale-model steamship. Of course, the steamship got away, capsized, and sank. Of course, Mueller fell into the river and, had it not been for a very ancient lady chancing by, who resolutely fished him out of the water with her cane, he would not have co-authored this book.

Use of "don't go near the water," that ancient injunction, is one method of avoiding crime on the waterways. It usually doesn't work. The call of the oceans—especially in the face of an injunction to the contrary—proves stronger. Besides, the chances of being victimized by crime are considerably greater on land than they are on water, unless you happen to live in one of those few countries mentioned in Adler's book *Nations Not Obsessed With Crime,* [1] those fortunate few countries with exceedingly low crime rates. No, we suggest you *do* go near the water and *do* your share to fight crime on the oceans.

Don't Go Overboard!

Crime and punishment. We hear this ancient distinctive cry for revenge and retribution each time we hear of a crime committed, a fellow human victimized. The thought of potential crime makes us call for punishment—as deterrence. The history of punishment for crimes committed on the sea, and particularly the use of ships for punishment, constitutes one of the darkest chapters of human evolution. To this day, some believe that the harsher the punishment, the greater the security of the seas from crime. Remember Caesar's crucifying the pirates! But the crucifixions didn't drive the pirates out of the Mediterranean. Pompeius' naval task force cleansed that sea of its criminals.

By the late Middle Ages even petty crimes and disciplinary infractions were subjected to cruel punishments; abandonment on isolated islands, keelhauling (which normally left the poor culprit dead), and whipping with the cat-o'-nine-tails. Capital sentences included walking the plank, hanging from the yard-arm, or, as happened to poor Mary Lee on board the ship *Charity* en route to the province of Maryland in 1654, torturing and then hanging on charges of being a witch.[2] The brutal sea was brutal because man made it so! An escalation, reminiscent of the modern arms race, ultimately led to staggering brutality by law enforcers and lawbreakers alike, devoid of human sentiment, oblivious to meaningful regulation of human conduct. These were the true Dark Ages of the Oceans—despite the great voyages of discovery that led others to proclaim those days to be the Renaissance. What did the pirate say? I'd hang for stealing a pound. I might as well hang for stealing a thousand!

As for arbitrary and brutal punishments inflicted by ships' captains or crew members for violation of ships' discipline or other infractions, rampant throughout the nineteenth century, the laws of most countries have put a definite stop to it. For the United States, Article 2191 of the Federal Criminal Code (Title 18, U.S.C.), provides:

> Whoever, being the master or officer of a vessel of the United States, on the high seas, or on any other waters within the admirality and maritime jurisdiction of the United States, flogs, beats, wounds, or without justifiable cause, imprisons any of the crew of such vessel, or withholds from them suitable food and nourishment, or inflicts upon them any corporal or other cruel and unusual punishment, shall be fined not more than $1,000 or imprisoned not more than five years, or both.

Our recital of the horrors of punishment is not a rejection of the use of criminal justice sanctions for dealing with those who have committed offenses on the seas. But it is a warning against penal overkill for maritime crime, and a rejection of any brutalizing punishments. Obviously, those apprehended for crimes on the high seas must be temporarily detained on shipboard and delivered to justice ashore—either that of the law of the flag, or that of the next port of call, or that of the law-enforcement vessel that takes the accused persons aboard. The penal disposition that follows upon trial and conviction, however, to be effective can only be consonant with a wise and progressive overall criminal-justice policy, and that is the same for landbound offenders and seaborne criminals. History teaches us nothing else. The control of crime on the ocean, however, requires far more than a wise criminal-justice policy. Here as elsewhere, penology is simply an aid.

Thumbtacks Scattered Topside: Prevention

"Let those barefooted bastards come to surprise me," said the skipper of a thirty-eight-footer we met in the Caribbean. "I'll be ready for them!"

"But if they sneak aboard barefooted, as if with cats' paws, how can you hear them in your sleep, especially after that nightcap of rum?"

"Very simply," he said. "Their screams and howls will wake me up! You see, I never go to sleep in those parts until after I have liberally sprinkled the cockpit with thumbtacks!"

An ounce of thumbtacks is better than a pound of—no, no, that's the wrong tack. We simply mean to say that every good sailor is alert to dangers reasonably to be anticipated. These dangers have always included the sea and the wind, weather conditions in general, rotting timber, and missing buoys on a dark night. Until ten years ago, the fear of crime was not a danger to be considered in the yachting community, or among fishermen, or in the tanker fleet, or among merchant sailors in general, except for precontainerization cargo pilferages dockside. That has certainly changed. In "Fear and the Cruising Sailor," Michael Lewis lists the fear of "yacht violence" among six major contemporary concerns.[3] The fear of crime has definitely invaded the realm of Neptune. The fear of crime, however, should be distinguished from the reality of crime. Although the reality of crime—its prevalence, increase, or ferocity —gives rise to the fear of crime, land-based studies demonstrate that fear soon runs away from reality, ultimately standing in no relation to reality. Our first recommendation, then, is: Stop worrying. The chance of being victimized by criminals of the watery world is still very small, and the last thing we want to achieve with this book is a *Jaws*-like hysteria. Nor do we want to minimize the seaborne crime situation, as has been attempted by some Caribbean-based charter boat operators who fear loss of business. Let us be realistic, then:

On the whole, the entire maritime industry has reacted responsibly, by individual and collective self-help. In the various chapters we have related the reactions of the big shipping companies, whether to container theft, fraud, or piracy. We referred to the work of voluntary organizations whose work, especially in registering shipping and transactions, increasingly contributes to greater safety on the seas. We have also related the prudent responses of the yachting community and the rules of thumb offered by experienced sailors—ranging all the way from "Don't sail in dangerous waters" to "Arm yourself to the teeth and let it be known that you are armed." Let us dwell on the question of arming oneself and one's vessel. When Greeley wrote his *Law for Yachtsmen* in 1952, he began the topic of arming with this statement: "Firearms are neither necessary nor advisable equipment on a pleasure craft. There are no boarders to repel nor mutinies to suppress."[4] How things have changed! Americans, as a people never really averse to carrying firearms, have armed themselves as never before, on land and on the water. This defensive reaction to crime is just another example of fear outstripping reality. Perhaps more deaths and injuries are caused by privately owned firearms than criminals have been repelled by them, though that is conjecture. There is another problem: the licensing laws, which vary from port to port and from state to state, particularly in foreign countries. Use of a firearm in foreign waters may entail even greater dangers in the form of unpleasantries with police, courts, and jails, even when a gun is used in self-defense or in defense of one's property. Clearly, guns are a nuisance, and everyone would agree that in the ideal world, a world cruise without a gun would be ideal.

While sailing aboard the U.S. Coast Guard cutter *Steadfast,* hailing suspected drug runners in the Gulf of Mexico and the Caribbean, it was standard procedure for the officer of the watch to inquire by radio or loud-hailer: "Do you have weapons aboard?" Every one of the vessels we stopped answered in the affirmative—fishing vessels, freighters, and yachts alike. The crew was then told to bring the weapons topside for visible display, and to stand away from them—for example, on the fantail. Clearly, several of the vessels hailed turned out to have no connection with the drug or piracy trade. They were peaceful yachtsmen, but nevertheless armed.

A few years ago, during the height of yachtjackings, *Cruising World* ran an interesting question on arming one's vessel. The response was astonishing. The overwhelming majority of boat owners, responding by letter, carried firearms aboard, some of them virtual arsenals. A few placed their trust in their flare guns (the bigger the better, and six-shooters preferred), while a single responder, a very experienced sailor, saw no need for firearms.[5]

On the basis of our research and experience, we see no need to carry firearms aboard, other than a flare gun, when we sail our own well-policed North American waters. The U.S. Coast Guard is never far away and gets there fast in case of trouble. VHF Channel 16 is a blessing. Cruising in the combat zones of the drug ocean is simply a no-no as far as we are concerned. But on major voyages, outside the range of Coast Guard protection, especially if the trip leads through or to affected waters, as we have identified them earlier, we would recommend a firearm aboard. Of course, that raises all kinds of problems: Do you know how to use a firearm? Are you capable of firing at a human being when necessary? Do you have the presence of mind to assess a dangerous situation, or does your adrenaline cloud your judgment? And if you do arm yourself, do you take care of your weapon so it can function when needed? If you do carry a weapon, keep it under lock and key until a dangerous situation arises. Comply with licensing laws, and declare the weapon when you enter a foreign port. We hope you will never have to use the firearm. Of course, if you are attacked by Thai pirates in the Strait of Malacca, forget your rifle or revolver. Those guys have machine guns and grenade launchers. For such occasions, carry a Bible aboard. As for alarm systems to protect you aboard while docked, anchored, or moored, yes, we believe in them, and almost anything electronic is better than thumbtacks.

So far we have spoken only of defensive and protective reactions to the reality of crime on the water. It is time to turn to more strategic approaches for getting sea crimes under control.

A Colossal Achievement: The Law of the Sea Treaty

Like so many good ideas, this one came from the Greeks. To be more precise, it came from the Greek island of Rhodos (Rhodes)—the same island to which Caesar, centuries later, was sailing to study rhetoric with Professor Molon. Rhodos also harbored one of the Seven Wonders of the (ancient) World: the famous "Colossus," the giant statue of the god of the sun. Carved by one of Rhodos' famous sculptors, this enormous piece of art was erected to celebrate the achievement of the island's independence from Greece. No, that is not the good idea to which we are referring. The good idea from Rhodos was far more colossal than the long-toppled statue: It was the idea that all the oceans should be governed by one law. And the scholars and merchants of Rhodos wrote that law, which became highly respected throughout the Mediterranean. Its creation is shrouded in mystery, and not a single complete copy of it survives. Parts of it were incorporated into Roman law, and the Romans gave Rhodos credit for those passages. From there fragments and bits of the Rhodos law of the sea found their way into virtually every major attempt at recodifying the law of the sea by whatever nation happened to have a controlling influence over the oceans. None of these efforts amounted to a truly global law of the sea. Indeed, whatever international law of the sea there was, consisted of a myriad of international conventions and agreements, customs, and respected decisions of national and international tribunals—until the delegations of the world's governments got together at Montego Bay, Jamaica, on December 10, 1982, and signed the Convention and Final Act, known as the United Nations Convention on the Law of the Sea, or simply the Law of the Sea Treaty. It had been nearly three thousand years in the making! "Never have so many lawyers from so many states congregated for so many years to hatch so lengthy a legal document. . . ." wrote Professor Gerald J. Mangone about the Law of the Sea Treaty—and that had been only the draft version![6]

We shall not even attempt to retell what thousands of lawyers, representing some 160 countries, ultimately came up with. But this document, as embodying the contemporary law of the oceans, is of immense significance to the question of crime on the high seas. We therefore must point to those provisions that help or hinder achievement of a crime-free ocean.

This international maritime law is the result of the Third United Nations Conference on the Law of the Sea, which was chaired by Ambassador (of Singapore to the United Nations) and President Tommy T. G. Koh and his predecessor, Hamilton Shirely Amerasinghe, and serviced by the late Bernardo Zuleta, special representative of Secretary General Javier Perez de Cuellar. What does it mean when we say that this convention is the law of the sea of the world today? It means that by acceding to it, nations declare themselves to be bound by its provisions, making them part of their own law. A total of 119 nations voted in favor of the convention on the first day and are in the process of acceding to it. Seventeen nations abstained, and four nations voted against it.

However one may feel about individual provisions, the convention itself is a colossal human achievement. By replacing a plethora of conflicting claims over parts and aspects of the oceans and establishing agreed-upon limitations, it is calculated to reduce conflict. It regulates freedom of navigation in all types of zones, straits, and archipelagos, despite the recognition of new rights by coastal states. Both the preservation and the exploitation of living and nonliving resources of the ocean have been fairly well guaranteed. The convention contains new and stricter rules to protect the oceans and the marine environment from pollution. There is ample provision for peaceful resolution of disputes, through mediation and, ultimately, an international tribunal for the law of the sea. Above all, the convention recognizes an "area" composed of that part of the high seas not subject to the territorial claims of any state. This "area" is declared the common heritage of humankind (a concept developed by Ambassador Arvid Pardo of Malta). Its exploitation is entirely in the hands of a universal "enterprise," and all profits will go to the benefit of all humankind.

The convention has established four territorial zones in

which coastal states may exercise different types of sovereign rights. The first zone is the territorial sea (Article 3), which may not extend beyond twelve miles from shore. Of course, if they wish, some states may wish to stick to the old three-mile cannon-shot range, or to six or nine miles. In this zone, which must be respected by the vessels of all states, coastal states have exclusive jurisdiction, subject to the right of innocent passage by vessels of other countries (Articles 17–26). "Passage is innocent so long as it is not prejudicial to the peace, good order or security of the coastal state. . . ." (Article 19). There follows a long list of "prejudicial" activities, ranging from fishing by foreign vessels to military exercises and pollution. Submarines may not enter this zone submerged (Article 20)! The coastal state has full rights to ensure compliance but should not exercise criminal jurisdiction over crimes committed aboard foreign vessels in this zone except:

- if the consequences of the crime extend to the coastal state
- if the crime is of a kind to disturb the peace of the country or the good order of the territorial sea
- if the assistance of the local authorities has been requested by the master of the ship or by a diplomatic agent or consular officer of the flag state
- if such measures are necessary for the suppression of illicit traffic in narcotic drugs or psychotropic substances. [Article 27]

The second zone recognized by the convention is the "contiguous zone" (Article 33), which a coastal state may delimit to twenty-four miles from shore. In this zone the coastal state has special rights to prevent infringement of its Customs, fiscal, immigration, or sanitary laws and regulations, including the right to punish violators.

The third zone is the "exclusive economic zone" (Article 57), in which the coastal state has the exclusive right to fish, to exploit the seabed, and to enforce protective measures for the preservation of resources, subject to certain universal limitations. It stretches two hundred miles out.

The fourth zone is the "continental shelf" (Article 76), which may extend as far as 350 miles. Here the coastal state has the right to exploit the seabed but must pay up to 7 percent of the yield to the world community as administered by the "authority."

The convention's elaborate provisions to protect the oceans against pollution are to be enforced by the flag state of vessels or by coastal states. That, perhaps, points to the single most important shortcoming of the convention. Although an international tribunal for the law of the sea has been provided for, as well as an "authority" administering the activities on the oceans, an "assembly," and a "secretariat," there is no international enforcement agency. Compliance rests with the coastal states and the flag states. We know that most of the world's tonnage sails under the flags of states that have no capacity to enforce any compliance with national or international laws by their vessels, whether in port or at sea. Most coastal states of the Third World have diminutive maritime law-enforcement capacity. For that reason, earlier in this book we called for the establishment of a United Nations marine police force, with donated or seconded patrol vessels and multinational crews, to enforce the law on the oceans. In particular, such vessels should act as a peacekeeping force in areas where there are conflicting claims. If such a force were in existence, nine Spanish fishermen might not have been wounded by French shellfire on March 8, 1984.[7] There might not be constant gunfire in coastal waters where navigation is difficult, such as around Nicaragua.[8] Nor might the Bahamas have lost one of their star patrol vessels in a sea where nervous fighter pilots are all too quick on the trigger whenever they find somebody too close to their territorial waters.[9]

As far as American policy is concerned, we may be asking too much! An international maritime law-enforcement and peacekeeping force? Even the ideas of an "authority" and "enterprise" to exploit the "area" of the high seas was too much,[10] so that the United States government did not sign the convention on the Law of the Sea—one of the few governments that did not. Where does that leave United States interests? Since it appears that just about all the rest of the world will accede to the convention, we are going to be in a precarious position. If we were to mine the resources of the deep seabed outside the convention, we would "earn the universal condemnation of the international community and will incur grave political and legal consequences," as Ambassador Koh put it.[11]

But all is not bleak. The U.S.A.'s failure to sign the convention has been so controversial that a policy reversal may well take place sooner or later. But beyond that, the United States government did sign the first package of four international conventions, in 1958, covering the territorial sea, the high seas, the continental shelf, and conservation of living resources. This package, known as the First United Nations Conference of the Law of the Sea, has been incorporated into the comprehensive 1982 convention.[12] This first package is U.S. law, and most of the more important aspects of crime prevention on the high seas were covered therein.[13] Thus we are bound to prevent and punish the transportation of slaves (Article 13). We must cooperate in the repression of piracy (Article 14).[14] Our Coast Guard vessels may board foreign merchant vessels on the high seas when there is reasonable ground for suspecting that the ship is engaged in piracy, or in the slave trade, or that the vessel, though flying a foreign flag or refusing to show her flag, is in reality an American vessel (Article 22). Our Coast Guard vessels have the right of "hot pursuit" out of our territorial sea or contiguous zone of any vessel believed, for good reason, to have violated our laws (Article 23). This convention obliges us to take measures to prevent pollution (Articles 24 and 25). Nothing in the 1958 conventions restricts American criminal jurisdiction over crimes committed aboard American vessels, wherever they may be, or over foreign vessels in our ports.[15]

The truly international law of the sea has arrived, and with it the potential of controlling all criminality on the high seas. The United States has taken the first step in joining the world in this endeavor. We trust our government not only will take the next step but also will take a leading role in making the final step possible—the establishment of the international maritime law-enforcement and peacekeeping force.[16]

No longer can we go it alone. Crime on the oceans affects all nations, all people, though we may be particularly hard hit, especially through the drug world war on the oceans. But we are not the only ones who suffer, as we have amply demonstrated. We have created great task forces to stop the insidious flow of narcotic drugs into our country. That is undoubtedly the right kind of approach. Virtually every earlier crime wave on the oceans was ended by the task-force approach. The Greeks did it, and the Romans did it under Pompeius; the Hanseatic League was a task force, and the Spanish and the British used task forces in the Caribbean; so did President Monroe when he sent the Navy South; and our first Navy was a task force against the Barbary Coast pirates. Modern task forces can do even better than earlier ones. In the past, nature and geography were irremovable obstacles, affording criminals of the ocean shelter and escape among islands and inlets. Satellite surveillance, aircraft, and modern technology can overcome those ancient obstacles. But the problem has become internationally diffuse and global. The Greeks made every city-state contribute to their task-force fleet, making it international in scope. So did the Hanseatic League. But today we are largely alone in fighting crime on the ocean. Even a beefed up Coast Guard operating as the maritime enterprise of the task force has not been able to stop crime on the oceans; it has just made a dent in it. There is no doubt that it could make an even bigger dent, given a substantially larger fleet, substantially more operational support, and substantially more posse comitatus support by the armed forces. But even that would not really control crime in its myriad forms on the oceans. Commerce and interchange are totally global and internationally intertwined; so is ocean criminality. To come to grips with it, oceanic crime prevention must be equally global and internationally intertwined. Hopeful beginnings have been noted; the IMO is beginning to get a grip on marine insurance fraud, the United Nations has joined the battle against maritime fraud and piracy, and Customs unions have been formed. We are awakening to the need for addressing an international problem internationally. But the international task-force attack against hard-core crime on the oceans is yet to be initiated against the smuggling of narcotic drugs, the bloody piracy in all corners of the world, the incipient terrorism of the seas, against the cheats and frauds of the ocean lanes which bleed consumers, especially those of the Third World, against all who are poised to desecrate the peace of the oceans by crime. *Quo usque tandem?* How long yet? How long do we have to wait?

19

The "Nonclusion"

•

Around a cape he once would sail,
And thus it was that he did hail:
"I'll sail, I'll sail, I'll sail
    evermore!"
Huzza! Satan, he heard him hail!
    ho! heigho!
Huzza! Satan took him by his word!
    ho! heigho!
Huzza! And damned he! His ship,
    she leaps from wave to wave forever, evermore!

Richard Wagner,
The Flying Dutchman *

The book is done.
It is not done.
It's done!
"Let me have the manuscript," says the publisher.
"But it's not done! It will never be done!"
"Let me have the manuscript; we've got to go to press."
But this book describes life, now, as it is, on the oceans, and it's going on out there, right now! Look, we described in Chapter 15 how those alien creepy-peepy subs were committing neutrality violations under the Swedish penal code. They are still there! Only yesterday the Swedes reported they had one trapped in the archipelago of their naval base at Karlskrona! Three frogmen were spotted. They were maintaining communications between the trapped minisub and a mother sub out in the Baltic.[1] It's happening! Depth charges are being dropped, and hand grenades are detonating. How can we stop this book with all that crime on the seas around us?
How can one finish a book in which the United States Coast

*Metropolitan Opera libretto (New York: Fred Bullman, Inc., n.d.).

314

Guard plays a central role, when daily something is happening to affect that role? Somebody finally criticized the federal budget cuts for the Coast Guard,[2] and hearings are being scheduled that hopefully will result in an upgrading of the Coast Guard's budgetary priorities.[3] The Coast Guard may finally get its 614-foot blimp![4] That would increase the Coast Guard's drug search capacity immensely. Another jet may be thrown in for good measure.[5] And above all, we are happy to read how proud New Bedforders—with their tragic record of drug seizures—are about "their" cutters the *Bibb,* the *Unimac,* and the *Vigilant,* which in 1983 raked up a formidable record in the drug world war on the oceans while still helping fishermen in trouble.[6] Yet the poor Customs Service is faring badly, budgetwise. It was even claimed that the budget cut that crippled that service's air wing, was scheduled to improve office decor in Washington.[7]

How can we stop this manuscript when the drug world war is still raging out there? Off our old stomping grounds not far from the Isles of Shoals, the New York-based Coast Guard cutter *Tamaroa* has just seized the eighty-foot fishing vessel *Apollo III* with five tons of pot aboard, arrested the all-Colombian crew, and hauled the prize into Boston.[8] Another Coast Guard cutter, down South, had to use artillery to stop a seventy-foot shrimper with thirty-two tons of marijuana aboard. The Colombian crew of nine was arrested. While towing the shrimper toward Key West, the cutter seized another drug runner, a forty-two-foot sport-fishing boat, the *Night Hawk II,* with three Americans aboard.[9]

And remember the freighter *Hetty,* seized off the Jersey shore? Well, her Australian master just got a ten-year federal prison sentence in Newark, New Jersey, for "pouring poison into the veins" of America, the sentencing judge said. A total of $90 million worth was the pot on the *Hetty.* Three crew members got eight-year sentences each.[10]

In the meantime, the drug-armament plot begins to thicken. A major drug arrest in Miami revealed that the profits were to be used to purchase arms for Guatemala.[11] And remember the "Coronado Company"? After an earlier indictment of fifty-seven defendants, twenty-seven more were indicted for their share in this huge narcotics smuggling organization.[12] Kingpin arrests were made all over the country on narcotics and racketeering charges, including a former Tampa chief assistant state attorney,[13] while a Colombian kingpin, residing in Fort Wright, Kentucky, got a ten-year sentence and a fine of $525,000 for running $12 million worth of cocaine into the United States from Colombia.[14] The Customs Service has stepped up its crackdown on the Colombian cocaine trade,[15] yet federal officials had to concede that the amount of cocaine coming into the country has increased considerably. In 1982 the import probably was between forty-five and fifty-four metric tons. In 1983 it may have been twice as much, and heroin and marijuana imports have likewise increased.[16] Perhaps the drug ocean is not a bottle anymore. It's more like a sieve! The Far East continues to use the hard-line approach. Singapore hanged the fifteenth drug trafficker under its draconian laws.[17] Yet the results?

Speaking of the Far East, how can we conclude this book without reporting that the piracy, murder, and brutality against the Vietnamese boat people continues as ferociously as ever?[18] In March 1984, of sixty people on a refugee boat out of Vietnam, only two twelve-year-old girls and five males survived Thai pirates' savagery.[19]

Nor have fraud and corruption ceased with the completion of our chapter on that topic. Another kilogram of cocaine (over $500,000 worth) used as evidence at trial is missing.[20] And the U.S. government is trying to get back nearly $2 million that shipbuilding executives had bilked out of tanker and Trident nuclear submarine contracts. One of the cheats fled to Greece.[21]

Street crimes of the ocean lanes! They continue unabated, all the way up North,[22] and all the way down South, where a beautiful Hans Christian class 43-footer disappeared right out of a Fort Lauderdale marina. And off the Pacific coast of Nicaragua, the 1,000-ton Mexican freighter *Diana D* and the Costa Rican fishing vessel *Santus Petrus* have mysteriously disappeared, and all the navies of the region have not found a trace of them.[23] Again, the suspicion is that the stolen vessels are being used for the drug trade.[24] Street crimes of the ocean lanes are now popping up that we had not even thought of! Somebody impersonated the harbor master of Block Island and collected dockage fees from visiting boaters.[25] But this is where the fun stops: The 506-foot luxurious cruise liner *Scandinavian Sea,* ablaze, had to be towed into Cape Canaveral, with 946 people aboard.[26] According to radio news, a passenger had bragged about setting fire to the cruise liner with his lighter.

And then there are the less fortunate people who keep coming to our shores in anything but cruise liners. As we write this at least eighteen Cubans and Bangladeshis have made it to Boca Raton, Florida, on a twenty-foot boat at $1,200 per head![27] There is still very little hope for the seventy-two hundred Haitians who fled to America and spent up to a year there in jail.[28] The confused story of the Marielita, "Freedom Fleet" boatlift, had its next chapter. While the boatlift was hailed as a great exercise in freedom and generosity, many of the captains who ferried the Cubans to Key West had been fined $1,000 per alien transported, and their vessels had been seized, and then only conditionally released. Now a federal judge in Miami has ruled the $4.7 million in fines were illegally imposed and has ordered thirty-one vessels to be restored to their owners. Undoubtedly more litigation will follow.[29]

Nor is there any letup in maritime smuggling. The illicit trade between Taiwanese Chinese and mainland Chinese is now estimated to be in the tens of millions of dollars annually, while the "no questions asked" third-party trade between the two countries may run as high as $450 million a year.[30]

Hold it—don't tear that manuscript away from us! Don't you at least want to hear some good news about crime on the oceans? Remember our indignation about those sleek New York City EPA tankers trudging the city's raw sewage out of New York and dumping it twelve miles off the New Jersey shore? Well, that will stop. Those tankers may have to sail out as far as a hundred miles, where the ocean is eight-thousand-feet deep—and not sixty![31] All around us we can note the growing awareness of the need for clean waters and conservation of living marine life. New Jerseyites staged a conspicuous demonstration over New York City's dumping of raw sewage into the Hudson River.[32] Los Angeles has instituted a strict clean harbor control system. They have their "harbor cops on the pollution beat."[33] A Kansas City, Missouri, company, in the face of overwhelming evidence against it, pleaded guilty to major violations of the Federal Clean Water Act! Forty-five more grand-jury investigations are under way.[34] The Mississippi River and all other American rivers and waterways will be grateful! Courts are also getting tough on fishing-law violators. A Norwich, Connecticut, Superior Court judge actually sent a repeat violator to several months in jail for unlawful fishing and for fishing without a license.[35]

But the happiest news and our last item is this: World pressure has won, and the Canadians have called off their seal hunts. People simply stopped buying seal out of protest over the four-hundred-year-old practice of clubbing those cuddly, helpless baby seals to death for their pure white fur. Hundreds of thousands of those droll creatures with doll-like features will live.[36] Where there's a will, there's a way. We *can* stop crime and brutality on the oceans.

Now, dear publisher, you may have our manuscript—even though crime on the oceans is continuing, until . . . until . . .

References

Introduction

1. The merchant fleet rank order according to tonnage is Greece, Panama, U.S.S.R., Liberia, Japan, United Kingdom, China, Italy, Norway, Singapore, U.S.A., Spain. "U.S. Merchant Fleet Now 11th Worldwide," *The New York Times* (Dec. 4, 1983), p. 33.

2. O'Reilly, "Songs from the Southern Seas," in Frank Shay, *A Sailor's Treasury* (New York: W.W. Norton & Company, 1951), p. 16.

Chapter 1. Perspectives from the Crow's Nest

1. *Customs U.S.A.: A Report on the Activities of the U.S. Customs Service During Fiscal Year 1982* (Washington, D.C., 1983), pp. 36–37. Much of the cocaine is being imported by plane. Customs seized 94 planes in 1978; in 1981 there were 272 plane seizures, and 206 in 1982. Marijuana seizures by the Customs Service averaged around 4 million pounds annually between 1978 and 1982. These seizures occurred for the most part on vessels, or off-loaded from vessels at dockside.

2. *Miami News* (January 28, 1983), p. 5A.

3. Ibid.

4. Ibid.

5. Ibid.

6. Ibid.

7. Ibid.

8. Ibid.

9. Ibid., p. 6A.

10. *Miami Herald* (January 28, 1983), p. 14A.

11. Ibid., pp. 1, 3D.

12. Ibid., p. 7D.

13. Ibid. (January 27, 1983), p. 2B.

14. Ibid. (January 28, 1983), p. 6A.

15. *Miami News* (January 26, 1983), p. 5A.

16. Ibid.

17. Ibid., pp. 10A, 48.

18. Ibid.

19. *Miami Herald* (January 28, 1983), p. 12A.

20. *Miami News* (January 28, 1983), p. 9A.

21. Ibid. (January 27, 1983), p. 6.

22. E.g., the need for large expansion of jail and prison capacities in view of the vastly increased crime problem. See Wendy Tucker, "Overcrowded Jails vs. Early Release of Some Criminals—Hard Realities Facing Judges," *Key West Citizen* (January 28, 1983), p. 1; "State May Condemn Land to Get Sites for Prisons," ibid., p. 3.

23. Janet Rapaport, "A Short Take: U.S. Customs Pre-Clearance in Bermuda," *Customs Today*, Vol. 18, No. 1 (Winter 1983), p. 19.

24. See Donald L. Willey, "Customs Anti-Smuggling Activities," *International Drug Report*, Vol. 27, No. 10 (October 1981), pp. 43–45.

25. Timothy J. Flanagan, David J. van Alstyne, and Michael R. Gottfredson, eds., *Sourcebook of Criminal Justice Statistics* (Washington, D.C.: U.S. Government Printing Office, 1982).

26. Internal government statistics on file with authors.

27. Ibid.

28. "Secrecy of Swiss Banks Is Under Fire," *N.B.S.T.* * (October 3, 1983), p. 15.

29. Reginald Stuart, "U.S. Tax and Drug Indictments Trail Figures in Bahamian Trust Company," *The New York Times* (October 17, 1983), p. 19.

30. Arnold H. Lubash, "Court Told of 'Laundry' for Millions in Drug Funds," *The New York Times* (April 17, 1983), p. 35.

31. Mathea Falco, "The Big Business of Illicit Drugs," *The New York Times Magazine* (December 11, 1983), pp. 108–11.

32. "Coast Guard Drug Law Enforcement," hearings before the Subcommittee on Coast Guard and Navigation of the Committee on Merchant Marine and Fisheries, House of Representatives, Ninety-Sixth Congress, First Session, on H.R. 2538 (Washington, D.C., March 28, 1979; Key West, Fla., July 3, 1979), Serial No. 96-2D.

33. Under the directorship of J. Edgar Hoover, the FBI had stayed out of drug law enforcement. Hoover, it was said, feared contamination of his agents. Since 1973, when the Drug Enforcement Administration was established in the Department of Justice, the FBI's resources and expertise have been drawn

*This abbreviation is used throughout the Reference section for the *New Bedford* (Mass.) *Standard-Times.*

upon, and today there are narcotics coordinators at FBI headquarters in Washington as well as at each of the fifty-nine FBI field offices. "F.B.I. Support," *The Police Chief* (March 1977), p. 28.

34. News Release, the Vice President, office of the press secretary (February 16, 1982), remarks of Vice President George Bush at the Miami Citizens Against Crime luncheon, Omni Hotel, Miami, Fla. (February 16, 1982).

35. "Fifty Years Ago, the 'Noble Experiment' Met with Repeal," *N.B.S.T.* (December 4, 1983), p. 18.

36. There are, of course, many reliable accounts of the "rum war," but two stand out: Malcolm E. Willoughby, *Rum War at Sea* (Washington, D.C.: U.S. Government Printing Office, 1964), which for all intents and purposes is an official U.S. Coast Guard account; and Everett S. Allen, *The Black Ships— Rum-runners of Prohibition* (Boston: Little, Brown & Company, 1965), written by the salty former editor-in-chief of the *New Bedford (Mass.) Standard-Times* (herein referred to as *N.B.S.T.*), the paper that has served us so well in researching the New England situation.

37. Willoughby, op. cit., pp. 127–28; "Fifty Years Ago, the 'Noble Experiment' Met with Repeal," loc. cit.

38. Conversations with knowledgeable law-enforcement officers, and see Chapter 15.

39. James Coates and George DeLama, "Satellite Spying on Narcotics Operation Is a Promising Tool for Drug Task Force," *Miami Herald* (January 23, 1983).

40. "Feds Use Radar Balloons to Fight Drug Smuggling," *N.B.S.T.* (October 2, 1983), p. 2.

41. *Bulletin of the U.S.C.G. Academy*, Vol. 45, No. 5 (September/October 1983), p. 42. "Attention now focuses on the British-built 'Skyship 600.'" See *Arab News* (Riyadh, January 22, 1984), p. 11.

42. *Soundings* (January 1984), p. 8.

43. *EPIC Users Guide*, U.S. Department of Justice, Drug Enforcement Administration (Washington, D.C.: U.S. Government Printing Office), 0-295-205.

44. Vice President's news release (March 16, 1982).

45. *Miami Herald* (November 1981) (originally an investigative report in the *Miami Herald*).

46. *Miami Citizens Against Crime, Goals* (n.d.; prob. 1981).

47. Vice President's press releases (February 16, 1982, and March 16, 1980).

48. Bud Newman, "Drug Fight Trims Smuggling Here, Task Force Chief Says," *Miami News* (January 28, 1983), p. 5A.

49. Jane Stone, "U.S. Will Streamline Drug Force," *Miami Herald* (January 28, 1983), p. 6A.

50. "Busted—South Florida Drug Task Force to Be Disbanded," *Trenton Times*, clipping on file with authors.

51. "Lawmen Say Drug 'Czar' Isn't Needed," *N.B.S.T.* (November 1, 1983), p. 3.

52. Horace Cavitt, "National Narcotics Border Interdiction System," *Customs Today*, Vol. 18, No. 4 (Fall 1983), p. 9.

53. "More Drug and Organized Crime Task Forces Formed," I.A.C.P., *Newsletter*, Vol. IX, No. 2 (February 1983), p. 1.

54. Reginald Stuart, "Federal Strategy Is Debated at Drug Traffic Hearing," *The New York Times* (October 13, 1983), p. 22.

55. Paul Anderson, "Drug War Faces Cutbacks in Funds," *Miami Herald* (February 4, 1984), p. 1.

56. William D. Montalbano and Carl Hiaasen, *Trapline* (New York: Atheneum Publishers, 1982).

57. Carl Hiaasen, Susan Sacks, and Richard Marin, "Smuggler's Island," *Miami Herald* (1982).

Chapter 2. A Tangled Caribbean Web

1. For a personal-experience account of American yachtsmen sailing in the drug-infested waters of the Bahamas, see Bonnie Waitzkin, "Misadventures on the Great Bahama Bank," *Motor Boating and Sailing* (January 1984), p. 46, and "The Bahamas Report," ibid., p. 44.

2. "Bridge for Drugs," *Trinidad Guardian* (January 18, 1984), p. 5.

3. With apologies to Carl Hiaasen and his colleagues, who first used this title in their famous exposé of Key West, hereinafter referred to as "Smugglers' Island," *Miami Herald Record* (1982).

4. Alfred Hoyt Bill, *New Jersey and the Revolutionary War* (New Brunswick, N.J.: Rutgers University Press, 1964).

5. Lionel White, *A Death at Sea* (New York: E.P. Dutton & Company, 1961).

6. "Smuggler's Island," p. 4.

7. "Colombia Bars Extradition," *The New York Times* (November 14, 1983), p. 12.

8. "Crashing on Cocaine," *Time* (April 11, 1983).

9. Ibid.

10. George Stein, "The Nazi," *Tropic—The Miami Herald* (January 2, 1983).

11. "Gunmen in Colombia Kill 2 American Bus Riders," *The New York Times* (September 1, 1983), p. 5.

12. "Remains of 100 People Found in Colombia Cave," *The New York Times* (April 17, 1983), p. 7.

13. ABC News, "The Cocaine Cartel" (New York, August 20, 1983), pp. 1–2.

14. See "Conch Republic Goes to 'War' Again," *Orlando Sentinel* (February 9, 1984), p. C4.

15. S.N. 96-20, p. 109.

16. George Stein, "The Nazi," *Tropic—The Miami Herald* (January 2, 1983), pp. 6–9, 18–19; see also Brendan Murphy, *The Butcher of Lyons*, Acropolis Press, 1983; Tom Bower, *Klaus Barbie—The Butcher of Lyons* (New York: Pantheon, 1984).

17. "Ex-Nazi Enjoyed Torturing Jews, Two Victims Testify," *Miami News* (January 28, 1983), p. 9.

18. Barbara Goldsmith, "The Children of Izieu," *Sunday* (New Bedford) *Standard-Times* (*Parade* magazine) (January 22, 1983), p. 4.

19. James H. Rubin, "U.S. Aid to Barbie Admitted," *Hartford Courant* (August 17, 1983), pp. 1, 6. The investigation into Barbie's connection with U.S. military intelligence agencies had begun in April 1983, when the Department of Justice had sent an official to La Paz for initial inquiries. See *The New York Times* (April 21, 1983), p. 7.

20. Bolivia's new civilian government has since ordered the arrest of former President Luís Garcia Meza and twenty-nine members of his military regime on charges of corruption and economic crimes. Meza is living in exile in Argentina. *The New York Times* (May 25, 1983), p. 5. But with Argentina's return to democratically elected government by late 1983, Meza's days in Argentinian exile may be counted. "Hated Honcho They Call the King of Cocaine Dealers," *New York Post* (February 24, 1983), p. 13, documenting Altman-Barbie's close ties with ex-Interior Minister Luís Arce Gomez, "The Minister of Cocaine." But as this book goes to press, ex-President Meza is on the lam again. *Miami Herald* (February 9, 1984), p. 4. Finally Argentina ordered the expulsion of Meza and Gomez—if they can be found. "Argentina Orders Pair Expelled," *Miami Herald* (int'l. ed., February 4, 1984), p. 2.

21. "Ex Chief of Gestapo in Lyons Is Linked to U.S. Intelligence," *The New York Times* (February 8, 1983), pp. 1, 9. E.J. Dionne, Jr., "The Nazi 'Butcher': Lyons Looks Back in Loathing," *The New York Times* (February 8, 1983), p. 2; "A Butcher at Bay," *Miami Herald* (January 28, 1983), p. 20.

22. AP. "Chronology of Nazi Who Fled via Rat Line Begins and Ends in Lyon," *Hartford Courant* (August 17, 1983), p. 7.

23. "Bolivia Files New Charges Against Jailed Former Nazi," *Miami Herald* (January 27, 1983), p. 2. "Ex Nazi Ran Mercenaries, Bolivia says," *Miami Herald* (January 28, 1983), p. 4.

24. "Cocaine Hunt," *Trinidad Guardian* (January 6, 1984).

25. "Rooted in Poverty, Cocaine, Trade Grows Rapidly, Bolivian Minister Says," *N.B.S.T.* (October 18, 1983), p. 2 (with map on p. 1).

26. *Boston Globe* (August 6, 1983), p. 5.

27. "Crashing on Cocaine," *Time* (April 11, 1983).

28. Bernard D. Nossiter, "U.N. Warns of Effects," *The New York Times* (January 30, 1983), pp. 1, 18.

29. ABC News, "The Cocaine Cartel" (New York, April 20, 1983).

30. Leslie Martland, "U.S. Tries New Tack in Drug Fight as Global Supply and Use Mount. Enforcement Costs Tripled," *The New York Times* (January 30, 1983), pp. 1, 18; "Panel Votes Debt Ceiling Rise," *The New York Times* (May 25, 1983).

Chapter 3. **El Tiburón Blanco**

1. To alleviate our readers' anxiety, twenty-four hours after the incident the National Oceanic and Atmospheric Administration issued a notice to all shipping that an unusual condition of sunspots had created havoc with all radar equipment in the area. The notice did not account for the other equipment failures and Professor Mueller's "popped out" lenses.

2. "Damaged Cutter Sails to Port with Suspects," *Miami Herald* (February 9, 1984), p. 5.

3. Malcolm F. Willoughby, *Rum War at Sea* (Washington, D.C.: U.S. Government Printing Office, 1964), p. 65.

4. Ibid., p. 62.

5. Jean Waller, "False Mayday Spurs U.S. Search," *Soundings* (July 1983), pp. 3, 26.

6. "Hoax Sends Service on Wild Goose Chase," *Soundings*, Sec. II (February 1984), p. 52.

7. *United States* v. *Andies and Greenwood*, Case No. 753-593-CR-PF.

8. Mathea Falco, "The Big Business of Illicit Drugs," *The New York Times Magazine* (December 11, 1983), pp. 108, 110.

9. Testimony of Michael P. Sullivan, assistant U.S. attorney, Southern District, Florida, before the Subcommittee on Coast Guard and Navigation of the Committee on Merchant Marine and Fisheries, House of Representatives, Ninety-Sixth Congress, First Session, on H.R. 2538 (Key West, Fla., July 3, 1979), S.N. 96-20, p. 63; hereinafter referred to as S.N. 96-20.

10. *Sunday Guardian* (January 8, 1984), p. 4.

11. *Trinidad Guardian* (January 6, 1984), p. 5.

12. "Seaga Moves to Head Off Confrontation," *Trinidad Guardian* (January 6, 1984), p. 5.

13. CLEAR Center Study Group (G.O.W. Mueller, intro.), "Model Narcotic Drug Legislation," *Criminology* 8 (1970): 156, 157.

14. Timothy Green published his book *The Smugglers: An Investigation into the World of the Contemporary Smuggler* in 1969 (New York: Walker & Company). It is incredible how the scene has changed in fifteen years. Cocaine was virtually unknown in America. Peru and Bolivia were just beginning to grow it. There was practically no marijuana import from Colombia, and Americans got most of their drugs, in the form of heroin, from Turkey (via Marseille) or the Golden Triangle.

15. William K. Stevens, "Pakistani-Afghan Area Leads as Supplier of Heroin to U.S.," *The New York Times* (June 30, 1983), pp. 1, 13.

16. Colin Campbell, "Thais Hesitate to Wreck Opium Fields and Tribes," *The New York Times* (February 20, 1983).

17. *The New York Times* (December 5, 1982), p. 52.

18. Gerhard O.W. Mueller (with cooperation of M. Cherif Bassiouni and Freda Adler), *L'Abus de Drogues et sa Prevention,* published for CLEAR Center as Vol. 44, 3–4, *Revue Internationale de Droit Penal* (Rennes, France: Imprimeries Simon, 1974); Arthur D. Moffet, Freda Adler, Frederick B. Glaser, and Diane Horvitz, *Medical Lollypop, Junkie Insulin, or What?* (Philadelphia: Dorrance & Company, 1974); Freda Adler, Arthur D. Moffet, Frederick B. Glaser, John C. Ball, and Diane Horvitz, *A Systems Approach to Drug Treatment* (Philadelphia: Dorrance & Company, 1974).

19. *United States* v. *Winter,* 509 F.2d 975 (5th Cir. 1975).

20. Timothy J. Flannagan, David J. van Alstyne, and Michael R. Gottfredson, eds., *Sourcebook of Criminal Justice Statistics—1981,* U.S. Department of Justice, Bureau of Justice Statistics (Washington, D.C.: U.S. Government Printing Office, 1982), p. 378.

21. Internal Coast Guard statistics on file with the authors.

22. Flannagan, van Alstyne, and Gottfredson, eds., op. cit., p. 377.

23. *The New York Times* (June 2, 1982), p. 2. The *Lion Heart* seizure had topped Miami's previously largest seizure, of seven hundred pounds, on the Colombian vessel *Mar Azul* on December 4, 1982, *The New York Times* (December 5, 1982), p. 52.

24. *The New York Times* (August 20, 1983), p. 12.

25. S.N. 96-20, p. 46.

26. Doug Schryver, "Double Vision—How Close Can a Stock Boat Come to Its Racing Version? The Answer Is Surprising," *Boating* (July 1983).

27. "Coast Guard's Caribbean Trap Nets $3M in Pot," *New York Post* (December 9, 1983), p. 12.

28. Edna Buchanan, "680 Pounds of Cocaine Found in Ship, Car," *Miami Herald* (December 5, 1982).

29. Robert W. Wennerholm, "Forfeiture," *The Police Chief* (February 1983), p. 17.

30. E.g., *Yachting* (December 1983), p. 201 (January 1984), p. 293.

31. Patty Koller, "Dope Boats Deteriorate in Custody," *Soundings* (October 1, 1983), pp. 2, 29.

32. Patty Koller, "Towing Company Exports Refurbished Drug Boats," *Soundings* (March 1984), p. 32.

33. Including prisoner groups, motorcycle gangs, ethnic outlaw groups, and others facilitating the drug landing and distribution. Leslie Maitland Werner, "New Crime Groups Assailed by Smith—Motorcycle and Prisoner Groups Grow Rich Through Drugs, Attorney General Says," *The New York Times* (November 30, 1983), p. 27.

34. "Study Ties Cocaine to Theft," *The New York Times* (September 20, 1983), p. C3.

35. "Record Heroin, Cocaine Seized," *Trinidad Express* (January 5, 1984), p. 31.

36. "Organized Crime Nets $38 Billion Yearly," *Trinidad Guardian* (January 16, 1984), p. 15. "Organized Crime Nets $16 Billion in Canada," *Trinidad Express* (January 14, 1984), p. 3. The *Guardian*'s figures appear to be in Trinidad and Tobago dollars, the *Express*'s figures in Canadian dollars.

37. *The New York Times* (September 19, 1983), p. 18.

38. "Figures Show Alarming Rise in Narcotics Trade" (by-line Vienna), *Trinidad Guardian* (January 16, 1984), p. 15.

Chapter 4. Poseidon's Police

1. Freda Adler, *Nations Not Obsessed with Crime*, Chap. 6 (Littleton, Colo.: Fred B. Rothman & Company, 1983).

2. "Costa Rica: Nicaragua Using Patrol Boats," *N.B.S.T.* (September 15, 1983), p. 2; "Nicaragua Guerillas Laying Mines at a Key Port," *The New York Times* (October 8, 1983), p. 3.

3. "1,065 Pounds of Cocaine Seized on Ship in Miami," *The New York Times* (June 2, 1983).

4. "Grosser Kokain Fang in Costa Rica," *Neue Zürcher Zeitung* (October 21, 1983), p. 11.

5. Marlise Simmons, "Guerilla Fires in Nicaragua Put the Heat on Costa Rica," *The New York Times*, on file with authors.

6. Countries following this pattern include Angola, Australia, Belgium, Bolivia, Brazil, Brunei, Bulgaria, Burma, Cameroon, Cape Verde, Chile, China (People's Republic), Czechoslovakia, Denmark, Dominican Republic, Ecuador, Egypt, El Salvador, Equatorial Guinea, Ethiopia, Fiji, Gambia, German Democratic Republic, Ghana, Grenada, Guatemala, Guinea-Bissau, Guyana, Honduras, Hungary, Ireland, Ivory Coast, Democratic Kampuchea, Kenya, Democratic People's Republic of Korea, Laos, Lebanon, Mali, Mauritania, Mexico, Morocco, Mozambique, Netherlands, New Zealand, Pakistan, Papua-New Guinea, Paraguay, Poland, Portugal, Romania, Senegal, Seychelles, Sierra Leone, Somalia, South Africa (where naval coastal forces are part of the Navy), Spain, Sri Lanka, Sudan, Suriname, Syria, Taiwan, Tanzania, Thailand, Togo, Tonga, Tunisia, Turkey, U.S.S.R., United Kingdom, Uruguay, Vietnam, Arab Republic of Yemen, People's Democratic Republic of Yemen, Yugoslavia, Zaire, and Zanzibar.

7. That is certainly true in the case of Brunei, Grenada, Guatemala, Guyana, Honduras, Democratic Kampuchea, Kenya, Laos, Lebanon, Maldives, Mali, Mauritania, Mozambique, Papua-New Guinea, Sudan, Suriname, Togo, Tonga, Zaire, and Zanzibar, whose navies are equipped only for patrol duty.

8. These countries include Austria, Bahamas, Bahrain, Bermuda, Costa Rica, Haiti, Hong Kong, Iceland, Jamaica, Jordan, Kuwait, Liberia, Malawi, Malta, Mauritius, Montserrat, Nicaragua, Panama, Qatar, Sabah, St. Kitts, St. Lucia, St. Vincent and the Grenadines, Solomon Islands, Switzerland, Trinidad and Tobago, and the Virgin Islands (BWI).

9. The data on the world's marine police and naval forces are derived from *Jane's Fighting Ships 1980–81*, Captain John Moore, R.N., ed. (London, New York, and Sydney: Jane's Publishing Co., Ltd., 1980) and *Weyer's Flottentaschenbuch 1979/81 (Warships of the World)*, Gerhard Albrecht, ed. (München: Bernard und Graefe Verlag, 1979) as well as from personal interviews with officers of a number of national Coast Guard services in the U.S.A. and abroad. Re recent U.S. Coast Guard training assistance, see Frank J. Priel, "U.S. Teaching Defense in the Caribbean," *The New York Times* (February 19, 1984), p. 3.

10. Gerhard Albrecht, ed. *Weyer's*, op. cit., p. 5.

11. Timothy J. Flannagan, David J. van Alstyne, and Michael R. Gottfredson, eds., *Sourcebook of Criminal Justice Statistics—1981*, U.S. Department of Justice, Bureau of Justice Statistics (Washington, D.C.: U.S. Government Printing Office, 1982), pp. 377–78.

12. George J. Lyford, "Boat Theft—A High-Profit Low-Risk Business," *FBI Law Enforcement Bulletin* (May 1982), pp. 1, 4. For further details, see Chap. 13.

13. Florida Department of Law Enforcement, *1981 Annual Report: Crime in Florida*.

14. Michael Brody, "Boom in Piracy—There's a Rising Tide of Marine Fraud," *Barron's* (November 29, 1982).

15. Tetsuo Imarato, "The Safety of Maritime Traffic and Investigation on

Traffic Rules Violations," *Resource Material Series 16:244* (Fuchu [Tokyo]: UNAFEI, 1979).

16. *The New York Times* (September 19, 1983), p. 8.

17. Yoshio Wada, "Criminal Investigation at Sea," *Research Material Series 20:157* (Fuchu [Tokyo]: UNAFEI, 1980). It is noteworthy that in a single year (1978) the Japanese Maritime Safety Agency had to investigate 1,964 significant incidents of pollution. See Tatsuo Narikone, "Maritime Offenses," *Research Material Series 18:130* (Fuchu [Tokyo]: UNAFEI, 1979).

18. Stephen H. Evans, *The Black Ships* (Boston: Little, Brown & Co., 1965).

19. Malcolm F. Willoughby, *Rum War at Sea* (Washington, D.C.: U.S. Government Printing Office, 1964).

19. Ibid.

20. Ibid., p. 47.

21. Lieutenant John G. Tuttle, "Offshore Patrol Vessels . . . An Overview," *Bulletin of the U.S.C.G. Academy*, Vol. 45, No. 5 (September–October 1983), pp. 27–31.

22. Ibid.

23. Rear Admiral William A. Jenkins, U.S.C.G. (Ret.), "A New Dimension of Coast Guard Aviation," *Naval Aviation* (May–June 1983), pp. 6–7. We shall return to the use of Coast Guard and naval aviation in combating high-seas criminality.

24. "U.N. Permits Use of Its Flag in P.L.O. Pullout," *The New York Times* (December 4, 1983), p. 15; "P.L.O. Still Using U.N. Flag; Nothing Has Changed," *Sunday Guardian* (Trinidad) (December 18, 1983), p. 2; "Israel Calls off Bombardment," *Express* (Trinidad) (December 21, 1983), p. 62; "Umbrella Over Tripoli," *Express* (Trinidad) (December 21, 1983), p. 60; "Pro-Arafat Guerrillas Evacuated to Iraq," *Trinidad Guardian* (December 22, 1983), p. 2; "The Ships, Flying the United Nations Flags Were Located by French Naval Vessels." Also see "Israel Pounds Port to Block P.L.O.'s Flight," *N.B.S.T.* (December 19, 1983), p. 2. But Israel did not shell the vessels flying the U.N. flag: "Arafat's Forces Leave Lebanon," *N.B.S.T.* (December 20, 1983), p. 2.

25. United Nations, *The Law of the Sea*, U.N. Publication Sales No. E.83.V.5. (1983), p. 31.

Chapter 5. Posse Comitatus—The Navy Gets into the Act

1. "*Posse Comitatus.* The power of the county. Citizens summoned by the sheriff to assist him in the execution of process," *The Cyclopedic Law Dictionary* (Chicago: Callaghan & Company, 1940).

2. Timothy J. Christman, "Smugglers," *Naval Aviation* (May–June 1983), p. 47.

3. "Drug Smugglers Convicted in San Juan," *Miami News* (January 28, 1983).

4. "Judge Backs Navy in Smuggling Case," *Miami Herald* (January 28, 1983), p. 6.

5. Interview with Charles F. Rinkevitch, South Florida Task Force coordinator.

6. Christman, op. cit.

7. Jean Waller, "Navy Fires First Shots in Drug War," *Soundings* (September 1983), pp. 5, 38.

8. Jeanne Gray, "Patrolling the Skies," *Naval Aviation* (May–June 1983), pp. 42–43.

9. Christman, op. cit., p. 48.

10. 18 U.S.C. 1385.

11. *Jackson* v. *State of Alaska,* 572 F.2d 87 (1977); *United States* v. *Chapparo-Almeida,* 679 F.2d 423 (5th Cir. 1982).

12. *United States* v. *Walden,* 490 F.2d 372 (4th Cir.), *cert. den.,* 416 U.S. 983, 94 S. Ct. 2385 (1974); *People* v. *Blend,* 175 Cal. Rep. 263, 121 C.A.3rd 215 (1981).

13. Note, "Honored in the Breach: Presidential Authority to Execute the Laws with Military Force," *Yale L.J.* 83 (1973): 130.

14. Report to the Congress by the Comptroller General of the United States, "If Defense and Civil Agencies Work More Closely Together, More Efficient Search/Rescue and Coastal Law Enforcement Would Follow," CD-76-456 (May 26, 1977).

15. Ibid., p. 46.

16. Ibid., pp. 47–48, emphasis ours, with the following note reference: "The Justice Department's position regarding the propriety of indirect assistance to civil law-enforcement authorities by military personnel is supported by the opinion of Judge Andrew Bogue in *United States* v. *Red Feather,* 392 Fed. Supp. 916 (D.S.D., 1975)."

17. Ibid., p. 48.

18. James Coates and George De Lama, "Satellite Spying on Narcotics Operation Is a Promising Tool for Drug Task Force," *Miami Herald* (December 23, 1983).

19. "President Reagan Calls for Reform in Criminal Justice . . . use of . . . Military in All-Out War on Major Crime Violators and Drug Pushers," *International Drug Report,* Vol. 22, No. 10 (October 1981), p. 4.

20. Christman, op. cit., p. 49.

21. 10 U.S.C. 18, Secs. 371–78.

22. Title 32—National Defense, Secs. 213.1–11, 47 F.R. 11899.

23. DOD Directive 5525.5-1.

24. "Crash off Nassau," *Trinidad Guardian* (January 11, 1984), p. 1.

Chapter 6. Heading North

1. Lou Lichtveld, *Crusoe's Only Isle* (Trinidad: Syncreators Ltd., 1974).

2. *Trinidad Guardian* (December 15, 1983), p. 1.

3. "Yacht Sails Out with Its Arms," *Trinidad Guardian* (December 15, 1983); "U.S. Yacht Given Clean Slate," *Trinidad Guardian* (December 16, 1983), p. 1; "Embassy Mum on 'Dorcas Sue,' " *Express* (Trinidad) (December 17, 1983), p. 4; "Customs Launch Inquiry into Release of 'Dorcas Sue,' " *Express* (Trinidad) (December 16, 1983), p. 5; "Commissioner Is Taking Ac-

tion," *Express* (Trinidad) (December 16, 1983), p. 5; "Boat Was on Church Mission," *Sunday Express* (Trinidad) (January 1, 1984), p. 3.

4. Nathan M. Adams, "Inside the Cocaine War," a feature condensation, *Reader's Digest* (1983), pp. 91, 214.

5. Lyman V. Rutledge, *The Isles of Shoals in Lore and Legend* (Barre, Mass.: Barre Publishers, 1965), pp. 30 et seq.

6. *N.B.S.T.* (October 23, 1984), p. 1.

7. William Sinon, "Service Head Affirms 'Drug War,' " *Soundings* (January 1984), Sec. II, p. 3.

8. Keith Schneider, "Carolina's Become New Battlefield in War on Drugs," *Miami Herald* (March 31, 1983), p. 4B.

9. "Federal Jury Indicts 33 in Drug Smuggling Case," *The New York Times* (July 9, 1983), p. 5.

10. "Marijuana Found Aboard Freighter," *The New York Times* (September 17, 1983).

11. "Ship Carrying [eleven tons of] Hashish Seized off Jersey Coast," *The New York Times* (November 4, 1983); Patty Koller, "Huge Hashish Cargo Seized," *Soundings*, Sec. II (January 1984), p. 2.

12. "Largest N.Y. Cocaine Haul," *Trinidad Guardian* (December 19, 1983), p. 19.

13. Leonard Buder, "Major Heroin Ring Broken, Federal Officials Say," *The New York Times* (September 21, 1983).

14. "432 Pounds of Cocaine Is Seized," *The New York Times* (December 1, 1983), p. B3. The text of the news report refers to 442 pounds. Jim Flannery, "Agents Seize Cocaine Cache," *Soundings*, Sec. II (February 1984), p. 4.

15. CBS, "The Coronado Mob," *60 Minutes* (December 11, 1983).

16. "673 Pounds of Cocaine Seized on Coast Raid," *The New York Times* (October 16, 1983), p. 26.

17. *N.B.S.T.* (April 15, 1977).

18. Ibid. (August 19, 1977).

19. Ibid. (August 16, 1977).

20. Ibid. (September 7, 1978).

21. Ibid. (May 13, 1978).

22. Ibid. (May 26, 1978).

23. Ibid. (December 14, 1978).

24. Ibid. (October 21, 1980).

25. Ibid. (September 5, 1980).

26. Ibid. (September 4, 1980).

27. Ibid. (October 1, 1982).

28. Ibid. (August 25, 1982; January 11, 1983).

29. "$24 Million Connection—Former State Official Arrested in Big Maine Drug Bust," *Soundings*, Sec. II (December 1982), p. 19.

30. *N.B.S.T.* (September 13, 1983), p. 3.

31. *Soundings* (December 1982), p. 46.

32. *N.B.S.T.* (November 10, 1982; February 4, 1983).

33. *Time* (November 29, 1982).

34. Alan Levin, "The New England Connection: Mafia Gets into the Act,"

N.B.S.T. (October 23, 1983), pp. 1, 12; "Drug Task Force Bases Success on Planning, Leadership," *N.B.S.T.* (October 24, 1983), p. 3.

35. Peyton Fleming, Part I, "N.E. New Haven for Drug Trafficking," *Foster's Daily Democrat* (November 14, 1983), pp. 1, 10; Part II, "Law Enforcement Battling Smugglers" (November 15, 1983), pp. 1, 20; Part III, "Cop Pretends to Be Crooked to Catch Dealer" (November 16, 1983), pp. 1, 34.

36. Alan Levin, "Dukakis Creates Strike Force to Attack Drugs," *N.B.S.T.* (November 24, 1983), p. 5; "Drug Law Enforcement Plan Channels Existing Resources," *N.B.S.T.* (November 30, 1983), p. 6.

37. "New Patrol Mulled for State," *Soundings,* Sec. II (January 1984), p. 2.

38. John Birtwell, "$3M Pot Haul Found Floating in Harbor," *Boston Herald* (August 11, 1983), p. 4.

39. *Boston Globe* (August 11, 1983), p. 19.

40. Kevin Cullen, "Morning Walker Finds $50,000.—Pot Bale on Beach," *Boston Herald* (August 13, 1983), p. 6.

41. *N.B.S.T.* (August 12, 1983), p. 3.

42. "Missed Date Might Have Led to Hull Pot Bale Dumping," *N.B.S.T.* (August 12, 1983), p. 3; Jim Flannery, "Yacht Aground Yields Cargo of Marijuana," *Soundings,* Sec. II (September 1983), p. 2.

43. "Court Lets Quincy Destroy Marijuana," *N.B.S.T.* (August 12, 1983), p. 2.

44. "State Should Make Advance Arrangements to Guard Drugs," *N.B.S.T.* (September 25, 1983), p. 12.

45. Les Suzakarno, "Why Guard Tons of Pot? Just Have a Cannabis Cookout," *N.B.S.T.* (October 2, 1983), p. 5.

46. Les Suzakarno, "Dartmouth Can Burn Marijuana," *N.B.S.T.* (November 1, 1983), p. 9.

47. Alan Levin, "Dartmouth's Pot Problem Goes Up in Smoke," *N.B.S.T.* (November 8, 1983), p. 13.

48. Les Suzakarno, "Arrest Likely in Mishaum Pot Find," *N.B.S.T.* (August 19, 1983), p. 9.

49. Les Suzakarno, "Nationwide Alert Is Issued for Pot Suspect," *N.B.S.T.* (October 6, 1983), p. 12.

Chapter 7. The Tiki X

1. The Crumbling Courthouse Is Due for "A New Face for the Spring," *N.B.S.T.* (December 18, 1983), p. 4.

2. "Police Grab 30 Tons of Marijuana," *Soundings* (December 1982), p. 50.

3. Kevin Cullen, "Grab New Bedford Shoppers off Street for Jury Duty," *Boston Herald* (August 10, 1983), p. 12.

4. Ernest J. Corrigan, "Tiki X Jury Still Lacks Two After Long Delay," *N.B.S.T.* (August 11, 1983), pp. 1, 5.

5. Ernest J. Corrigan, "Jury of 15 Will Do for Drug Trial, Judge Rules," *N.B.S.T.* (August 12, 1983), p. 5.

6. Howard Manley, "Would-be Juror Tired of Court, Small Talk and Eddie Fisher," *N.B.S.T.* (August 13, 1983), p. 1.

7. Sandra A. Lopes, "Court Officers Abducted Citizens Right off Street

for Jury Duty," letter to the editor, *N.B.S.T.* (August 18, 1983), p. 4.

8. Margaret A. Charig, "Tiki X Jurors Tour Fairhaven's Waterfront," *N.B.S.T.* (August 13, 1983), p. 3.

9. Margaret A. Charig, "Jury Gets First Look at Marijuana from Tiki X," *N.B.S.T.* (August 16, 1983), p. 5.

10. Margaret A. Charig, "Drug Bust Reconstructed—Patrolman Tells Tiki X Jury How November Raid Occurred," *N.B.S.T.* (August 17, 1983), p. 5.

11. Margaret A. Charig, "What Does a Smuggler Wear? Tiki X Defense Battles Evidence Tied to Clothing," *N.B.S.T.* (August 18, 1983), p. 5.

12. Margaret A. Charig, "Prosecution Links Clothing to One Tiki X Defendant," *N.B.S.T.* (August 19, 1983), p. 5.

13. Margaret A. Charig, "Tiki Bales Are 'Herbs' to Defense," *N.B.S.T.* (August 20, 1983), p. 5.

14. Margaret A. Charig, "It Looks Small Like Pot, But Tiki X Defense Wants Proof," *N.B.S.T.* (August 23, 1983), p. 5.

15. Margaret A. Charig, "Tiki X Defendant Goes to Jail After Mystery Hearing," *N.B.S.T.* (August 24, 1983), p. 5.

16. Margaret A. Charig, "3rd Tiki X Defendant's Case is Withdrawn from Drug Trial," *N.B.S.T.* (September 2, 1983), p. 5.

17. Margaret A. Charig, "Tiki X Drug Trial to Resume Today," *N.B.S.T.* (September 7, 1983), p. 5.

18. Margaret A. Charig, "Tiki Defense Goes for Final Arguments," *N.B.S.T.* (September 8, 1983), p. 5.

19. Margaret A. Charig, "And Then There Were Six," *N.B.S.T.* (September 9, 1983), p. 7.

20. "Judge Slaps Tardy Lawyer in Tiki X Case with $100 Fine," *N.B.S.T.* (September 13, 1983), p. 5.

21. Margaret A. Charig, "Tiki X Trial Jurors Resume Deliberations Today," *N.B.S.T.* (September 13, 1983), p. 5; Margaret A. Charig, "Tiki X Trafficker Vanishes, Forfeits Bail," *N.B.S.T.* (September 15, 1983), p. 9.

22. Margaret A. Charig, "Jury Finds Five Guilty in Tiki X Pot Trial," *N.B.S.T.* (September 14, 1983), pp. 1, 5; Alan Levin, "Dukakis Enthusiastic About Pina Proposal," *N.B.S.T.* (September 14, 1983), pp. 1, 4.

23. Editorial, " 'Scorched Earth' Drug War Welcome, but Details Needed," *N.B.S.T.* (September 16, 1983), p. 6.

24. Ernest J. Corrigan, "Tiki X Sentences," *N.B.S.T.* (September 20, 1983), p. 4.

25. "Court Throws Out Pot Sentencing Law," *N.B.S.T.* (October 14, 1983), p. 3.

26. Margaret A. Charig, "Court Ruling May Change Tiki Sentences," *N.B.S.T.* (October 25, 1983), p. 5.

27. Margaret A. Charig, "Lawyers Dispute Sentences in Tiki X Drug Trial," *N.B.S.T.* (November 16, 1983), p. 39.

28. "Bill to Clarify Mandatory Drug Sentences Signed," *N.B.S.T.* (December 15, 1983), p. 13.

29. "Lawyers in Pot Smuggling Trial Agree to Test Law on Sentencing," *N.B.S.T.* (December 22, 1983), p. 22.

30. Margaret A. Charig, "Revised Trafficking Law Clouds Drug Case," *N.B.S.T.* (January 23, 1984), p. 5.

31. *N.B.S.T.* (February 4, 1983).

32. "Seized Fishing Boats Up for Auction," *N.B.S.T.* (November 17, 1983), p. 23.

33. David Foster, "Pot Auction Cancelled," *N.B.S.T.* (December 2, 1983), p. 12.

34. "Ads Expected for New Bids on Boats," *N.B.S.T.* (December 6, 1983), p. 5.

35. Margaret A. Charig, "4 Boats Involved in Drug Smuggling Are Sold at Auction," *N.B.S.T.* (December 29, 1983), p. 5.

36. Alan Levin, "Fairhaven Gets Paid for Guarding Pot," *N.B.S.T.* (October 5, 1983), p. 4.

37. Alan Levin, "Drug Units Seize Trawler," *N.B.S.T.* (January 21, 1984), p. 1.

38. "Unimac Crewmen Board Haitian Ship in Marijuana Bust," *N.B.S.T.* (December 12, 1983), p. 3; "Unimac Tows Seized Ship Toward Port," *N.B.S.T.* (December 13, 1983), p. 3; "Suspected Drug Ship's Crew Jailed," *N.B.S.T.* (December 15, 1983), p. 3.

39. "2 Arrested, Cocaine Seized in Chelsea," *Boston Globe* (August 13, 1983), p. 20.

40. "Trooper and His Dog Nab Pair in $2M Cocaine Bust," *N.B.S.T.* (September 15, 1983), pp. 1, 3; "Found with Cocaine," *N.B.S.T.* (September 15, 1983), p. 3.

41. "Defendants Say Pot Is Part of Their Worship," *N.B.S.T.* (September 14, 1983), p. 3; "Pot Worshipping Couple Convicted," *N.B.S.T.* (September 21, 1983), p. 3.

42. *N.B.S.T.* (September 13, 1983), p. 9.

43. Alan Levin, *N.B.S.T.* (September 13, 1983), p. 5.

44. Ibid. (September 10, 1983), pp. 1, 5.

45. "Profit Pays for Costly Land on Vineyard, Jury Is Told," *N.B.S.T.* (September 13, 1983), p. 3.

46. *N.B.S.T.* (August 17, 1983), p. 4.

47. Ibid. (September 24, 1983), p. 19.

48. Ibid. (September 6, 1983), p. 20.

49. Ibid. (October 8, 1983), p. 19.

50. Ibid. (October 20, 1983), p. 3.

51. Mark Vosburgh, *N.B.S.T.* (October 20, 1983), p. 2.

52. *N.B.S.T.* (November 4, 1983), p. 3.

53. Ibid. (November 6, 1983), p. 3.

54. Ibid. (October 30, 1983), p. 53.

55. Les Suzakarno, *N.B.S.T.* (November 10, 1983), p. 4.

56. *N.B.S.T.* (November 23, 1983), p. 20.

57. Ibid. (January 17, 1984), p. 3.

58. Ibid. (December 14, 1983), p. 40.

59. Ibid. (December 18, 1983), p. 6.

60. Ibid. (January 1, 1983), p. 41, emphasis on drug busts.

61. Ibid. (January 12, 1984), p. 5, by David Foster.

62. John Lempesis, "Parents: Kids Need Fun—Without Drugs," *N.B.S.T.* (November 14, 1984), pp. 1, 5; "Fall River Benefits Most with Officer in Drug Unit," editorial, *N.B.S.T.* (October 3, 1983), p. 14; "Dukakis' Tour

Spotlights Local Economy, Drug Crackdown," *N.B.S.T.* (November 14, 1983), p. 1.

63. Reginald Stuart, "Florida's Tourism Shifts from South," *The New York Times* (February 19, 1983), p. 31.

64. "Marijuana Ships Seized off Massachusetts," *The New York Times* (July 25, 1983); Alan Levin, "The New England Connection: Mafia Gets into the Act," *N.B.S.T.* (October 23, 1983), pp. 1, 12; Alan Levin, "Area Fishermen Say Profits from Smuggling Almost Too Good to Ignore," *N.B.S.T.* (October 23, 1983), p. 12; Alan Levin, "Drug Task Force Bases Success on Planning, Leadership," *N.B.S.T.* (October 24, 1983), p. 3; "Three Hundred Bales of Marijuana . . . ," *The Advocate* (Fairhaven) (August 4, 1983), p. 18.

65. Alan Levin, "Third Fire Devastates Verdeans' Building," *N.B.S.T.* (September 12, 1983), p. 4.

66. Alan Levin, "Local Man Is Official in Firm That Owns Boat Seized in City Pot Bust," *N.B.S.T.* (August 13, 1983), pp. 1, 3.

67. "17 Suspects Arrested in Pot Busts Plead Innocent," *N.B.S.T.* (August 16, 1983), p. 5.

68. Bess Zarafonitis, "Defense in Drug Smuggling Case Forfeits Trawler," *N.B.S.T.* (September 7, 1983), p. 7.

69. Howard Manley, "Taxpayers Face a Whopping Tab for Guarding Pot," *N.B.S.T.* (September 22, 1983), p. 5; Les Suzakarno, "$13 Million Up in Smoke —Marijuana Burned in Fall River Incinerator," *N.B.S.T.* (September 30, 1983), pp. 1, 5.

70. "2 Men Indicted by U.S. on Drug Law Charges," *The New York Times* (August 16, 1983), p. 24; Bob Pape, "Two Indicted as Kingpins of Nationwide Pot, Hash Ring," *N.B.S.T.* (August 16, 1983), pp. 1, 3.

71. Todd Heath, "U.S. Says Leaders of Huge International Drug Ring Indicted," *Hartford Courant* (August 16, 1983), p. 3.

72. "Major Pot Smuggling Ring Broken, Feds Say," *N.B.S.T.* (November 30, 1983), p. 3.

73. *The New York Times* (January 24, 1984); *N.B.S.T.* (January 24, 1984), p. 18; *Saudi Gazette* (Riyadh) (January 25, 1984), p. 4.

74. Arnold H. Lubasch, "13 Indicted on Conspiracy in Wholesale Cocaine Ring," *The New York Times* (January 24, 1984), p. B3.

75. "Fugitive Financier Is Called Drug Kingpin," *N.B.S.T.* (September 7, 1983), p. 2.

76. "New Drug 'Cartels' Are Constant Threat, Attorney General Says," *N.B.S.T.* (December 1, 1983), p. 3.

Chapter 8. Hailing, Boarding, Searching, Seizing

1. See, e.g., "So Much for 4th Amendment," *Cruising World* (November 1983), p. 19.

2. Mike Smith, "Boarded!," *Yachting* (September 1983), p. 20.

3. L. Conway, "Boarded," *Yachting* (December 1983), p. 17.

4. George F. Hurley, "Boarded," *Yachting* (November 1983), p. 10.

5. Nancy Trimble, "Sailboat Racer Indicted in Drug Smuggling Plot," *Soundings*, Sec. II (March 1984), pp. 1, 62.

6. Ernest J. Corrigan, "Angry Fishermen Tell Studds of Coast Guard Boardings," *N.B.S.T.* (December 6, 1983), p. 4. There was an instant response: "Coast Guard's Inspections Need Not Rattle Fishermen," *N.B.S.T.* (December 9, 1983), p. 6.

7. 19 U.S.C. §158(a).

8. *United States* v. *Villamonte-Marquez,* 77 L.Ed. 2d 22, 103 S.Ct. 2573 (1983).

9. See also Bill Tuttle, "Random Boardings Are Backed by Supreme Court's Majority," *Soundings* (August 1983), pp. 3, 32.

10. "Federal Government Steps Up Drug Battle," *Soundings* (January 1984), p. 8.

11. 14 U.S.C. §89(a).

12. *United States* v. *Williams,* 617 F.2d 1063 (*en banc,* 1980).

13. *United States* v. *Williams,* 1088, n. 30.

14. *United States* v. *Conroy,* 589 F.2d 1258 (5th Cir., 1979).

15. Note: "Fifth Circuit Cases Concerning Search and Seizure Upon the High Seas: The Need for a Limiting Doctrine," 10 Georgia Journal of International and Comparative Law (1980): 167, 183 and as "untenable," comment: *"Smoke on the Water": Coast Guard Authority to Seize Foreign Vessels Beyond the Contiguous Zone,* 13 International Law and Politics (1980): 249, 323. Accord: *United States* v. *Mann,* 462 F.Supp. 933 (1979) (search of American ship in Mexican contiguous zone upheld).

16. *See* comment, *"Smoke on the Water,"* supra, 320–22.

17. See *The Ship Richmond,* 23 U.S. (9 Cranch.) 102 (1815).

18. Note: "Search and Seizure of Foreign Vessels on the High Seas Permissible if the Vessel Is Subject to the Operation of the United States Law, and Evidence Acquired in Violation of International Law Does Not Require Exclusion," 15 Vanderbilt Journal of Transnational Law 227: 230–33. Article 6(1) Convention on the High Seas: "Ships shall sail under the flag of one State only and, save in exceptional cases expressly provided for in international treaties or in these articles, shall be subject to its exclusive jurisdiction on the high seas," TIAS 5200.

19. *United States* v. *Williams,* 1082.

20. Ibid., 1083

21. Ibid., 1070. The Convention on the High Seas offers no protection to stateless vessels. *United States* v. *Cortes,* 588 F.2d 106 (5th Cir., 1979). Statelessness can be shown by failure to show registration papers, *United States* v. *Cortes,* ibid., or by changing flags to avoid boarding, *United States* v. *Dominguez,* 604 F.2d 304, 308 (4th Cir., 1979). Failure to fly the flag of the country of registry is not alone sufficient to warrant an inference of statelessness, *United States* v. *Postal,* 589, F.2d 862 (5th Cir., 1979).

22. Convention on the High Seas, adopted April 27, 1958; 13 UST 2312; TIAS 5200; 450 UNTS 82. The textual reference is to Article 15, which reads:

ARTICLE 15

Piracy consists of any of the following acts:

1. Any illegal acts of violence, detention or any act of depredation, committed for private ends by the crew or the passengers of a private ship or a private aircraft, and *directed:*

a. On the high seas, against another ship or aircraft, or against persons or property on board such ship or aircraft;

b. Against a ship, aircraft, persons or property in a place outside the jurisdiction of any State;

2. Any act of voluntary participation in the operation of a ship or of any aircraft with knowledge of facts making it a pirate ship or aircraft;

3. Any act of inciting or of intentionally facilitating an act described in sub-paragraph 1 or sub-paragraph 2 of this article.

Where piracy is shown, the pirate ship and personnel may be seized, and force commensurate with necessity may be used to effect the seizure. Major R.W. Gehring, "Defense Against Insurgents on the High Seas: The Lyla Express and Johnny Express," XXVII *J.A.G. Journal* 317 (1974): 320, 329, 330, 343.

23. *The Marianna Flora,* 11 Wheat. 1, 42, 6 L.Ed. 405, 415.

24. *United States* v. *Cortes,* 588 F.2d 106 (5th Cir. 1979).

25. Ibid., 110–11.

26. *United States* v. *Williams,* 1082.

Chapter 9. Piracy: The Jolly Roger Flies Again

1. Chairman, Committee on Merchant Marine and Fisheries, in cosponsoring H.R. 2538, in hearings before the Subcommittee on Coast Guard and Navigation of the Committee on Merchant Marine and Fisheries, House of Representatives, Ninety-Sixth Congress, First Session, S.N. 96-20 (Washington, D.C.: U.S. Government Printing Office, 1982), p. 3; hereinafter referred to as S.N. 96-20.

2. Carl Hiaasen, "Bloody Cruise in the Bahamas: Mystery Shrouds Couple's Fate," *Miami Herald* (September 1, 1980), pp. 1, 4. William Robbins, "Legislature Tells of a Bahamian Sea Mystery," *The New York Times* (August 30, 1980), p. 20.

3. Red Marstan, "Yachtsmen Cleared in Bahamian Shooting," *Yachting* (June 1, 1982), pp. 24–25.

4. We promised the Coast Guard to omit statements on the characteristics, etc., of suspects.

5. S.N. 96-20, p. 3.

6. Carl Hiaasen, "Troubled Waters," *Miami Herald* (July 31, 1982).

7. Ibid., and Coast Guard report on file with authors.

8. Ibid.

9. "Vigilance Urged in Reports on Hijacking and Piracy," *The New York Times,* Sec. 8 (October 16, 1977), p. 9.

10. *The New York Times* (May 22, 1977), p. 50.

11. "Coast Guard Warns Boaters of Piracy and Hijackings," *Crime Control Digest* (September 26, 1977), p. 8.

12. "Drugs and Death on the High Seas," *Time* (September 22, 1980), p. 24.

13. Don Street, "The Pirates of Paradise," *Yachting World* (December 1982), p. 40.

14. Ibid.

15. E.g., George Gardon, "The Pirate Packs Who Leave Blackbeard Behind," *Daily Mail* (London) (March 3, 1982).

16. David Cox, "Caribbean Pirates," *Yachting World* (May 1982).

17. Ibid. and editor's response.

18. E.g., E.F. Bull, "Disputed Piracy," *Yachting World* (February 1982), p. 33, and following letters by Chris Doyle and Bonne Rose.

19. Margaret B. Hicks, "Pirates: What Pirates?," *Yachting World* (July 1982), p. 31.

20. Street, op. cit., p. 43.

21. Ibid.

22. Carl Hiaasen, "Troubled Waters," op. cit.

23. Ibid.

24. See Chap. 12.

25. "Yacht Stolen," *Express* (Trinidad) (January 9, 1984), p. 7. "Venezuela cops find Baltoa yacht," *Trinidad Guardian* (January 10, 1984), p. 1.

26. "Vi ska stoppa sjörövarna, Palme," *Aftonbladet* (Stockholm) (January 19, 1983), p. 12; "Piraterna är besegrade," *Expressen* (Stockholm) (January 19, 1983), p. 5.

27. Poster on file with authors. Swedish pirates had seized a vessel off Lagos, Nigeria.

28. Gregory James, "Pirates of Lagos: Once an Annoyance, Now a Major Threat," *The New York Times* (March 14, 1981), p. 4.

29. "Five Nations Insist Nigeria Act to Curb Port Pirates," *New York Times* (November 23, 1977), p. 6.

30. "Pirates of Lagos," op. cit.

31. Ibid.

32. Ibid.

33. "Nigeria Curbs Fishermen in Drive to Halt Pirates," *The New York Times* (November 25, 1977), p. 17.

34. "Pirates of Lagos," op. cit.

35. "Sticks and Stones Hurt Pirates' Bones," *Bergen* (N.J.) *Record* (March 2, 1983).

36. "Pirates of Lagos," op. cit.

37. "Sticks and Stones," op. cit.

38. Ibid., p. 4.

39. Ibid.

40. Ibid.

41. John Darnton, "Pirates Plying Nigerian Seas," *The New York Times* (January 9, 1977), p. 1.

42. "Freighter Disappears off Africa," *The New York Times* (January 21, 1978), p. 6.

43. "Stepping Up the Search" (by-line Lagos), *Express* (Trinidad) (January 14, 1984), p. 31.

44. S. Sindahmed, "GCC Security Accord May Be Signed Soon," *Arab News* (Riyadh) (January 24, 1984), p. 2.

45. Fedell L. Posce, "Norway Ready to Help in Construction of Ports," *Arab*

News (Riyadh) (January 22, 1984), p. 2; "Norway Minister Tours Damman," *Arab News* (Riyadh) (January 24, 1984), p. 2.

46. "Färg och pengar nytt piratvapen," *Aftonbladet* (Stockholm) (November 12, 1979), p. 5; Victor Walker, "Greek Government, Shipowners Clash Over Proposed 'Piracy' Laws," *Journal of Commerce* (March 5, 1980), p. 10.

47. Doyle McManus, "Lebanese Ports a Bonanza for Pirates," *International Herald Tribune* (October 16, 1979).

48. Ibid.

49. Homer, *The Odyssey,* Robert Fitzgerald (transl.) (Garden City, N.Y.: Doubleday & Co., 1961), p. 94 and *passim.*

50. Ibid.

51. Walker, "Greek Government, Shipowners," op. cit., p. 10.

52. Ibid.

53. Ibid.

54. Victor Walker, "Little Chance Seen for 'Piracy' Laws Proposed in Greece," *Journal of Commerce* (May 5, 1980), p. 34.

55. Ibid.

56. Ibid.

57. Walker, "Greek Government, Shipowners," op. cit.

58. Walker, "Little Chance Seen," op. cit.

59. Ibid.

60. Ibid.

61. "The Jolly Roger Still Flies," *Time* (July 31, 1978), p. 35.

62. Vincent W. Stove, "Australian Ship Line Issues Pirate Alert," *Journal of Commerce* (September 29, 1981), p. 11.

63. "Please Repel Our Boarders," *Far Eastern Economic Review* (October 9, 1981), p. 43.

64. Ibid.

65. "Australian Ship Line Issues Pirate Alert," op. cit., p. 11.

66. "Pirates Still Running High on the Seas of Indochina," *International Herald Tribune* (October 17, 1978), p. 1.

67. "Letter from Singapore," *Far Eastern Economic Review* (February 17, 1978), p. 58.

68. "Pirates Still Running High," op. cit.

69. "Please Repel Our Boarders," op. cit.

70. "Troubled Waters of Sabah," *Far Eastern Economic Review* (December 7, 1979), p. 25.

71. "Jaguars at Sea," *Far Eastern Economic Review* (March 24, 1978), p. 5.

72. "Please Repel Our Boarders," op. cit.

73. "Pirates Still Running High," op. cit.

74. Ibid.

75. "Thai Piracy Against Boat People Seems Relentless," *The New York Times* (May 7, 1980), p. 6.

76. "Excerpts From U.S. Message Recounting a Refugee's Ordeal," *The New York Times* (January 11, 1982), p. 4.

77. "The Agony of Vietnam Refugee Boat 0105," *The New York Times* (July 25, 1979), p. 1.

78. "Thai Pirates Kill 70 'Boat People,'" *The New York Times* (January 11, 1980), p. 3.

79. Ibid.; "Thai Piracy Against Boat People," op. cit.

80. "Thai Piracy Against Boat People," op. cit.

81. Ibid.

82. "Thailand's Part-Timers in Terror," *Far Eastern Economic Review* (February 1, 1980), p. 27.

83. "The Thai Pirates," *Newsweek* (August 13, 1979), p. 33.

84. Ibid.

85. "U.N. Office Sets Effort to Protect Asian Refugees," *The New York Times* (May 30, 1980), p. 5.

86. "Thailand's Part-Timers in Terror," op. cit.; Jack Anderson, "Pirates Elude Navy," *Star Ledger* (Newark, N.J.) (March 14, 1983).

87. One citation for many: "Drifting Refugees Find Sanctuary on British Ship," *The Times* (London) (August 8, 1980), p. 5.

88. "West German Ship Saves Refugees from Pirates," *The New York Times* (February 20, 1982), p. 5.

89. Tim Severin, *The Sindbad Voyage* (London: Hutchinson, 1982), p. 217.

90. "Cambodian Seizure of U.S. Ship Decried," *Journal of Commerce* (May 13, 1975), p. 11.

91. " 'Piracy' Storm Over Israeli Cargo Ship," *Time* (June 26, 1976), p. 5.

92. "Cuban Delegates Visiting Nassau in Boat Incident," *The New York Times* (May 13, 1980), p. 14.

93. "Japanese Freighter Hijacked by Bandits in Philippine Port," *The New York Times* (September 27, 1975), p. 7.

94. "Philippine Navy Forces Rebels to Yield Ship and 29 Hostages," *The New York Times* (September 30, 1975), p. 3.

95. "Mystery Boat Under Attack," *Trinidad Guardian* (January 14, 1984), p. 2.

Chapter 10. Where Land and Law End: Terrorism at Sea

1. Tom Sawyer, "Bomb Threat Disrupts State Race," *Soundings* (August 30, 1983), p. 30.

2. A.L.I. Model Penal Code, Sec. 211.3, "Terroristic Threats." See, e.g., New Jersey Code of Criminal Justice, Sec. 2C: 12-3.

3. Proceedings of the International Conference on the Repression of Terrorism (1937); C.94, 447 (1938).

4. There are exceptions. Thus, Ronald D. Crelinsten, Dannielle Laberge-Alamejd, and Denis Szabo, *Terrorism and Criminal Justice* (Lexington, Mass.: Lexington Books, 1978), lists "offshore oil wells, gas and oil pipelines and submarine cables" among technology vulnerable to terrorist attacks; p. 7.

5. M. Cherif Bassiouni, ed., *International Terrorism and Political Crime* (Springfield, Ill.: Charles C. Thomas, Publisher, 1975); Yonah Alexander, ed., *International Terrorism: National, Regional and Global Perspectives* (New York: Praeger Publishers, 1976).

6. Gerhard O.W. Mueller and Edward M. Wise, *International Criminal Law*, Chap. 5 (South Hackensack, N.J.: Fred B. Rothman & Company; London: Sweet & Maxwell, 1965). Gerhard O.W. Mueller and Douglas Besharov, "The Existence of International Criminal Law and Its Evolution to the Point of Its

Enforcement Crisis," M. Cherif Bassiouni and Ved Nanda, eds., *A Treatise on International Criminal Law*, Vol. 1, Chap. 1, Sec. 1 (Springfield, Ill.: Charles C. Thomas, Publisher, 1973).

7. Ernest Lehman, *The French Atlantic Affair* (New York: Atheneum Publishers, 1977).

8. Account based on world press reports of January 1961, esp. *The New York Times* (January 21, 1961), pp. 1, 3; *The New York Times* (January 31, 1961), pp. 1, 3; *U.S. News and World Report* (February 6, 1961), pp. 46–47.

9. Neil C. Livingstone, *The War Against Terrorism* (Lexington, Mass.: Lexington Books, 1982), p. 154.

10. John Malcolm Brinnin, *The Sway of the Grand Saloon—A Social History of the North Atlantic* (London: Macmillan, 1972), p. 477.

11. Jack Higgins, *Luciano's Luck* (New York: Dell Publishing Company, 1981), p. 20.

12. B. M. Jenkins and J. Johnson, *International Terrorism: A Chronology, 1968–1974* (Rand Corp., 1975), p. 39.

13. Frederick Forsythe, *The Devil's Alternative* (New York: Ahiara International Corporation, S.A., 1979), p. 244.

14. J. Bowyer Bell, *A Time for Terror* (New York: Basic Books, 1978), p. 106.

15. Livingstone, op. cit., p. 138.

16. Peter van der Linde, *Time Bomb* (Garden City, N.Y.: Doubleday & Company, 1978), esp. Chap. 10.

17. Livingstone, op. cit., p. 137.

18. Elizabeth Drake and Robert C. Reid, "The Transportation of Liquefied Natural Gas," *Scientific American* (April 1977), p. 28.

19. Merle Macbain, "Will Terrorism Go to Sea?," *Security Management* 24(8) (1980): 76, 82.

20. Alistair MacLean, *Seawitch* (Garden City, N.Y.: Doubleday & Company, 1977).

21. Glenn Fowler, "Exxon to Check Harbor Blast," *The New York Times* (October 19, 1983), p. 4.

22. Livingstone, op. cit., p. 137.

23. "Probe: Training Could Have Saved Rig," *N.B.S.T.* (December 22, 1983).

24. "Shipyard Puts Barricades Outside Gates," *N.B.S.T.* (December 28, 1983), p. 4.

25. Enfoque de Panama, Vol. 13, No. 1 (Panama: Focus Publishers, S.A., 1983), p. 30.

26. "Participan 500 abogados en la XXIV Convención," *Estrella de Panama* (February 8, 1984); "21 Nations Attend XXIV Conference of the Inter-American Bar Association," *Star and Herald* (Panama) (February 8, 1984), p. B6.

27. *Diario La Estrella de Panama, Suplemento el Istmo* (November 6, 1983).

28. *Diario La Estrella de Panama* (December 5, 1983).

29. Bernard Lewis, *The Assassins* (New York, Basic Books, 1968), pp. 96–124.

30. Ley 20, Gazete Oficial, Año LXXX, No. 19, 909 (September 30, 1983), governing the armed forces and the defense of the canal.

31. Luís Arrieta Aleman, "La Protección del Canal de Panama contra Ac-

ciones Terroristas," paper presented at the XXIVth Congress of the Inter-American Bar Association (Panama, 1984).

32. Richard T. Meislin, "Panama's President Abruptly Resigns," *The New York Times* (February 14, 1984), p. 3.

33. Livingstone, op. cit., p. 136.

34. B. Drummond Ayres, Jr., "U.S. Marines Diverted to Grenada," *The New York Times* (October 22, 1983), pp. 1, 5.

35. Francis J. Reynolds, *The United States Navy from the Revolution to Date* (New York: P.F. Collier & Son, 1918).

36. "Forget the 'Maine'!," *Parade Magazine* (January 8, 1984), p. 20, suggests that the *Maine* explosion may have been due to a spontaneous combustion in one of the ship's coal bunkers that, in turn, resulted in the explosion of an adjacent munitions magazine.

37. R.W. Barnett, "The U.S. Navy's Role in Countering Maritime Terrorism," *Terrorism: An International Journal* 6(3) (1983): 469. See *Washington Post* (August 15, 1981), p. 1; (October 3, 1981), p. A-16; (November 3, 1981), p. 2.

38. "Hey, Let's Steal a Sub!," *Newsweek* (October 16, 1970), p. 38.

39. R.W. Barnett, op. cit.

40. Douglas R. Barnett, "Dolphins, Naval Warfare, and International Law," *U.S. Naval Institute Proceedings* 107(9) (September 1981): 117–22.

41. "High Rise—Coast Guard Boats form a Cordon Around the Nuclear-powered Aircraft Carrier USS 'Enterprise' as the Flat-top Steams Slowly in San Francisco Bay During Fleet Week," *Soundings* (January 1984), p. 16.

42. William Borders, "Lord Mountbatten Is Killed as His Fishing Boat Explodes, I.R.A. Faction Says It Set Bomb," *The New York Times* (May 28, 1979), pp. 1, 10, 11.

43. Ibid.

44. "100 Terrorist Organizations Identified," *N.B.S.T.* (January 31, 1984), p. 8.

45. "Presidential Protection Called Weak—Fake Bombs Planted, Ex-investigator Says," *Miami Herald* (February 8, 1984), p. 1.

46. Cdr. A. Robert Matt, "Trouble on the Water!," *The Police Chief* (September 1979), pp. 68–70.

47. Carlos A. Calderon, "Big Coast Guard Fleet for Olympian Task," *Soundings* (January 1984), p. 14.

48. Ronald Clarke, "Warning of Terrorism at Olympics," *Trinidad Guardian* (January 2, 1984), p. 15.

49. R.W. Barnett, op. cit.

50. Merle Macbain, op. cit.

51. J. D. Nyhart and J. Christian Kessler, "Ocean Vessels and Offshore Structures," *Legal Aspects of International Terrorism*, ed. Alona E. Evans and John F. Murphy (Lexington, Mass.: Lexington Books, 1978).

Chapter 11. Tempting Tides: Corruption

1. Carl Hiaasen, Susan Sacks, and Richard Merin, "Smugglers' Island," *Miami Herald*, 1982, p. 11.

2. Ibid., p. 2.

3. Ibid.

4. Ibid., p. 21.

5. P. Bradley Nutting, "The Madagascar Connection: Parliament and Piracy, 1660–1701," *North American Journal of Legal History,* Vol. XXII (1978), p. 211.

6. Frank Browning and John Gerassi, *The American Way of Crime* (New York: G.P. Putnam's Sons, 1980), p. 56.

7. Ibid.

8. Ibid., p. 66.

9. Hamilton Cochran, *Free Booters of the Red Sea* (Indianapolis, Ind.: The Bobbs-Merrill Company, 1965), p. 71.

10. N.Y. Docs., 221–24, Osgood, Eighteenth Century, as quoted in Browning and Gerassi, op. cit., p. 68.

11. Ibid., p. 210.

12. Robert Carse, *The Age of Piracy* (New York: Rinehart & Company, 1957), p. 213.

13. Ibid.

14. Ibid.

15. Ibid.

16. P. Bradley Nutting, op. cit., p. 212.

17. Browning and Gerassi, op. cit., p. 60.

18. Ibid., pp. 64–65.

19. Malcolm F. Willoughby, *Rum War at Sea* (Washington, D.C.: U.S. Government Printing Office, 1964), p. 70.

20. Ibid., pp. 67–68.

21. Ibid., p. 78.

22. *Soundings* (December 1982), p. 9.

23. "Coast Guardsmen Guilty in Selling Antidrug Plans," *The New York Times* (March 5, 1983), p. 16.

24. Ralph Blumenthal, "Ship Inspectors' Costs Paid Directly," *The New York Times* (November 30, 1983), p. B4.

25. Ralph Blumenthal, "Business Gives Sports Tickets to Coast Guardsmen," *The New York Times* (November 20, 1983), p. 41.

26. "Customs Agent Faces Drug Charges," *N.B.S.T.* (September 23, 1983), p. 2.

27. "Ex-Miami Officer to Be Sentenced," *Miami News* (June 28, 1983).

28. Jim Quirk, "Witness in Missing Cocaine Case Disappears," *N.B.S.T.* (August 19, 1983), p. 5.

29. Betsy A. Lehman, "Police Report Cocaine Theft at Barracks," *Boston Globe* (August 13, 1983), p. 1; Jim Quirk, "Drugs Gone—Troopers Were Holding Cocaine in Middleboro," *N.B.S.T.* (August 13, 1983), p. 1; Timothy Clifford, "$½M Drug Haul Stolen from Cops' Strongroom," *Boston Herald* (August 13, 1983), p. 5.

30. "Stolen Cocaine Is Still a Mystery," *N.B.S.T.* (September 4, 1983), p. 4.

31. "Trooper Is Linked to Middleboro Drug Theft," *N.B.S.T.* (October 3, 1983), p. 1.

32. "Trooper Indicted in Drug Theft," *N.B.S.T.* (October 4, 1983), p. 1.

33. Jim Quirk, "State Trooper's Arraignment Means Task Force Did Duty, Officer Says," *N.B.S.T.* (October 5, 1983), p. 5.

34. Jim Quirk, "Cocaine Theft Cuts Charges," *N.B.S.T.* (November 5, 1983), p. 1.

35.   ARTICLE 7

Law enforcement officials shall not commit any act of corruption. They shall also rigorously oppose and combat all such acts.

Commentary:

a. Any act of corruption, in the same way as any other abuse of authority, is incompatible with the profession of law enforcement officials. The law must be enforced fully with respect to any law enforcement official who commits an act of corruption, as Governments cannot expect to enforce the law among their citizens if they cannot, or will not, enforce the law against their own agents and within their own agencies.

b. While the definition of corruption must be subject to national law, it should be understood to encompass the commission or mission of an act in the performance of or in connexion with one's duties, in response to gifts, promises or incentives demanded or accepted, or the wrongful receipt of these once the act has been committed or omitted.

c. The expression "act of corruption" referred to above should be understood to encompass attempted corruption.

"Code of Conduct for Law Enforcement Officials," A/RES/34/169 (February 5, 1980).

36. "Ex-Prosecutor Is Sentenced," *The New York Times* (May 22, 1983), p. 26.

37. "Cuba Disputes Reagan on Drugs," *The New York Times* (May 25, 1983), p. A4.

38. Reginald Stuart, "Bahamian Leader Denies Drug Link," *The New York Times* (September 15, 1983), p. 13; Reginald Stuart, "U.S.-Bahamian Relations Are Straining Under Drug Investigations," *The New York Times* (September 28, 1983), p. 21.

39. Nicki Kelly, "Drugs Focus on Bahamas—Pindling Determined to Uncover the Facts," *Trinidad Guardian* (January 13, 1984), p. 14.

40. Paul West, "The Turks and Caicos, Quietly," *The New York Times* (March 6, 1983), pp. xx, 51.

41. Report of Schmahl and Schmahl on file with authors.

42. "Concentrate on Easing Traffic in 1984, Burroughs Tells Cops," *Trinidad Guardian* (December 24, 1983), p. 1.

Chapter 12. Vanishing Vessels: Marine Insurance Fraud

1. Leslie Buglass, *Marine Insurance Claims, American Law and Practice*, 2nd ed. (Cambridge, Md.: Cornell Maritime Press, 1972), p. 6. Readers interested in the technical aspects of marine insurance law underlying this discussion of

marine insurance fraud are well advised to consult, for American practice, William D. Winter, *Marine Insurance: Its Principles and Practice,* 3rd ed. (New York: McGraw-Hill Book Company, 1952), and for English practice, J. Kenneth Goodacre, *Marine Insurance Claims,* 2nd ed. (London: Witherby and Company, 1981).

2. Burglass, op. cit., p. 9.

3. Michael Brody, "Boom in Piracy—There's a Rising Tide of Marine Fraud," *Barron's* (November 29, 1982), p. 19.

4. Eric Ellen and Donald Campbell, *International Maritime Fraud* (London: Sweet & Maxwell, 1981), p. 3.

5. Michael Brody, op. cit., p. 19.

6. Peter van der Linde, *Time Bomb* (Garden City, N.Y.: Doubleday & Company, 1978), pp. 95–96.

7. Ellen and Campbell, op. cit., p. 2.

8. Michael Brody, op. cit., p. 18.

9. Ellen and Campbell, op. cit., p. 24; see also "Dagens 'sjörövare' förfalskar, sanker," *Hufvudstadsbladet* (November 11, 1983), p. 15.

10. International Maritime Bureau, ICC, Publication 380-3 (1981).

11. Ellen and Campbell, op. cit., p. 27.

12. Speech presented by Jack Wilson, former assistant commissioner, Scotland Yard, at a meeting of the Association of the Bar of the City of New York, program titled "Crime in the Maritime Industry" (New York, December 6, 1983).

13. Ibid., Ellen and Campbell, op. cit., pp. 45–48.

14. "New Perspectives in Crime Prevention and Criminal Justice and Development: The Role of International Cooperation," working paper prepared by the Secretariat, A/CONF., 87/10 (July 29, 1980).

15. Wilson, op. cit.; Ellen and Campbell, op. cit., pp. 49–52.

16. *Guide to Prevention of Maritime Fraud* (International Chamber of Commerce, 1980).

17. United Nations Development Program (UNDP), Governing Council, "Progress Report on the Proposed World Maritime University—Report of the Administrator," D.P./1983/3 (December 16, 1983).

Chapter 13. Street Crimes of the Ocean Lanes

1. "Wenn ich den Beweisantrag so sehe . . . ," *Der Spiegel,* No. 45 (1983), pp. 77, 80. The peculiarities of shipboard homicides have been recognized only by Hans von Hentig, the famed German criminologist, who had spent his years of exile in the United States. See his book *Der Schiffsmord und neun andere Verbrechensstudien* (Hamburg: Kriminalistik Verlag, 1967). (Vol. 35, Kriminologische Schriftenreihe aus der Deutschen Kriminologischen Gesellschaft.)

2. Louise B. Davidson and Eddie Doherty, *Strange Crimes at Sea* (New York: Grosset & Dunlap, 1966), p. 9.

3. *FBI Uniform Crime Reports* (Washington, D.C.: U.S. Government Printing Office), annually.

4. "Crime Prevention and Control," report of the Secretary General, A/32/199 (September 22, 1977).

5. Hal Burton, *The Morro Castle* (New York: Viking Press, 1973); Gordon Thomas and Max Morgan Witts, *Shipwreck: The Strange Fate of the Morro Castle* (New York: Stein and Day, 1972); Thomas Michael Gallagher, *Fire at Sea: The Story of the Morro Castle* (New York: Rinehart & Company, 1959).

6. William Sisson, "Prosecutor Punctures 'Perfect' Raft Slaying," *Soundings* (February 1984), p. 5.

7. Cheryl McCall, "A Bloody, Baffling Mass Murder Shakes the Peaceful Spirit of a Small Town in Washington," *People* (September 12, 1983), pp. 74–80.

8. Robert Hanley, "Boat Recovered in Boston Search for Student, 25," *The New York Times* (September 28, 1983), p. B2.

9. "Skipper: 'Too Rough' to Save Crewmen," *New York Post* (May 13, 1976), p. 14.

10. *Regina* v. *Dudley and Stephens*, 14 Q.B.D. 273 (1884).

11. *United States* v. *Holmes*, 1 Wall. Jr. 1, 26 Fed. Cas. 360 (No. 15383) (U.S. Circuit Court, E.D. Pa., 1842).

12. Davidson and Doherty, op. cit., pp. 176–95.

13. M. Cherif Bassiouni, *Working Paper, International Norms and Standards in International Criminal Law, Crime Prevention and Criminal Justice in the Context of Development: Challenges for the Future*, Siracusa, Italy: International Institute for Higher Studies in Criminal Law, (1983), pp. 78–81.

14. See Part I.

15. "4 Arrested on a Boat in Raid on Gambling," *The New York Times* (October 17, 1983), p. B7.

16. Jim Flannery, "Festivities Marred by Alleged Hit and Run Collision," *Soundings* (July 1983).

17. "Police Seize Party Boat Liquor," *Soundings* (September 1983), p. 80.

18. Jean Waller, "Stiff Penalties Spelled Out in Bill Against Tipsy Boating," *Soundings* (February 1984), p. 2.

19. "Briefs," *Soundings* (January 1984), p. 16.

20. Jim Flannery, "New York Wrestles with Boat Theft Problems," *Soundings*, Sec. II (January 1984), p. 41; "Congress and Nautical Boozing," *Yachting* (February 1984), p. 23.

21. "2 on Boat Arrested on Deer Charges," *N.B.S.T.* (December 3, 1983), p. 5.

22. "Owner's Hopes Raised—2 Sightings of Stolen Toddywax," *Soundings* (December 1982), p. 12; "Toddywax Theft Still a Mystery," *Soundings*, Sec. II (September 1983), p. 24.

23. George Lyford, "Boat Theft, a High Profit/Low Risk Business," National Crime Information Center, *FBI Law Enforcement Bulletin* (Washington, D.C., May 1982), p. 2.

24. Ibid., p. 4.

25. Ibid., p. 5.

26. 1981 Annual Report: *Crime in Florida*.

27. William Sisson, "Researchers See 36 Percent Crime Rate for City Boats," *Soundings*, Sec. II (July 1983), p. 3.

28. Jerome Hall, *Theft, Law and Society* (Indianapolis, Ind.: The Bobbs-Merrill Company, 1952).

29. Ibid., p. 234.

30. "Kids Steal Ferry, Head for Miami," *N.B.S.T.* (February 11, 1984), p. 2.

31. 1981 Annual Report, *Crime in Florida,* p. 43.

32. John J. Connors, "New England Police Target Boat Thefts," *Soundings,* Sec. II (August 1983), pp. 1, 18.

33. Flannery, "New York Wrestles with Boat Theft Problems," loc. cit.

34. "Police Add 4 Launches," *The New York Times* (June 30, 1983), p. B2.

35. "U.S. Report Outlines Theft Prevention Laws," *Soundings* (January 1984), p. 16.

36. Hall, op. cit., p. 287.

37. Lyford, op. cit., p. 4.

38. Lynda Morris, "Burglar, Burglar, Burglar," *Cruising World* (July 1983), pp. 185–91; "On Board Alarm Systems," *Yachting* (January 1984), pp. 92, 157, et seq.

39. "Making Things Work," *Sail* (February 1984), p. 24.

40. "An Open Invitation," *Yachting Monthly* (October 1983), p. 194.

41. Morris, op. cit., p. 191.

42. Wilson, see Chap. 12, note 12.

43. Eric Ellen and Donald Campbell, *International Maritime Fraud* (London: Sweet & Maxwell, 1981), p. 32.

44. For a discussion of policing the ports, see Henry C. Collier, "Policing the Ports of Hampton Roads," *The Police Chief* (October 1977), p. 20.

45. Anne L. Millet, "Pilot Blamed for Tug Sinking in Cape Cod Canal," *N.B.S.T.* (November 1, 1983), p. 7.

46. Charles F. Chapman, *Piloting, Seamanship and Small Boat Handling* (New York: The Hearst Corporation, 1963).

47. N.J. Code of Criminal Justice 2C:12-2.a.

48. 18 U.S.C. §2191.

49. 18 U.S.C. §2192–95.

50. 18 U.S.C. §2198.

Chapter 14. People for Profit: The Alien Smuggle

1. "Death in the Morning," *Time* (November 9, 1981).

2. Anders Gyllenhaal and John MacCormack, "Bahamas: A Sieve for Refugees," *Miami Herald* (December 6, 1982), p. 1A.

3. "The People Smugglers," *Miami Herald* (December 8, 1982); pp. 1, 14, 15; "Hundreds of Taiwanese, Cubans Enter U.S. Using Bogus Costa Rican Passports," *Star and Herald* (Panama) (February 8, 1984), p. B6.

4. Gyllenhaal and MacCormack, op. cit., p. 14A.

5. *Haitian Flow,* U.S. Immigration and Naturalization Service (1982).

6. *Fort Lauderdale News* (December 12, 1983), p. 12A.

7. Ibid.

8. "Crushed by Ship," *Trinidad Guardian* (December 28, 1983), p. 1.

9. "Journey Was Deadly for Some Refugees," *Miami Herald* (December 7, 1982), p. 12A.

10. Anders Gyllenhaal and John MacCormack, "Transient Haitians Wait for Ships That Never Come," *Miami Herald* (December 6, 1982), p. 15A.

11. "Haitians Held," *Trinidad Guardian* (January 7, 1984); *Orlando Sentinel* (February 8, 1984), p. A20.

12. Gary Kriss, "Lawyers for Haitian Refugees Ask Cases Be Heard in County," *The New York Times,* Sec. II (February 27, 1983), pp. 1, 13; "Aliens Held in Miami Go On a Hunger Strike," *The New York Times* (February 4, 1984).

13. Our discussion of America's detention policy vis-à-vis Haitian illegal aliens is based in part on Jill Adler's research memorandum on file with authors.

14. John Arnold, "Haitians' Boats Deposit 'Crew' in Miami," *Miami Herald* (December 6, 1982), p. 14A.

15. Ibid.

16. Edward Schumacher, " 'Mutiny' in Cuban Harbor: Relatives Demand U.S. Boat Await Refugees," *The New York Times* (May 15, 1980), p. 14.

17. Ibid.

18. "Two Fugitives Arrested Among Cuban Refugees," *The New York Times* (May 13, 1980), p. 5.

19. Reginald Stuart, "Cubans' Lawyers Question Deportation Plans," *The New York Times* (May 29, 1983), p. 22.

20. Tracy Thompson, "Suit Questions Where Cubans' Rights Begin," *Atlanta Constitution* (January 17, 1983).

21. Ibid.

22. The information on the Colombian people-smuggling operation was derived from interviews with Mexican officials, Mr. Andrew Antippes, members of the South Florida Task Force, and the following news exposés: Gyllenhaal and MacCormack, "Bahamas: A Sieve for Refugees," op. cit., p. 14A; John MacCormack, "3 Portraits from a Shady but Profitable World," *Miami Herald* (December 7, 1982), pp. 1, 12A.

23. MacCormack, ibid., pp. 1A, 12A.

24. "The Journey Was Deadly for Some Refugees," *Miami Herald* (December 7, 1982), p. 12A.

25. Anders Gyllenhaal and John MacCormack, "Bahamas: A Sieve for Refugees," op. cit., pp. 1, 14A.

26. Timothy Green, *The Smugglers: An Investigation into the World of the Contemporary Smuggler* (New York: Walker & Company, 1969), p. 166.

27. Ibid.

28. Ibid., p. 153.

29. Robert Lindsey, "Bigger Border Patrol Can't Halt Influx, Agents Say," *The New York Times* (February 13, 1984), p. A12.

Chapter 15. Security at Stake: The Murky Waters of Espionage and Treasonous Trade

1. Francis Joseph, "Police Seize Cache of Arms in Raid at Arina," *Trinidad Guardian* (December 28, 1983), p. 1.

2. Timothy Green, *The Smugglers: An Investigation into the World of the Contemporary Smuggler* (New York: Walker & Company, 1969), provides an excellent introduction.

3. Neil C. Livingstone, *The War Against Terrorism* (Lexington, Mass.: Lexington Books, 1982).

4. Leonidas Escobar, Cristóbal Interco Press, "Looks Like Soviet Ships Are Carrying Weapons in Canal," *Trinidad Guardian* (January 10, 1984), p. 12.

5. "Eight Arrested for Plot to Kill Burnham," *Trinidad Guardian* (December 24, 1983), p. 1.

6. "Police Station in Guadeloupe Damaged by Bomb Explosion," *The New York Times* (November 21, 1983), p. 5; Barbara Crossette, "When Fear Pays a Visit to Caribbean Paradise," *The New York Times* (February 14, 1984), p. 2.

7. *Star and Herald* (Panama) (February 6, 1984), p. 2.

8. Paper presented by Robin Montano, Esq., of Trinidad, on file with authors.

9. *Saudi Gazette* (Riyadh) (January 24, 1984), p. 4.

10. Phillip Taubman, "U.S. Said to Have Set Up Large Spy Network in Latin America," *The New York Times* (March 19, 1983).

11. "High Seas—Strange Cargo—A Curious Trove of Soviet Arms," *Time* (July 4, 1983), p. 33.

12. *The Penal Code of Sweden*, trans. Thorsten Sellin, Vol. 17, American Series of Foreign Penal Codes (G.O.W. Mueller, director) (South Hackensack, N.J.: Fred B. Rothman & Company; London: Sweet & Maxwell, 1972).

13. Vora objudna besökare, 7080 (February 1983), Försvarsstabens—och Marinstabens info. Adv./Dahlback & Berglund/Tintatryck.

14. Att Mota Ubåtshotet, Ubåtskrängningarna och Svensk Säkerhetspolitik, SOU Betänkande av Ubåtsskyddskommissionan (1983:13).

15. "Sweden Letting Navy Attack Foreign Subs," *The New York Times* (July 2, 1983).

16. "Sweden Improves Defenses Against Submarine Intruders," *The New York Times* (September 18, 1983), p. 3.

17. *Express* (Trinidad) (December 22, 1983), p. 51.

18. "Swedes, Hunting a Sub, Drop Depth Charges," *The New York Times* (February 15, 1984), p. 5; "Swedes Seek Intruder Sub," *The New York Times* (February 12, 1984), p. 5.

19. *International Herald Tribune* (June 4–5, 1983), p. 1.

20. "Norwegians Fire At a Suspected Sub," *The New York Times* (June 30, 1983).

21. Drew Middleton, "Antisub Warfare: Soviet Trying to Catch Up," *The New York Times* (November 20, 1983), p. 21.

22. "U.S. and Soviet Seek to Prevent a Surprise Attack," *The New York Times* (December 8, 1983), p. A6.

23. *Svenska Dagbladet* (June 11, 1983), p. 1.

24. Tom Keene with Brian Haynes, *Spy Ship* (New York: Dell Publishing Company, 1983), p. 84.

25. "Soviet Spy Ship Detected off Hawaii," *N.B.S.T.* (September 16, 1983), p. 2.

26. "South Korea Reports Sinking 'Spy Boat' from North Korea," *Boston Globe* (August 6, 1983), p. 6.

27. "Excarcelan a tres marinos japoneses en Corea del Norte," *La Estrella de Panama* (February 8, 1984), p. B-10.

28. Anthony Grey, *The Prime Minister Was a Spy* (1983).

29. "Australian's Drowning Was Faked, Book Says," *The New York Times* (November 21, 1983), p. A5.

30. William C. Mann, "Spying, North Europe Top Game," *Star and Herald* (Panama) (February 5, 1984), p. 2.

31. Jon Zonderman, "Policing High-Tech Exports," *The New York Times Magazine* (November 27, 1983), p. 99.

32. Ibid., p. 102.

33. Ibid., p. 99; "Office of Investigations—*Operation Exodus,*" Customs U.S.A., a report on the activities of the U.S. Customs Service during fiscal year 1982, pp. 10–11.

34. Zonderman, op. cit., pp. 103, 125.

35. Andres Oppenheimer, "Reagan Seeks Funding to Slow Illegal Trade," *Miami Herald* (February 6, 1984), p. 70.

36. Amity Shlaes, "Soviet Watchers Face Growing Secrecy on Kremlin's Economic, Crop Statistics," *The Wall Street Journal* (February 10, 1984), p. 30.

37. Charles P. Hanley, "Now Castro Makes Use of the Expert Vesco Connection," *Trinidad Guardian* (January 14, 1984), p. 7.

38. "3 Patrol Boats Seized on Way to Nicaragua," *The New York Times* (December 10, 1983), p. 9.

39. Jim Flannery, "Seized Boat Gear Judged 'Average,' " *Soundings* (March 1984), pp. 3, 39.

40. "Chicago Company and Executive Guilty of Shipping Parts to Libya," *The New York Times* (August 16, 1983), p. 15.

41. Clyde H. Farnsworth, "For Something Short of War, Export Controls," *The New York Times* (September 2, 1983), p. B6.

42. Zonderman, op. cit., pp. 99, 102.

43. Edward C. Burks, "Moscow-Bound Computer Is Seized," *The New York Times* (November 21, 1983), p. 5.

44. "Swedes Say Shipment 'Frozen,' " *The New York Times* (November 21, 1983), p. 5.

45. "Swedes Seize 2nd Shipment of Equipment," *The New York Times* (November 25, 1983), p. 3; "Computer Programs Seized En Route to the Soviet Union," *The New York Times* (November 29, 1983), p. 11.

46. "Computer-Smuggling Route Is Uncovered," *N.B.S.T.* (December 2, 1983), p. 2.

47. "British Customs Seizes Computers," *N.B.S.T.* (December 12, 1984), p. 2.

48. Maureen Dowd, "5 Named in Plot to Send Peking High-Tech Gear," *The New York Times* (February 13, 1984), pp. 1, B2.

49. For excellent, albeit slightly dated treatment of smuggling in general, and the work of Customs officers in particular, see Timothy Green, *The Smuggling Business* (London: Aldus Press, 1977) and *The Smugglers: An Investigation*

into the World of the Contemporary Smuggler (New York: Walker & Company, 1969). Among the English classics are Lord Teignmouth and Charles G. Harper, *The Smugglers: Picturesque Chapters in the History of Contraband*, 2 vols. (London: Cecil Palmer, 1923) and E. Keble Chatterton, *Kings Cutters and Smugglers* (London: George Allen & Unwin, Co., Ltd., 1912).

50. "The Customs Cooperation Council," *Customs Today*, Vol. 18, No. 1 (Winter 1981), p. 5.

51. Friedrich Klein, "The European Community's Customs Union," *Customs Today*, Vol. 18, No. 1 (Winter 1983), p. 9.

Chapter 16. The Ocean Is the Victim

1. Paul Ress, "Sea Sickness," *Secretariat News* (New York: United Nations, February 28, 1983), pp. 4–5.

2. Peter Hulm, *A Strategy for the Seas, the Regional Seas Programme Past and Future* (UNEP, 1983), p. 3.

3. *The Siren*, news from UNEP's Regional Seas Programme, No. 19 (January 1983).

4. Jim Flannery, "River Protectors Put Heat on Exxon," *Soundings*, Sec. II (November/December 1983), p. 4.

5. Note, *American Criminal Law Review*, Vol. 18, No. 169 (1980), p. 368.

6. "Belgium Seized Oil Slick Imperils Persian Gulf," *The New York Times* (March 31, 1983), p. 5.

7. "Oil Tanker Breaks off S. Africa," *Boston Globe* (August 7, 1983), p. 16.

8. Herman Conrad, "Congress Works on Oil Spill Fund," *Soundings* (October 1983), p. 10.

9. M.F. Torq, "Oil Pollution, Legislation and Combat," *Journal of the Arab Maritime Transport Academy*, Vol. 8, No. 16, p. 28.

10. "Judge Refuses to Bar Ocean Burning of PCB's," *The New York Times* (November 20, 1983), p. 26; "Plan to Burn PCB's in the Gulf Protested at Hearing in Texas," *The New York Times* (November 22, 1983), p. 22; "Aide Says Gulf Burning of Wastes May Go Ahead," *The New York Times* (December 8, 1983), p. 25.

11. Rick Tirsch, "Toxic Chemical Dumped Near Canal, Officials Say," *Miami Herald* (January 28, 1983), pp. 1, 14A.

12. " 'Windscale' Casts Shadow on N-Industry," *Saudi Gazette* (January 25, 1984), p. 8.

13. Ibid.

14. Hulm, *A Strategy for the Seas*, op. cit., p. 1.

15. Peter Hulm, "The Regional Seas Program: What Fate for UNEP's Crown Jewels?," *Ambio*, Royal Swedish Academy of Sciences, Pergamon Press, Vol. XII, No. 1 (1983), p. 7.

16. Ibid., p. 7.

17. "U.S. Study to Identify Chesapeake Polluters," *The New York Times* (December 18, 1983).

18. Judy Foreman, "Court Gets Plan to Clean Boston Harbor," *Boston Globe* (August 11, 1983), p. 1.

19. John T. McQuiston, "Dispute Continues on Dumping in Sound," *The New York Times*, Sec. II (November 1983), p. 1; Patty Koller, "U.S. Dumping Rule Awaited," *Soundings*, Sec. II (March 1984), p. 2.

20. "PCB Levels in Striped Bass in the Hudson Decline," *The New York Times* (November 20, 1983), p. 45.

21. "Pollution Prompts Warning to Limit Eating of Bluefish," *The New York Times* (November 6, 1983), p. 69.

22. Bess Zarofonitis, "Banned in N.Y., Eaten in Mass.?," *N.B.S.T.* (October 2, 1983), p. 1.

23. Jim Flannery, "Focus: Fish Contamination," *Soundings*, Sec. II (November/December 1983), p. 18; William Sisson, "Focus: U.S. Study Finds Pollutants Hurt Bass Larvae," *Soundings*, Sec. II (November/December 1983), p. 19; William Sisson, "Focus: Critic Probes Genetic Link," *Soundings*, Sec. II (November/December 1983), p. 21.

24. Ernest J. Corrigan, "2 City Firms Sued Over Harbor PCB's," *N.B.S.T.* (December 13, 1983), pp. 1, 5.

25. Virginia Pool, "William Sargent Delivers Talk on Battle Over Georges Bank," *Vineyard Gazette* (Martha's Vineyard) (August 12, 1983).

26. Jill M. Higgins, "Westport Shellfish Beds to Stay Closed," *N.B.S.T.* (December 7, 1983), p. 4.

27. "Once Tainted Clam Bed Reopens in New Jersey," *The New York Times* (November 5, 1983), p. 30.

28. "L.I. Clam Beds May Remain Shut," *The New York Times* (July 9, 1983), p. 24.

29. "High Mercury Levels Spur Swordfish Tests," *Soundings* (March 1984), p. 12.

30. Jim Flannery, "Study Finds Muddied Sound," *Soundings*, Sec. II (January 1984), p. 58.

31. "Fish Stories and Empty Offices," *Time* (April 11, 1983), p. 18.

32. Bess Zarofonitis, "Permanent Shellfishing Ban Is Imminent for Polluted Cove," *N.B.S.T.* (January 4, 1984), p. 4; "More Testing Needed Before Long-Term Clarks Cove Closing," *N.B.S.T.* (December 7, 1983).

33. "GESAMP IMCO, FAO, UNESCO/WMO/WHO/IAEA/UN/UNEP Joint Group of Experts on the Scientific Aspects of Marine Pollution," *The Health of the Oceans*, UNEP Regional Seas Report and Studies No. 16 (UNEP, 1982), p. 51.

34. "Death Toll 13," *Trinidad Guardian* (January 17, 1984), p. 2.

35. "Saving Whales," *Newsweek* (July 23, 1979), pp. 64–65; "Trawler's Crew Vows to Ram Seal-Hunting Ship off Canada," *The New York Times* (February 13, 1983), p. 15.

36. "Bass Fishermen Fear New Law Means Ruin," *The New York Times* (November 14, 1983); Susan Pollack, "Saving Stripers Isn't Simple," *National Fisherman* (December 1983).

37. Jim Flannery, "Fishery Managers Adopt Emergency Bass Limits," *Soundings*, Sec. II (March 1984), p. 17.

38. Christopher Simpson, "New Mid-Atlantic Trawling Laws Protect Summer Flounder Stocks," *National Fisherman* (December 1983), p. 18.

39. Russ Fee, "Catch Adjustments Recommended for King Mackerel," *National Fisherman* (December 1983), p. 11.

40. Chris Blackburn, "Red King Crab Closure Is Step 1 in Regulating Stocks," *National Fisherman* (December 1983), p. 8.

41. "U.S. Boat Crew Seized in Brazil," *New York Post* (August 4, 1983), p. 22.

42. "Coast Guard Holds an Italian Trawler," *The New York Times* (October 25, 1983), p. B3.

43. "Venezuela Fisherman Fined After Guilty Plea," *Trinidad Guardian* (December 23, 1983), p. 5.

44. Jim Flannery, "Lobstermen Battle Over Sites," *Soundings*, Sec. II (March 1984), p. 46.

45. "Limit on Licensing Is Proposed to Ease Strife in Mississippi," *National Fisherman* (December 1983), p. 11.

46. From statement by Tom Falvey to *Newsweek* (August 1, 1983).

47. *Newsweek* (August 1, 1983); "Foes of Whaling Say Colleagues Will Be Freed," *The New York Times* (July 22, 1983).

48. *The Globe and Mail* (Toronto) (January 18, 1984), p. 12.

49. "Trawler's Crew Vows to Ram Seal Hunting Ship off Canada," *The New York Times* (February 13, 1983), p. 15.

50. Bess Zarofonitis, "Frionor Parent Firm to Stop Marketing Whale Meat," *N.B.S.T.* (October 10, 1983), p. 5.

51. "Shipment of Turtle Soup Is Seized," *Miami Herald* (January 28, 1983), p. 12A.

52. George Will, "Saving the Whales Helps Humanity, Too," *Miami News* (January 26, 1983); "Flotilla of Japanese Whalers Leaves on Antarctic Voyage," *The New York Times* (October 23, 1983), p. 10.

53. As quoted in "Saving Whales," *Newsweek* (July 23, 1979), p. 65.

54. G.O.W. Mueller, "Offenses Against the Environment and Their Prevention, An International Appraisal," *Annals*, American Academy for Social and Political Sciences, 444 (July 1979).

55. G.O.W. Mueller and Douglas Besharov, "The Existence of International Criminal Law and Its Evolution to the Point of Its Enforcement Crisis," Sec. 1 in "The Scope and Significance of International Criminal Law," *A Treatise on International Criminal Law*, ed. M. Cherif Bassiouni and Ved Nanda (Springfield, Ill.: Charles C Thomas, 1973).

56. United Nations Convention on the Law of the Sea, Arts. 116–20.

57. Stacy C. Hall, "U.S. and Mexico May Work Out Tuna Agreement Yet," *National Fisherman* (December 1983), p. 16.

58. "OECS Wants More Fishing $," *Trinidad Express* (January 10, 1984), p. 10.

59. "Island's Puzzle: Drop in Cod Catch," *The New York Times* (February 12, 1984).

60. UN Convention on the Law of the Sea, Art. 230.

61. Peter Hulm, The Regional Seas Program," op. cit., p. 3.

62. Ibid., p. 2.

63. See G.O.W. Mueller, "Offenses Against the Environment," op. cit., p. 61.

64. "Missouri Company Pleads Guilty to Violations of Clean Water Act," *The New York Times* (February 20, 1984), p. A20.

65. Note, *American Criminal Law Review*, Vol. 18, No. 169 (1980), p. 346.

66. Ibid., p. 347.

67. Jim Flannery, "New Boats Patrolling N.Y. Coastline," *Soundings*, Sec. II (November/December 1983), p. 10.

Chapter 17. Lessons of History

1. The various accounts of Caesar's encounter with the pirates differ slightly. Compare Suetonius's account with that of Plutarch's, and see Gerard Walter, *Caesar—A Biography* (New York: Charles Scribner's Sons, 1952). The account of the affair by Gaius Suetonius Tragpuilius (born about A.D. 70) may be found in Suetonius, *The Twelve Caesars*, trans. Corbert Graves (New York: Penguin Books, 1979), pp. 14–15. The account of Plutarch (A.D. 66–120) may be found in Plutarch, *Fall of the Roman Republic*, trans. Rex Warner (New York: Penguin Books, 1972), pp. 244–45.

2. Homer, *The Odyssey*, trans. Robert Fitzgerald (Garden City, N.Y.: Doubleday & Company, 1961), p. 94.

3. Rudolf His, *Deutsches Strafrecht bis zur Karolina* (München and Berlin: R. Oldenbourg, 1928), pp. 84, 85.

4. Walter Heichen, *Klaus Störtebecker* (Berlin: A. Weichart, 1938), p. 160.

5. Lyman V. Rutledge, *The Isles of Shoals in Lore and Legend* (Barre, Mass.: Barre Publishers, 1965), p. 30 et seq.

6. Irvin Haas, *America's Historic Ships, Replicas and Restorations* (New York: Arco Publishing Company, 1975), pp. 61–64.

7. Douglas Bottin, *The Pirates* (Alexandria, Va.: Time-Life Books, 1978), p. 31.

8. The historical summary in this chapter is based on a variety of books, especially the following:

- *The Lives and Bloody Exploits of the Most Noted Pirates, Their Trials and Executions . . .* (Hartford, Conn.: Ezra Strong, 1839).
- Douglas Botting, *The Pirates* (Alexandria, Va.: Time-Life Books, 1978).
- Hamilton Cochran, *Freebooters of the Red Sea: Pirates, Politicians and Pieces of Eight*, Indianapolis, Ind.: The Bobbs-Merrill Company, 1965).
- Robert Carse, *The Age of Piracy* (New York: Rinehart & Company, 1957).
- J. Franklin Jameson, *Privateering and Piracy in the Colonial Period* (New York: Augustus M. Kelley, Publisher, 1970).
- Alexander Isquemelin, *Buccaneers of America* (London, 1684–85).
- Daniel Defoe, reprinted; William Graves (ed.), *A General History of the Robberies and Murders of the Most Notorious Pyrates* (New York and London, Garland Publishing, Inc., 1972).
- P. Bradley Nutting, "The Madagascar Connection: Parliament and Piracy, 1690–1701," *The American Journal of Legal History*, Vol. XXII (1978), pp. 202–15.
- Kenneth R. Andrews, *Elizabethan Privateering* (Cambridge: Cambridge University Press, 1964).
- David Mitchell, *Pirates* (New York: Dial Press, 1976).

9. "Underwater Wreck Called Treasure Ship," *The New York Times* (December 5, 1982), p. 48; " 'Pirate' Vessel Sets Off a Hunt for Booty," *The New York Times* (December 12, 1982); Kenneth J. Looper, "Divers Comb Ocean Floor in Search of Ship's Booty," *Boston Globe* (August 7, 1983), p. 32.

10. "Senators Warned of Damage Facing Historic Shipwrecks," *The New York Times* (November 6, 1983), p. 76.

Chapter 18. Charting a Course for the Future

1. Freda Adler, *Nations Not Obsessed with Crime* (Littleton, Colo.: Fred B. Rothman & Company, 1983).

2. Proceedings of the Council of Maryland, Liber B, p. 611 (June 23, 1654).

3. Michael Lewis, "Fear and the Cruising Sailor," *Cruising World* (February 1984), pp. 88–89.

4. Harold Dudley Greeley, *Law for Yachtsmen* (New York: A.S. Barnes & Company), 1952, p. 208.

5. Betsy Hitz, "Is It Time to Arm for Cruising?" *Cruising World* (October 1980), pp. 106–16.

6. Gerald J. Mangone, *Law for the World Ocean* (London: Stevens & Sons, 1981), p. 38.

7. *The New York Times* (March 9, 1984), p. 8.

8. "Americans Detained Offshore," *Soundings* (July 1983); "Avoiding Tropical Trouble," *Soundings* (July 1983), p. 4.

9. "2 Cuban Fighters Buzz U.S. [Coast Guard] Plane in Bahamas," *The New York Times* (May 13, 1980), p. 5.

10. Norton S. Ginsburg, "Should the United States Sign the 'Constitution for the Oceans'?," *The University of Chicago Magazine* (Winter 1983), pp. 24–37.

11. *The Law of the Sea*, New York: United Nations, p. xxxiv, 1983.

12. On the effort of the House Merchant Marine and Fisheries Committee to review the Administration's controversial position on the convention, see "Washington Briefs," *Soundings* (August 1983), p. 14.

13. Convention on the High Seas of August 29, 1958, UNTS, No. 6465 (1963), pp. 82–102.

14. For the convention's definition of "piracy" see Chap. 8.

15. Peter D. Clark, "Criminal Jurisdiction Over Merchant Vessels Engaged in International Trade," *Journal of Maritime Law and Commerce*, Vol. 11 (1979–80), pp. 219–37.

16. The study that, in our view, got the United States position off on the wrong tack was Robert E. Osgood, Ann L. Hollick, Charles S. Pearson, and James C. Orr, *Toward a National Ocean Policy: 1976 and Beyond* (Washington, D.C.: U.S. Government Printing Office, 1974). For relevant congressional debates on the issue, see *Law of the Sea Negotiations*, Wash., D.C.: U.S. Govt. Printing Office, hearing before the Subcommittee on Arms Control, Oceans, International Operations, and Environment of the Committee on Foreign Relations, United States Senate, Ninety-Seventh Congress, Second Session

(September 15, 1982). Of scholarly interest is Gerald J. Mangone, *Law for the World Ocean* (London: Stevens & Sons, 1981). See also Myres S. McDouglas and William T. Burke, *The Public Order of the Oceans—A Contemporary International Law of the Sea* (New Haven, Conn.: Yale University Press, 1962) and R.P. Barston and Patricia Birnie, *The Maritime Dimension* (London: George Allen & Unwin, 1980).

Chapter 19. The "Nonclusion"

1. "Swedes Spot 'Person'; He Skips into the Sea," *The New York Times* (March 2, 1984), p. 3; "Swedes Hunt 3 Frogmen on Isles Near Navy Base," *The New York Times* (March 5, 1984), p. 5.

2. "Coast Guard Budget Cut Is Criticized," *N.B.S.T.* (February 24, 1984), p. 3.

3. "Hearing on Coast Guard Policies Is March 2," *N.B.S.T.* (February 22, 1984), p. 7.

4. "U.S. May Float Blimp in Drug War," *Soundings* (April 1984), p. 13.

5. Anne L. Millet, "Coast Guard Due to Get Jet Before 3 Cape Copters Go," *N.B.S.T.* (February 28, 1984), p. 3.

6. Bess Zarafonitis, "Cutters Sail on Seas of Adventure," *N.B.S.T.* (February 26, 1984), pp. 3–4B.

7. "Office Decor Plan Took Drug Force Funds, Official Claims," *N.B.S.T.* (February 25, 1984), p. 2.

8. "Coast Guard Seizes Boat with 5 Tons of Pot," *N.B.S.T.* (February 26, 1984), p. 3; "A Net Full of Pot," *N.B.S.T.* (February 28, 1984), p. 3.

9. "2 Boats Seized for Drugs," *The New York Times* (February 21, 1984), p. 12.

10. "4 Sentenced as Drug Runners," *The New York Times* (February 28, 1984), p. B2.

11. Carl Hiaasen, "Miami Drug Deal Might Have Been Part of Guatemalan Plot, Police Say," *Philadelphia Inquirer* (February 18, 1984), p. 10C.

12. "Washington Grand Jury Indicts 27 in Drug Ring," *N.B.S.T.* (February 25, 1984), p. 2.

13. "U.S. Agents Say Ring Is Cracked," *Miami Herald* (February 4, 1984), p. 2B.

14. "10 Años Para Traficante Internacional," *La Estrella de Panama* (February 8, 1984), p. 10B.

15. "Drug Crackdown Confirmed," *The New York Times* (March 8, 1984), p. B20.

16. "Cocaine Smuggling Up Despite War on Drugs," *N.B.S.T.* (February 19, 1984), p. 2.

17. *Arab News* (January 22, 1984), p. 6.

18. Al Suntoli, "Thailand—The Gulf Pirates," *The Atlantic* (February 1984), pp. 25–30.

19. "53 Missing After Attack on Boat from Vietnam," *The New York Times* (March 3, 1984), p. 9.

20. "Drug Evidence 'Lost' During Georgia Trial," *Star and Herald* (Panama) (February 5, 1984), p. 2.

21. "Shipbuilding Fraud Suit," *The New York Times* (February 21, 1984), p. D9.

22. "Two Charged in Boat Theft," *Soundings*, Sec. II (April 1984), p. 47.

23. "Intensifican Busqueda de Carguero Mexicano," *La Nación* (Costa Rica) (February 3, 1984), p. 10; "Tacsan Califica de Frustranto Investigación Sobre Los Barcos," *La Nación* (February 18, 1984); "Los Barcos Fantasmas" (editorial), *La Nación* (February 16, 1984), p. 14.

24. Bill Tuttle, "Cruiser Finds Base Is Stolen," *Soundings*, Sec. II (April 1984), p. 1.

25. "Imposter Takes Harbor Fee," *Soundings*, Sec. II (April 1984), p. 2.

26. "Blaze on Cruise Ship Forces 946 to Flee," *The New York Times* (March 11, 1984), p. 24, and front-page photograph.

27. "Border Officers Hold 16 Who Landed in Florida," *The New York Times* (February 21, 1984), p. 12.

28. "The Haitians and the Lucky Law," editorial, *The New York Times* (February 22, 1984), p. 18.

29. Russ Oleson, "U.S. Seizures of Boatlift Vessels Held Illegal," *Soundings*, Sec. II (April 1984), p. 24.

30. Christopher S. Wren, "China and Taiwan: A Web of Unofficial Contacts," *The New York Times* (February 22, 1984), p. 4.

31. "A Longer Trudge for the Sludge," *The New York Times* (March 4, 1984), p. 6E; Ralph Blumenthal, "Policy to Change on Ocean Dumping," *The New York Times* (March 2, 1984), pp. 1, B4; "Dump Site Distance Debated," *Soundings*, Sec. II (April 1984), p. 49.

32. William G. Blair, "Jersey Protests Dumping by City—[Senator Frank R.] Lautenberg Cites Discharges of Sewage into Hudson," *The New York Times* (March 4, 1984), p. 34.

33. John Davies, "This Harbor Cop Is on the Pollution Beat," *Soundings* (April 1984), p. 19.

34. "Missouri Company Pleads Guilty to Violations of Clean Water Act," *The New York Times* (February 20, 1984), p. 20.

35. Jim Flannery, "Angler Serves Time for Suspended License," *Soundings*, Sec. II (April 1984), p. 7.

36. Douglas Martin, "Canadians, Yielding to Furor, Call off Hunt for Baby Seals," *The New York Times* (March 9, 1984), pp. 1, 6; "Baby Seals Are Reprieved," *The New York Times* (March 11, 1984), p. E9.

Index

•